FALLSCHIRM PANZER DIVISION 'HERMANN GÖRING'

FALLSCHIRM PANZER DIVISION 'HERMANN GÖRING'

A HISTORY OF THE LUFTWAFFE'S ONLY ARMOURED DIVISION 1939–1945

Lawrence Paterson

Foreword by
Richard Overy

Greenhill Books

Fallschirm-Panzer-Division 'Hermann Göring'
First published in 2021 by
Greenhill Books,
c/o Pen & Sword Books Ltd,
47 Church Street, Barnsley,
S. Yorkshire, S70 2AS

www.greenhillbooks.com
contact@greenhillbooks.com

ISBN: 978-1-78438-610-8

CIP data records for this title are available from the British Library

Designed and typeset by Donald Sommerville

MIX
Paper from responsible sources
FSC® C013604

Printed and bound by CPI Group (UK) Ltd, Croydon CR0 4YY

Typeset in 10.6/14.3 pt Adobe Caslon Pro

Contents

I'd like to dedicate this book to the memory of the great Edward Lodewijk van Halen.

Plates

Images are from the author's collection unless noted otherwise.

Plate Section 1

Adolf Hitler and Hermann Göring.

Göring and Walther Wecke inspecting Landespolizeigruppe 'General Göring'; Walther Wecke, commander of Polizei Abteilung z.b.V. 'Wecke'; Friedrich-Wilhelm Jakoby; men of Landespolizeigruppe 'General Göring'.

Men of the Wach Bataillon 'Hermann Göring' at Carinhall; Regiment 'General Göring' troops with a 37-mm flak gun; Walther von Axthelm, an early commander of Regiment 'General Göring'.

SdKfz 231 armoured cars of Detachment 'Kluge' in Norway; motorcycle-sidecar combination showing the Viking ship emblem applied to all Detachment 'Kluge' vehicles used in Norway; a towed 88-mm anti-aircraft gun of Regiment 'General Göring', France 1940.

Guns of the 14th (Heavy) Railway Flak Battery; men of 6th Company with a ditched 88-mm gun, May 1940; Generalmajor Paul Conrath.

The highly decorated Karl Rossmann; Soviet KV-2 heavy tank destroyed by 'Hermann Göring' guns near Dubno, 1941; Oberleutnant Musil of 11. Kompanie (Panzer Pionier) of the Panzer Regiment; a 'Hermann Göring' soldier wearing a Waffen-SS camouflaged smock.

'Hermann Göring' combat engineers training in the use of 'storm boats'; 'Hermann Göring' armour and infantry training (*Alan Scheckenbach*); men formerly of Fallschirmjäger Regiment 5 in Tunisia after their redesignation as Jäger Regiment 'Hermann Göring'; Hauptmann Hans Jungwirth with a British prisoner whom Jungwirth saved from summary execution.

'Hermann Göring' motorcycle messenger; 'Hermann Göring' command post, Tunisia; 'Hermann Göring' troops in Sicily (*Alan Scheckenbach*).

'Hermann Göring' Panzer IV crew in Sicily (*Alan Scheckenbach*); 'Hermann Göring' men in Sicily wearing a mixture of uniforms (*Alan Scheckenbach*).

Plate Section 2

A 'Hermann Göring' Panzer man wearing a 'Hermann Meyer' peaked cap and standard Heer panzer insignia; Adolf Scheckenbach, wearing the white-backed Panzer insignia peculiar to 'Hermann Göring' troops (*Alan Scheckenbach*); Sturmgeschütz IIIB used for training at Harderwijk in 1944 (*Alan Scheckenbach*).

A new Panzer IV for the 'Hermann Göring' Division (*Alan Scheckenbach*); Oberst Wilhelm Schmalz; a 'Hermann Göring' Panzer IV commander.

A 'Hermann Göring' *Sturmgeschütz*; 'Hermann Göring' Panzers deployed in Sicily (*Alan Scheckenbach*); 'Hermann Göring' men being evacuated from Sicily (*Alan Scheckenbach*).

'Hermann Göring' Division recruiting pamphlet, 1943; Hermann Göring inspecting reinforcements for his division; an 88-mm gun of 2. Batterie, I./Flak-Regiment 'Hermann Göring', Italy.

A wrecked Panzer IV near Salerno; Knight's Cross holder Gerhard Tschierschwitz; 'Hermann Göring' Panzergrenadier prisoners of war, Mount Porchia, January 1944; 'Hermann Göring' troops ready for action, Italy, 1944.

'Hermann Göring' troops helping safeguard the treasures of Monte Cassino; bringing fresh water to the front lines, Italy, 1944; training Panzer recruits near Utrecht, 1944 (*Alan Scheckenbach*); Oberst Georg-Henning von Heydebreck.

Wreckage left behind by the 'Hermann Göring' Division after a reprisal action in Italy, July 1944 (*Canadian National Archives*); Hauptmann Wolfram Stronk; Major Hans Briegel; Generalmajor Schmalz and SS-Gruppenführer Heinz Reinefarth, Warsaw, 1944.

Oberst Hans Horst von Necker; Franz Lürbke (*Franz Lürbke*); Knight's Cross award ceremony, East Prussia, December 1944; Generalmajor Erich Walther; Karl Rossmann and Gerhard Tschierschwitz.

Hermann Göring inspects the men of his Wachregiment near his Reichsjägerhof on the Rominte Heath.

Foreword

Hermann Göring was the only National Socialist leader apart from Hitler to have a military division named after him. The Leibstandarte SS Adolf Hitler was a unit with a ferocious fighting record. By contrast, the 'Hermann Göring' Division, only formally constituted as such in late 1942, had a slow gestation and a chequered wartime experience. 'Wherever it fights,' announced the eponymous commander-in-chief, 'no enemy can succeed.' Yet the division, or a part of it, was captured in Tunisia, pushed out of Sicily, driven back from the Gustav Line, overwhelmed and captured in East Prussia. The history of the division is also the history of German defeat.

There was nevertheless a long prehistory to the founding of the division, meticulously reconstructed here by Lawrence Paterson. The division began life early in 1933, like the 'Leibstandarte', as a small mobile police unit dedicated to protecting the government quarter, and in particular the person of Hermann Göring himself – president of the German parliament, interior minister for Prussia and soon head of an Air Ministry. In 1935, once the infant Luftwaffe was officially founded, the police unit became the Regiment 'General Göring' under air force control. This was an unconventional force, soon to be a confusion of guard units, anti-aircraft batteries and paratroopers, regarded by German Army commanders as a 'vanity project' for the ambitious and egotistical commander-in-chief of the air force. It was the same story with Göring's role as economic dictator once he was appointed to head the Four-Year Plan organisation in 1936. The giant state holding company, set up to produce iron and steel, and later armaments, for the German war effort, was known as the Reichswerke 'Hermann Göring'.

The small multi-function regiment performed an incoherent mixture of roles throughout its early history, partly a product of the odd mix of duties the soldiers were expected to perform. Remarkably, some part of the regiment, whether guards, anti-aircraft units, or infantry, popped up in almost every major operation in the story of German territorial expansion and war: a guard unit watched over the Czech Skoda Works (later incorporated in Göring's Reichswerke) when Czechoslovakia was invaded and occupied; the regiment protected German leaders when they went to war against Poland in 1939; anti-aircraft units aided the invasion of Denmark and Norway before moving to France; part of the regiment transferred to Romania in March 1941 to safeguard the oil of Ploesti, in case the Soviets threatened a vital war resource; in summer 1941 a section of the unit was placed under Army Group South for the Barbarossa operation. Unlike most Army units, the regiment never worked as a whole, split both functionally and geographically. Given the confusion surrounding its use, it is surprising it managed to function at all.

Although the regiment was in some respects Göring's military pet, he seems from Paterson's account to have been a distant godfather. Once the regiment was raised to brigade strength in March 1942, then to a whole division in October, it was at the beck and call of the Army for operations in France (where Allied invasion was anticipated as early as 1942), North Africa, Italy, the Eastern Front, and the defence of the western Reich in 1944 at the time of Arnhem. In the process the unit became the Panzer Division 'Hermann Göring' in summer 1943, and then, with paratroopers attached once again, the Fallschirm-Panzer Division 'Hermann Göring'. Though short of troops and inadequately armed, the division became one half of the Fallschirm-Panzer-Korps 'Hermann Göring' in September 1944, its final iteration before defeat in May 1945. The unit was all but destroyed with defeat and capture in Tunisia in May 1943, but it was reconstituted and despite problems in training and equipment, fought well enough in Sicily and Italy for the Allies to develop a certain respect for it.

The unit suffered, like most of the German armed forces, from the over-ambitious strategy pursued by Hitler and his headquarters. Sending part of the division to Tunisia was a pointless waste given the hopeless logistical position facing Axis forces. Defending Italy south of Rome eventually decimated the division when the German forces could have moved north to a more defensible line. Sending elements of the division hither and thither in 1944 merely reflected Hitler's failuure to decide on priorities or to accept that the war could not be won. What is striking from this account is the willingness of German soldiers and airmen to carry on a dogged fighting defence, often in desperate situations, with little chance of success. The stoical resistance slowed down Allied armies everywhere and accounts for why it took more than two years after El Alamein and Stalingrad to bring the German armed forces to defeat. The division was just one among dozens to become adept at entrenched defensive fighting, spoiling counter-attacks, and well-organised withdrawal. Ironically, given Göring's habitual boasting about his air force, it was the absence of effective German air power from 1942 onwards that fatally weakened the determined efforts on the ground.

Inevitably, any account of the Fallschirm-Panzer Division 'Hermann Göring' must confront its postwar reputation as one of the German units notorious for atrocities against civilians. In the anti-partisan campaign in Italy, elements of the division took part in the programme of burning down villages, murdering or deporting the male inhabitants, occasionally killing women, children and the elderly, part of a tally of more than 19,000 murdered Italian civilians. All of this was sanctioned from above by commanding generals, including Field Marshal Kesselring, supreme commander in Italy, who all regarded softness against the civilian population as a betrayal of the fighting soldier. It must also be the case that soldiers who were constantly subject to Allied air attack, fighting an unwinnable war, took out their rage and frustration on civilians who were blamed for harbouring the 'bandits' responsible for terror attacks on German forces. The key was sanction from above, but after the war Kesselring, and many other German commanders, got away with brief prison sentences or no sentence at all, while lower-ranking officers in the 'Hermann Göring' Division were put on trial and imprisoned.

Göring liked to boast that his regiment, then his division, was the most National Socialist of all, but the truth seems more mundane. The soldiers were all volunteers, checked for physical appearance and fitness, likely to be former members of the Hitler Youth, but whether they were more ardent than other recruits as a result is difficult to demonstrate. The Luftwaffe was a creation of the Hitler state, which perhaps explains why it was thought to be more staunchly National Socialist, but the evidence is ambiguous where in the case of the SS, subject to hours of ideological training, there is less room for doubt. The division fought to defend Germany's new empire and to prevent or postpone German defeat; some were no doubt fanatical supporters of the regime, some not. It would be useful to know what form of political education was targeted at the division, and how receptive the ordinary soldier was to the ideological package of the dictatorship.

The history of the Fallschirm-Panzer Division 'Hermann Göring' illustrates both the strengths and weaknesses of the German military effort.

Nominally under the distant supreme command of Hitler's paladin and Luftwaffe chief, the division fell between two stools, air force and army, replicating a wider tension between the two services. The need to fight on three fronts meant a constant juggling of resources, which were never adequate enough anywhere to achieve strategic advantage. The distant campaigns strained Germany's logistic capability, and left units short of ammunition, equipment, even at times food. The difficulty in recovering and repairing the division's tanks could be repeated across the battlefronts. Nevertheless, for all these drawbacks, the German armed forces continued to manage the battlefield effectively enough to postpone defeat and to exact a high and bloody cost from the approaching Allied armies. When Göring sought out American captivity in May 1945 along with his trainload of loot, the troops of 'his' division were still in combat around Dresden and in Czechoslovakia, fighting indeed to the bitter end.

Richard Overy,
University of Exeter

Introduction

'If you mean "go for them" Field Marshal, then I'm your man.'
Paul Conrath to Albert Kesselring, July 1943

The 'Hermann Göring' Division is one of the Wehrmacht's more enigmatic formations. Created from a militarised police force to operate at the behest of Hermann Göring, head of the Prussian Police, it was a 'private army' in the making. Göring hoped to rival the challenge presented by Heinrich Himmler's burgeoning SS empire, but in this endeavour he failed. Instead, the unit became, to all intents, an Army regiment operated by Göring's Luftwaffe, thereby condemned to be an organisation with two masters. However, it more closely resembled the Waffen-SS than the Heer of the Wehrmacht. While maintaining exacting physical standards, high political motivation and a purely voluntary composition, the regiment nonetheless expanded to become a brigade and then a division by 1943. However, it rarely entered active service as a complete force, more regularly being divided into battle groups of whichever troops were available and trained. Frequently on the back foot because seldom granted the time required to reach full establishment as a combat-ready division, the 'Hermann Göring' troops were rarely optimally prepared for action. Reassignment of previously created *Fallschirmjäger* formations often helped bolster the unit's organisational weaknesses as well as providing a cadre of experienced soldiers to help mould the men alongside whom they served.

However, despite these major obstacles, the 'Hermann Göring' troops swiftly carved a major niche for themselves by their actions on battlefields in Africa, Italy and on the Eastern Front. Their reputation almost appears to have exceeded their actual achievements, though a steadfast aggression in combat became a hallmark of the division. Unfortunately, like the Waffen-SS, so did incidents of brutality against civilian populations. The same duality and complexities that affected Himmler's fighting troops are evident within at least some of the ranks of the 'Hermann Göring' units.

The division's military reputation was forged by a seeming fearlessness in attack, perfectly embodied by its main wartime commander, Paul Conrath. However, this zeal for the offensive also resulted in frequent criticism from Conrath's contemporaries that this was a wasteful means by which to wage war, once again reminiscent of accusations levelled at some officers of the Waffen-SS such as Josef 'Sepp' Dietrich and Theodore Eicke. Nonetheless, the Allies developed a wary respect for the fighting ardour of men who wore the 'Hermann Göring' cuff title. Göring had once boasted that he was commander-in-chief of the most politically motivated of the Wehrmacht's three arms of service, though the line between nationalism and political extremism is extremely fine and frequently difficult to see. The young volunteers who formed the original division were certainly motivated by patriotism and a desire to be part of what was considered an elite formation. However, to label the fighting men of the division as fanatical Nazis – as is so often done – is as facile as it is inaccurate. By contrast, the accusation cannot be dismissed in a blanket fashion. The complications of studying a 'first-echelon' fighting unit that waged war under the swastika flag are as prevalent within the 'Hermann Göring' history as they are for any of those that comprised the original Waffen-SS.

This book includes many organisational tables, which, though they may possibly slow down the narrative, do illustrate the interchanging of officers between different units and unit types. Unfortunately, some unit commanding officers and similar details could not be firmly identified and, rather than rely on supposition, I have left those spaces vacant.

This is not a book that focuses on uniforms and insignia of this unusual unit; there are several excellent such resources already available. Rather, this book is an operational history beginning with the formation's prewar inception as a Bavarian police unit and taking the story to the end of the war by which stage it had become a sprawling – albeit constantly understrength – Panzerkorps.

Acknowledgements

I would like to take the opportunity once again to thank people who have helped with this project. Firstly, my wife Anna and children Megan and James who continue to put up with the tribulations of being around an obsessive author. Thanks to Audrey 'Mumbles' Paterson for constant support from the other side of the world and Don 'Mr Mumbles' Tasker. Also thanks to Michael Leventhal, my esteemed publisher at Greenhill

Greenhill and Donald Sommerville for his hard work at editing another one of my manuscripts.

I am deeply indebted to the author Stephen Robinson, who has written a number of superb books, and who helped connect me with Alan Scheckenbach. Mr Scheckenbach provided priceless personal information and photos that had belonged to his Uncle Adolf, who served with the 'Hermann Göring' Division after transferring from the Heer. This insight is incredibly useful, and I have included many quotations directly from Adolf Scheckenbach rather than attempting to paraphrase his words. I believe that it is far more useful to have such 'eyewitness' accounts than to fictionalise history as seems to be prevalent among authors today. As in my other books, I have not done this. Novelising history to me produces neither a workable novel nor exact history.

Another 'Hermann Göring' veteran who allowed use of his words and life story is Franz Lürbke, who has recorded his experiences on an excellent website (www.franzluerbke.de) and who, through his son Dierk, allowed me to use whatever I wanted. Also, Bill and Carol Schiers permitted use of the diary of 'Hermann Göring' soldier Rolf Wallburg that Bill's father, Master Sergeant Robert Schiers, recovered from an abandoned motorcycle in North Africa. They have since returned it to Herr Wallburg's family – an amazing story that I recommend reading about in full on their website (www.billcarol.com). Many thanks go as well to Professor Dr Detlef Stronk who kindly filled in some gaps in my information regarding his father Wolfram Stronk who was badly wounded near Warsaw in 1944.

Chapter One

Police

'Patriotism is when love for your own country comes first; nationalism, when hate for people other than your own comes first.'
General Charles de Gaulle

At the end of the First World War, Germany was held accountable for the previous four years of conflict, the likes of which the world had never witnessed. The newly created republic of the Deutsches Reich – colloquially known as the 'Weimar Republic' due to its constitutional assembly meeting being held in the Thurungian city of Weimar – inherited a chaotic state in 1918 as the previous constitutional monarchy of Kaiser Wilhelm II was deposed and men returned from the front line to a country wracked by revolution. The subsequent Treaty of Versailles emasculated the country militarily: no U-boats or air force were allowed, and the remaining German Army, re-formed as the Reichswehr, was strictly limited in strength to 100,000 men; times were tough economically, too.

Republican Germany was divided into a series of constituent federal states (*Länder*), each with its own governmental infrastructure that mirrored that of the sovereign Weimar government, responsible for running major public services such as education and police. Though the Reichswehr had only 100,000 men, there had been no limitations placed on police force membership and many military and *Freikorps* veterans enlisted in the Landespolizei, creating a disciplined militarised police force, useful for keeping control of the greatest perceived threat to the republic – communist revolutionaries – while also maintaining a valuable reserve of trained men for potential future military purposes.

Though relative peace settled over the German *Länder* from 1924, the Weimar Republic remained inherently unpopular among much of the population. Adolf Hitler's Nazi Party (NSDAP) prospered in the hard times that followed the 1929 world economic crash. Elections in 1932 failed to yield a clear majority government: the NSDAP achieved 196 of the 293 required seats. Facing political and social turmoil, the ageing President Paul von Hindenburg was persuaded to pre-empt further elections and appoint Adolf Hitler as Chancellor of Germany, which he did on 30 January 1933. However, there had been no sweeping Nazi victory and Germany still lay on the brink of political disaster with six million people unemployed and a resurgent communist party determined never to concede defeat to the National Socialists. As was his prerogative as Chancellor, Hitler was able to appoint a new Minister of the Interior for Prussia, the largest and most important *Land*. To this post, Hitler despatched the politically astute Hermann Göring: former First World War fighter 'ace', loyal member of the NSDAP since 1922, former head of the SA and, from 2 February, Reich Commissar for Aviation (whereupon he instigated the covert reconstruction of a German air force).

Göring immediately set about clearing the Prussian Ministry of the Interior of all but adherents to the NSDAP, dismissing twenty-two of the thirty-two Prussian police chiefs and 1,457 men in total, as well as dissolving the Prussian state parliament and replacing it with an 'Advisory State Council'. In his purge of Prussia's huge Landespolizei Göring was assisted by Major Walther Wecke. A former artillery officer and member of a *Freikorps*, 'Freiwilligen Brigade Reinhard', Wecke had joined the Berlin Schutzpolizei on 24 June 1919. An early adherent to the principles of National Socialism, Wecke became Chairman of the National Socialist Association of Police Officials and during March 1932 he compiled dossiers on the 'ideological reliability' of individual Prussian policemen – later used by Göring and the newly appointed Prussian police chief, Generalmajor der Landespolizei (and SS Obergruppenführer) Kurt Daluege – before officially joining the NSDAP that November. On 5 January 1933, Wecke was elected chairman of the Association of Prussian Police Officers and later became a key contact point between the NSDAP and Prussian police force.

To consolidate his hold on Prussian security, on 23 February 1933, Göring ordered the formation of a motorised police unit under Wecke's command that would be devoted primarily to the National Socialist cause above all other considerations and principally concerned with protection of the Reich government. Thus two days later the Polizei Abteilung z.b.V. 'Wecke' (z.b.V. = *zur besonderen Verwendung*, 'for special duties') was activated in Berlin, formed from fourteen officers and 400 men of the Prussian Landespolizei.[1] Honouring its original members, a decree issued by Göring ruled that the police emblem of the former German East African colony was to be worn by men of the first *Hundertschaft* (approximately a company, 100 men strong); that one of the first identifying insignias displayed by this new formation was the 'Cross of the South' – a small woven shield worn on the lower left sleeve – displayed a traditional connection to Germany's imperial past.

Wecke's unit comprised a command *Abteilung*, three *Polizeibereitschaften* (each a company strong), a motorcycle platoon (*Zug*) and signals platoon. The three main components were:

1. Kompanie/Polizei-Abt. z.b.V. 'Wecke'	*Polizeihauptmann Bruno Bräuer*
2. Kompanie/Polizei-Abt. z.b.V. 'Wecke'	*Polizeihauptmann Otto Sydow*
3. Kompanie/Polizei-Abt. z.b.V. 'Wecke'	*Polizeihauptmann Wilhelm Köppen*

Before long the unit also received two armoured cars (*Polizei Sonderwagen*) each armed with a pair of turreted heavy machine guns. Wecke's men were initially quartered in Berlin's Kreuzberg quarter, within the former barracks of the Imperial Prussian Königin Augusta Garde-Grenadier-Regiment Nr. 4 on Jüterboger Straße, the men recognisable as police in their standard dark blue Schutzpolizei uniforms with shako. While undergoing a military training regime, they mounted their first raids on Berlin's Communist headquarters during the early morning of 2 March 1933. During this, Police Battalion 'Wecke' arrested twenty-seven communist leaders and seized significant quantities of weapons and explosive material. Over the days that followed, workers' quarters were repeatedly raided in an attempt to destroy Berlin's Communist Party infrastructure. This concerted assault followed on the heels of the Reichstag Fire and subsequent passing by Hindenburg of the 'Decree of the Reich President for the Protection of People and State' that suspended civil liberties and invoked what was, to all intents and purposes, martial law. The suppression of German communists was legally intensified, ultimately resulting in a Nazi coalition government with the conservative German National People's Party (DNVP) emerging from fresh elections on 5 March, subsequent passing of Hitler's Enabling Act – the power to enact laws without the involvement of the Reichstag – and the final triumph of Hitler as dictatorial leader of Germany.

Early attempts to create a more consistent national police service had been met with strong opposition from each of the *Länder*, which were unwilling to relinquish their differing legal codes. The predominantly Catholic Bavaria was particularly vociferous in its refusal as it feared encroachment on its legal decision-making by Protestant Prussia. However, the rise of the National Socialists ended this wrangle and Reichsführer-SS Heinrich Himmler was determined to amalgamate the sixteen separate *Land* police forces into a single nationwide entity. Eventually he created the national Ordnungspolizei that incorporated all uniformed police forces after being named Chief of German Police in the Interior Ministry on 17 June 1936 following a decree by Hitler unifying 'control of police duties within the Reich'.

Göring was in control of Prussia's police forces for years before Himmler's success. Wecke's unit was redesignated Landespolizeigruppe 'Wecke' z.b.V. on 17 July 1933 and its appearance changed: it became the first police unit to be equipped with a Reichswehr green uniform, complete with light green arm-of-service piping (*Waffenfarbe*), on trouser seams and around the collar. The same uniform would become standard among Prussian police units by June the following year. Wecke's *Gruppe* now more closely resembled infantrymen than policemen, with the traditional police shako being replaced by a Reichswehr steel helmet, its left side bearing the national tricolour emblem, the right a large swastika. They were also presented with a special Landespolizei standard on 13 September in a ceremony presided over by Göring in his Reichswehr general's uniform. The standard comprised a large white swastika with the Prussian eagle at its centre set on a green background. During the ceremony, Göring sketched his burgeoning desire for a private army when he stated that his goal was to 'make the Prussian state police a sharp weapon for Germany and, if the day comes that we are called against an external enemy, to hand it over to Führer on equal terms to the Reichswehr'.[2] Further change followed on 22 December of that same year when the unit became Landespolizeigruppe 'General Göring'. Men of the renamed formation were also authorised to wear a new cuff-title on the lower left sleeve: a dark green band with the words 'L.P.G. General Göring' machine-embroidered in white Gothic script, edged with white borders top and bottom for NCOs, executed in hand-woven silver-grey wire for officers.

Göring had secured the germ of his own personal army, one he envisioned would reach a strength of 56,000 men and initially intended to rival both Himmler's SS and the Reichswehr, though neither ambition would be realised. Nonetheless, as an instrument of solidifying his own power-base, his Landespolizeigruppe operated with considerable autonomy at the behest of their namesake commander-in-chief and in a clearly politically motivated manner. Indeed, on 2 December 1933 Wecke remarked in a letter to SS-Obergruppenführer Kurt Daluege: 'We now have a National Socialist police force.'[3] Wecke, promoted to *Polizei Generalmajor* at the beginning of 1934, steadily accumulated volunteers until the number of men available to him amounted to a force of six battalions.

On 6 June 1934 the architect of the unit, Wecke, was sidelined when he was transferred from his command position to the operations staff (*Führungsstab*) of the Prussian Police, replaced by Oberstleutnant Friedrich-Wilhelm Jakoby. The new man was a former infantryman, Jakoby having volunteered for the 5. Westfälischen Infanterie-Regiments Nr. 53 in 1915 and ended the war a *Leutnant der Reserve*. He left the Army in October 1919, entering the Prussian Landespolizei as a *Polizeileutnant*, reaching the rank of *Polizeihauptmann* by August 1932. The day following the formation of Hitler's government, 31 January 1933, Jakoby was appointed adjutant to the newly appointed Minister of Aviation and Prussian Minister of the Interior, Hermann Göring. Promoted to *Polizeimajor* on 20 April 1933, Jakoby had assisted Wecke in the purge of non-National Socialist officers from the Landespolizei headquarters before succeeding him as commander.

Jakoby was in command when, on 30 June 1934, Landespolizeigruppe 'General Göring' took part in the 'Night of the Long Knives', the Nazis' purge of SA officers who were alleged to have been plotting revolution against their Führer. Jakoby and his men occupied sandbagged machine-gun posts in the streets of Berlin, guarding the Prussian State Ministry and Göring's nearby private villa ensconced within the protected enclave of government buildings. The purge of SA officers was so complete that Wecke took temporary charge of SA-Obergruppe III (Berlin-Brandenburg) for most of July following the execution of its former commander, SA-Gruppenführer Karl Ernst. Following this bloodletting, the 'General Göring' unit was gradually expanded still more and moved its barracks to that formerly of the Königin-Elizabeth-Garde-Grenadier-Regiment Nr. 3 in Charlottenburg.

The departed Wecke eventually returned to Army logistics during October 1935 at the rank of *Generalmajor*, before moving to the Luftwaffe two years later. Initially commander of the Reichsluftschutz-Schule, Berlin-Wannsee, he later became commander of the Luftwaffe contingent of 'Protection Zone' (Schutzzone) Slovakia until his active service ended because of ill health at the rank of *General der Flieger*. Wecke died of an unspecified illness in a Luftwaffe hospital in Gotha (Luftwaffen-Lazarett 8/III) on 16 December 1943, his ashes later being interred in a Berlin cemetery. The official German newspaper report of Wecke's urn arriving in Berlin provided Allied propaganda with material for a small newspaper article that inferred Wecke was murdered as part of an internal purge similar to that which had decimated the SA. The brief article, entitled 'Ein Röhm'scher General' concluded:

> The dead General Wecke has never been mentioned before, neither in the newspaper nor on the radio. So he obviously neither 'fell' nor died of an illness. What's going on? Is this a 'Röhmian' end that has been prepared for Göring's general?

On 16 March 1935 Adolf Hitler revealed to the world Germany's covert rearmament, the existence of the Luftwaffe, and the reintroduction of conscription in a final abrogation of the Treaty of Versailles. Göring, with exceptional assistance from his deputy, former Lufthansa executive Erhard Milch, had consolidated the power of Germany's fledgling air force and the Luftwaffe had come into being as an independent service arm on 15 May 1934, albeit still under the camouflage required by this contravention of the Versailles Treaty. With the deception now discarded, Göring was named Luftwaffe Commander-in-Chief (Oberbefehlshaber der Luftwaffe), directly subordinate to Hitler as the head of the armed forces. Various units previously disguised as the flying clubs of police formations – generally comprised of SA paramilitaries – were handed over officially to the strength of the Luftwaffe. While this restructuring of Göring's departments took place, Jakoby's ground unit remained a part of the Landespolizei but was once again redesignated on the first day of April, this time as Regiment 'General Göring'.

By now the fully motorised complement numbered some 1,856 men and comprised the following units:

Regimental Staff	
Band [Musikkorps]	(formed at the beginning of 1935 from an Army cadre for ceremonial purposes, often performing the regimental parade march, Gottfried Rode's 'Der Jäger aus Kurpfalz')
1st Light Infantry Battalion [I. Jäger Abteilung]	*Polizeihauptmann Bruno Bräuer*
2nd Light Infantry Battalion	
13th Motorcycle Company [13. Kradschützen Kompanie]	
14th Engineer Company	*Polizeioberleutnant Karl-Lothar Schulz*
Mounted Reconnaissance Platoon [Reiterzug]	
Signals Platoon [Nachricten Zug]	*Polizeioberleutnant Eberhard Lüdecke*

During the autumn 3rd (Light) Flak Battalion [III. (leichte) Flak Abteilung] was added to the Regiment (under the command of Polizeihauptmann Adolf Wolf), and on 24 September, Regiment 'General Göring' was finally officially transferred to the Luftwaffe and Jakoby commissioned into the Luftwaffe as an acting *Oberstleutnant*. Former Army infantry and engineering officer Major Josef Kammhuber was attached for two months as tactical advisor – he had just returned from a trip to South America aboard the 'Graf Zeppelin' airship.

Outwardly the men of the regiment changed little about their appearance other than the addition of a Luftwaffe eagle on the right breast and the winged oakleaves in place of the Polizei cockade on peaked caps. Not until 23 March 1936 were they ordered to exchange the Reichswehr green uniform for Luftwaffe blue. The unit was also provided with distinctive white Luftwaffe rank patches, fringed by orthodox Wehrmacht *Waffenfarbe* colours; for example NCOs and men of the Jäger were identified by rifle-green *Waffenfarbe*, with red for flak artillery. The cuff title also changed, now dark blue with 'General Göring' embroidered in silver wire for officers, with a silver border above and below, embroidered in matt grey thread for NCOs and without the border for enlisted men.

By October, with an influx of fresh volunteers, the regiment reached a strength of 108 officers and 2,935 men and Jakoby's troops were placed under the command of Generalmajor Hubert Weise as Höherer Kommandeur der Flakartillerie in Luftkreis II. Almost totally motorised with the repurposing of its mounted troops, the constituent units now comprised:

Regiment Staff	with Band, Signals, Mounted Platoons att.
1st Light Infantry Battalion	*Hauptmann Bruno Bräuer*
Signals Platoon	*Oblt. Eberhard Lüdecke*
Engineer Platoon [Pionier Zug]	
1st, 2nd, 3rd Light Infantry Companies	
4th Machine-gun Company	
2nd Light Infantry Battalion	
Signals Platoon	
Engineer Platoon	
5th, 6th, 7th Light Infantry Companies	
8th Machine-gun Company	
3rd Light Flak Battalion]	*Hptm. Wilhelm Köppen*
Staff Battery	
9th Battery, 6 x 37-mm guns	

10th Battery, 6 x 20-mm guns	
11th Battery, 6 x 20-mm guns	
12th Battery, 6 x searchlights	
13th Motorcycle Company	with attached Armoured Car Platoon [Panzerspäh Zug]
14th Engineer Company	*Oberleutnant Karl-Lothar Schulz*
15th and 16th Guard [Wach] Companies	(added in July 1936 and April 1937 respectively)

Hermann Göring now controlled a highly trained infantry unit that matched Himmler's embryonic Waffen-SS in its dedication to National Socialism and its commander-in-chief. The vainglorious Luftwaffe head was determined to create an elite military formation in his name to rival both the Army's 'Großdeutschland' and Himmler's Leibstandarte SS 'Adolf Hitler' though numerically Göring's unit was eclipsed by what was then called the SS Verfügungstruppe. Further differentiating his troops from their opposites, Göring directed them to explore a path that diverged from that of his SS rivals.

The origins of German experiments with parachute troops can be traced to an event in 1931 when invited Reichswehr observers witnessed a Red Army demonstration parachute drop; a second massed exercise also open to foreign military observers then took place at Kiev in 1935. In total 1,500 men and their supporting equipment were successfully parachuted into 'action'. Among the assembled German officers observing was Oberst Kurt Student who immediately recognised the latent possibilities of pursuing development of a German parachute arm. On 29 January 1936, Göring's deputy, Erhard Milch, issued a secret communiqué requesting volunteers for the formation of Germany's first *Fallschirmjäger* unit within the framework of the Regiment 'General Göring'.

Such volunteers were concentrated in Bruno Bräuer's 1st Battalion and, along with Oberleutnant Karl-Lothar Schulz's recently renumbered 15th Engineer Company, were sent to a newly established Luftwaffe parachute training school (Fallschirmschule 1) at Stendal-Bostel airfield in Anhalt, northwest of Berlin. Bruno Bräuer himself – later a leading light of the *Fallschirmjäger* – made his first jump on 11 May 1936. While the embryonic parachute unit exercised, the remainder of the regiment moved to a training ground near Altengrabow, in Saxony near Magdeburg, to continue instruction as a conventional motorised infantry formation with supporting units.

On 13 August, Jakoby was transferred to Luftkreis-Fliegerschule for signals training, handing command of the regiment over to Major Walther Moritz Heinrich Wolfgang von Axthelm.[4] Axthelm was the first commanding officer who had not served in the Landespolizei; he had been an artillery officer throughout the First World War and thereafter in the Reichswehr. Transferred to the Air Ministry in April 1935 he had been appointed Gruppenleiter bei der Inspektion der Flakartillerie before being given command of Regiment 'General Göring' following Jakoby's departure. The appointment of an experienced artillery officer perhaps indicated the direction in which the regiment would proceed, although from September 1937, for the first-time, a paratrooper sub-unit was officially included in the regimental strength: Major Bruno Bräuer's 4th Paratroop Battalion [IV. Fallschirmschützen Abteilung/RGG] which would soon absorb Hptm. Karl-Lothar Schulz's 15th Paratroop Engineer Company.

A general reorganisation took place shortly thereafter at the beginning of October, at which point the 2nd Jäger Battalion disappears from the regimental order of battle. It is likely that it was broken up and used to expand other constituent parts; it is frequently noted as having 'converted' to the heavy flak battalion that would be a core feature of the regiment in the years to follow. On 1 October 1937 Regiment 'General Göring' comprised:

Regiment 'General Göring'	***Obstlt. Walther von Axthelm***	
Chief of Staff:	*Hptm. Bernhard von Oppeln-Bronikowski*	
Adjutant:	*Hptm. Karl-Erich Bertram*	
Signals Platoon		
Band		
1st (Heavy) Flak Battalion	*Hptm. Werner Hullmann*	
Staff		
Staff Battery	*Oblt. Hans Joachim von Jablonowski*	
1st Battery (88-mm)	*Hptm. Erich Rösner*	
2nd Battery (88-mm)	*Oblt. Werner Geicke*	
3rd Battery (88-mm)	*Oblt. Alfred Schröder*	
4th Battery (37-mm)	*Hptm. Karl Thimm*	
2nd (Light) Flak Battalion	*Maj. Paul Conrath*	replaced by Maj. Ernst Rüdel when Conrath became Chief Adjutant, Ob.d.L.
Staff		
Staff Battery	*Oblt. Robert Schulz*	
5th Battery (20-mm)	*Hptm. Walter Barg*	
6th Battery (20-mm)	*Hptm. Eberhard Lüdecke*	
7th Battery (20-mm)	*Hptm. Neubauer*	

3rd Guard [Wach] Battalion	Maj. Otto Sydow	formed from Mounted Platoon, both Guard Companies and Motorcycle Coy.
Staff Signals Platoon		
Mounted Platoon		
8th Motorcycle Company	*Hptm. Joachim Preuss*	with attached armoured car platoon, disbanded in November
9th Guard Company	*Oblt. Heinz Zorn*	
10th Guard Company	*Hptm. Waldemar Kluge*	
11th Guard Company	*Lt. Gustav Altmann*	added on 1 April 1938
4th Paratroop Battalion	*Maj. Bruno Bräuer*	
Staff		
Signals Platoon		
11th Paratroop Company	*Oblt. Walter Gericke*	
12th Paratroop Company	*Oblt. Vogel*	
13th Paratroop Company	*Oblt. Merten*	
14th Paratroop MG Company	*Oblt. Noster*	
15th Paratroop Engineer Company	*Hptm. Karl-Lothar Schulz*	

In March 1938, elements of 'Regiment General Göring' – including 8th Motorcycle Company – went into action for the first time during the so-called 'Blumenkrieg' as Germany annexed Austria. In only three days, elements of the regiment reached an Austrian bridge over the Leitha River, a tributary of the Danube near the Hungarian border. The entire Regiment later took part in the parade before Hitler in Vienna on 15 March before being stationed in the Theresian Military Academy, Wiener-Neustadt, and Bad Fischbach for brief garrison duties. The military academy would later host a Wehrmacht NCO school, its first commander Oberst Erwin Rommel.

Later that month, Bräuer's 4th Battalion was detached permanently to form the 1st Battalion of 1st Paratroop Regiment as part of the inaugural German airborne formation, 7th Flieger Division. Major Otto Sydow was soon appointed commander of a new air-landing training unit, Luftlande-Bataillon/Regiment 'General Göring', that remained on strength until it too transferred to 7th Flieger Division as its 3rd Battalion during November.[5] Sydow's place as commander of the Guard Battalion was taken by Maj. Willi Weber; its members were tasked with guard duty at the Reich Air Ministry, Göring's Berlin villa and his palatial and expanding Carinhall, northeast of Berlin in the Schorfheide forest, between the lakes Großdöllner See and Wuckersee.

Carinhall had been named in honour of Göring's Swedish first wife who had died of natural causes in 1931. Although she had been initially interred in Sweden, the distraught Göring had her remains moved to a mausoleum on the Carinhall grounds in 1934. The residence itself was built as a grand hunting lodge in stages from 1933 onwards, becoming a luxuriously appointed private residence protected by his troops, including part of the RGG cavalry unit. Friedrich Gerlach was a young recruit who joined the Mounted Platoon in 1943:

> Here in the Reiterzug we had to do a lot of guard duty. Once there was the patrol day and night. For this, three men were always assigned. The guard room for these three men was over by the guard company, which was located about 200 m away from us and was right on the street that led to Groß Schönebeck, and every three hours the patrol followed the path from our barracks to the street and back again. Then there was the stable guard, also day and night and relieved every two hours. There were also three men assigned to the stable guard, which means that we always had four hours of free time between guard duty but were, of course, on duty during the day. At five in the morning all three men had to feed the horses. Feeding usually went on until shortly before six o'clock and then at seven we were woken up again. In addition, there were daytime patrol rides through the Schorfheide. Each lasted about two hours and was carried out by two men, two patrols a day, one in the morning and one in the afternoon. The route was prescribed by our security guard and followed extensive paths around Hermann Göring's residence.
>
> The guard company, which was based beside the country road, had a main post on the road and two more near Göring's residence as well as another post immediately in front of the house. The house was about a kilometre from the company's accommodation, in the middle of the forest. On one occasion, at night, enemy aircraft came over – from Carinhall you could see this well – Hermann Göring came out of his house and said to the guards: 'Well, they will surely fly on to Berlin.'
>
> On Sundays we went up to Göring's residence with two or three comrades. Here we also guarded the crypt of Hermann Göring's first wife . . . One descended about six to eight steps to this crypt. The room was about four metres square. In the middle was a bronze

> coffin on a base with a bronze oak wreath on it. This crypt was across the street from the entrance to the courtyard of Göring's residence.
>
> Another task of our Reiterzug was to accompany Hermann Göring on the hunt. The escort consisted of three men fully equipped with sub-machine guns and live ammunition. This ride then proceeded as follows. The plan for the hunting trip would be announced by Hermann Göring in the morning. Three men were then assigned to escort protection. Since Göring always went out hunting in the afternoon, the riders had to report to the company at 1 p.m. The carriage or hunting wagon was stationed there. A security guard called Banke drove this carriage, which was pulled by two horses. This guard picked up the three escorts from Oberforstmeister Schade, who was not far from the company, then drove up to the Waldhof and picked Göring up. Any game that Göring shot was retrieved by two of the riders while the third stayed with the horses; the game was then put in a special storage area at the back of the carriage. Then it went back home.[6]

In October 1938 the regiment also participated in the occupation of the Sudetenland, before yet another reorganisation of what was, essentially, now an anti-aircraft unit with attached guard battalion. From members of the heavy anti-aircraft battalion, the 3rd Searchlight [Scheinwerfer] Battalion was created, commanded by former regimental staff officer Maj. Bernhard von Oppeln-Bronikowski. Similarly, the 5th (Light) Battery was detached to form a cadre around which a second light anti-aircraft battalion was created, 4th Flak Battalion, under the command of Oberstleutnant Walter von Hippel (former Chief of Staff to Generalmajor Hubert Weise). Its composite batteries were initially designated 1st–3rd, but later renumbered 15th–17th; two batteries had 20-mm and one had 37-mm cannon.

The regiment continued to accept only volunteers, each man signing on for a period of twelve years after fulfilling rigorous criteria similar to that of the Waffen-SS. Applicants had to be aged between 18 and 25 and no less than 1.68 metres (5 ft 6 in.) tall. They were required to be German citizens – no *Volksdeutsche* were accepted – eligible for military service, of proven Aryan descent, unmarried and with no previous criminal convictions. More tellingly for a military formation created as an elite part of Göring's empire, they were required to 'guarantee that they would always openly support the National Socialist state'.

Göring oversaw the construction of a luxurious new barracks for his men, situated in Berlin's Reinickendorf district. On a site formerly used by an imperial airship battalion, designer Oberbaurat Schneidt developed a complex of 130 buildings arranged around a central axis and accessed by an oval internal ring road. Alongside the impeccably kept accommodation, workshop and eating areas was an extensive sports facility complete with running track and indoor and outdoor swimming pools.

The regiment took an active part in the occupation of Czechoslovakia, marching into Prague on 14 March 1939 as part of Hitler's final bloodless conquest and spending several weeks on guard at the important Plzeň Skoda works. Young recruit Rolf Wallburg had joined the Regiment 'General Göring' in November 1938 after completing his compulsory Reich Labour Service duty. Assigned to 11th Battery of 3rd Searchlight Battalion, he took part in the invasion of the Czech Republic.

> For the first time the entire battery is marching into war. During extreme cold, icy roads and severe snowfall we are leaving Berlin. The drive itself is even getting worse. The drivers do not yet have driving licences, we haven't fired a single bullet yet, and we go to war anyway. Everything turns out well. Via Dresden and Bodenbach we reach Prague. We are welcomed with enthusiasm in the Sudeten German area, but in Prague people are against us with clenched fists. Our mission is to get Prague under control and establish order. Setting up patrols and guarding, things was not hazard free but we succeed and after a few weeks everything in Prague is streamlined after German patterns. Glorious days they were; everything is very inexpensive, cake, beer and food are excellent. Then we have to return. Our training time is being completed in Prague before marching back. Two days before Easter we are back in Berlin.[7]

Hitler's bluster and bullying of British and French governments had now expanded the Third Reich successfully into two neighbouring countries, but his increasing agitation against Poland and planned reoccupation of the 'Danzig corridor' would prove a step too far. With declared French and British intentions to counter any aggression against Poland with military action, German mobilisation was ordered on 15 August and existing elements of the regiment were enlarged and reorganised: the Mounted Platoon to a Cavalry Squadron [Reiterschwadron], while 9–11 Companies of the Guard Battalion were renumbered 1–3 respectively.

Four new units were created:

Reserve Searchlight Battalion (*Maj. Hermann Römer*) – 1st–3rd Batteries (subsequently transferred out of the regiment and redesignated during 1941 as 3rd Battalion, Flak-Regiment 32);

Ersatz Battalion (*Maj. Ludwig Grauert* from 16 May 1940)– a training and replacement unit;

1st (Heavy) Railway [Eisenbahn] Flak Battery (*Oblt. Arnold*) – formed from members of 1st (Heavy) Flak Battalion and later renamed 14th (Heavy) Railway Flak Battery – armed with four 105-mm guns and two 20-mm flak weapons and later subordinated to 3rd Battalion;

8th (Light) Flak Battery (*Hptm. Wolfgang Seewald*) – equipped with mobile 20-mm anti-aircraft guns mounted on railway cars. This unit was under Göring's direct control as Oberbefehlshaber der Luftwaffe and was therefore entirely independent of the regiment; it was initially tasked with anti-aircraft escort for Göring himself and Foreign Minister von Ribbentrop and flak protection of Berlin's Führerhauptquartier.

Arnold's Heavy Railway Battery remained distinct from that operating as part of the train used by Adolf Hitler – the *Führerzug* – and Göring's 'Amerika' command train and conformed to what became a standard Wehrmacht railway flak configuration. Each flatcar mounting a large calibre weapon was of the same configuration, with a single gun mounted dead centre with folding panels on either side to be lowered to provide a stable crew platform when in action. Raised portions at each end of the car provided stowage for ammunition and maintenance material, while the crews were housed in accommodation boxcars – not specifically designed for flak troops but a stopgap measure at the war's beginning – with separate canteen car and headquarters car for battery commander Oblt. Arnold. The smaller calibre 20-mm cannon – one at each end of the train – were housed integrally in the roof of the same car in which the crew was accommodated.

Railway flak provided the Luftwaffe with an effective and highly mobile anti-aircraft capability that was considerably expanded as the war progressed, occasionally also used in the anti-tank role on the Eastern Front. The 14th (Heavy) Railway Flak Battery, RGG was initially deployed to Berlin in September 1939, thereafter travelling to the Western Front and providing anti-aircraft firepower at the French border in the Rhineland, ranging between Bad Krotzingen and Saarbrücken until the attack on France in May 1940.

Chapter Two

Early Successes in War

'A war, even the most victorious, is a national misfortune.'
Field Marshal Helmuth Graf von Moltke

At the outbreak of war, 7th Light Battery, RGG was posted to Berlin in the air defence role, the men of 2nd Guard Company also present as protection for Führer headquarters. Providing anti-aircraft defence for their head of state was the Führer Flak Abteilung, which in 1939 was comprised of Maj. Conrath's 2nd (Light) Flak Battalion; the motorised 20-mm Flak guns of 7th Battery were under the command of Hptm. Walter Barg (his immediate subordinate being Leutnant Karl Rossmann who was soon to rise to prominence in the regiment) designated part of the Führer Escort Command [Führerbegleitkommando] and set to accompany Hitler into Poland after hostilities began.

At the beginning of October 1939, the Führerbegleitbataillon was formed in the 'Hermann Göring' barracks in Berlin-Reinickendorf under the command of Generalmajor Erwin Rommel; Barg's 7th Battery, RGG was attached alongside three infantry companies (rifle, '*schnelle*' – equipped with motorcycles and armoured cars – and '*schwere*' – equipped with 37-mm anti-tank and 20-mm flak cannon).[1] Furthermore, the 9th Railway Escort [Eisenbahn-Begleit] Battery, RGG was created under the command of Oblt. Herbert Tilcher, equipped with train-mounted 20-mm cannon, later superseded by the fearsome four-barrelled 'Vierling', and divided into two detachments allocated for the protection of trains used by Göring, Hitler and Foreign Minister Joachim von Ribbentrop.

While other regimental flak units were retained in Berlin for anti-aircraft protection when the invasion of Poland began, Maj. Otto Sydow led 3rd Guard Battalion into Poland as second echelon troops behind the German spearheads. While most were transported by truck towards Warsaw, which finally fell to German besieging forces on 28 September, Hptm. Waldemar Kluge's 10th Guard Company was flown in by Junkers Ju 52 aircraft to provide security for the Warsaw-Okecie airfield and its associated PZL state aircraft factory that had produced fighters and bombers.

Born in Kupferburg, Lower Silesia, in 1904, Kluge had already experienced combat against the Poles, having taken part in fighting against the Silesian uprisings at the age of seventeen; he was awarded the Silesian Eagle Order (Schlesischen Adlerorden) First and Second Class after being wounded in the battle of Annaberg in May 1921. Following a period working as a miner in Upper Silesia, during 1925 he had joined the Schutzpolizei as an officer candidate in Brandenburg, was commissioned as a *Polizeileutnant* and transferred to the Luftwaffe and the 'General Göring' Regiment when Wehrmacht conscription was introduced.

These troops took no active part in the fighting in Poland, while the anti-aircraft units stationed in Berlin faced only a leaflet raid mounted by Whitleys of 10 Squadron, RAF, at the beginning of October. Following Poland's surrender on 6 October, three RGG flak battalions were transferred west and provided a temporary redesignation as cover for their movements: Axthelm's Regimental Staff, 1st (Heavy) Battalion and 4th (Light) Battalion were officially redesignated 103rd Flak Regiment, headquartered in Erkelenz in the Rhineland and subordinated to II. Flakkorps, Army Group B.[2] The 3rd Searchlight Battalion, meanwhile, was attached to 101st Flak Regiment (I. Flakkorps, Army Group A) in support of the Twelfth Army, relocated first to Trier until 25 January, and then Neuerberg until May. Only Maj. Conrad's 2nd (Light) Flak Battalion initially remained in the Berlin area on air defence duty.[3]

While the Western Front may have settled into what the British jokingly referred to as the 'Phoney War' German attention had now turned to the difficult process of planning for an invasion of the Low Countries and northeastern France. However, fears of a British occupation of Norway steadily increased in Berlin and, following the Royal Navy raid on the German prison ship *Altmark* in Norwegian territorial waters on 15 February 1940, Hitler's vacillation between concentrating his forces against Western Europe or countering a potential threat to Scandinavia – and thence the Baltic – ended. The invasion of Norway and Denmark would come before the attack on France and the Low Countries and, on 1 March 1940, detailed instructions were issued to the Wehrmacht for the invasion, code-named 'Weserübung'; 'Wesertag' was set for 9 April 1940.

The RGG contributed one battle group to Weserübung; designated 'Detachment Kluge' under the command of Hptm. Waldemar Kluge and attached to XXXI Army Corps. This pattern of forming battle groups (*Kampfgruppen*) from regimental forces would become an operational standard until such time as the unit was of a size to be deployed intact for battle in 1942. The Wehrmacht frequently excelled at the use of such ad hoc formations, particularly in the later war years, and the regiment provided an early example of this tactical system.

There were, in essence, two distinct types of *Kampfgruppe*; the first was a deliberate temporary grouping of units assembled to achieve a specific purpose, while the second was an assembly of units thrown together by circumstances under a single command, commonly encountered during the German defensive fighting in the war's later stages. Most *Kampfgruppen* carried two designations, the first and most used being the commander's name – for example, Kampfgruppe 'Schmalz' in Sicily in 1943 – the second being a more militarily punctilious designation, generally numbered. The principle of *Kampfgruppen* was enabled by German military doctrine which practised *Auftragstaktik*; the art of military delegation filtering down the chain of command. In practice, junior officers were briefed by their superiors on what task they were to accomplish, but how they chose to do it was left to their own discretion. Although Adolf Hitler later interfered with this principle as his authoritarian grip over the military was tightened from 1942 onwards, the Wehrmacht and Waffen-SS were served consistently well by *Auftragstaktik* except in those rare cases where commanding officers were simply not up to the task.

Kluge's small unit was led by a battalion headquarters with attached motorised signals platoon. Under his command was a motorcycle platoon led by Hptm. Joachim Preuss which also included three eight-wheeled heavy SdKfz 231 reconnaissance armoured cars. Alongside the lightly armoured reconnaissance vehicles, the platoon counted nine heavy machine guns, three light machine guns and three light mortars as its heaviest weapons. Hauptmann Helmut Funck's 1st Guard Company, RGG was attached, a motorised infantry company that also carried six heavy and four light machine guns and three light mortars alongside its individual small arms. Finally, Hptm. Wolfgang Seewald led four platoons totalling twelve flak vehicles armed with 20-mm cannon of the 8th (Light) Flak Battery. For the attack on Denmark – 'Weserübung Süd' – Kluge's unit was directly supported by an Army reconnaissance squadron from the Kavallerie und Panzertruppenschule (Cavalry and Panzer Troops School) at Krampnitz, comprising mixed heavy SdKfz 231s and four-wheeled SdKfz 222s and apparently under the command of an officer named Hessel. The entire formation was subordinated to Oberst Günther Angern's 11th (motorised) Rifle Brigade [Schützenbrigade (mot.)]; an independent Army brigade that would later form the infantry component of the 11th Panzer Division.

These units were to operate in western Denmark alongside the 170th Infantry Division, which would advance along the two main north–south roads on either side of the Jutland Peninsula. Angern's brigade, with Kluge's detachment, would hasten north between these spearheads, aiming to reach the important Aalborg airport, to relieve and reinforce a battalion of the 69th Infantry Division that was to be airlifted in to seize the field during the early morning of the offensive's opening day. En route, they would also secure the major town and fishing port of Esbjerg, this latter task allocated to Kluge.

Though reports of German troop movements and warnings of an impending attack were received in Copenhagen, the Danish authorities did little to prepare for invasion and the bulk of the German troops were kept some distance from the border until the early hours of 7 April to at least maintain the illusion of secrecy. Kluge and his men accompanied 11th Brigade to Heide, less than 100 kilometres from the Danish border, before making a final dash to the jumping-off point at Bramstedtlund, travelling in convoy overnight at speeds of up to 65 km/h without lights.

There was no preparatory artillery or aerial bombardment. Instead, Brandenburger commandos operated to the east securing railway lines, while aerial and seaborne landings were launched by surprise elsewhere. Kluge's part of 'Weserübung Süd' began at 0515 hours, when Hessel's armoured cars spearheaded the movement across the border. There was no opposition until Kluge's unit reached the crossroads in the small town of Bredevad, 15 km within Danish territory. There, elements of the Danish 4th Battalion had deployed from Camp Søgaard; a 1st Company Bicycle Platoon, with one light machine gun, and a single 20-mm anti-tank weapon detached from the 4th Motorcycle Company had established a makeshift defensive position in residential gardens after being placed on alert and leaving their barracks only three-quarters of an hour before the invasion began. Without time to establish a roadblock, the Danes observed the approaching armoured cars and motorcyclists and opened fire at a range of only 300 metres, disabling the leading vehicle from the Krampnitz squadron and killing its driver. Kluge deployed troops of the Guard Company and a brief but fierce battle followed in which two further armoured cars were disabled and a number of German troops killed. With German armoured support approaching from the southeast, the Danish defenders were cut off from retreat and soon overwhelmed; two were killed and five wounded before they surrendered to Kluge's men at 0715.

Thereafter Kluge's rapid advance was barely delayed by Danish defenders, infantry being used to outflank any position found by the spearhead armoured cars, all the while covered by Bf 110 fighters above. Esbjerg and the small airfield at nearby Oksbøl were soon captured after brief defence by a Danish flak unit and with Copenhagen taken by seaborne troops, the Danish government capitulated at 0834.

Kluge's men were assigned coastal defence duties in the Jammerbugt area until 19 April when they moved to Aalborg to be shipped to Oslo aboard the freighter *Campina* and join the fighting in Norway where 'Weserübung Nord' had raged for nine days. The detachment left Denmark late on 20 April, arriving the following day to be attached to Kampfgruppe 'Fischer', comprising the bulk of Oberst Hermann Fischer's 340th Infantry Regiment with two attached Panzer platoons (including a single Neubaufahrzeug, an experimental heavy tank design used primarily for propaganda purposes in Norway). Fischer's *Kampfgruppe* was a component of Generalleutnant Richard Pellengahr's 196th Infantry Division, under whose command it remained, and the rest of this unit comprised Kampfgruppe 'Pellengahr' with a small amount of supporting armour attached, including the two remaining Neubaufahrzeuge.

Pellengahr began his drive north into central Norway towards Trondheim, his two *Kampfgruppen* advancing on either side of Lake Mjøsa, taking the western Gudbrandsdal himself and Fischer the eastern Østerdal. Kluge arrived at the front line as the battle for Lillehammer ended with the defeat of the British 148th Brigade and its subsequent retreat towards Andalsnes.

Kampfgruppe 'Fischer' was then placed directly under the command of Group XXI and on 23 April, Fischer pushed Kluge's motorised troops and his armour from Rena along the shores of Lake Storsjøen, reaching the northern end of the lake on 24 April before moving on to Tynset. Kluge's motorcycle platoon was split off to follow the railway spur to Røros and its valuable copper mine, which was occupied on 25 April, a single minor casualty being suffered when one man fell from his motorcycle.

Kampfgruppe 'Fischer' met heavy resistance from Norwegian troops in the steep sided Østerdal at a small farm named Naaverdalen, battering its way with Luftwaffe support towards Ulsberg before swinging north to Berkåk where, shortly before noon on 30 April, they met troops from 181st Infantry Division that had landed at Trondheim and moved south, finally linking the southern German forces with those in central Norway. Contact was also shortly regained with Kampfgruppe 'Pellengahr' to the west and the surviving 123 officers and 2,500 men of Norwegian 2nd Division, trapped between the advancing *Kampfgruppen*, surrendered soon afterwards. The 'General Göring' units lost two men during the fighting and eleven badly wounded, who included Hptm. Funck, replaced as 1st Guard Company commander by Oblt. Budig.

Kluge moved onwards to Trondheim during 1 May, briefly attached to 181st Infantry Division before pushing north towards Namsos with GenLt. Valentin Feurstein's 2nd Mountain [Gebirgs] Division which had been ordered to advance on Narvik where German troops were being hard-pressed by Allied forces. Despite British belief that the route north could not be traversed by German forces either in strength or at speed, Feurstein mounted a lightning advance using an ever-changing array of the spearhead troops at his disposal, including Kluge's men. Namsos was rapidly occupied before several sharp battles culminating at Bodø from where the retreating Allied troops were evacuated by sea and the town taken by German troops on 1 June.

Though Feurstein's mountain troops would push on through inhospitable terrain to relieve Narvik, Kluge and his men were relegated to airfield security at the small aerodrome at Hattfjelldal, 46 km southeast of Mosjøen, simultaneously guarding the Swedish frontier against Allied stragglers attempting to flee a defeated Norway. The Norwegian government signed an armistice on 9 June, the day after the Germans discovered that Allied forces had successfully evacuated Narvik. Kluge's men soon returned to Germany, beginning their march south from Trondheim on 11 June, by which time Allied forces in France were reeling before a fresh German onslaught.

Kluge's Wachbataillon remained in Berlin as guard for the Luftwaffe's command centre and Göring's residence. On occasion, Göring retreated from the capital to his Reichsjägerhof on the Rominte Heath, the majestic East Prussian hunting lodge that he had had constructed in 1936 in his capacity as Reichsjägermeister and known as 'Emmyhall' after his second wife. There the battalion provided a bodyguard for him.

Preuss's motorcycle unit was expanded to company size. Numbering six officers, fifty-nine NCOs and 180 men it formed the nucleus of a new rifle battalion, under the command of a recuperated Hptm. Funck, ready in time for deployment to the Balkans in early 1941.

Fall Gelb and Fall Rot

With the Jäger and reconnaissance units already deployed to Weserübung, it was the regiment's flak units that took part in the invasion of the Low Countries and France, spread between Army Groups A and B in independent *Kampfgruppen* in support of fast-moving Panzer troops. For the invasion the expanded 1st Battalion, RGG (under its 'cover' as 103rd Flak Regiment) was comprised of three heavy batteries of 88-mm cannon (1st–3rd/RGG) with the addition of the light 4th Battery's 37-mm and 5th Battery's 20-mm cannon.[4] Two attached Luftwaffe flak units – 1st Battalion, 7th Regiment and 2nd Battalion, 43rd – completed the regimental order of battle.

On 10 May, Axthelm led 103rd Flak Regiment from Erkelenz over the Belgian border in the direction of Hasselt, reaching the town within three days by which time 5th Battery had already claimed two RAF Bristol Blenheims and a French Amiot bomber shot down. In total, gunners of Regiment 'General Göring' would claim sixteen French and British aircraft shot down by the end of the Western campaign. The flak batteries were frequently sited near crucial river crossings to protect often fragile pontoon bridges from aerial bombardment and ensure maintenance of the continued German advance.

Such flak regiments were of crucial importance, but it was perhaps their anti-tank capability that was of most profound value to the German operations. Though fast-moving, many of Germany's armoured formations were not well-matched against heavily armoured – though frequently under-gunned – French and British tanks.

Alongside infantry formations, the 4th and 5th Panzer Divisions, moving into the area of the Mormal Forest through the weaker northern fringe of the Maginot Line, fought a four-day battle with French armour of the 1e DLM (Division Légère Mécanique, Light Mechanised Division; S35 and H35 tanks) and 39e BCC (Bataillon de Chars de Combat, R35 tanks) strongly supported by French colonial troops, beginning on 20 May. Casualties were heavy on both sides but the Regiment 'General Göring' gunners contributed greatly to the French defeat, particularly by use of 88-mm cannon at short range. Near Engelfontaine alone, 1st Battery claimed five tanks destroyed. By the end of the French campaign 2nd Battery had destroyed two, while 3rd Battery claimed thirteen tanks in total. Their contribution to the fighting in the Mormal Forest was profound; by the end of the battle the French had lost every tank of both commands, and bewildered infantrymen were soon pushed out of the wooded areas as German troops overcame the scattered fortified positions that had been established as a planned extension of the Maginot Line.

While the Mormal battle raged, Panzers reached the English Channel, pinning the bulk of the BEF into the Dunkirk and Calais pockets. The line of march taken by 1st Battalion, RGG led to Cambrai by 23 May and Amiens two days later. Crucial pontoon crossings of the Somme River were heavily defended by the time they were attacked by Fairey Battles of RAF 103 Squadron during the early afternoon of 28 May. Flying Officer Roy Douglas Max's aircraft was heavily damaged and later claimed as shot down by 2nd Battery established on high ground overlooking three sides of the pontoons. Max was hit in the left knee by shrapnel, his gunner, Aircraftman Dubois, also wounded and the Battle hit in the engine and leaking glycol before Max managed to break away to make a forced landing at a French airfield near Châlons.

Axthelm's 103rd Flak Regiment protected the Somme crossing until the start of 'Fall Rot', the second stage of the conquest of France. Army Group B then crossed the Somme, heading towards the Seine River. Axthelm's men reached Beauvais by 9 June before moving east towards Laon and advancing along a different axis toward Château-Thierry and the crossing of the Marne on 13 June. Within three days they had reached Villeneuve-la-Guyard.

Elsewhere, 3rd Battalion, RGG had covered bridges over the Sûre River in Luxembourg for the opening three days of the invasion before moving into Belgium and taking part in combat at Bertrix and Libramont-Chevigny between 14 and 16 May. Their searchlights were integral to the anti-aircraft security of the Meuse crossing at Charleville–Mézières until 21 May when 45-year-old Maj. Bernhard von Oppeln-Bronikowski led his men to the captured French airfields around Guise, heavily used for the duration of the campaign by Luftwaffe fighter units and transport aircraft as a major supply hub which, though deactivated following the French surrender, was integral to Luftwaffe forward operations. The battalion also provided security for Ghent airfield and oil storage.

At the time of France's surrender, 3rd Battalion was operational in Boulogne where it would stay until February 1941 under a new commander, Hptm. Hans Dietrich Lindenberg, covering the harbour, airfield and artillery positions. The battalion would not return to Germany until 10

February 1941 to serve in the defence of the German capital for a full year.[5] Rolf Wallburg wrote of his battalion's time in Boulogne in his diary, despite this being forbidden by military regulations:

> In the city are just a few navy units. They are highly appreciative that we arrived. The Tommy attacks the port and the city night by night and often also during the day. We are about to change this. We take a great position at the outskirts of the city in a way that we have an excellent overview of the entire port, the city and also the area outside the city. Straight from the first day we have intense enemy contact with the Tommy. We never thought we would be able to keep this position that long – but we did it. Surely, it was a tough time for us and demanded a lot of nerves; but it was also a good time. At dusk our work started. It was impossible to sleep during the night and so we all gathered in our community tent. Only the air-raid look-out was outside and he had to perform exceptionally. He was the first to hear the Tommies approaching and per his notification the entire coast sounded the alarm. Then we ran outside to our machinery and machine guns and it was only a few nights that we were not successful. Often, we were alerted up to twenty times per night but we never got tired. Then we were standing outside in the rain of falling anti-aircraft gun shrapnel, the bombs were howling and exploding in and around our position. Yes, and often the Tommy attacked our position, flying low with bombs and onboard guns. Then we returned fire as much as we could. It was best when we brought one down; and that was often the case in Boulogne . . . At dawn it got quiet and we could finally sleep. But often even then it was not possible to sleep; either it was the Tommies or the German squadrons going to England that did not let us rest. Then we were lying outside in front of our tents and gazed at our birds flying over and saw how the bombs over there were detonating. Another time it was a convoy of ships that was sunk and often we looked at the air fights that happened over the Channel.[6]

Independent of the remainder of the regiment, 14th (Heavy) Railway Battery had remained in the Rhineland until taking part in Operation 'Tiger', launched on 14 June as the first German troops entered Paris. The railway guns engaged bunkers of the Maginot Line in support of the assault on the formidable defences by Army Group C. Seven divisions advanced from Saarbrücken towards St Avold in what was a largely unnecessary – and costly – operation.

Axthelm and the 103rd Flak Regiment were in the Parisian suburb of St Denis at the time of the French Armistice; Oblt. Walter Dieke and a platoon from 7th Battery were present during the ceremonial signing of the agreement at Compiègne on 21 June while the remaining units proceeded to Nantes and northwards into Brittany as a mobile anti-aircraft force in freshly occupied territory, spending five days stationed at the major harbour of Brest before returning to Paris in early July to spend a period in anti-aircraft defence at the Villacoublay airfield complex and Paris-Orly.

The 14th Railway Battery spent time stationed in Paris, Cherbourg and Bordeaux before returning to mobile flak duties in Germany. Ultimately, after covering 12,377 kilometres in the course of the first two years of war, in October 1941 the battery passed out of the Regiment 'General Göring' and became 4th Battery, Railway Flak Battalion 321, though Oblt. Arnold, his officers, and most of the NCOs and enlisted men opted to remain with the regiment.

On 1 June Axthelm handed command of the Regiment 'General Göring' to Oberst Paul Conrath as he moved on to command 1st Flak Brigade; Axthelm was promoted to *Generalmajor* that September.[7] Conrath was a veteran of the First World War, enlisting as a volunteer in the 4. Garde-Feld-artillerie-Regiment on 10 August, 1914 and then being assigned to Reserve-Feldartillerie-Regiment 44. He fought on the Western Front until 1917 when promoted to *Leutnant* and transferred to 4. Badischen Feldartillerie-Regiment Nr. 66 as an officer of the General Staff. Following the end of the war, the demobilised officer joined the Polizei before being transferred to the Luftwaffe as a *Major* and adjutant to Reichsmarschall Göring. He commanded 3rd (Light) Flak Battalion, RGG, in the later part of 1937, but returned to the post of Göring's adjutant until promoted to *Oberst* and given command of the Regiment 'General Göring', which at that time was still officially designated 103rd Flak Regiment. Conrath led his elements of RGG back to Germany where they remained in training until 29 March 1941, expanded by an additional rifle battalion, until transfer to the Balkans.

Meanwhile, 2nd (Light) Battalion, RGG was transferred from Berlin and allocated security anti-aircraft duties in the Netherlands and would remain on security duties in that country until September 1941.

'Marita' and 'Barbarossa'

On 23 March 1939, the governments of Germany and Romania had signed a bilateral economic agreement for the fostering of economic relations between the two nations. Germany was essentially granted considerable control of major aspects of the Romanian economy guaranteeing the delivery of quantities of agricultural goods, timber and, perhaps most crucial to Germany's military machine, oil. In return, the Germans offered technical advances and military equipment. A small unit of Brandenburgers was active from Christmas that year to oversee the security of the oil installations near Ploeşti.

During 1940 Romania began constructing extensive air defences around the city of Ploeşti and the Prahova oil region. Following the occupation of Bessarabia and northern Bukovina by the Soviet Union in June and a period of internal instability, Romania signed the Tripartite Pact in November and joined the Axis. Despite its own anti-aircraft installations – and before officially joining the Axis – Bucharest sought on 17 September to nullify the threat posed by the Soviet military which now sat across the left tributary of the Danube. A German military mission was requested, with specialised units, modern weapons and instructors for Romanian personnel. The request was approved, and the first German troops entered the Prahova Valley during October. However, that month Mussolini launched an ill-considered war against Greece which soon degenerated into a disastrous failure as Greek forces punished the invading Italians and pushed them back beyond their Albanian starting points. Worse, the attack settled any question of Greece's obscure political alignment and it joined the Allies, providing a Balkan staging post for British and Commonwealth aircraft placing the Royal Air Force now within striking distance of the Ploeşti oilfield. Hitler immediately ordered additional Luftwaffe units to Romania and had plans prepared for an invasion of Greece (Operation 'Marita').

Major components of Conrath's 'Regiment General Göring' left Germany for Romania on 29 March 1941 and travelled from Berlin via Dresden, Prague, Vienna and Budapest until arriving at bases situated at various points around the Ploeşti refineries. Both 1st and 4th Flak Battalions and the newly formed Motorised Rifle Battalion – led by Hptm. Helmut Funck – were despatched and placed under the command of Generalleutnant Georg-Hans Reinhardt's XLI Panzer Corps (Twelfth Army) that had been sent to Romania in preparation for the Balkans offensive.[8] While the flak units remained near Ploești, Funck's infantry were only briefly in Romania for training, relocating in stages through Kraków and Sandomierz to the Polish city of Zamość during May , only 20 km from the Soviet frontier, as they had been earmarked to take part in the spearhead of Operation 'Barbarossa'.

Plans for 'Marita' demanded Bulgarian cooperation for troops crossing their territory, the nation bowing to German pressure and going one step further by joining the Axis on 1 March 1941. A hesitant Yugoslavia followed twenty-four days later, on the proviso that German troops would not transit the country for any aggressive move against Greece. However, a bloodless coup d'état led by the former commander of the Yugoslav Air Force, General Dušan Simović, deposed Yugoslavia's government, Simović renouncing the Tripartite Pact and sealing the country's borders. An incensed Hitler met his military chiefs on 27 March and demanded that Yugoslavia be destroyed as a 'military power and a sovereign state'. Directive No. 25 was hurriedly prepared and signed and Yugoslavia would be first to fall in Operation 'Marita', which had now become an attack on the last politically independent Balkan states.

Generalfeldmarschall Wilhelm List's Twelfth Army was tasked with conquering Yugoslavia; the majority of his troops were already in Bulgaria preparing for the Greek campaign. List was compelled to split his command hurriedly in response to the new directive. Though the conventional Yugoslavian military was vastly inferior to the Wehrmacht, the geography itself posed daunting problems for a mobile invasion: mountainous with limited communications networks and major river obstacles including the Danube marking the border of Yugoslavia and Romania and swollen with melted ice from the spring thaw.

Bridges were therefore key and to that end Brandenburgers would spearhead the attack at various points. Oberleutnant Kutschke's 7th Company of the Brandenburger Regiment was positioned near the 'Iron Gates' of the Danube, a river gorge separating Romania from Serbia and an area in which Yugoslavian border defences had been visibly strengthened, The Brandenburgers became part of an assault group led by Engineer Oberst Richard Bazing, with a supporting reserve of bridging and engineer units, light anti-aircraft weapons of 5th Company, Flak Regt. 501 and the towed 88-mm guns of Hptm. Alfred Schröder's 3rd Battery, RGG. Bazing gathered his forces near Orsova where the river was a kilometre wide and, at dawn on 6 April, the Brandenburgers and engineers crossed the Danube;

Yugoslavian positions on the western bank were assaulted and overrun after brief though fierce fighting. The narrow beachhead was swiftly reinforced as the battle moved away from the river. To maintain their grip on the crossing area, Security Group Iron Gates (Sicherungsgruppe Eisernes Tor) was established and half of 3rd Battery remained on station to provide anti-aircraft cover.

The remainder of 'Marita' passed with no further involvement of the regiment, which was soon reorganised and expanded before gathering in Poland at the end of May for the impending attack on the Soviet Union, code-named Operation 'Barbarossa', Hitler's overly-ambitious attempt to destroy Stalin's sprawling country. Part of Army Group South, Conrath's Regiment was subordinated to Generalleutnant Otto Deßloch's II. Flakkorps (in turn subordinate to Luftflotte 4) supporting Generaloberst Ludwig Ewald von Kleist's First Panzer Group. The organisation of Regiment 'General Göring' on 15 June 1941 stood at the following:

Regiment 'General Göring'	***Oberst Paul Conrath***	
Adjutant	*Hptm. Walter Stauch*	Staff: 8 officers, 28 NCOs, 74 men
Transport Group	*Hptm. Kumacsek*	5 NCOs and 26 men; (from 12./XVII, 2.5-ton ammunition trucks)
Signals Platoon	*Oblt. Schirmer*	1 officer 12 NCOs and 64 men
Motorised Workshop Platoon	*Amtmann Karl Gmelch*	1 Amtmann, 6 NCOs and 47 men
1st Battalion	*Maj. Werner Hullmann*	
Adjutant	*Lt. Nikolai Jahr*	HQ of 7 officers 28 NCOs, 129 men
1st Battery,	*Oblt. Rudolf Graf*	33 NCOs, 139 men, 4x88-mm
2nd Battery	*Hptm. Robert Schulz*	5 officers, 27 NCOs, 140 men, 4x88-mm
3rd Battery	*Hptm. Alfred Schröder*†	5 officers, 23 NCOs, 130 men, 4x88-mm; †Schröder killed 23 June 1941
5th Battery	*Hptm. Paul Neubauer*	3 officers, 35 NCOs, 183 men, 12x20-mm
Motor Transport Train	*Lt. von Lochow*	42 vehicles, 9 NCOs, 45 men
4th Battalion	*Hptm. Werner Geicke*	
Adjutant	*Oblt. Claus-Peter Bock*	HQ of 12 officers, 25 NCOs, 77 men
6th Battery	*Oblt. Engelbert Berends*	3 officers, 30 NCOs, 154 men, 9x37-mm
15th Battery	*Hptm. Hans Beinhofer*	6 x each calibre, 5 officers, 36 NCOs, 194 men, 20-mm, 37-mm
16th Battery	*Oblt. Karl Roßmann*	4 officers, 33 NCOs, 178 men, 12x20-mm half-tracks
Motor Transport Train	*Oblt. Fischer*	20 vehicles, 1 officer, 9 NCOs, 43 men

Rifle Battalion	*Hptm. Helmut Funck*	
Adjutant	*Oblt. Robert Rebholz*	HQ of 9 officers, 24 NCOs, 59 men
8th Battery, 20-mm	*Hptm. Wolfgang Seewald*	12 vehicles, 4 officers, 33 NCOs, 175 men
1st Rifle Company	*Oblt. Alfred Krohn*	4 officers, 32 NCOs, 160 men
3rd Rifle Company	*Hptm. Otto Brandenburg*	4 officers, 31 NCOs, 155 men
(Both companies equipped with 9 x LMG, 3 x 50-mm mortars and three light anti-tank weapons)		
Motorcycle Company	*Hptm. Joachim Preuß*	6 officers, 59 NCOs, 180 men; 9 x LMG, 2 x HMG, 3 x 50-mm mortars and 6 light anti-tank weapons, + motorcycles and 3 x 8-wheeled armoured cars)
Motor Transport Supply Train	*Hptm. Wendt*	20 vehicles, 1 officer, 16 NCOs, 40 men
2nd Btn, Flak Regiment 43	*Maj. Alfred Karlhuber*	attached to RGG
Adjutant	*Oblt. Walter-Ernst Grothe*	
6th Battery, 4 x 88-mm	*Oblt. Otto Rengermann*	5 officers, 20 NCOs, 136 men
7th Battery, 4 x 88-mm	*Oblt. Martin Wittkowsky*	4 officers, 19 NCOs, 137 men
8th Battery, 4 x 88-mm	*Oblt. Josef Hagel*	4 officers, 21 NCOs, 137 men
9th Battery, 12 x 20-mm	*Oblt. Egbert Belau*	6 officers, 30 NCOs,183 men
10th Battery	*Hptm. Ernst Schlechtweg*	5 officers, 30 NCOs, 185 men; 12 x 20-mm
Motor Transport Train	*Hptm. Otto Petri*	42 vehicles, 2 officers, 8 NCOs, 47 men

Conrath's troops were to support Generalleutnant Ludwig Crüwell's 11th Panzer Division, a spearhead of General der Panzertruppe Werner Kempf's XLVIII Corps (mot.) that would be used swiftly to exploit the crossing of the Bug River made by men of the 57th and 75th Infantry Divisions. Their strategic objective was Kiev, though numerous rivers and densely wooded swathes of the western Ukraine would need to be passed first. On 22 June, the opening day of 'Barbarossa', several of the Regiment's 88-mm guns engaged a scattering of Soviet bunkers on high ground north of the town of Sokal before Conrath's men crossed the Bug behind the first Panzers at midday.[9] Though infantrymen encountered several defensive lines, defending Russian troops soon crumbled, and reconnaissance units of 11th Panzer reached as far as Stoyaniv by 2300 that night, where they clashed with leading elements of the Soviet 10th Armoured Division before halting during the hours of darkness.

Facing Kleist's Panzer Group was the Red Army's Southwestern Front (roughly equivalent to a Wehrmacht army group) commanded by Ukrainian Colonel General Mikhail Kirponos. Unlike many of his contemporaries, Kirponos had ignored instructions to disregard the rumours of impending German invasion, and therefore the units of the Southwestern Front were at least partially prepared to face the German attack. Stavka's Chief of Staff, Georgy Zhukov, had issued the 'Directive of Peoples' Commissariat of Defence No. 3' on 'Barbarossa's opening day, in which he ordered Kirponos to mount an immediate counter-attack with the strategic aim of securing Lublin. Kirponos, a pragmatic man with meritorious experience from the Russo-Finnish War, was unconvinced by such an obviously ambitious plan, but Zhukov himself arrived at Kirponos's headquarters at Teropil to direct the operation. The resultant clash was catastrophic for the Red Army and launched what became the single largest tank battle of the Second World War, bigger even than the now-famous colossal armoured clash around Kursk in 1943.

On 23 June RGG opened fire on Russian tanks for the first time, as 11th Panzer battered its way the 11 km southwards from Stoyaniv to Radekhiv from where Russian tanks had advanced. By the end of this first engagement, which lasted nearly six hours, twenty-six burning Russian tanks (six T-34s and twenty BT tanks) littered the field, seven destroyed by 36-year-old Hptm. Alfred Schröder's 88s of 3rd Battery. However, the battle had been far from one-sided, with twenty Panzers destroyed or disabled and the Russians abandoning the field due to a lack of ammunition rather than being bested in combat. Among the German casualties suffered that day was Schröder himself, killed by Russian gunfire. As in France, the Germans had been shocked to see smaller-calibre shells fired by their Panzers bouncing off the armour of the enemy tanks – T-34s in this case, an extremely advanced design with a near-perfect armour combination of thickness and sloping angle – and the large flak weapons became invaluable in their anti-tank role. While the 88s of 3rd Battery engaged enemy armour, anti-aircraft cover was provided by Hptm. Neubauer's 5th Battery's 20-mm cannon; a single Petlyakov Pe-2 twin-engine dive bomber was brought down just after noon.

On 24 June, spearheads of 15th Panzer Regiment reached the small village of Shchurovychi on the Styr River over which German troops established a minor bridgehead before the bridge itself was destroyed by Russian Tupolev SB bombers. Though the Red Air Force suffered grievous losses at the hands of the Luftwaffe both on the ground and in the air during the early days of 'Barbarossa', it steadfastly mounted repeated attacks on Kleist's axis of advance, contributing to a growing traffic jam at Radekhiv where leading elements of 16th Panzer Division had begun arriving after being released from reserve. The 88s of 3rd Battery claimed a single SB II shot down over that town while 2nd Battery, which had advanced with the leading troops, claimed three SB IIIs shot down that morning over Shchurovychi to the east.

Neubauer's 5th Battery spent the day spread along the route of advance, covering numerous river crossings as the Wehrmacht raced to attack the strategic road junction at Dubno in a giant pincer movement. Their 20-mm guns destroyed a single light tank near the village of Kozyn, and nine Russian bombers between Berestechko and Merva on the Styr River. The Germans advanced, seizing Khmil'no, Lopatyn and as far east as Ostroh on the Horyn River with little resistance. Dubno, attacked from north and south, fell the next day – 25 June – the same time that Hptm. Karl Thimm's 4th Battery (37-mm flak guns) appears on strength for the first time in German records; it claimed two Russian fighters shot down at Kopytiv and Zboivs'ka. The German forces then readied themselves to face an expected strong Soviet counter-attack after aerial reconnaissance reported large Russian armoured units approaching both west and the east of the Styr River towards the southern flank of 11th Panzer Division's line of advance. During the previous day, leading Soviet elements had reached Brody and made progress northwest towards Radekhiv.

Fortunately for the Germans, the Red Army counter-offensive was mired in problems. In total, six mechanised corps launched an uncoordinated attack hamstrung by contradictory orders and poor – frequently non-existent – communications. Their thrusts were also disorganised through a lack of transport for supporting troops, patches of poor, swampy terrain for the heavier KV tanks and no clearly stated objective. Zhukov and Kirponos issued conflicting orders, many of which were not received in any event. The struggle that unfolded has since become known as the Battle of Brody as the armoured clash concentrated in the triangle between Dubno, Lutsk and Brody. In total the Red Army threw approximately 5,000 tanks towards the battle, 3,000 of which engaged the German force that mustered some 1,000 Panzers and supporting infantry and artillery.

By 26 June, despite their confusion, Kirponos's forces had managed to seize the initiative, forcing some German units to withdraw locally and cutting off troops near the Styr, who prepared recently captured bridges for demolition lest they fall back into Soviet hands. Conrath's anti-tank capability was thrown into the line and between 27 and 30 June 1st Battery swiftly destroyed a confirmed four tanks, 2nd Battery eleven at Dubno, and 5th Battery six. On 7 July the daily Wehrmacht news communiqué – *Die*

Wehrmachtberichte – mentioned the regiment for the first time, singling out 2nd Battery for attention:

> During the armoured battle near Dubno a battery of the Anti-aircraft Regiment 'General Göring' under the leadership of Hptm. Schulz and also Lt. Wilmskötter particularly distinguished itself.[10]

Another account of the battle for Dubno was penned by Unteroffzier Jägeler of 2nd Battery in Russia on 10 September 1941. The piece that Jägeler wrote may have been destined for one of the Wehrmacht's propaganda publications or may simply have been kept on file in the regimental records.

> On 26 June we reached Dubno very early and noticed that the Russians were already busy flying. The city had been the destination of our march and when we reached it, we immediately established positions against both possible air and ground attack. Soon there is an air raid alarm and, as an introduction to the battle, we achieve a great success. A direct hit by our heavy anti-aircraft guns tears a Russian bomber [Tupolev SB III] into pieces, a wonderful sight for us with all the individual fragments spinning around in the air.
>
> The Panzer Division spearhead had advanced rapidly and taken Dubno and the path for units following was open. But in the surrounding forests there were still strong Russian forces, including tanks. The city's own defences were weak and it goes without saying that we took over the task of protection against enemy tanks. However, the Russians clearly hadn't yet recovered from the shock of our advance, because the night passed quietly.
>
> Early the following morning we are in action again against aircraft, when reports reach us that in the village of Tarakaniv – about 4 km west of Dubno – several enemy tanks have attacked a German column and are now heading towards Dubno. Only a short time later, we are ready to fight again, this time in our anti-tank positions. A motorcyclist arrives and reports that there are two of our own vehicles immediately behind him, but that four Russian tanks are approaching approximately two and a half kilometres away. The first is a heavy goose, with three smaller ones in staggered formation to the rear. What are they up to? Do they want to probe and reconnoitre us first? Soon our own vehicles are long gone and then we sight the colossus. It is a 64-ton command tank [KV-2] with a 15-cm cannon.

We are well camouflaged in our position and let him get closer, because we know that his armour is exceptionally strong. At 800 m the first shell from the heavy anti-aircraft gun is fired at the beast. Hit! But the tank keeps rolling. He shoots aimlessly towards us with his cannon. He is already approaching; 400 m, and now he must have discovered us as his barrel swings to point in our direction. He shoots and his fire lands to left and right. The tank rolls ever closer and starts taking hit after hit. Now, at around 200 metres, we target him again. Firing – followed immediately by a blinding explosion and flames; the whole gun crew have to take cover so as not to be killed by the pieces of shattered iron flying around. The shot went right into his ammunition locker and the tank dissolved into nothing but its components. A hole in the street remains and in it some bent iron parts; the turret and tracks are later found in a nearby field.

The other three Russian tanks have followed to that point at a respectful distance and when they see the fate of their big brother, they quickly turn around and retreat. Unfortunately, we can't send them our blessings in the form of some shells, because they soon disappear into the adjacent forest.

What will the Russians do now? Reports from prisoner interrogations have confirmed that Dubno is very important to them, because this is where their food and gasoline supplies are. Since the enemy has been encircled, he will undoubtedly try to break out to retake Dubno. But we won't let this happen and all available weapons are to be used to ward off the inevitable attack. Nothing further occurs that night and the following morning all is still quiet. But there is tension in the air and everyone feels that something is coming. The battery chief reports that strong Russian armoured forces are being prepared in the village of Tarakaniv, reinforced by infantry. The enemy is far superior in numbers and there are only a few companies on our side, which is why every available man is assigned to the battery as protection against infantry. In order to keep our back free, the bridge at Strakow is blown up. However, we want to forestall the hostile attack and attack the village of Tarakaniv at 1500 hrs. We advance quickly but resistance stiffens in the village and the attack soon stalls. Enemy tanks have positioned themselves well and are heavily involved in the defence. At 2000 hrs, the Russians counter-attack. With tanks in the lead they break through our newly won infantry positions and the sheer weight of their numbers means we have to give up ground slowly until the first Russian tanks hit our defences.

Infantry guns become involved in the battle and anti-tank guns fire relentlessly. The gunners of the heavy anti-aircraft guns fearlessly allow tanks to approach closely, as the darkness makes it difficult to aim properly. Finally, it is time to open fire and after a short fight, two tanks go up in bright flames. We fight the attacking infantry that have moved forward bunched tightly together with time-fused shells and together with hand grenades and machine-gun fire we knock off the enemy.

Where are the other tanks? They open fire, shells landing again to left and right of us. But they encounter another 88-mm position and after another firefight the position is held. Will the Russians attack at night? We don't believe so, because they would have very poor visibility from inside their tanks.

During the night, gun 'Anton' is moved to a new protected position, the third night in a row that the crew has got no sleep. The main thrust of the Russian forces is now obvious to us and the moved gun has barely been cleared for action when the guard reports: 'Enemy tanks approaching!' It is 0315 hrs and we can see how the tanks slowly and successively disengage from their cover. We are located on the edge of a somewhat elevated cemetery and can see the southern and southwestern edge of the city very well, as well as the hinterland held by the enemy.

The tanks roll towards the city, often providing potential easy targets. However, experience has shown that we have to let the monsters come much closer to us . . . The 64-ton lead tank [KV-2] rolls ahead, others following closely behind . . . 'Anti-tank round – Range 500 – Fire!' the order is given to target this largest tank. With his 150-mm cannon he wants to put us out of action and his fire is landing close to our gun, but our shells are bouncing off the giant's body without hindering him at all. There! He stopped and we can clearly see one of his left rollers breaking away and the track hanging down. However, he continues to fire his gun and an assault gun that had been assigned to us for close defense is disabled by his fire. The enemy's turret is targeted and finally after a few shots the crew tries to bail out. Confused, they run straight into infantry fire. Covered by the large tank, a 32-tonner [T-34] opens fire on us, but this is soon on fire after our first shots. This time the tanks that are following do not reverse but try to reach the street. Just when one shows us his full broadside, he takes a direct hit. A flash of flame and the crackle that follows shows us that stored ammunition is detonating inside the tank.

In the meantime, another tank has reached the street and in no time will reach the entrance to the town. But his shooting is wild and after taking more than three hits a shell explodes just under the hull and the tank is lifted up and tipped into the ditch. 'The same range,' the next command comes, and in the blink of an eye, another shot rips it apart just as the crew tries to get out. Two tanks are then sighted to the left. The range-finder makes the perfect setting and when the monsters arrive in the cross hairs both go up in blinding flames with three shots each.

When another 52-tonner approaches from the right, it suddenly becomes clear to us that the Soviets have planned a two-pronged attack on the city. But this tank is also soon knocked out, and its ammunition ignites 15 minutes after it was first hit. To counter further simultaneous two-pronged attacks and secure our flank, another 88-mm is brought into a new position and just in time as two more enemy tanks try to attack our guns from behind but come across this other gun. After the wheels of the leading tank are hit, he turns quickly; but the second drives straight towards the 88. Only seconds later, after a short fire-fight, his fate is sealed. With burning clothing, two crewmen manage to escape. It's only 0600 hrs and eight tanks are already done. What will come next?

There are occasional mortar hits in our position. We decide that our lines of vision and field of fire must be enlarged and, on all fours, gunners crawl up to the trees and laboriously chop some down. It turns out to be a good idea as two mortars are discovered in the trees, to which a tank can be seen moving at intervals, surely bringing them ammunition. Unfortunately, the tank is too far away to attack effectively, but the mortars are soon put out of action with shellfire.

By noon, enemy artillery fire is increasing and with this preparation we expect an attack by the enemy soon. We are given infantry as close-range security in plenty of time before the attack. Suddenly

> the fire stops and we can hardly believe our eyes. Masses of enemy infantry come surging over the heights, the golden yellow cornfield teeming with them. Together with the artillery, we start shooting at them; our shots are perfect and while the artillery shells detonate on the ground, ours [anti-aircraft shells] burst a few metres above the heads of the Russians. We sow death and destruction in their ranks and the masses dissolve into a wildly racing mob. They manage to work their way individually into the village of Tarakaniv and are finally within rifle range of us. Machine guns rattle incessantly, and we have to set fire to a few houses with the heavy anti-aircraft gun to flush the Russians from their cover. Enemy aircraft arrive to support the attack, but these too are ineffective due to well-aimed defensive fire of the light flak guns. When another enemy tank reaches the 88's field of fire, it is destroyed immediately.
>
> This final Russian attack collapses completely and it is primarily thanks to the anti-aircraft battery of Regiment 'General Göring' that Dubno remains in German hands despite the most powerful enemy assaults. Finally, early on 30 June 1941, two of our divisions reach Dubno and roll up the enemy front.[11]

The battle had been against Lieutenant General Nikolai Popel's force of nearly 300 tanks of 8th Mechanised Corps – including 100 T-34 and KV tanks – that had thrust towards Dubno into the rear of 11th Panzer Division, successfully cutting German supply lines to their forces to the east. However, unsupplied, unsupported and lacking clear instructions, Popel's force was whittled down until pushed back on 1 July; Jägeler and 2nd Battery destroyed eleven tanks over a three-day period.

Though the situation had presented a serious problem for Army Group South, ultimately the counter-attack was defeated as disagreements between Zhukhov and Kirponos escalated, creating debilitating hesitation and confusion between subordinate units. The Red Army lost 2,648 tanks during the four days of fighting of the Battle of Brody. Though German losses are more difficult to quantify they are thought to number approximately 100 armoured vehicles. Luftwaffe air support had also greatly contributed to the Soviet defeat and the Soviets' subsequent chaotic withdrawal accelerated the great encirclement battles that exacted a terrible toll of their forces. However, the brief crisis faced by Army Group South had drawn significant resources away from the central thrust towards Moscow.[12]

The Russian Southwestern Front was ordered to retreat to the Stalin Line, a system of fortifications that marked the pre-war border with Poland but which was largely abandoned and stripped of weapons after a second set of fortifications – the Molotov Line – was started further west after the invasion of Poland. The denuded Stalin Line stood no chance of holding and elements of Kempf's LXVIII Corps pierced the line and threatened the right flank of the retreating Soviet 6th Army. In desperation, the Red Army counter-attacked towards Berdychiv to where 1st Battalion, RGG had moved in support of the Panzers and where Oblt. Graf's 1st Battery destroyed two more tanks on 8 July. The 3rd Battery was heavily engaged over the days that followed and by 12 July had confirmed the destruction of eight more Soviet tanks. However, German losses were equally heavy with 11th Panzer Division suffering nearly 2,000 casualties.

Losses among Regiment 'General Göring' are more difficult to calculate, but among them was Lt. Dirk Itzen, observation officer of the 3rd Battery, killed on 13 July near Berdychiv. Itzen was posthumously awarded the Knight's Cross on 23 November, his citation reading: 'While subordinated to a Panzer division, Itzen and his battery destroyed sixteen enemy tanks, two aircraft and a tanker. Throughout this time Itzen proved to be a shining example to his subordinates up until his death in mid-July 1941.'

Army Group South bypassed the Ukrainian capital Kiev and began to close the ring around Soviet forces in the area of Uman. On 21 July Preuss's motorcycle company advanced southeast from Berdychiv to establish communication with the advancing SS Division 'Wiking', only to be bombed mistakenly by Ju 87 Stukas on 23 July, and then fight alongside the SS men as they and elements of 1st SS 'Leibstandarte Adolf Hitler' closed the ring near Korsun, trapping the remains of the Soviet 6th and 12th Armies.

The bulk of the RGG fought alongside 'Wiking' in the weeks that followed, Oblt. Karl Rossmann's 16th Battery 20-mm flak half-tracks suffering particularly heavy losses in the area of the small village of Sverdlykove as trapped Soviet troops attempted to break out to the east. The RGG and SS men held the village and bridge over the Syniukha River, periodically encircled by Soviet troops in the confusing pitched battles that followed; one major clash lasted for fourteen uninterrupted hours. The village itself was recaptured by Red Army troops as Rossmann hung grimly on to the bridge until reinforcements drove the Russians back out of the remains of Sverdlykove. For his leadership during the battle, Rossmann was later awarded the Knight's Cross on 12 November, the award presented to him in Vilnius.[13]

The attached 2nd Battalion, Flak Regiment 43, commanded by Maj. Alfred Karlhuber, took part in defending Buzivka against Red Army troops trying to break their encirclement and suffered significant losses. The battalion was briefly transferred north to Zhashkiv to regroup before being committed to the fighting in the Ukraine throughout August. It was located in Kryvyi Rih on 20 August, only a little over 50 km from the Dnieper.

During the afternoon of 7 August Soviet troops trapped in the Uman pocket began surrendering en masse; this confirmed the destruction of both the 6th and 12th Armies and elements of the 18th and netted nearly 103,000 prisoners, including both army commanders, four corps commanders, and eleven divisional commanders.

As Army Group South raced for the Dneiper, Conrath's regiment was in Kirovohrad on 17 August where it was divided to support three separate thrusts: towards Cherkasy in the northeast, Aleksandriya to the east (which was abandoned by the Red Army without a fight), and Krivoy Rog to the southeast and onwards to Nikopol. The first of the regiment's elements to reach the great river on 19 August were near Zaporizhzhia, site of the huge Dnieper Hydroelectric Station, which was partially destroyed by NKVD troops, the resultant tidal surge killing several Red Army officers crossing the river at that time and anywhere between 20,000 and 100,000 civilians from riverbank settlements downstream.

The constituent parts of the regiment were involved in mopping up Soviet resistance in the Dnieper bend until 25 August, supporting the 9th Panzer Division in the elimination of a small Soviet bridgehead that had been tenaciously held on the Dnieper's western bank. Flak elements then supported the crossing of the Dnieper, before following on 13 September, traversing the river at Kremenchuk whereupon they were subordinated to 59th Motorcycle Battalion of the 9th Panzer Division, commanded by Maj. Wilhelm Schmalz, who would later feature heavily in 'Hermann Göring' history. By this stage, as a result of the successful handling of his men, Oberst Paul Conrath had also received the Knight's Cross, awarded on 4 September.

The various regimental components were then moved into LXVIII Corps reserve as the autumn rains turned the churned roads to a morass of mud, complicating vehicle movement. Conrath was seconded to security duties within the region until mid-September, headquartered at Lokhvytsya but, after a brief rest, RGG was returned to the fighting east of Kiev after II Flak Corps was transferred to Luftflotte 2 and the support of Guderian's Panzer Group in Army Group Centre. Between 2 and 20 October, the RGG took part in the battle of Briansk, during which the commander of 1st Battery, Oblt. Rudolf Graf, won the Knight's Cross on 6 October. This battle resulted in the encirclement and capture of over 665,000 Red Army prisoners. The majority of the battered regiment was then pulled from the line and given security duties until 6 November on the German communication lines in recently occupied eastern Ukraine. By this stage of the war Conrath's men had destroyed an estimated 161 aircraft, 324 armoured vehicles and 45 bunkers as well as taking 11,000 prisoners.

Those few flak elements that remained with Guderian's Panzer Group penetrated nearly as far as Tula, a bare 200 km from Moscow, as the first winter snows began to bite and Soviet resistance to the invading Germans stiffened considerably. After suffering severe casualties, the majority of Conrath's men were regrouped as the remains of Regiment 'General Göring' and transferred to Vilnius until 22 November, when the regiment began a return to Germany.

Behind them, however, a small contingent of RGG riflemen remained in Russia. Surviving infantrymen of Rifle Battalion 'General Göring' were placed under the command of Hptm. Paul Neubauer – formerly of 5th Battery – after Funck was wounded during November. They were used to reinforce the composite Luftwaffe Kampfverbände 'Meindl' holding the strategically important airfield at Yukhov against fierce Soviet counter-attacks. Melded into a cohesive fighting unit alongside fragments of other Wehrmacht and Waffen-SS formations, Neubauer's men helped repel repeated Red Army attacks in thick snow amidst appalling winter conditions.

On 13 February 1942 approximately 100 survivors of Rifle Battalion 'General Göring', including Neubauer, were airlifted to reinforce 1st Battalion, Air-Landing Regiment, under the command of Maj. Walter Koch that were holding Schaikowka airfield.

> Strong attacks on Prijut from south (two Russian battalions). Large-scale attack by the Russians in several waves on Wypolsowo with about 420 men. The enemy lost 230 dead, 107 prisoners, 290 rifles, 25 LMG, 2 HMG, 6 light mortars and two 20-mm flak weapons.[14]

Neubauer was severely injured on the first night of combat as part of Kampfgruppe 'Koch', his place taken by Oblt. Käfer who was also wounded shortly afterward. Oberleutnant Robert Rebholz, commander of the heavy weapons platoon, took charge, though at that time only he, six NCOs and fifty-two men remained combat-fit. They helped defend the airfield at Anisovo-Gorodishche before the surviving forty-two men were relieved on 23 March and began the long rail journey to Berlin and reunion with the remainder of the regiment. Amidst the awards of Iron Crosses liberally sprinkled throughout the regiment for the veterans of the 'Barbarossa' campaign, the cherished Luftwaffe ground combat badge was also subsequently granted for participation in three or more actions at designated places in Russia.

Chapter Three

Growing Pains

'It's not the big armies that win battles, it's the good ones.'
Field Marshal Maurice Comte de Saxe

During March 1942 Göring ordered the regiment increased to brigade strength, and subsequently renamed as Brigade 'Hermann Göring'. An order dated 22 May 1942 instructed all ranks to replace the previous 'General Göring' cuff-titles with ones bearing their new name, the change to be completed no later than August. Initial versions issued to troops were written in Gothic script but this was superseded by block capitals shortly thereafter. The main combat units were despatched to France and gradually gathered in camps of the Seventh Army reserve (Army Group D) within the area of Uzel, Loudéac, St Brieuc and Pontivy in Brittany, northeast of Lorient.

Rolf Wallburg, now promoted to *Unteroffizier*, had repeatedly requested a transfer from the searchlight battalion to a combat unit during 1941, even considering volunteering for the *Fallschirmjäger*:

> At the end of [January] there is finally light at the end of the tunnel. It is Sunday evening and we are all sitting in the common room when the boss asks who would be interested in reporting to the infantry. I immediately volunteer alongside only one other of my men. I am speechless; first they moan every day but now they are not taking this opportunity. I talk to them and address their morale and after a few minutes everybody is thrilled and all volunteer . . . In the first days of [February] it is being decided which branch of the service everybody wants to join and every day we enthusiastically discuss it; nobody is interested any longer in the anti-aircraft service. I report to the motorcycle marksmen [*Kradschtüzen*]. If you are going to do something, then do it, and nearly all my men report to the same branch. Hopefully, we will start soon, but it will certainly begin

> eventually because the re-organization of the regiment was ordered by the Führer . . .
> 2 March: I pack my kit and relocate to the 10th Motorcycle Company in Reinickendorf. A new time starts for me here. Company commander is my old battery chief Oblt. Lübke; senior NCO is my old Oberfeldwebel Teller. Of my old comrades Beckmann, Dietrich, Kreutzfeld, Mattes, Knabe and Voitzek are still there; other than that, there are only new faces. A tough time starts. I have to catch up quite a bit and need to learn a lot, but I enjoy it. It is a completely different life with the *Kradschützen* and I am looking forward to a mission.[1]

On 5 June near Vannes, regimental-scale exercises in conjunction with Junkers Ju 88 aircraft were held in the presence of Conrath and Generalfeldmarschall Hugo Sperrle, commander of Luftflotte 3. Sperrle expressed great satisfaction with the regiment's performance, the simulated combined-arms manoeuvres marking the end of the brigade's initial training period.

A Führer Directive of 9 July concerning the strengthening of defensive measures in the West articulated fresh German fears of an attempted British landing in France to open a second front and relieve pressure on Russia. To that end, available Waffen-SS units were to be transferred to France and cooperate with the 'Hermann Göring' Brigade:

> The SS Motorised Command is to be organised speedily and transferred to the Commanding General, Armed Forces, West. All SS units in the West, if possible, also the Göring Brigade, are to be combined under this command.

However, this idea appears to have been relatively short-lived, though the Luftwaffe was also ordered to concentrate all available forces of both 7. Fliegerdivision and the 'Hermann Göring' Brigade in their assembly areas for immediate commitment if required.

The brigade was to be issued new camouflage smocks and helmet covers according to a memorandum circulated on 21 July 1942, with initial priority given to brigade staff, as well as the combat troops of the Rifle and Flak Regiments. The remainder would receive theirs as stock became available, the new clothing being provided from a surplus of camouflage clothing held by the Waffen-SS, though supplies were exhausted by the summer. This frequently leads to misidentification of 'Hermann Göring' men as Waffen-SS troops in contemporary photographs. Not until 1943 were the three-quarter length camouflage jackets worn by Luftwaffe field divisions provided for 'Hermann Göring' troops, leading to a frequently mismatched appearance of men when on active service. As *Fallschirmjäger* men were also transferred in and out of the division over the months that followed, some 'Hermann Göring' members were also seen in the three-quarter-length jump smocks, adding to the profusion of uniforms available to the unit. Generally, at least Panzer and self-propelled gun crews wore the same-pattern uniforms as their Heer equivalents, with the addition of Luftwaffe insignia and items peculiar to 'Hermann Göring' such as cuff-titles.

From July the expansion and reorganisation of Conrath's unit was overseen by a newly established Sonderstab 'HG' that existed for three months as an administrative liaison and coordinating staff directing the flow of new recruits to their relevant units. This staff was headed by Maj. Gerhard Schmudlach, former commander of 3rd Battalion, which had been dissolved and its unit designation later attributed to the 'catch-all' battalion of specialist troops of the Rifle Regiment.

Though many Wehrmacht officers considered the Hermann Göring Regiment a mere vanity project, assistance was freely given by Heer commands in the training of the Luftwaffe men. For example, during the second half of August, thirteen of 9th (Heavy Infantry Gun) Company were despatched by train to Quimper for training in the use of 150-mm cannon by Oblt. Schmidt of 13th Company, 95th Infantry Regiment (17th Infantry Division). A fully rehabilitated Oblt. Wilmskötter, company commander, reported to the Infantry Regiment commander at the beginning and end of the training session to be apprised of his men's performance.[2] Also observing the sessions was Maj. Geicke, commander 2nd Battalion, Flak Artillery Regiment 'HG', who established contact with the 95th Infantry in order to ascertain the level of command training given during the course. Engineer training for 'Hermann Göring' 'shock-troops' was undertaken at Angers at the Army's Pionier Schule 7 during November, including advanced use of flamethrowers, minesweeping equipment, assault boats and welding and cutting torches.

The Brigade's armoured contingent was expanded slightly, Oblt. Lübke, having moved from command of the Motorcycle Company during April to 13th Panzer Company, received three Panzer IIIs (armed with 50-mm anti-tank guns) and two Sturmgeschütz III assault guns (75-mm cannon). In short order, four platoons were established, two of each vehicle: Oblt.

Heidrich and Lt. Wolfram Stronk taking command of a pair of StuG platoons, Lts. Lahusen and Blonk the Panzers. Lübke's armoured company then moved to France where its heavy weapons were incorporated into Preuss's 3rd (Heavy) Rifle Battalion.

Paul Conrath was promoted to the rank of *Generalmajor* on 11 July 1942 and his unit was officially granted the title of Brigade 'Hermann Göring' four days later. The combat units remained stationed in France and accounted for one of three separate components of the overall 'Hermann Göring' structure.[3] The strength and organisation of the brigade as of September 1942 was as follows:

Brigade 'Hermann Göring'	***Generalmajor Paul Conrath***	
Adjutant	*Hptm. Hans Beinhofer*	
Staff Company	*Oblt. Borchardt*	
Rifle Regiment 'HG'	*Oberst Hans Heidemeyer*	
1st Rifle Battalion	*Major Helmut Funck*	
1st Rifle Company	*Oblt. Franz Josef Grüne*	
2nd Rifle Company	*Hptm. Theodor [?] Weber*	
3rd Rifle Company	*Hptm. Walter Stauch*	
4th Rifle Heavy Weapons Company	*Hptm. Christian Spieler*	
2nd Rifle Battalion	*Hptm. Kurt Schreiber*	
5th Rifle Company	*Hptm. Gerhard Nagorny*	
6th Rifle Company	*Hptm. Robert Rebholz*	
7th Rifle Company	*Hptm. Horst Oehme*	
8th Rifle Heavy Weapons Company	*Hptm. Johann Dingelstedt*	
9th Heavy Infantry Gun Company	*Oblt. Friedrich Wilmskötter*	
3rd (Heavy) Rifle Battalion	*Maj. Joachim Preuss*	
Transport Column [Kolonne]	*Hptfw. Franke*	
10th Motorcycle Company	*Hptm. Eduard Kiefer*[4]	
11th Armoured Engineer Company	*Oblt. Musil*	
12th Panzerjäger [Anti-tank] Coy	*Oblt. Norbert Stiller*	
13th Panzer Company	*Hptm. Martin Lübke*	(including Armoured Car Platoon, previously att. to 10th Company)
Panzer Workshop Platoon	*Oblt. Joachim Zacher*	
Flak Regiment 'HG'	*Obstlt. Werner Hullmann*	
1st Battalion	*Maj. Fritz Schröter*	
Transport Column	*Oblt. Engelham*	
1st (Heavy) Battery	*Oblt. Heinrich Schaare*	
2nd (Heavy) Battery	*Hptm. Eduard Graf von Uxküll-Gyllenband*	

3rd (Heavy) Battery	*Obtl. Hans Arnold*	
4th (Light) Battery	*Oblt. Walter Wöhlert*	
5th (Light) Battery	*Hptm. Gerhard Gustmann*	
14th (Light) Battery	*Hptm. Dieke*	
2nd Battalion	*Maj. Geicke*	
Transport Column	*Oblt. von Löper*	
6th (Heavy) Battery	*Hptm. Röhme*	
7th (Heavy) Battery	*Hptm. Koch*	
8th (Heavy) Battery	*Oblt. Günther Norden*	
9th (Light) Battery	*Oblt. Klaus-Peter Bock*	
10th (Light) Battery	*Hptm. Karl Rossmann*	(experimental)
11th Howitzer Battery	*Oblt. Rudolf Graf*	

The second 'Hermann Göring' component remained in Berlin. Headed by Schmudlach's Sonderstab, it also included the Band, Guard Battalion and 4th Flak Battalion detailed to protect the government quarter, VIP trains and personal residences:

Sonderstab 'HG'	*Maj. Gerhard Schmudlach*
Band 'HG'	*Musikmeister Hans Friess*
4th (Führer) Flak Battalion 'HG'	*Maj. Paul Neubauer*
15th Battery	*Oblt. Reimer*
16th Battery	*Oblt. Heimann*
17th Battery	
Führer Zug	*Oblt. Gerdes*
Foreign Minister [Aussenminister] Zug	*Oblt. Hacker*
Reichsmarschall Zug (I and II)	*Oblt. Flügel*
Guard Battalion 'HG'	*Maj. Waldemar Kluge*
Staff Company	*Oblt. Otto Heyne*
1st Guard Company	*Hptm. Adolf Zillmann*
2nd Guard Company	*Hptm. Alfred Krohn*
3rd Guard Company:	*Oblt. Fritz Truckenmüller*

The men of the Guard Battalion were frequently rotated through combat units, also providing opportunities to remove men from the front line without any blemish on their record should such a transfer be required. In one instance on 23 October 1942, Conrath authorised the transfer of Obgef. Heinrich Stelter from 1st Battalion, Panzer Regiment 'HG' to 3rd Guard Company in Berlin. Stelter was the last of three sons left alive from a farming family, the others killed in action of the Eastern Front. In exchange, Gef. Schmidt of 3rd Guard Company was posted to take his place in the armoured unit, which was still being formed.[5]

Until the end of 1940, a unit of the Wach Battalion, RGG was only relocated from Berlin and stationed at the Reichsjägerhof during major military operations. This was Göring's majestic East Prussian hunting lodge that he had had constructed in 1936 in his role as Reichsjägermeister (Reich Master of the Hunt), on the Rominte Heath. The 'lodge' became, in reality, a network of buildings as Göring ordered its almost continual expansion, an attached game reserve covering an expanse of 260 km² supporting his passion for hunting. However, from the opening of Operation 'Barbarossa' and transfer of the Luftwaffe High Command from Berlin's Air Ministry to East Prussia, an entire company of the Guard Regiment was permanently stationed at the Rominte Heath, regardless of whether Göring was in residence or not.

The third brigade component was the replacement training battalion located in Utrecht, the Netherlands, and comprised:

Ersatz Battalion	*Maj. Robert Schulz*
1st Staff Company	*Oblt. Schütte*
2nd Rifle Company	*Oblt. Wenzel*
3rd Rifle Company	*Oblt. Vollmann*
4th Heavy Infantry Gun Battery	*Oblt. Gehrke*
5th Driver Company	*Oblt. Schink*
6th Motorcycle Company	*Oblt. Sailer*
7th (Heavy) Battery	*Oblt. Lorenz*
8th (Light) Battery	*Oblt. Mayer*
9th Howitzer Battery	*Oblt. Niedermayer*
10th Convalescent [Genesenden] Company	

Extensive training was required as the brigade had been rapidly expanded by a reshuffling of existing units then bolstered by an influx of volunteers. On 15 September Conrath issued a memorandum entitled 'Guidelines for Continued Training' in which he detailed every facet of preparation for Brigade operations from the correct use of motorcycles to gas defence. The central point of his instructions was contained on the second page of his nine-page document and provides an insight into the moulding of the 'Hermann Göring' troops into a formidable ideologically driven fighting force (underlining as in original):

> Focus of training:
> The Rifle Regiment's training is based on mastery of the tactics of the fast troops in cooperation with tanks, tank destroyers, pioneers and the weapons of the anti-aircraft regiment.
> The Flak Regiment must be fully employable for all air and ground defence roles in cooperation with, and providing protection for, armoured Brigade units.
> Success in combat is not achieved solely through leadership and weapon performance, but, above all, through the spirit of the troops. Education and training must always be matched with this.
>
> Every single commander must therefore be particularly concerned with the mental and spiritual education and ideological training of his soldiers. In weekly classes on daily issues, he must influence his officers, non-commissioned officers and men.[6]

However, the brigade's composition had created problems, deriving as it did from a single motorised infantry regiment. It would be unable to survive self-sufficiently in its current form and certainly unable to operate with any kind of autonomy on the battlefield. Thus it was that no sooner had the brigade begun combined-arms training than, on 15 October 1942, Hitler authorised the expansion of Conrath's unit to full division size, with the ultimate aim of forming a complete Panzer division, though with a confused and somewhat chaotic development plan. Conrath issued an order that same day that illustrated the desired haste with which this new division would be created:

> Fundamental reasons prohibit leave of absence for soldiers of the 'Hermann Göring' Division for study purposes. The implementation of the realignments ordered by the Führer and the establishment of operational readiness on 1 January 1943 require the exertion of all forces of every soldier in the 'Hermann Göring' Division.[7]

Indeed, though perhaps not yet apparent to the men of the division, they had already been earmarked for deployment to North Africa where the situation of German and Italian forces had deteriorated. As an omen of pending transfer, on 21 October, twenty-two NCOs and enlisted men from both artillery and infantry units, led by Waffenoberinspektor Wagner of the staff of 1st Battalion, Flak Artillery Regiment 'HG', began training in adapting their weapons to tropical use.

In Berlin, Schmudlach's Sonderstab 'HG' was disbanded to be replaced by Organisationsstab F under the command of former flak commander Oberstleutnant Wilhelm Fuchs from the Luftwaffe General Staff. The divisional expansion required an influx of men and 5,000 Luftwaffe volunteers were enlisted and farmed out to the various units by Fuchs as existing units were divided and reinforced to create the new component parts.

The Musikmeister and 120 men of the 'Hermann Göring' Band were also present in France during October, used as support troops for training by 3rd Battalion, Grenadier Regiment 'HG', the Reconnaissance Battalion and 11th Armoured Engineer Company. Alongside combat training, the Band gave a series of concerts in Meucon, Locmine and Josselin, the musicians marching to each location while their instruments were transported by truck. Though held in high regard for their musical proficiency and performing well-received concerts both at ceremonial occasions in Germany and for troops in occupied territories, the role of the Band steadily shrank as the war situation deteriorated over the years to follow. Eventually, its members were folded into the divisional Feldgendarmerie and transformed from musicians into military police.

During November, after Vichy France was occupied by the Wehrmacht following the Allied Operation 'Torch' landings in North Africa, the divisional combat units relocated from Brittany to villages in the area of Mont de Marsan, south of Bordeaux and continued their rigorous training regime, including anti-invasion measures practised on the coastline between Bordeaux and Biarritz as part of the First Army reserve.

One of the newest divisional elements was the Panzer Regiment, the entire personnel of 3rd (Heavy) Battalion of the Rifle Regiment becoming 1st Battalion, Panzer Regiment 'HG', still commanded by Hptm. Preuss.

1st Battalion, Panzer Regt. 'HG'	*Hptm. Preuss*
Adjutant	*Oblt. Wolfram Stronk*
Signals Platoon	*Lt. Groll*
13th (Panzer) Company	*Hptm. Lübke*
10th (Motorcycle) Company	*Hptm. Paulus*
11th Company (Armoured Engineer)	*Oblt. Musil*

By the year's end the complete divisional organisation had been decided, though major components existed as yet only on paper. A simple procedure was followed by which personnel and equipment levels of an existing cadre unit were increased to reach its desired strength, its expansion determined by the rate of vehicle and weapon acquisition as well as training and recruiting levels. An undated document from the end of 1942 provides the first anticipated organisational chart, including units either not yet created or not yet officially amalgamated:

Division 'Hermann Göring'	***Generalmajor Paul Conrath***	
Grenadier Regiment 1 'HG'	*Oberst Herbert Ewert*	formerly Rifle Regiment
1st Battalion	*Hptm. Konstantin Hahm*	mechanised, 1st–4th Companies, plus HQ Coy. with Mortar, Anti-Tank, Engineer Platoons
2nd Battalion		mechanised, 5th–8th Companies, HQ Company
3rd Battalion	*Maj. Helmut Funck*	mechanised, 9th–12th Companies, HQ Company
13th Company		heavy infantry guns
14th Company	*Oblt. Norbert Stiller*	Panzerjäger
Grenadier Regiment 2 'HG'	*Oberst Dr Edgar Johann*	4th, 5th, 6th Battalions, organised as above, no sub-units yet formed
Grenadier Regiment 3 'HG'		7th, 8th, 9th Battalions, organised as above, no sub-units yet formed
Flak Regiment 'HG'	*Obstlt. Werner Hullmann*	
1st Flak Battalion		1st–5th Batteries, plus HQ Battery
2nd Flak Battalion	*Maj. Werner Geicke*	6th–11th Batteries, plus HQ Battery; formed apart from 10th Battery
3rd Flak Battalion	*Hptm. Friedrich Fährmann*	12th–16th Batteries, plus HQ Battery; partially formed
4th (Führer) Flak Btn. 'HG':	*Maj. Paul Neubauer*	
Panzer-Regiment 'HG'	*Obstlt. Walter Straub*	
1st Panzer Battalion	*Maj. Preuss*	1st–3rd Companies, plus HQ Company; partially formed
2nd Panzer Battalion		4th–6th Companies, plus HQ Company; partially formed
Artillery Regiment 'HG'	*Oberst Oehring*	
1st Artillery Battalion		1st–3rd Batteries, plus HQ Battery; partially formed
2nd Artillery Battalion		4th–6th Batteries, plus HQ Battery; partially formed
3rd Artillery Battalion		7th–9th Batteries, plus HQ Battery; not yet formed

4th Artillery Battalion		10th–12th Batteries, plus HQ Battery; not yet formed
5th Artillery Battalion		Sturmgeschütz, 13th–15th Batteries, plus HQ Battery
Panzer Recce. Btn 'HG'	*Hptm. Otto Brandenburg*	
Adjutant	*Lt. Rennmayr*	
Staff Company	*Lt. May*	with Armoured Car Platoon
1st Motorcycle Company	*Hptm. Kiefer*	
2nd Volkswagen Company	*Oblt. Rolf Gerhardt*	
3rd Armoured Car Coy.	*Hptm. Paulus*	not yet formed
4th Panzerjäger Company	*Oblt. Jahr*	
5th (Heavy) Company	*Oblt. Dingelstedt*	
Engineer Platoon	*Oblt. Lambrecht*	
Infantry Gun Platoon	*Lt. Jende*	
6th Flak Company	*Hptm. Walter Dieke*	20-mm
Armoured Engineer Battalion 'HG':		
1st Armoured Engineer Company		
2nd Armoured Engineer Company		not yet formed
3rd Armoured Engineer Company		not yet formed
4th Armoured Engineer Company		not yet formed
Panzer Signals Battalion 'HG'	*Maj. Bettlewski*	
Staff Company		
1st Panzer Signals Company		radio
2nd Panzer Signals Company		teletype [Fernsprech]; not yet formed
Medical [Sanitäts] Btn 'HG'	*Oberfeldarzt Dr Blackstein*	
1st Medical Detachment		
2nd Medical Detachment		not yet formed
3rd Medical Detachment		not yet formed
Supply [Nachschub] Regiment 'HG'		
1st Supply Battalion	*Obstlt. Rahlfs*	
2nd Supply Battalion		partially formed
Maintenance Battalion	*Obstlt. Schlegel*	partially formed

Military Police Troop; Field Post Detachment [Feldpostamt]; Ground Readiness Team [Flugbereitschaft]; Divisional support units such as blacksmith, bakery and butchery [Verwaltungsdienste]

Utrecht

Ersatz und Ausbildungs Regt. 'HG'	*Maj. Robert Schulz*

Berlin

Guard Regiment 'HG'

Grenadier Regiment 2 and 3 were never completely formed, although Oberst Dr Edgar Johann, former battalion commander in 1st Luftwaffe Field Division, was transferred to the 'Hermann Göring' Division on 6 November 1942 to command the 2nd Regiment, on paper at least.

Oberst Wilhelm Schmalz – formerly of 59th Motorcycle Battalion (9th Panzer Division), subsequent commander of 11th Panzergrenadier Regiment and holder of the German Cross in Gold – was seconded from the Heer as head of training for the Luftwaffe troops stationed in Mont de Marsan during January 1943. Schmalz had already encountered the 'Hermann Göring' troops in Russia and would prove instrumental in turning the unit into the elite formation of its future reputation. While Conrath and most of his senior officers were undoubtedly capable, their experience was no doubt limited. Schmalz, on the other hand, had first entered the German cavalry in April 1919 and thereafter served continuously in the armed forces from that point onwards as they morphed from the Reichswehr to Wehrmacht.

> When I arrived in January 43, I was informed that a Panzer division was to be organised from those elements which had not gone to Africa, and from new volunteers. I found a planned organisation devised by Luftwaffe officers at their own discretion and bearing little resemblance to the organisation of a Panzer division of the Heer. It was an impracticable plan. One had to decide whether to create a Panzer division, or an infantry division with armoured elements. In the event of the adoption of the first solution, it was necessary to concentrate on tanks, supported by infantry mounted on armoured vehicles. If the second plan were selected, the infantry would need no armoured vehicles. The planned organisation was, therefore, illogical: nine infantry battalions mounted on armoured vehicles was excessive for two tank battalions. Furthermore, the Heer furnished all armoured material, including artillery. Since Panzer divisions of the Heer had only two tank battalions and four infantry battalions (and only one infantry battalion was mounted in armoured vehicles), it was inconceivable that the Heer would equip nine armoured infantry battalions.[8]

Schmalz's recommendations provided a firm footing for the organisation of the division along more conventional Heer lines. He immediately emphasised the comparatively high number of specialists that would be required, particularly personnel experienced in the use of armoured vehicles, assault guns, anti-tank weapons and engineers. He strongly advocated the continued recruiting of volunteers while also requesting that the Heer provide experienced officers and NCOs from its armoured forces to act both as instructors and combat officers. In return, inexperienced Luftwaffe officers would be rotated into Heer units for 'on the spot' training. The division would also require equipment to continue to be provided from Army stocks (with the exception of flak weapons), though the increased anti-aircraft contingent of an entire flak regiment, negated the requirement for an independent anti-tank battalion. Up to 20,000 men would be required per year, at a rate of 1,500 per month, a target that was successfully met by Luftwaffe recruiting.

Ultimately, though he remained integral to its creation, Schmalz fundamentally opposed the entire rationale of the 'Hermann Göring' Division's existence within the Luftwaffe. He was already well aware of the problems that would likely be encountered by the reliance on a competing service arm for equipment – something that he would become all too familiar with the following year when he was placed in command of the division – and realised that the absorption of excellent volunteers into the Luftwaffe deprived the Heer of badly needed men. Indeed, the battle for manpower between the Wehrmacht's three branches (and the Waffen-SS) had intensified as the 'Hermann Göring' Division was now no longer the only Luftwaffe ground formation to have become a reality.

The creation of Luftwaffe field divisions had been authorised during October 1942 because of Göring's jealous hold on the power of his air force and all men connected to it. With the decline of the Luftwaffe at the hands of growing Allied aerial power and confused testing and construction programmes, the service had become bloated with trained ground personnel who could no longer be suitably employed. In 1941 the Luftwaffe accounted for 20 per cent of Germany's overall manpower pool, with only a minority being actual air crew. During September 1942, facing exhaustion of his ground forces and a growing crisis at Stalingrad, Hitler ordered Göring to release 200,000 men for use by the Heer. Incensed at the loss of so many men that he considered politically committed and fully indoctrinated with National Socialist zeal, unlike the reactionary Heer, Göring instead offered to form twenty field divisions using those troops, with these to remain under Luftwaffe control. Hitler acquiesced and within two months seven Luftwaffe field regiments had been created; the field divisions soon became a reality, though with predictably mixed results. Skilled technicians many of these men may have been, but they were not sufficiently trained in front-line land combat. Substantially smaller than equivalent Heer divisions, Göring ordered that they be used on defensive duties in quieter sectors of the front, though the deteriorating war situation would see them frequently thrust into the front line. These units were entirely distinct from both the *Fallschirmjäger* and 'Hermann Göring' formations and there was barely any interchange of personnel between them at all.

As part of the divisional expansion, the decision was made at the Reich Air Ministry to transfer Oberstleutnant Walter Koch's entire 5th Paratroop Regiment to Conrath's command. It would become the Rifle [Jäger] Regiment 'Hermann Göring', an instant means by which the division's infantry capability was immediately increased to the recommended two regiments, moreover with a strong core of experienced fighters. These paratroopers included veterans of the battle for Crete and most had previously been part of Meindl's Luftlande-Sturm-Regiment alongside whom men of the Schützen Bataillon had fought at Yukhov and Schaikowa airfields during the arduous winter battles before Moscow. The battered unit had been relieved from the line and moved to France where, after reinforcement, it undertook extensive training in the old French Army exercise area near Mourmelon, southeast of Reims, in preparation for the expected assault on Malta (Operation Hercules).

However, due to the exigencies of reinforcement requirements for North Africa, Koch's 2nd Battalion, commanded by Maj. Friedrich Hübner, was detached in the summer of 1942 to join Ramcke's Paratroop Brigade that had been sent to Libya to bolster Rommel's relatively small Afrika Korps in its final drive towards the Suez Canal. Though this offensive would end at El Alamein, at no point was Hübner's battalion returned or amalgamated into the 'Hermann Göring' Division. The remaining elements earmarked for incorporation in Conrath's division were:

Rifle Regiment 'Hermann Göring'	***Obstlt. Walter Koch***
1st Battalion	*Hptm. Hans Jungwirth*
HQ Company	
1st Company	*Lt. Erich Schuster*
2nd Company	*Oblt. Gerd Maier*
3rd Company	*Hptm. Otto Langbein*
4th Company	*Hptm. Hugo Paul*

3rd Battalion	*Hptm. Wilhelm Knoche*
HQ Company	
9th Company	*Hptm. Rudolf Becker*
10th Company	*Oblt. Ulrich Jahn*
11th Company	*Oblt. Arthur Schneider*
12th Company	*Oblt. Hans Hoge*

The Rifle Regiment remained 'incomplete' as it moved to its new parent unit, though some confusion remains as to the official date when Koch's men became part of the 'Hermann Göring' Division; many of the *Fallschirmjäger* were completely unaware of their new parent unit, receiving no direct communication from Conrath or additional cuff-titles or identifying insignia. Nonetheless, the *Soldbuch* of Obergefreiter Heinrich Hoffmann of 2nd Company at least contains notation of the official change from 2nd Company, 5th Paratroop Regiment to 2nd Company, Rifle Regiment 'HG' on 15 October 1942.[9]

Additionally, as the Flak Regiment also languished in a semi-completed state, the Luftwaffe's 221st Flak Battalion was transferred intact to become 3rd Flak Battalion 'HG'.

However, almost as soon as the *Jäger* transferred to Conrath's command, Kesselring grabbed Koch's troops for immediate posting to North Africa as a fresh crisis developed in November 1942. They thereby became the first 'Hermann Göring' unit to serve in Tunisia and claimed the credit for maintaining the Axis hold on the region following the Allies' Operation 'Torch'. Three beachheads were taken in the vicinity of Casablanca, Oran and Algiers by a force of 73,500 Anglo-American troops. Once well established ashore, Allied commanders planned to squeeze Axis forces between their advance from the west and Montgomery's Eighth Army forces pushing from Egypt, Rommel's front line on the eve of 'Torch' resting at Sidi Barrani. At the time of the Allied landing there were no German forces in Tunisia except a small liaison staff monitoring compliance with the terms of the armistice with France.

Tunisian topography alone would challenge the Allied invaders. While coastal movement was possible using the railway and road linking Tunis with Algeria, this was a dangerously exposed and predictable path. The country's interior was dominated by rocky alluvial plains and high mountains connected by valleys, frequently cut by wadis which provided natural anti-tank obstacles when dry and were subject to flash flood in rain.

Movement inland was confined to primitive roads through narrow passes of the Dorsal mountains, which could readily be covered by determined defenders. Armoured operations were limited to the Medjez valley and plains to the south of Feriana–Sbeitla–Pichon. The 10 km-wide ridge running from Medjez-el-Bab towards Tunis that sloped down to the plain was under cultivation and free from anti-tank obstacles. However, the ground frequently turned into a thick glutinous quagmire in rains – and the rainy season was just beginning, proving to be longer than normal and lasting into April. West of Mateur, isolated peaks and ridges dominated the terrain for a depth of ten or more kilometres, making possession of this high ground essential, but also requiring strong defending forces to hold the area.

The German High Command had already held discussions before the 'Torch' landings – and before the decision to amalgamate Koch's regiment with the 'Hermann Göring' division – that concluded the regiment should be transferred to North Africa to reinforce a beleaguered Rommel; though the 'Torch' landings hastened their departure to Tunisia and the rear of the German occupied territory rather than at the front lines in Libya.[10] The 1st and 3rd Battalions of Koch's Regiment had been ordered to transfer from Mourmelon-le Petit to Guingamp on 26 October in anticipation of integration into the division, but the unfolding crisis in the Mediterranean took precedence and their stay in Brittany was brief. The regiment began moving again on 10 November 1942, first by train to Caserta, Italy, where they were concentrated before an advance group of an officer and men from 10th Company were emplaned aboard Ju 52 transport aircraft near Naples and flown via a refuelling stop in Sicily to El Aouina airfield near Tunis on the evening of the 11th. Two squads of *Fallschirmjäger* engineers were also flown to Bizerte, led by Feldwebel Peter Ahrendt, to seize and hold the airfield there.

The German decision to hold Tunisia was as much motivated by a desire to keep Italy as an active member of the Axis as to delay any attempted Allied landing on European Mediterranean soil. Thus, instead of backing up Rommel's success of the previous year, Hitler instead chose to reinforce what, with hindsight, now seems inevitable failure. Kesselring had been ordered by Hitler to 'throw everything into it that you have available' and immediately set about locating troops that could be shuttled into Tunisia as part of Operation 'Braun', to seize and hold ports and airfields, establishing a defensive perimeter around the city of Tunis until regular infantry and armoured troops could arrive. Once this Tunisian bridgehead was established, Rommel's back would be considered secure and he could withdraw to positions on the Tunisian–Libyan border, Hitler's vagaries notwithstanding. On 14 November the OKW War Diary outlined the future of 'Braun':

> The bridgehead is fully subordinate to Oberbefehlshaber Süd [Kesselring], to whom General der Panzertruppe Nehring is subordinate as the local command authority in Tunis. The Italians agree and the Duce has told the Führer that he will send troops to Tunisia as soon possible. It is important to establish the bridgehead in a race with the Americans. Large units are to be transferred: the 10th Panzer Division (Marseille), the 'Göring' Division (Cognac) and the 334th Infantry Division (Kriemhilde, ordered to the home war zone on 8 November to incorporate replacement troops). The order of their transfer [to Tunisa] should solely depend on which division can move first, which of course depends on the timely provision of rolling stock. An SD task force of 7 officers and 17 men is to be dispatched to Tunis.[11]

Kesselring's personal security troops and leading Luftwaffe elements of a new fighter command, Fliegerführer Tunis, had begun landing on 11 November. The airfield came under bombing attack as Koch's *Fallschirmjäger* arrived; his men were immediately ordered to drive through the city and cover roads leading to the west. The following day the remainder of 3rd Battalion began landing, Jungwirth's 1st Rifle Battalion following on 15 November. The confusion of German reinforcement to Tunis left Koch's men without a signals unit, reliant instead on runners using the Tunis tram network. Indeed, the hastily announced LXXXX Corps that would control all Wehrmacht units gathered in Tunisia was headed by the gifted General der Panzertruppe Walther Nehring whose initial communications resources were a civilian taxi and a hotel telephone.

Koch, mindful of the need for a wide perimeter into which Rommel's retreating forces in the east could withdraw, immediately proposed to Nehring a determined assault by his two battalions against French forces at Medjez-el-Bab. Six colonial garrisons under the command of Vichy military governor General Georges Barré had retreated to the town in the face of the Allied landings and begun employing delaying tactics against German forces in order to allow the Allies to reach them before they were forced to declare for which side they would fight.

With Vichy troops outnumbering Axis forces, Hptm. Knoche and his French-speaking adjutant Oblt. Fritz Quednow, accompanied by Lt. Klein of 14th Company, 104th Infantry Regiment, rode by motorcycle sidecar combination to meet French Colonel Le Couteux in Tebourda to request that French troops evacuate the area along the Medjerda River and allow the establishment of three German bridgeheads on the western bank. However, despite their invoking Pétain's proclamation that any Allied advance into Vichy territory was illegal and thereby German defences acceptable, Le Couteax rejected the request and referred them to Barré for adjudication of the issue. After a brief meeting and exaggeration of Axis strength, Tebourda and Djedeida were ceded to the Germans, though French troops refused to give up Medjez-el-Bab.

Nehring, concerned that his meagre forces would be exposed and over-stretched, proposed instead that Koch form *Kampfgruppen* with which to seize the town and its important bridge over the Medjerda River, thereby thwarting the Allied race for Tunis. Hauptmann Knoche led his 3rd Battalion, reinforced by an Italian anti-tank company, two dual purpose 88-mm guns from the 10th Panzer Division and a *Kampfgruppe* from the 190th Panzer Battalion, towards the town and, after Barré refused a final ultimatum from Kesselring, went into action following a brief Stuka attack. The battle was ferocious, the town's railway station changing hands three times before the French defenders prevailed and the *Fallschirmjäger* were forced to retreat, losing control of the bridge but fortifying their hold on the eastern river bank.

Allied spearhead forces were approaching from the west as elements of the British First Army – 11th Brigade (78th Infantry Division), 2nd Lancashire Fusiliers and 5th Northamptons – attempted to wrest the town from the *Fallschirmjäger* on 25 November. A frontal assault by 2nd Lancashire Fusiliers was repulsed with heavy losses and a crossing upstream by the Northamptons was also thrown back by the timely arrival of German tanks.

However, a penetration by a small number of M3 Light tanks of the U.S. 1st Armored Division attacked Djedeida airfield and Nehring momentarily panicked, ordering Koch to retreat to the east and form a defensive perimeter nearer to Tunis; the *Fallschirmjäger* withdrew to another position just west of Massicault (now Borj el Amri). After conferring with Kesselring and being informed of impending reinforcement, Nehring regained the initiative and with armoured reinforcements from 10th Panzer Division – including a company of formidable Tiger Is – Koch was ordered to advance on Medjez where they clashed once more with British 11th Infantry Brigade on 30 November.

While Koch's battalions advanced a small British parachute landing had been made by Lt-Col John Frost's 2nd Parachute Battalion on 29 November with the aim of seizing enemy airfields. The plan was to drop on Pont du Fahs airfield and then march on Depienne twelve miles to the north, followed by Oudna a further twelve miles distant. Once established there, Frost was instructed to await ground forces.[12]

Take-off was troublesome for the British force as a result of thick mud while last-minute intelligence also revealed that neither Pont du Fahs nor Depienne airfields were actually in German use. Instead, Frost would drop on Depienne and march immediately for Oudna, thought to be an active Luftwaffe base. Frost subsequently suffered nearly twenty casualties in the drop alone, which commenced at 1400 hrs, his men being dispersed to such an extent that the remaining daylight was used concentrating his forces. Lieutenant Denis 'Bucky' Boiteux-Buchanan, commander of C Company, was instructed by Frost to remain at Depienne and guard the injured men while also collecting silk parachutes scattered nearby. The small British force was captured at midday the following day by Italian troops.

On hearing of the parachute drop, Koch immediately diverted two companies – Lt. Erich Schuster's 1st Company and Oblt. Ullrich Jahn's 10th Company – with supporting armoured vehicles from 90th Armoured Reconnaissance Battalion (10th Panzer Division) – to engage the new threat. Koch and Jungwirth also travelled towards the reported parachute drop by car to reconnoitre the area while the remainder of their riflemen pressed on finally to take the bridge at Medjez.

Boiteux-Buchanan's men were fortunate that those two officers had decided to head to Depienne, as a surly officer of 90th Armoured Reconnaissance Battalion had arrived just before them and ordered the Italians to shoot the captured paratroopers. He believed he was acting in accordance with Hitler's October order that all commandos 'whether they be soldiers in uniform' and 'whether they land by parachute . . . [and] on discovery make obvious their intention of giving themselves up as prisoners, no pardon is on any account to be given'. However, as the prisoners were being lined up against a wall, Koch and Jungwirth arrived on the scene, Koch leaping from his vehicle and engaging in a fierce argument with the reconnaissance officer, bluntly declaring that the captured men would be treated in accordance with international law and transported to a prisoner of war camp.

By the following morning the remainder of Frost's men had established a defensive position on high ground south of Oudna when leading elements of Jahn's 10th Company made contact and fighting began which lasted until nightfall. Frost later expressed admiration for the German machine-gun teams:

> Admittedly the Germans were fresh compared with us, but there could be no doubt that their weapon handling was superior, for time and again they got into action first, and while our men were still groping for good fire positions, the opposing gun numbers would bring long and accurate bursts to bear. Nevertheless we managed to prevent them from being able to call the top of the hill their own and, despite the help their tanks could give them, we clung firmly to the reverse slope and were able to enfilade any who became too adventurous.[13]

Faced with potential encirclement, Frost opted to divide his troops into smaller parties and move west towards Massicault, though French farmers encountered on the way strongly advised against such a move as it was occupied by Germans. One small party led by Lt. Peter Stainforth had stopped to rest at a farm when a German motorcycle combination approached; Leutnant Schuster was riding in a sidecar with another man, attached to eighteen-year-old Gefreiter Hans Teske's motorcycle. Schuster dismounted to question the French farmer regarding reported British troops, while Teske went behind a nearby haystack to relieve himself, leaving his rifle propped against the motorcycle. As the Frenchman explained that British troops had been there but moved on, the hidden British paratroopers kept their weapons trained on the unsuspecting Germans.

> The watching British officers kept their Bren and Sten guns trained on the three Germans, staying well back. Teske, now more comfortable, was suddenly aware of some Arab children playing close by and then, to his horror, of a British soldier standing in the barn door, covering him with his gun . . . Teske was a quick thinker, and I later learned that he reasoned that if he gave no sign of recognition, he would probably walk away alive. Hopefully, this British soldier was merely covering a wounded comrade . . . So

> Teske buttoned up his flies and sauntered off, knowing full well that a false move would result in a holocaust of shooting.
>
> The Germans remounted and drove off, Teske still feeling hot and cold. He was also in a fearful quandary. He could not now admit what he had seen for fear of the consequences, even though his silence had undoubtedly saved all their lives. He decided to say nothing, and the patrol continued on its way.[14]

The main body of retreating British troops, led by Frost, congregated at an Arab farm named El Fedja, the buildings surrounded by thick cactus and the farm providing water and plenty of sturdy cover; it was thereafter known to the British as 'Cactus Farm'. At 1000 on 1 December, Oblt. Ulrich Jahn's 10th Company located Frost's men, spotted by Frost observing the British positions through binoculars from a distant ridge. After a mortar barrage the 26-year-old company commander led the first exploratory probe of the British positions and was killed by close range defensive fire from A Company, Lt. Werner Kempa taking charge of the German unit.[15] An offer to lay down their arms and surrender was rebuffed by Frost and the Germans commenced limited attacks supported by intense mortar and machine-gun fire.

With casualties mounting, Frost's men waited until they had defeated another German assault before beginning their withdrawal from Cactus Farm at 1815 on 2 December, eventually stumbling across some American half-tracks and reaching Medjez-el-Bab on 4 December; the town was still held by French colonial troops. It had been a costly exercise for the British with over 300 casualties, while Koch's 5th Paratroop Regiment had also suffered badly; his adjutant Lt. Johannes Ismer was among those killed in one of the attacks on Cactus Farm.

During December, the Paratroop Regiment was again engaged in heavy fighting at Tébourba and Fourna that pushed Allied troops back in the region of El Battan and ultimately prevented an Allied breakthrough to Tunis itself. The German operations thus stalled the Allied advance and rendered the front line relatively quiet for several weeks. While these battles were being fought, Nehring was abruptly ordered to return to Germany, handing over control of his troops to Generaloberst Hans-Jürgen von Arnim as LXXXX Corps became Fifth Panzer Army.[16]

Although it is recorded that it was February before Koch's men were officially amalgamated into the new 'Hermann Göring' Division, their inclusion had been confirmed by OKL the previous November, although for a period they were in the confusing administrative position of being listed on the strength of both the new division and XI Fliegerkorps (responsible for Mediterranean *Fallschirmjäger*) at the same time. Despite this, they were clearly already considered part of the division by the end of 1942, further evidenced by their inclusion in Conrath's end of year message to his troops issued on 29 December:

> At the turn of the year I convey my most sincere best wishes to all officers, technicians, NCOs, soldiers, staff and workers. A year of tireless work to build up our division is behind us.
>
> Parts of the division were used in the tough defensive battles on the Eastern Front from January to March, and the Jäger Regiment has been involved in the victorious fighting around Tunis since the beginning of November.
>
> I thank all members of the division for their outstanding performance.
>
> We thank our fallen comrades with grieving pride, who give their lives in the struggle for Germany's freedom. Their sacrifice is the most sacred legacy for all of us. The new year will present us with large and difficult tasks. The division will fight decisive battles. We trust our soldier's oath for Germany and will do our duty for the Führer.

During November, as Koch's men had been heading to North Africa, other units of Conrath's division had begun moving to Italy, the first troop trains leaving on the 16th of the month despite objections from Conrath that his men were not yet ready. Major Christoph Walter Werner, a former flak officer before Luftwaffe General Staff training, had been transferred during July to be the divisional Chief of Staff. He later recalled the predicament for a post-war case study prepared for the U.S. Army.

> At that time the elements of the division which were ready to be sent to the front were transferred into the area between Rouen and Bordeaux, however without any definite assignment. Since additional transfers had to be anticipated, especially to the coast of southern France where an enemy attack was not unlikely, it was no longer feasible to carry out organisational training on a higher level. Owing to the fact that it was impossible to make decisions about the

special units which were being formed, in most cases on separate training grounds, moreover, owing to delays and curtailments in training on the organisational level, which applied also to the units and organisations stationed in southwestern France, the division at that moment was ready for combat or ready to be sent to the front only to a limited extent. If the disturbing alarm conditions should persist . . . the entire [divisional] activation programme would be endangered and the schedule for its completion (1 February 1943) would be greatly delayed.

In addition to the current progress the division submitted a pertinent report to the OKL requesting that employment of the division prior to completion of activation be avoided.[17]

Nevertheless, first the Paratroop Regiment, and then those elements of the division deemed combat-ready were ordered to the front via Italy as the Wehrmacht possessed barely any operational reserves capable of being despatched to Africa. Conrath established his headquarters in an Italian Army barracks in Santa Maria Capua Vetere, about 25 km north of Naples. The camp lay just outside the town limits, only 400 metres from a ruined Roman amphitheatre – the second largest in the world and made famous as the arena in which Spartacus fought – and initially provided insufficient vehicle parking as well as still housing a large contingent of Italian troops whom the German arrivals viewed as dragging their heels in leaving the barracks lest they be posted to North Africa. Protracted negotiations with the Italian authorities finally ousted the previous occupants and, while many divisional vehicles were parked along the approach roads, troops set about digging trenches and other fieldworks both within and immediately beyond its wired perimeter, perfect for the continued training of the Luftwaffe troops. The truck workshop company (Kraftwagen Werkstatt Kompanie) was soon situated on the Caserta to Naples road, while the armoured workshop company (Panzer Werkstatt Kompanie) was established adjacent to Santa Maria's main town parking area. The truck depot in particular was soon busy adapting vehicles for tropical use. Meanwhile, Obstlt. Hullmann's Flak Regiment had been assigned to air defence in the Naples area: 1st Battalion (minus 5th Battery) stationed in Santa Maria Capua Vetere–Caserta–Marcianise; 2nd Battalion (minus 8th, 9th and 10th Batteries but with 11th Battery and 6th (Light) Battery attached) was stationed north of Naples harbour.

The Sturmgeschütz Battalion had been established with the assistance of a cadre of officers, NCOs and men transferred from various Army training and combat units, as well as specialist workshop personnel and inspectors. The senior officer of the ex-Army men was Hptm. Gerhard Schmock, former commander of 1st Battery, 226th Sturmgeschütz Battalion and most recently attached to the training staff of XIII. Fliegerkorps (formed from Luftwaffe Division Meindl), Bergen.[18]

The first Sturmgeschütz Platoon with four long-barrelled assault guns had been established at the beginning of June 1942 under command of Oblt. Wolfram Stronk (later replaced by Oblt. Heidrich). By the beginning of November, after divisional expansion had been confirmed, twenty-one *Sturmgeschütze* had been assembled in Magdeburg and entrained for northern France whereupon, by divisional order 716/42, they were incorporated into the 'Hermann Göring' Artillery Regiment.

The *Sturmgeschütze* arrived in Saintes on 12 November and were officially accepted by Hptm. Rossmann of the Panzer Regiment while it was still forming and initially designated 7th, 8th and 9th Batteries of 3rd Battalion, Artillery Regiment 'HG'. Rossmann, who had transferred from the Flak Regiment to a company command in the newly established Panzer Regiment, then led the guns and a hundred men by train to Italy. They were mistakenly sent to Bari before meeting up with fresh troops transferred from Utrecht to Santa Maria for incorporation in the *Sturmgeschütz* unit.

On 6 December, Hptm. Schmock arrived as battalion commander and training began in earnest, thirty-two men from the original Army cadre also being taken on the strength of the Staff Battery as 3rd (StuG) Battalion was renumbered as 5th (StuG) Battalion, Artillery Regiment 'HG'. Furthermore, twenty-two ex-Army men were folded into 13th Battery (formerly 7th Battery), twenty-five for 14th Battery (formerly 8th Battery), twenty-six for 15th Battery (formerly 9th) and four for the 5th (StuG) transport column.

The assault-gun unit was finally considered fully activated on 7 December 1942 and officially welcomed into the division by Conrath at the beginning of January in a personal address at Santa Maria. Shooting practice began at the coastal community of Castelvolturno, north of Naples, and soon in combined arms exercises around Capua with the newly arrived Grenadier Regiment after its transit from France.

13th Battery	*Oblt. Wilmskötter*
1st Platoon	*Lt. Scaper*
2nd Platoon	*Lt. König*
3rd Platoon	*Lt. Poetter*
14th Battery	*Oblt. Heidrich*
1st Platoon	*Lt. Block*
2nd Platoon	*Lt. Wolfram Stronk*
3rd Platoon	*Obfw. Sturm*
15th Battery	*Oblt. Hagemann*
1st Platoon	*Lt. Wibbelt*
2nd Platoon	*Lt. Wittschonke*
3rd Platoon	*Lt. Karl-Heinz Wallhäusser*

In the search for reinforcements for the war in Russia, an Army application for the *Sturmgeschütze* to be transferred to the East was rejected. Their rationale had been that the difficulties of using armoured and motorised troops in inhospitable Tunisian terrain rendered the armoured vehicles extremely unsuitable. Instead they offered an exchange for either a mountain or infantry division from the Eastern Front, something that Conrath actually fully endorsed. However, it was not to be, and on 19 December the final confirmed order from OKW was received at Conrath's headquarters. The 'Hermann Göring' Division was headed to Tunisia.

Chapter Four

Tunisia

'In war the issues are decided not by isolated acts of heroism but by the general training and spirit of an army.'
Field Marshal Albert Kesselring

Divisional elements continued to trickle to Italy by train from Bordeaux; the transfer of the division from First Army was announced as completed by 28 December. Though committed to an estimated four trains every day, the divisional troop trains passing through Austria were considerably delayed by a bottleneck at the Brenner Pass where only a limited amount of traffic was permitted. Those sent via southern France and the Riviera fared considerably better, though through administrative error at Kesselring's Oberbefehlshaber Süd headquarters, many trains – including those of the the StuG unit – were instead routed via Foggia and Bari rather than the western Italian coast. Meanwhile, in Tunisia, Koch's Jäger Regiment had been strengthened with the attachment of Africa Battalion 24, Tunisia Battalion 5, 14th Panzerjäger Company, 104th Panzergrenadier Regiment and 9th Company, 69th Panzergrenadier Regiment.

Beginning in mid-November the Jäger Regiment had also been re-organised to replace the battalion posted to Ramcke's command and bring it back to the strength of three battalions, at least on paper. The existing 3rd Battalion was divided and placed under the command of Hptm. Gerhard Schirmer while Knoche headed a short-lived, ad hoc 2nd Battalion. Existing officers in the newly created battalion were promoted to assist in the creation of fresh company commands.

Conrath continued to make his case to Göring that the division was unready for commitment to action. When orders for the Flak Regiment to relocate to Tunisia were received during the final days of December, he submitted a detailed report on the general lack of preparedness in his division, urgently attempting to dissuade Göring from ordering his men to Tunisia and firmly stating that only 50 per cent of the division was combat-ready. Furthermore, as almost all armoured and artillery units were included in those not yet ready to be employed, the division essentially existed merely on paper. The finishing touch to Conrath's argument was that because of the Allied air and naval dominance over Axis transport routes to North Africa, it was entirely possible that units would take 50 per cent losses en route, an unacceptable loss to the fledgling division.

> In view of the valuable contingent of men and of the excellent technical equipment of the division, such a percentage of expected loss, especially only a few weeks prior to the completion of the organisation, would mean not only taking a risky chance but inviting complete failure.
>
> The stated purpose, of strengthening the Tunisian front with Panzer organisations, will by no means be achieved through the planned procedure. The actual final result, consisting more or less in strengthening the infantry forces in Tunisia, could be achieved much better by employing an infantry or mountain division.[1]

Instead Conrath proposed that the division remain in Europe and continue its recruitment and training schedule in order to be battle-ready by February. Then it could be sent to Russia as a complete Panzer division for which it would be well prepared from an organisational, equipment and morale standpoint. Regardless, his suggestion was flatly denied by the Reichsmarschall at the beginning of January.

A Führer Directive of 14 January 1943 commanded that, due to the situation at Stalingrad, the entirety of armaments production for the Heer, and of all motor vehicles until 15 March, were to be put at the disposal of Army units either on or bound for the Russian Front. Such equipment could only be given to other Wehrmacht branches if considered necessary for maintaining operations on the southern part of the Eastern Front. However, no doubt due to Göring's privileged position in the National Socialist hierarchy, there were some notable exceptions to this stringent rule. As well as the urgent equipping of six Luftwaffe field divisions and three regiments, the 'Hermann Göring' Division would also receive new equipment on 'an equal basis with the combat divisions in the east'.

As the division commenced final preparations for moving an order was issued by the administration office (IVa) on 21 December calling for the immediate return of issued tropical helmets from all armoured units, specifically: Panzer Regiment; 3rd Sturmgeschütz Battalion; Armoured

Car Platoon, 3rd Company, Armoured Reconnaissance Battalion; as well as the 14th Company (Panzerjäger) of Grenadier Regiments 1 and 2, and the Jäger Regiment. The unwieldy pith helmet had proven unpopular with troops, and incompatible in use and storage in the cramped confines of armoured vehicles. While standard steel helmets, peaked hats and sidecaps were predominantly worn, there was also the peaked visor cap known as the 'Hermann Meyer'; this was peculiar to the Luftwaffe and had the appearance of an officer's cap though it was intended to be worn by all ranks. However, this cap was also eventually replaced as it was relatively expensive to produce because its detachable neck cloth made it a complicated design.

In January an advanced staff (*Vorkommando*) of the 'Hermann Göring' Division was sent to Tunisia to oversee the transfer of combat units from Italy to North Africa; the release of units in Italy was to be coordinated in Santa Maria by the divisional Quartermaster (Ib) Maj. Ulrich Bobrowski. This *Vorkommando* would attempt to prevent the confusion created by at least four different offices being directly involved in the actual transportation, and conflicting demands being issued by the swiftly created Wehrmacht administration in Tunisia for armour and anti-tank units to be given priority. The *Vorkommando* was headed by Oberst Josef 'Beppo' Schmid, formerly Göring's chief intelligence officer and soon to command all divisional units posted to Tunisia. These were thereafter collectively known as Kampfgruppe 'Schmid' and were bolstered by the addition of myriad non-Luftwaffe and even Italian units. The situation in Tunisia had been remedied by shovelling any available manpower into the battle to prevent the capture of Tunis and not until April would Kampfgruppe 'Schmid' actually be referred to officially in Wehrmacht records as the Division 'Hermann Göring'; even at this stage divisional headquarters and some of Conrath's men were still spread between France and Italy. The piecemeal transporting of the division during January was briefly delayed on Hitler's orders until it could, he hoped, be assembled in Italy and transferred en masse. Instead precedence was given to 10th Panzer, 164th Light and 334th Infantry Divisions. This too created its own logistical problems as Conrath wanted his division transported either intact or at the very least as integral tactical units, and Schmid's task was to prevent them being assigned after landing to scattered Wehrmacht formations from which it would be extremely difficult to recover them for divisional control once committed to the front line.

Among the additional 'bolt-on' units for Schmid's command were the replacement units Afrika Marsch Bataillon [Draft Replacement Battalion] 24 and Hptm. Karl Mickley's Tunis Field-Bataillon T5 (formerly Afrika Marsch Bataillon 23).[2] Assigned originally to the 334th Infantry Division, Mickley's troops were later transferred to Kampfgruppe 'Schmid'. These battalions were not originally conceived as combat units but rather intended as replacement pools for the Afrika Korps and composed of a variety of specialists as well as combat troops; they did not bring any equipment with them, only their personal weapons. Lacking heavy weaponry, vehicles, field kitchens and communications equipment they did, however, provide a ready manpower supply for Kesselring as he rushed men into the Tunisian bridgehead to occupy ground before the Allied advance.

Viewing the 'Hermann Göring' units – including Koch's Jäger Regiment – in isolation from the other Axis troops engaged in the Tunisian battles between January and March is difficult as formations were frequently moved about the battlefield as available and as required. To those 'Hermann Göring' troops who were already veterans of combat, this process was probably expected as they had never yet operated as a cohesive single entity in combat. Interestingly, General der Panzertruppe Gustav von Vaerst later noted that the Hermann Göring 'Division' in Tunisia had the combat value of 'two-thirds of an infantry division (motorised) without its artillery'.[3]

During January the Flak Regiment began transferring to Bizerte, followed by other divisional units as the rate of transfer increased throughout February. Ju 52 aircraft were used for personnel and the most important small equipment pieces and personal weapons, while some guns and special vehicles were shuttled from Naples or Foggia via refuelling in Sicily to Tunis or Bizerta aboard six-engine Me 323 'Gigants'. Flat-bottomed Luftwaffe Siebel ferries carried flak guns and their crews as well as ammunition from Naples, Salerno, Reggio or Trapani to Tunisia, frequently unloading on any convenient patch of Tunisian coastline. The heaviest equipment – Panzers, assault guns, vehicles and wheeled guns accompanied by the minimum of personnel – were despatched by Italian freighters through waters that were being strongly contested by Allied air and naval forces.

Attempts were made to streamline the transfer of the Luftwaffe troops by appointing divisional liaison officers at the points of departure, intermediate refuelling and arrival, but they were unable to achieve the desired frictionless movement of men and supplies. The precedence already given to 10th Panzer, 164th Light and 334th Infantry Divisions delayed the 'Hermann Göring' Division's shipment and resulted in the feared piecemeal despatch of small, fragmented units. The aerial transfer of men and equipment created further problems. Suitable numbers of men were required to accumulate in distant airbases such as those around Foggia, leaving some units temporarily immobilised. Equipment was also lost, left at intermediate refuelling staging airfields in Sicily either through aircraft engine trouble or bomb damage to the airfields. Such material was rarely successfully reintegrated into the flow of reinforcement to Tunisia.

While the 'Hermann Göring' troops were painfully shuttled into the Tunisian enclave, Koch's Jäger remained in action. Arnim had placed them alongside 10th Panzer Division and 334th Infantry Division in the centre of the German defensive line. Koch's men were involved in the battle of Bou Arada, some 30 km south of Medjez. Northeast of the town was a low hill with two trees on top, from which lookouts could cover much of the surrounding terrain and even see the coast itself. Gefreiter Hans Teske of 1st Company, Jäger. Regt. 'HG', remembered the battle that followed.

> It was 11 January, the beginning of the Battle for Two-Tree Hill . . . my personal initiation in the real war – trench warfare with all its horrors and cruelties. Most of us were between 18 and 21 years of age. This type of war made men of all of us. It formed a comradeship which became eternal for the few who survived.
>
> Two Tree Hill was situated near the British lines. It had been left unoccupied for many weeks. Now that we took an interest in it, this hill became important to the British – yet only two days earlier they could have taken the hill without bloodshed, and dug themselves in.
>
> Our opponents turned out to be members of the Inniskillings, now forming part of the 6th Armoured Division. Ceaselessly they were thrown into the attack. They were brave men, taking very heavy losses – but despite this they were unable to gain any ground.
>
> Artillery was peppering our positions. British tanks were in action. Some wounded arrived, blood over their faces, some shot through the lungs, gasping for air, German, Italian, British. One German was seriously hurt, his skull was shot open. I was to take him in the sidecar to the first aid post, only about two miles away. Alas, I could not. A piece of shrapnel had smashed the fuel tap of the motorcycle. So one of my comrades and I carried him on an improvised stretcher through murderous shellfire to safety . . . On my return to the front, I learned that during my few hours of absence we had advanced, but at a terrible cost. My company had lost

> every officer, either wounded or missing, presumed killed. Leutnant Fleming had just been brought in, shot through the hip, the last of our officers, so Leutnant Kleinfeld of HQ Company, formerly of the 1st, was brought up and given command of 1st Company.
>
> I reported back. Nowacki, our observer, came down the hill past me. He gave me the news we all dreaded – Leutnant Schuster was dead. Schuster, CO of 1st Company, who had survived Eben Emael, Crete and Russia, and who won the Knight's Cross as a *Feldwebel* on Crete, was dead. His body had been recovered.
>
> The war was ferocious and the hill, now strewn with bodies, changed hands many times. During the night, with some tanks in support, we took the hill. Many prisoners were taken. I remember a dazed British artillery observer sitting on the edge of a trench, holding his head, as if he was on exercise. His comrade was dead beside him. Bullets were whistling past, yet he sat there as if this was of no concern, completely shocked.
>
> Later that day, when German paras prepared for an attack, our artillery fired short. Hermann Geerz and Heinrich Krauter were blown to pieces. Unknown to us, the enemy had brought in a large concentration of artillery. They wanted to break through in this area and thrust into Tunis. Into this build-up we advanced on 18 January. Our men with battle experience from Russia and Crete said they had never experienced anything like this. The ground shook. The whole area became full of craters and was littered with shrapnel. At the end of the day, we had gained very little. Losses were heavy. The 3rd Company suffered most – 31 killed, three times as many wounded. Infantry battalion [Afrika Marsch Bataillon] A24 was almost wiped out.[4]

The fighting was confused and bloody and both British and German stretcher bearers later cooperated to retrieve wounded men from the carnage; Erich Schuster's body was found by German stretcher bearers and carried back to their lines. The young officer had been shot in the thigh, his femoral artery severed, and the incapacitated man bled to death. The same day an order for his promotion to *Oberleutnant* was received by his company. After five days, the German attack was broken off, having achieved its objective, claiming 4,000 British prisoners and the capture or destruction of 24 tanks, 52 guns and 228 vehicles. The Germans had pushed Allied forces back and won a valued new defensive line, though at high cost. The *Jäger* dug in to defend their hard-won gains.

Despite the division having officially been removed from First Army control on the French Atlantic coast, during February Paul Conrath toured those units still undergoing training in France as well as the armoured contingents working up in Germany's training grounds. On 26 January, Hptm. Rossmann, formerly of 16th Company, Flak Regiment, welcomed the first volunteers for the new Panzer Regiment at the Bergen training area in the southern part of the Lüneburg Heath.[5] From there, once sufficient men were assembled, they were transported by train to Münsingen and formed into 4th Company to start their combat training. On 10 February they were transferred to Mont-de-Marsan and billeted in the small town of Garlin as they began advanced exercises in combined infantry and Panzer tactics, activity that would last until 25 May. Rossmann was later promoted to command 1st Battalion, his 4th Company being taken over by Hptm. Schmidt, and the three sections of the company headed by Leutnants Saab, Zotter and Petschke respectively. By this stage, the other companies of 1st Battalion had already started to form along this established pattern.

As the arduous transfer of units continued to North Africa an estimated strength of those troops still at Santa Maria during the last two weeks of February listed some 3,650 men from nearly every component of the division. Furthermore, rather than accompany his division to Tunisia, Conrath was ordered to concentrate on establishing new units; he subsequently issued Division Order Nr. 2 on 9 March which outlined the distribution of responsibilities for the shell of the division that remained in Italy.

> The Reichsmarschall has ordered me to visit and train the division's new units in Germany and France. The parts of the division deployed in Tunis will continue to be managed by Generalmajor Schmid for the time being.
>
> The commander of the divisional components located in Italy is Oberst Ewert, who receives the disciplinary powers of a regimental commander.
>
> After relocation of most of the divisional staff to Tunis, the remaining staff officers in Santa Maria will be:
>
> Oblt. Poetter, 5th Battalion, Artillery Regt, as Ordnance Officer; Lt. Netzel, Panzer Signals Battalion, as Signals Officer; Regierungsoberinspektor Janssen, Staff, Flak Regiment, as IVa

> [divisional administrator]; Stabsarzt Dr Ewersberger, Divisional Supply Officer, as IVb [divisional medical officer]; Regierungsinspektor Gerlach, Divisional Staff 'HG', as Registrar [civilian role].
>
> The remainder of the command is subordinate to Oberst Ewert; after the division's transport staff has moved away . . .
>
> After the movement of the Armoured Reconnaissance Battalion, 5th (StuG) Battalion, Artillery Regiment HG and the 1st Battalion, Panzer Regiment from Italy, Oberst Ewert will take over the 1st Grenadier Regiment 'HG'. Also, Hptm. Vogel is ordered to France as Signals Officer for the new divisional units under Kommandeur der Gruppe Neuaufstellungen (Oberst Schmalz).[6]

By the end of February Kampfgruppe 'Schmid' had been loosely formed, although the majority of its components were not Luftwaffe troops. It was initially divided into three sub-groups, but only Gruppe 'Koch' contained 'Hermann Göring' men. However, the transfer of personnel began in earnest in February after Hitler's previous postponement order expired. Schmid's mixed bag of assembled troops initially held a 50 km stretch of the front line from immediately south of Medjez to the mountainous region south of Bou Arada; fresh divisional units trickled into Tunis and marched immediately to the line. On 3 March 3rd Battalion, Jäger Regt. 'HG' was withdrawn after three days of tough fighting 10 km west of Quballat as part of Operation 'Ochsenkopf', the Jäger Regiment advancing from the Goubellat Plain and attempting to encircle and destroy the British at Medjez-el-Bab and Bou Arada.[7] Ultimately, despite an impressive number of British prisoners being taken, Arnim's offensive ground to a halt with losses it could ill afford and Quballat was taken by Allied troops, though the salient created by 'Ochsenkopf' continued to be held by the remaining *Jäger*.

Divisional reinforcements continued to arrive, or at least receive scheduled departure times from European ports. However, although casualties among units transported by air were remarkably low, several ships carrying vehicles and heavy equipment were lost, with a resultant adverse effect on the division's subsequent action in Tunisia. On 10 March the 5th Sturmgeschütz Battalion was ordered to Sicily; two transport vehicles were loaded in Caserta on 17 March under the command of Oblt. Hohlbein. The following day Oblt. Wilmskötter supervised a second shipment; both of them were unloaded in Reggio Calabria by the 20th and within four days shipped across the straits to Messina. From there they travelled by road to

Trapani before arriving at their destination 3 km to the south at Paceco, a primary terminus for the seaborne supply of North Africa. There, they constructed a bivouac close to the Trapani–Marsala road before awaiting onward movement to North Africa.

On 24 March the motorcycle company of Armoured Reconnaissance Battalion 'HG' was transferred to Tunisia. Unteroffizier Rolf Wallburg wrote in his diary:

> Airfield Naples: Now the time has come. After waiting for this moment day after day in the last few weeks – again and again in vain – we eventually had an alarm last night. We went straight out to the airfield and now we have everything loaded around 9 a.m. We should start at 10:30; hopefully everything works. The first group with Hauptmann Kiefer started at 6 in the morning; if all went well, they are already over there. The weather is excellent.
> Tunis, 24 March: Africa! The first impression? I do not know, but I imagined something different. But in many ways, it's very African. The flight over here was fine; it took exactly 3½ hours and we felt completely safe in the old Ju. At 10:30 a.m. we started in Naples with about 40 aircraft, flew past Vesuvius again and then we flew at 50 to 60 m height above the Mediterranean. Gradually you got used to the bouncing of the aircraft and near Capri you did not notice anything any more. Then came Sicily, and our group was joined by another 40 aircraft. We were now a whole squadron and it was a very nice sight. We also had fighters escorting us from Sicily onwards. At 1:30 p.m. the African coast came in sight and at 2 p.m. we landed. There was just an air raid alarm; over Bizerte stood a huge explosive cloud and we hurried to unload. The aircraft left again in no time. Now we stand with the 1st Platoon which has been waiting for us on the main road and wait for our onward journey. It is an outrageous bustle here and the supply system rolls along quite nicely.
> Ferme Mangba, 25 March: We got here yesterday evening and will probably stay for the time being on this French farm; at least until the company has completely arrived here. The 3rd Platoon and 4th Platoon did not yet arrive today; other things were flown over instead. The area here is as we had imagined: partly plain and then again hilly and severely intersected. The climate is still in our bones, you always feel a bit tired and droopy.

> Ferme Mangba, 26 March: Now we start digging in the motorcycles, you never know and it's better that way. Strong storm for days, you can only walk around with galoshes. The other two platoons are still not here. From the front line you can hear only the artillery fire; air activity very low.[8]

Hitler ordered on 28 March all remaining combat-ready parts of the division transferred to Tunis, though he also instructed that from mid-April, outfitting of the 4th Flak Battalion and 1st Panzer Battalion with weapons and vehicles was to be postponed due to the demands for equipment of the Eastern Front as the ramifications of the catastrophe at Stalingrad still rippled through the Wehrmacht.

Almost immediately, the recently arrived Motorcycle Company was divided into smaller components to man a thinly held line.

> Ferme Robinson, 1 April: Last night we moved into the front positions and replaced the comrades from the army. It was a great relief, pitch dark – and we even tapped in minefields for a while. I now lie with my group in an advanced base, a farm; our mission is to hold this base until the last man. The location of the farm is very unfavourable; from all sides, the enemy can approach almost unseen and, moreover, we are only seven men strong. A base and seven men. The connection to our company is as good as non-existent. The platoon command post is 900–1000 m behind me in a large wadi, Popp's group is there too, and Kreutzfeld's group 800 m to my left in a small wadi. Under these circumstances the enemy can get through everywhere and it is therefore necessary for us to keep our eyes open. Proper sleep is out of the question; at night we all lie in the holes or run patrols and during the day we watch the field. In between, but only in daytime, a little nap can be taken.
>
> Base Robinson, 2 April: The last night was okay, in general it was calm. Some fire attacks by artillery, as well as during the day and mutual reconnaissance activity. At 2 in the morning a fierce firefight between Grote's reconnaissance patrol and an enemy camp. A *Feldwebel* of the army, who went along as an instructor, died. Now during the day artillery again – harassing fire. Weather still very bad and stormy; food good except drinks. In the last 48 hours, only one canteen full for seven men; a bit too little to drink. The mood in the base otherwise good.

> Base Robinson, 3 April: Tonight, Tommy was at our base for the first time. In the time between 2 and 3:30 a.m. he tried to come in with a patrol. We kept calm and wanted him to get up close. After he had approached from all sides, he pulled back again. Now assume that he will move in in the coming night with a stronger, powerful reconnaissance platoon. During the day everything calm except light artillery fire. Weather is getting better, food is good. Only too little to drink and hardly any sleep.
>
> Base Wallburg, 4 April: In the company we have now got the name 'Base Wallburg'. It must be held in any case. Last night we got quite some artillery fire, but everything went well. The rest of the company – 3rd and 4th Platoons – have finally arrived too and I got, after the boss looked at the base tonight, an S.M.G. as reinforcement. Thank God, now I feel better again, because now we are in a better position to repel an attack. We are now 2 NCOs, 10 men strong. Gefreiter Sprießler joined us and a B position is also supposed to come here. With my 6 men I really could not do much and was shaking sometimes in my boots. Now it's time to upgrade our positions and sleep is not possible at all any longer. Superior enemy air activity and artillery fire during the day. Kreutzfeld also got his blessing today; you cannot even put your head out. Otherwise very good weather and outrageously many fleas. The beasts cost you even the last bit of sleep. Mood nevertheless still good!
>
> Base Wallburg, 5 April: Everything is the same here. The night was quiet, only it is always freezing cold. If you lie there ten hours in your hole, you are stiff in the morning like a board. To the left of us were hand-grenade fights; it was the patrol that we saw descending, Gefreiter Stegemeier was wounded. During the day a lot of artillery shelling and English fighter aircraft. Sun and flies become unbearable.[9]

The resolve of Wallburg's men remained firm, fostered by a sense of belonging to an elite unit and also because discipline behind the lines remained rigid and strong. On 4 April, Gefreiter Wilhelm Staatz was executed for cowardice after having been found guilty of deserting his company during heavy fighting between 24 and 28 February. Schmid issued a proclamation regarding the sentence that was circulated in divisional orders during April.

> The dutiful soldier, who fights with self-sacrifice and confidence in the flag, must be given the firm conviction that the slacker and coward will always suffer the greatest misfortune. The deed could therefore only be punished with the death penalty.[10]

By mid-April Kampfgruppe 'Schmid' began to be referred to officially as Division 'Hermann Göring' in reports from Tunisia as the transport of men and material reached full swing. As an example, in a report from the Chief of Staff (Ia) of Panzer Regiment 'Hermann Göring' on 15 April, the following personnel and vehicles were listed as freshly available for deployment on African soil:

from 1st Battalion, Panzer Regiment 'HG'

Staff Company — *Hptm. Konstantin Hahm*

9 officers, 11 NCOS, 50 men; 6 heavy motorcycles, 10 motorcycles with sidecars, 1 light passenger car, 1 truck; 70 Kar 98k, 116 bayonets, 18 .08 pistols, 26 MP38/40, 4 MG 34

from Panzer Regiment 'HG'

3rd Company

3 officers, 34 NCOs. 42 men; 1 heavy motorcycle, 3 motorcycles with sidecars, 1 light truck, 1 light car (2/40),[11] 2 Panzer III (50-mm cannon), 8 Panzer IV (75-mm cannon); 10 Kar 98k, 63 .08 pistols, 16 MP38/40, 1 MG 34, 20 MG34 (in Panzers)

from Grenadier Regiment 'HG'

14th Company — *Oblt. Werner Kahrass*

4 officers, 16 NCOs, 46 men; 1 light motorcycle, 2 heavy motorcycles, 3 motorcycles with sidecars, 1 light car (2/40), 1 Kfz 15 medium signals vehicle, 1 Opel truck, 9 Panzer IIF; 14 Kar 98k, 44 .08 pistols, 14 MP38/40, 10 MG 34, 9 75-mm PaK 40[12]

from Flak Regiment 'HG'

18th Company

5 officers, 22 NCOs, 105 men; 2 heavy motorcycles, 1 heavy motorcycle with sidecar, 3 Kfz 1 (light troop car), 1 towing machine, 13 armoured halftracks; 73 Kar 98k, 84 .08 pistols, 12 MP38/40, 19 MG 34, 9 20-mm Flak 38 (Vierling) on halftracks.

Panzer Workshop Company 'HG' — *Oblt. Joachim Zacher*

1 officer, 8 men; 2 heavy motorcycle sidecar combinations, 1 light car (Kfz 1), 1 Opel truck; 8 Kar 98k, 1 .08 pistol; spare parts and engine for Panzer II, transmissions for Panzer II and III

At 1300 hrs on 8 April the first five Panzers of 3rd Company, Panzer Regt. 'HG' were driven from their unloading dock to the front line in the Medjez Valley without incident apart from occasional British harassing fire. Three Panzer IVs joined the advance group the following afternoon and they took up new positions either side of the road leading west at 0130 on 10 April. Long after daylight had illuminated the ground ahead, enemy tanks were sighted and the Panzers began receiving more sustained artillery fire. Nineteen-year-old Lt. Heinz Lahusen – 1st Platoon leader of the 3rd Company, having transferred from Lübke's 13th Panzer Company, Rifle Regiment during October – counted as many as thirty-three visible tanks in the distance; the same pattern of distant sighting but no engagement was repeated the next day. The right-hand group of Panzer IVs took more artillery fire and withdrew to a hull-down position for shelter; two Panzers were briefly out of action with idler wheel and roller damage from the shelling.

As British artillery fire abated, the damaged vehicles returned from repairs to retake their previous position during the following day and for the next five days waited for any serious threat to develop. By that time, the 50 km divisional front had lengthened slightly, held with whatever means had become available, the Grenadier Regiment being responsible for particularly difficult terrain in a salient west of the lake Sebkhet el Kourzia. From the north, flanked by the 745th Grenadier Regt., the 1st and 2nd Battalions, Jäger Regiment 'HG' occupied the line from Medjez to immediately south of Quballat with artillery support from 1st Battalion, 90th Panzer Artillery Regt.[13] The 2nd and 3rd Battalions, 1st Grenadier Regiment 'HG' held the southern flank, supported by the guns of 2nd Battalion, 190th Artillery Regt. and the Italian 2nd Battalion, 21st Artillery Regt. East of Bou Arada, 4th Company (Panzer Jäger), Armoured Reconnaissance Battalion 'HG' and Tunis Field Battalion T5 were grouped together as Regiment 'Ewert', with 1st Battalion, 999th Artillery Regt. and the Italian 1st Battalion, 3rd Artillery Regiment in support. South of the T5 Battalion the 10th Panzer Division held the line. In reserve near 'HG' divisional headquarters, the Flak Regiment was positioned east of the banks of the Miliane River near Djebel Oust.

Allied air forces mounted a determined assault on the German supply bridge to North Africa – 'Operation Flax' between 5 and 27 April – and supplies of fuel, ammunition and men steadily dwindled as both aerial and seaborne transports were savaged. On 14 April Göring sent what he hoped would be an encouraging message to Schmid:

> Under your leadership, the parts of my division deployed in Tunis have fared extremely well in the fight. I would like to thank you and the team for this and offer my appreciation. The decisive struggle

> in Tunisia is now in full swing. I know that I can fully rely on my division in the coming hard days of the fight. In tough doggedness, wherever it is used, my squad will wrestle bitterly for every inch of the ground. Wherever it fights, no enemy can succeed.[14]

At 2300 on 18 April, following a brief, heavy-artillery barrage, a British reconnaissance patrol of approximately thirty men was spotted by the 'HG' Panzers still occupying ground in the Toungar Valley. Following a two-hour battle in which the Panzers were supported by infantry of Marsch Battalion A24, the British withdrew. However, by that point there appeared little doubt to German leaders of the likely outcome of the Tunisian struggle and the remainder of the 'HG' Panzer Regiment had received clear instructions not to proceed to North Africa, but to remain in Italy as reinforcement for a battle group to be assembled for the likely required defence of Italy itself. Only eight tanks of the regiment's already transferred 3rd Company would see action in North Africa. Instead, the division's *Sturmgeschütze* were still to be shipped to Africa, the decision to send them being confirmed by OKW on 20 April, but ultimately never being carried out.

The Anglo-American armies in the west were now poised to launch Operation 'Vulcan' and the final drive on Tunis. However, Arnim mounted what he hoped would be his own spoiling attack, Operation 'Fliederblüte', launched on the night of 20 April. For the assault, the 'Hermann Göring' Division was subdivided into three attack groups (*Angriffsgruppen*), under Schmid's overall command: Gruppe 'Audorff' in the north, Gruppe 'Schirmer', the central 'shock group', and Gruppe 'Funck' holding the southern flank.

From north to south, Obstlt. Paul Audorff, commander of the 754th Grenadier Regiment (334th Infantry Division), was placed in control of one 'Hermann Göring' Grenadier battalion, one Flak battery and 1st Platoon, 5th Engineer Company. The centrally located Hptm. Gerhard Schirmer commanded the largest *Kampfgruppe* of the three, subdivided into 'Nord' and 'Süd'. Schirmer had been elevated to command the Jäger Regiment after Walter Koch had been hospitalised once again during February and flown back to Germany. Schirmer's Nord sub-group boasted 1st Battalion, Jäger Regt. 'HG', 2nd Battalion, Panzer Regt. 7 (10th Panzer Division, known as 'Panzer Battalion Burk' and also including Tiger Is of 504th Heavy Panzer Battalion), two-thirds of 4th (Panzerjäger) Company, Armoured Reconnaissance Battalion 'HG' and half of the 1st Company, Armoured

Engineer Battalion 'HG'. Untergruppe Süd contained 2nd Company, Jäger Regt. 'HG', 1st Battalion, 7th Panzer Regt. and the other half of 1st Company, Armoured Engineer Battalion 'HG'. Meanwhile Hptm. Kurt Hubert, Adjutant of the Flak Regiment 'HG', headed two infantry companies made from men of his regiment brought forward from their reserve position. This small formation – 'Einheit Hubert' – was added to the strength of Schirmer's *Fallschirmjäger*.

As well as artillery support for all three combat zones, additional heavy weapons were supplied for Schirmer's forces. Two howitzer batteries, the 1st Battalion, 90th Panzer Artillery Regt, one 88-mm battery and the 75-mm anti-tank weapons of 14th Company, 1st Grenadier Regt. 'HG' were behind Schirmer's Untergruppe Nord; a single heavy flak battery supported his southern group. In the most southerly of the three *Kampfgruppen*, Maj. Helmut Funck controlled part of 2nd Battalion, 1st Grenadier Regt 'HG'.

The German attack began at 0500 hrs and immediately struggled to make headway. Gruppe 'Audorff' failed to reach its planned objectives in the face of heavy resistance while Schirmer's northern group encountered an unexpectedly well-developed and strengthened British defensive sector. Gruppe 'Süd' was likewise heavily engaged and mired amidst defences created in depth. After overcoming initial confusion caused by the German offensive, British infantry and armoured forces pressed forward throughout the day. Gruppe 'Audorff' occupied high ground east of Medjez (Hills 101 and 109), their eastward-facing front line coming under increasing pressure and placing Gruppe 'Nord's northern wing in peril. With no choice, Schirmer withdrew the latter to its starting positions from 1400 after providing infantry cover for Panzer Battalion Burk. Gruppe 'Nord' did manage to overrun British artillery positions and took Height 166 (Henchir el Mallaha, known to the Allies as 'Banana Ridge') 5.5 km southeast of Medjez-el-Bab, while Gruppe 'Süd' attacked towards Djebel Djaffa, taking the hill northwest of Quballat and destroying some Churchill tanks of 48th Royal Tank Regiment (RTR) while repulsing strong British infantry counter-attacks and coming within half a mile of the British 4th Division's headquarters. Funck's battlegroup occupied territory in the northeastern foothills of the Dejebel Rihane.[15]

However, the main British line did not break and at 1800 after relocating his headquarters to Ain el Asker, Schmid ordered all units to disengage and return to their original jumping-off points in defensive hedgehogs.

Adolf Hitler and Hermann Göring. During the inter-war years the former First World War fighter ace became more adept politically than militarily.

eft: Göring and Walther Wecke inspecting andespolizeigruppe 'General Göring', the newly uthorised cuff-titles visible on the men's lower left leeves.

elow left: Walther Wecke (pictured here during the var as a Luftwaffe general), commander of Polizei Abteilung z.b.V. 'Wecke' that formed the original ucleus of Regiment 'General Göring'.

Right: Friedrich-Wilhelm Jakoby, pictured here luring the war.

Below: Men of Landespolizeigruppe 'General Göring' showing a mix of Polizei, Reichswehr and unit insignia and uniform.

Men of the Wach Bataillon 'Hermann Göring' at Carinhall. The flag is the divisional standard, unchanged since presented to Landespolizeigruppe 'Wecke' z.b.V in July 1933.

Regiment 'General Göring' troops training with a 37-mm flak weapon.

Walther von Axthelm was appointed to command the Regiment 'General Göring' in 1937. He is pictured here as a *Generalmajor*, commander of I. Flakkorps during the war.

Top: SdKfz. 231 armoured cars of Detachment 'Kluge' being entrained in Norway for return to Germany.

Above: Motorcycle-sidecar combination showing the distinctive Viking Ship emblem applied to all vehicles that had taken part in 'Weserübung' with Detachment 'Kluge'.

The towed 88-mm anti-aircraft guns of Regiment 'General Göring' proved particularly effective against ground targets during the exhausting advance in France and the Low Countries, 1940.

Above: Paul Conrath (*right*) pictured here as a *Generalmajor* during training in France.

Top left: Guns of the 14th (Heavy) Railway Flak Battery went into action against the Maginot Line, though pictured here in Italy in 1943.

Left: Men of 6th Company attempting to right their towed 88-mm that has slid into a French roadside ditch, May 1940.

Karl Rossmann, one of the most distinguished and highly decorated members of the 'Hermann Göring' units.

Soviet KV-2 heavy tank destroyed by 'Hermann Göring' guns during the fierce fighting around Dubno.

Oberleutnant Musil of 11. Kompanie (Panzer Pionier) of the new Panzer Regiment; his 'General Göring' cuff title is highly visible against the black uniform of armoured troops.

A 'Hermann Göring' soldier equipped with a Waffen-SS surplus camouflage smock.

'Hermann Göring' combat engineers training in the use of 'storm boats'.

Joint 'Hermann Göring' armour and infantry training. (*Alan Scheckenbach*)

Men of Fallschirmjäger Regiment 5 in Tunisia after they had been transferred en masse to Conrath's division as Jäger Regiment 'Hermann Göring'.

Hauptmann Hans Jungwirth, I./Jäger Regt. 'Hermann Göring' (*left*) and British prisoner Corporal Gavin Cadden, 2nd Btn. Parachute Regt., Depienne November 1943. Cadden narrowly escaped summary execution thanks to Jungwirth's and Oberstleutnant Walter Koch's timely arrival.

'Hermann Göring' motorcycle messenger using an Italian Bianchi motorcycle, Tunisia 1943.

'Hermann Göring' command post, Tunisia.

'Hermann Göring' troops encamped in Sicily. (*Alan Scheckenbach*)

'Hermann Göring' Panzer IV crew, Sicily. (*Alan Scheckenbach*)

The mixture of uniforms worn by 'Hermann Göring' men in Sicily is apparent in this photo, from orthodox tropical uniform, to surplus Waffen-SS gear and an outdated pith helmet. (*Alan Scheckenbach*)

Concentrated British artillery fire was taking its toll on infantry formations and 17-pounder guns brought up for the intended assault on Tunis caused heavy losses among the Panzers. Though by the end of the first day 'Hermann Göring' troops had captured 12 officers and 306 men, they had lost a confirmed 34 dead, 92 wounded and 201 men missing. The Germans gave ground, while British forces launched rapid local counter-attacks. British losses were heavy against determined defensive fire, but Schmid's men reported local penetration by British tanks and the Allies began to gain traction as the 'Hermann Göring' troops ran short on ammunition, fuel and energy.

With the failure of the offensive, inevitable defeat in Tunisia had already been registered by officers of the 'Hermann Göring' Division. Two days after 'Fliederblüte' had misfired, messages were exchanged between the armoured elements regarding the fitting of explosive charges to gun barrels in preparation for demolition. Neither the Staff Company nor Panzers had yet attached theirs, though the 14th Panzerjäger Company reported to Preuss in Italy that all demolition charges were fitted and ready. Nevertheless, Schmid's after-action report dated 5 May placed a positive spin on a battle that could never be conclusive beyond its ambition of denting the inevitable attack on Tunis:

> On the night of our attack, the enemy had stopped deploying his forces for a scheduled major attack. The division's attack destroyed the enemy supply in its sector of the front line and caused the enemy severe material and personnel losses. Furthermore, the enemy attack on the section facing the Jäger Regiment 'HG' did not take place and the British attacked on 22 April 1943 only in the area held by 1st Grenadier Regiment 'HG'. The enemy was therefore unable to carry out his major attack in its intended form in terms of time and space.[16]

At the southern flank of the 'Hermann Göring' front line, on 22 April, 11th Company, 1st Grenadier Regt. 'HG' was heavily engaged in resisting an Allied assault on Hill 304 near Bou Arada. Severe losses were suffered by both sides and the company commander killed, squad-leader Oberfeldwebel Johannes Scheid taking over leadership and successfully defending the hill until the exhausted Allies withdrew. Scheid was subsequently awarded the Knight's Cross on 21 June 1943, publicly announced by Hitler on the same day as Oberstleutnant Paul Audorff received the coveted award.

Within that same portion of the main battle line, in action area Djebel Zaghouan, Hptm. Eduard-Heinrich Kiefer, formerly commander of 10th Motorcycle Company and by now commander of 2nd Company, Armoured Reconnaissance Battalion 'HG', was also awarded the Knight's Cross, granted on 18 May 1943. Furthermore, Hptm. Kurt Schreiber, commander of 2nd Battalion, 1st Grenadier Regt. 'HG', was awarded the Knight's Cross on 21 June 1943. However, all three 'Hermann Göring' recipients received their awards in captivity.

British probing of the German lines had been relentless and the Armoured Reconnaissance Battalion had continuously manned isolated outposts before the main battle line. Unteroffizier Wallburg held his post at 'Base Wallburg', renamed the 'Sanatorium' as a cover in case of radio interception.

> Sanatorium, 14 April: The night before last night I was at [Point] 08 near the enemy, so we had him breathing down our neck last night and this morning. The first time he came at 9:50 p.m. and I discovered him with my standing patrol. We, Wörndle and I, walked in parallel next to him towards Sanatorium, and we shot at them 250 yards in front of our base. They were 15 men and they ran like rabbits. The second time I went out at 2 a.m.; they came with two reconnaissance patrols, and as we stalked one, suddenly the other appeared at our backs. But we were able to make it through. We were lucky and at 5 a.m. we were back home. Tonight, we go out again, only that today it is very dark and stormy. In any case, this sneaking up and scouting is more fun than lying here in the base and to lurk on the opponent. Otherwise, everything is the same here and the mood is good. Klaus Lehmann is also dead as I just heard. In general, the 2nd Company has been affected significantly more.
>
> Sanatorium, 15 April: The reconnaissance patrol last night was unsuccessful; nobody came from the other side or we ran past each other. Therefore, we have been plastered with artillery fire for 1¾ hours tonight like never before. The whole house was shot to pieces, Feldwebel Gutjahr wounded and [Private] Kittler was buried under rubble; it was nearly like being in hell. Guess that they eventually will come tonight . . .
>
> Sanatorium, 19 April: In the last several days and nights it was fairly quiet, except for a tank attack at Buri . . . nothing noteworthy was recorded. Yesterday evening I was again on reconnaissance patrol

> with Zuber and Scheffler, and it was again a very special situation. We were just 1,000 metres beyond Sanatorium and stalked 244, when we were suddenly shot from behind with machine pistols. Probably an enemy reconnaissance patrol. We moved on, slowly approached 04 and believed it would be clear of the enemy, but when we got 30 m from it hand grenades were thrown at us and fire from two M.G.s. Then I broke into a sweat and we had to crawl backwards quite a bit. We had lost Scheffler and when we went to get him from the front, we got fired at again. When we realized that they wanted to pinch us off, we retreated and a quarter of an hour later Scheffler also arrived. God, how happy I was then.
>
> Sanatorium, 20 April: Tonight, we wanted to smoke out 244 and 04 with a raiding patrol, but unfortunately, the birds were all flown. I went again with Zuber, Simonsen and Fischer on reconnaissance patrol and came back home at 4:20 a.m. No enemy contact, but our bones trembled [so much] that I'm still completely smashed now. We had not eaten anything for 24 hours.
>
> Base Sanatorium has now been abandoned, everything has moved back to the HKL [main front line] and I'm only here with three men. We must be on alert day and night; sleeping is soon unthinkable and I'm curious when they want to catch us here. They will come soon; and if they do, we are prepared for it . . .

Wallburg and his men were fortunately granted permission to retreat from their advance positions immediately before a British assault on 26 April, leaving as the first shells of a fearsome artillery bombardment rained on their outpost and destroyed what had been left standing of the farm buildings.

Three days previously, on 23 April, as the British counter-attacked on the heels of the retreating 'Fliederblüte' troops, 'Hermann Göring' flak guns were in action against enemy armour. East of Medjez, Obergefreiter Heinrich Witte's guns of 7th Company, Flak Regiment 'HG' were heavily engaged and suffered severe casualties. With some members of his crew wounded during a period of less than two minutes, Witte acting as gunlayer destroyed nine British tanks in close-quarter fighting. Killed in action on 8 May during the final retreat to Tunis, he was posthumously awarded the Knight's Cross over a year later on 18 May 1944.

The Jäger defending Hill 107 between Medjez el Bab and Quballat were finally overrun by British troops, but wrested back control of the peak once again two days later. However, they were not to hold it for long as further determined British attacks drove them inexorably eastwards. Now the focal point of the battle for the Medjez Valley swirled around Cactus Farm and the ridge on which it sat, defended by forty-eight *Fallschirmjäger* of 4th Company, Jäger Regiment 'HG' led by Feldwebel Heinrich Schäfer. Gefreiter Paul Beck of 1st Battalion was employed as a motorcycle runner at the time.

> In the middle of March 1943, I was seconded to the 4th Company, the HQ being at the Cactus Farm near Peter's Corner. Here it was like a holiday centre, disrupted only by the odd run to forward positions such as Point 107 or Point 133. However, on 27 April, a British attack on Point 107 and Point 133 succeeded, changing the situation completely. Point 137 (Sidi Abdallah) and the Cactus Farm became the German main line of defence on the important Tunis to Medjez-el-Bab highway. The Cactus Farm was held by a total of forty-eight paras under Sergeant Schäfer.
>
> That evening I experienced the first attack on this farm. British infantry [1st Battalion, Royal West Kent Regiment], supported by artillery, advanced towards us. We held fire until the enemy was a few yards away. Surprised by the heavy fire which opened up so suddenly, they withdrew. Next morning, we observed sappers clearing a passage through the minefield. We were unable to do anything about it, lest we display our own weakness. We also had to conserve ammunition. Soon we understood the meaning of the sappers' efforts, sixteen Churchills [12th Royal Tank Regiment], supported by infantry, advanced towards our farm.
>
> Again, we only opened up at very close range. Our sole anti-tank gun destroyed or immobilised several British tanks. A few British infantrymen who had succeeded in penetrating into the farm defences were again ejected. In the desperate situation, we asked our artillery to shell our own positions. The enemy withdrew. We picked up enemy wounded and took prisoner some men who were hiding.
>
> We succeeded in rescuing the crew of a burning Churchill tank. They were all seriously wounded and one of them died during the night. He kept asking for water. Water we didn't have – the only liquid we had was wine, and plenty of it.

> In the afternoon, the enemy attacked in several waves, supported by tanks. They managed to penetrate in places; however, this time, Tiger tanks arrived on the scene, just in time. It was sheer hell. It was night before we were in control of the farm again.
>
> In the early hours of 30 April, British infantry and tanks came in force and penetrated our positions. Desperately we defended ourselves. Again, we requested our own artillery to shell our positions. A lone Focke-Wulf 190 flew in to our aid and destroyed a tank through a direct hit with a bomb. In the afternoon, the enemy sent over a man protected by a white flag. He asked us to surrender honourably. He did not get a reply and departed. This was followed by a large British attack. Our positions were penetrated in places and only after more hand-to-hand fighting, destruction of tanks by 3 kg charges, magnetic charges or Molotov cocktails, did we succeed in regaining control of the situation.
>
> By the evening of 30 April, a new defensive line had been completed and HQ ordered us to leave Cactus Farm and take our place in the new line. We left the farm under cover of darkness. To our knowledge there were over 300 British soldiers who lost their lives and 30 tanks or armoured vehicles littered the battleground. We had lost three men killed.[17]

The *Jäger* withdrew north to new defensive positions around Massicault (now Borj El Amri) only 30 km southwest of Tunis. A *Leutnant* who had arrived on the penultimate day of their stand at Cactus Farm with orders from regimental headquarters to hold for one more day counted 37 destroyed enemy tanks and an estimated 400 British dead littering the battlefield. He recommended Schäfer for the Knight's Cross, which was eventually awarded on 8 August 1944, by which time he and his men were prisoners of war in the United States, Schäfer being held at Camp Harne, Texas.[18]

The prowess of the veteran *Jäger* as they continued to mount isolated and aggressive patrols against enemy lines was later noted by American military intelligence. Though their tendency to move in groups of 30 to 40 men at night in close formation rendered them vulnerable to ambush and they were considered to not patrol as deeply into enemy territory as their Allied opposites, their achievements in Tunisia were noteworthy.

> Of the offensive patrols that were undertaken, virtually all were made by the 'Hermann Göring' Jäger Regiment. Sometimes three

> men went forward to reconnoitre while the main body of the patrol waited under cover. The technique was first to make a penetration into a position and then to employ grenades and light machine guns. In the resulting confusion the Germans would attempt to withdraw with prisoners. Daylight offensive patrols were exceptional, but the striking feature of one such raid was its evidently careful planning. The raid was made by a platoon of the 'Hermann Göring' Jäger Regiment, divided into a fire party, with light machine guns and grenades; an assault party, with grenades and fixed bayonets; and a demolition party. The timing was perfect, no signals were used, and the raid appeared to have been rehearsed. The three parties attacked successively from three directions and the demolition group succeeded in damaging a field gun.[19]

It is difficult to establish what happened to all of the elements of 1st Battalion, Panzer Regt. 'HG' that had reached North Africa. In entirety, nine 20-mm flak half-tracks, nine Marder II tank destroyers (75-mm Pak 40 mounted on Panzer II chassis), two Panzer IIIs and eight Panzer IVF2s saw action in Tunisia. They were not directly involved in the 'Fliederblüte' attack but held in reserve and suffered no more than harassing fire during that period of time, interspersed briefly with concentrated British bombardments. However, on 22 April, Lt. Lahusen was informed by the commander of 3rd Company, A24 of British troops assembling in a wadi immediately in front of the main battle line, though nothing disturbed the German defences during the night that followed.

The Panzers of 3rd Company had been formed into Kampfgruppe 'Irkens', a composite force created by Arnim from his last available armoured units. Arnim had succeeded Rommel as chief of Heeresgruppe Afrika (Army Group Africa) on the latter's return to Germany in March, while command of Fifth Panzer Army passed to General der Panzertruppe Gustav von Vaerst.

The morning of 23 April dawned cold, but clear and twelve British tanks were sighted, attacking troops of 754th Infantry Regiment on the Panzers' right flank. The enemy tanks moved across the eastern face of Djebel el Rhar, coming to a halt approximately 2,500 metres from the Panzers of 3rd Company. Four of the Panzer IVs opened fire; two British tanks were soon seen to be hit and burning, while the remainder turned and began moving away as British artillery fire rained down on 3rd Company. The infantry of 754th Regiment fought throughout the day, and at 2200 Lahusen led four Panzer IVs closer to the action to provide direct support, while company commander Oblt. Hermann Münzner led the remaining five with supporting infantry from 3rd Company, A24 to repulse a British platoon that had broken through the main defensive line.[20]

From 0300, three Panzer IVs secured the flank of Hptm. Lersch's T3 Battalion as the infantry gradually disengaged and withdrew. In less than two hours, Münzner had concentrated all eight of his Panzers, covering T3 while it established a hedgehog defensive formation, the Panzers dispersed throughout the hedgehog. Sporadic artillery fire continued to fall, though only a single Panzer crewman was slightly wounded by shell fragments.

As evening fell, at 1830 Feldwebel Fragel was ordered to reconnoitre the area immediately before the German position and, with an accompanying infantry group, destroyed an enemy artillery observation post and threw back a recently arrived American infantry company. From midnight, Lersch would begin pulling back T3, and the Panzers took up a hull-down position in a wadi near the Anserine Farms, a huge French colonial estate that had proved popular with both British and German patrols after artillery fire had ruptured its wine vats making their contents easier to retrieve. The next day saw no action and the following night the Germans pulled back yet further, taking up alert positions in the mountains before moving once again the following day to positions immediately behind 5th Company, 734th, north of the Medjerda Valley.

Here the British renewed their assault on the afternoon of 29 April, and during the night that followed Lt. Lahusen and Unteroffizier Sondermann counter-attacked a British infantry unit with their respective Panzer IVs, driving the British from the ridge they had occupied and standing guard over the captured ground until morning.

At 1300 on 30 April, urgent messages were received from 5th Company of the 754th Grenadier Regiment (334th Infantry Division) holding the line below the hill of Djebal al Ghar north of Medjez-el-Bab. This bitterly contested peak dominated the entrance to the Medjerda Valley that led directly to Tunis, barely 50 km distant, and had finally fallen to British troops six days previously after ferocious fighting. The grenadiers estimated the British to be attacking in battalion strength and supported by at least eighteen tanks approaching from Djebel el Rhar. Münzner divided his company in two, moving into position amongst the German grenadiers and exchanging fire with the approaching tanks. Before long, Lahusen was forced to disengage under heavy fire from his right-hand position after his four Panzers received damaging shell hits to a gun, gearbox and drive sprocket. On the left flank, Münzner spotted four British tanks on the slope in which 5th Company was entrenched, their fire still concentrated on Lahusen's retreating group. Oberfeldwebel Gerhard Kirschbaum laid down a smoke screen from his Panzer, covering a depression in the ground and allowing Münzner to approach undetected and open fire from a range of only twenty-five metres, hitting two tanks before the British reacted and began to withdraw. One of the tanks was seen to burst into flames, while the crew abandoned the other before it too started to burn slowly.

The Grenadiers then reported a fresh attack by nine British tanks from the nearby heights and Münzner's group changed direction, Kirschbaum leading the attack towards another ridge. However, as his Panzer crested the rise it was hit by fire from another undetected hull-down tank only thirty metres from the German line. A single shell penetrated the turret causing carnage inside.

The driver let the damaged tank roll back; Kirschbaum, however, had been killed instantly, his gunner and loader both wounded. Münzner opened fire on a mosque on the heights above, guessing correctly that it contained an artillery observer responsible for the accurate shelling they had endured, as the battle ebbed away. The British temporarily withdrew and a German reconnaissance patrol later found no sign of them in or around the shattered mosque while damaged Panzers were towed back to the company workshop for repairs that night.

Kampfgruppe 'Irkens' had been formed to wrest the combat initiative from the British and regain control of the dominant heights at Djebel Bou Aoukaz, thereby halting the advance of British V Corps. This they did temporarily, although they also exhausted their final fuel stocks. There was now no longer any room for manoeuvre for the beleaguered troops in Tunisia. Nonetheless, as late as 28 April, fresh elements of the 'Hermann Göring' Division remained earmarked for transfer to Tunisia from Italy, Conrath requesting priority shipping space be given to the division's equipment. Experienced officers were requested urgently in Tunisia to replace heavy losses and men were periodically loaded aboard Italian destroyers and the German destroyer ZG3 *Hermes* for the dangerous run between Sicily and Tunis – the Italian *Leone Pancaldo* was sunk by Allied aircraft on 29 April within sight of the African coastline. A number of 'Hermann Göring' troops were aboard and after rescue were subsequently returned to Italy by hospital ship before being ordered at the beginning of May immediately to make a second attempt to reach Tunis; the special leave normally granted shipwrecked survivors was curtailed.

At the end of April, the remaining men of the Armoured Reconnaissance Battalion had relocated to a threatened sector at Pont du Fahs.

> Last night we had an alarm and moved into the endangered section. We immediately dug in as Tommy put heavy artillery fire over us – and one can only say: Thank God. In the morning he attacked with a battalion of foreign legionnaires, but the attack was totally smashed. Now, in the afternoon, we have been pulled out again and are now to be deployed to the north, at Bizerte at another weak point of the front; you cannot relax here anytime.
> Mountain position near Bizerte, 30 April: After a 120 km ride on our bikes (we are so thankful that we still have them) we are now landed here in the high mountains. We were barely dismounted when the climb started – with full ammunition, weapons, etc. It was horrible, everyone gave his last energy reserves and when we were up, everybody was completely exhausted. Overnight, we stayed so wet, sweaty as we were, just lying, without blankets – without everything. In the morning we were stiff from the cold and the rain, like a board. Now we have moved into position; but when it gets serious, we cannot hold it. Opposite us are very belligerent Englishmen, Americans, blacks, snipers and a lot of artillery. The losses on our side are increasing. I dread the coming night.[21]

The inevitable final Allied push for Tunis through the Medjez Valley that began on 6 May was tenaciously opposed by the 'Hermann Göring' troops, though the weight of numbers against them forced a relentless retreat. The command structure changed once more. The Deutsches Afrika Korps that had faced the Eighth Army's advance from Libya had been forced back to Zaghouan and was subsequently given command of what remained of the 'Hermann Göring' and 10th Panzer Divisions. The surviving Panzers of Münzner's company made their last stand at La Mornaghia, a one-sided battle that ended with the destruction of the last of the 'Hermann Göring' tanks. The division had been out of contact with Arnim for two crucial days during which time the Panzerarmee commander had no idea where the 'Hermann Göring' troops were, nor in what condition. Schmid's men continued to suffer heavy losses, withdrawing before the onslaught with almost no transport or fuel. Unbelievably, it was only then – 9 May – that the transfer of any further personnel of the 'Hermann Göring' Division to Tunisia was officially halted.

Command and control all but collapsed inside the shrinking perimeter around Tunis. A last-ditch evacuation of troops and equipment using any possible craft was briefly undertaken, though Allied air and naval power proved an easy counter and officially only 632 men from mixed units were evacuated by sea. On 10 May Kesselring suspended all seaborne evacuation transport from noon following a discussion between OKW and Arnim. Arnim's Heeresgruppe Afrika HQ had at last re-established contact with the hitherto 'missing' 'Hermann Göring' Division, however.

By this stage remaining units of the division had also finally been placed under new command. At 1045 on 10 May, Generaleutnant Gotthard Frantz, commanding officer of 19th Flak Division, an ardent National Socialist who was a virtual caricature of a Prussian general always resplendent in full uniform and with a monocle clamped into his left eye, even beneath sunglasses, replaced Schmid, who had been recalled to Germany. Arnim later expressed his personal disgust at the fact that Conrath never appeared in North Africa and the subsequent departure of Schmid.

> On 9 May, the missing (deputy) commander of the 'Hermann Göring' Division appears before me. In answer to my complaint addressed to OKW during recent days that even at this serious point in time before the Allies began their final attack, the real commander of the division [Conrath] did not make an appearance with his division in Africa, was finally answered personally by Hermann Göring in a radio message. 'It need not concern us at all as the mass (!) of the division has other tasks and the right commander would stay there.' So, in a sense: it is no longer worth sending anything to you in Africa! Now the deputy appears with a radio command from his Reichsmarschall calling him back to Italy. All other commanders stayed with their troops.[22]

Under cover of darkness later that night, Schmid and divisional transport officer Hptm. August Wolf were picked up by a transport Junkers under fighter escort at Menzel Temime, ferrying the pair out of the Tunisian trap. Schmid was being returned to Santa Maria in Italy 'by order of the Führer' as he was considered 'a repository of secret knowledge' due to his previous intelligence work, arriving at the barracks the following day. On the afternoon when he assumed command Frantz sent a signal to Göring's

Adjutant and to Luftflotte 2 as the divisional staff and other 'Hermann Göring' elements were now completely surrounded by Allied troops:

> The Staffs of Division 'Hermann Göring' and 19th Flak Division are fighting shoulder to shoulder as infantry in the all-round front line held by German forces, to the last round. We salute our Reichsmarschall! Long live the Führer!

At noon the following day, a second signal was sent:

> The final battle is beginning. Long live the Führer![23]

Some 'Hermann Göring' elements continued to resist. At Jebel Ichkeul, a scrub-covered mountain southwest of Bizerte, approximately 300 of the division's men still doggedly occupied the peaks under the command of Hptm. Otto Brandenburg, CO of the Armoured Reconnaissance Battalion 'HG'. Brandenburg and two of his company commanders – Kiefer and Gerhardt – had been directly ordered by Vaerst to take and hold the heights overlooking the northern approaches to Tunis. Besieged by the U.S. 91st Reconnaissance Battalion, the western half of Jebel Ichkeul had fallen to the Americans, while Brandenburg's troops stubbornly resisted from the eastern half. The battle all but over, General Omar Bradley instructed Colonel Benjamin 'Monk' Dickson, Intelligence Officer at II Corps HQ, to convey a note written by the recently captured Vaerst to Hptm. Brandenburg 'or his successor' ordering them and any remnants of the Fifth Panzer Army to lay down their arms and surrender. By this time, Brandenburg had become seriously ill and was indeed incapacitated as commander, Kiefer deputising for him at this final hour. Dickson ascended the hill under a flag of truce and returned with a wounded Luftwaffe Oberleutnant representing the 'HG' troops. The German officer requested verification of the note's authenticity, to which the American battalion commander whose men surrounded the eastern hill enclave told him via a translator to 'go to hell'. In response the German officer then requested a certificate attesting to the fact that the men of the 'HG' division were the last to lay down their arms on the northern Tunisian front.

> 'Brother,' the battalion commander retorted, 'either you'll come down right now and cut out this monkey business or we'll carve that certificate on your headstone.' Three hundred troops marched down with the 'Hermann Göring' flash stitched to their sleeves.[24]

On 13 May Axis forces in North Africa finally surrendered and 275,000 men went into captivity, led by Arnim, who had refused to be evacuated and forever lamented the fact that he had never been given clear operational instructions and had been misled about the level of supply that his forces would receive. The 'Hermann Göring' Division, as it existed in Tunisia, was virtually completely lost; commander of 3rd Battalion, 1st Grenadier Regt. 'HG', Major Helmut Funck, Jäger Regt. 'HG' commander Hptm. Horst Zimmermann, commander of 1st Grenadier Regt. 'HG', and Oberst Herbert Ewert, Divisional Chief of Staff Major Christoph Wilhelm Werner were among the senior officers who were taken into captivity. Otto Brandenburg, taken prisoner while seriously ill and promoted to *Major* in November, eventually died in American captivity. The German war in Africa was over.

A great many of the 'Hermann Göring' prisoners were shipped to camps in the United States, after interrogation by Allied intelligence officers. One such report offers an interesting insight into the mindset of at least one of Göring's officers.

> Of all their enemies, the German soldier seems to respect the English most. Those who had fought in Russia described Russians as animals. After Russia, Tunisia was 'a rest cure.' The Englishman was a 'good fellow' . . . There was, on the other hand, one officer of the 'Hermann Goering' Division who remarked, much to the alarm of the interrogating officer, 'If there is one type I detest more than a Jew, it is an Englishman; I would strangle one gladly with my bare hands, here and now.'[25]

Indeed, such sentiment was prevalent in the the Heer – many Army men had formed an immediate dislike to Göring's favoured troops; viewing them – rightly or wrongly – with the same jaundiced eye as Himmler's private army, the Waffen-SS. After his capture in Tunisia at the head of 86th Panzergrenadier Regiment (10th Panzer Division), Oberst Hans Reimann expressed his low opinion of the division to British interrogators:

> The famous or infamous 'Hermann Göring' Division was there, a lot of swine, nothing but puffed up – the officers were so loud-mouthed – young puppies and the older ones as well, they were so loud-mouthed that you simply didn't know what sort of people they were; at the first attack they were scattered and ran away so fast from the tanks that we had to stop them![26]

Chapter Five

Rebirth

'All that can be done with the soldier is to give him *esprit de corps* – a higher opinion of his own regiment than all other troops in the country.'

Frederick the Great

The disaster in Tunisia decimated the 'Hermann Göring' Division. A post-war account written by Conrath for the benefit of the U.S. Army archives allows a glimpse of his state of mind following the destruction of most of his division. Oberst Bogislaw von Bonin of the Heer General Staff had written a highly critical essay for the Canadian military regarding the battles for Sicily and Italy, prefacing his account with a brief indictment of 'this rank amateur strategy, this unjustifiable optimism, this criminal frivolity' that had seen the Wehrmacht reinforce an untenable hold on Tunisia with troops neither requested nor able to function effectively after losses suffered in transport.[1] Conrath echoed Bonin's view:

> Oberst von Bonin's comments regarding the senseless transfer of German troops to Africa applies to the 'Hermann Göring' Division. All combat components of the division had been transported to Tunis between February and April 1943 and were lost there without being able to influence the course of the campaign in any way. These troops were sorely missing in Sicily and during the later fighting in Italy. Only the logistic, transport and rear-area units remained with the division in the Naples area.[2]

The original training schedule for the 'Hermann Göring' Division before its piecemeal despatch to North Africa had called for completion by February, revised to as late as April as units began moving to the front. However, the loss of so many men in Tunisia threw the entire plan into confusion as Schmalz later recalled:

> The assembly of the division as an integral unit became highly questionable. To replace the departed battalions, new recruits were trained immediately at a training area in Germany. During the summer of 1943, troops of the Division were assembled from all corners of the Reich and transferred to the vicinity of Naples, Italy, where the units of company level and above were fully trained. New recruits were not concentrated in the replacement and training regiment, some parts of which were located in Holland and others in Berlin. At that time the division was also charged with the mission of sending replacements to the Guard Battalion 'Göring' and to the anti-aircraft regiment which was responsible for the protection of Hitler's headquarters. Thus, the entire personnel situation was under the control of the Division, but material and tactical employment were controlled by the Heer.[3]

Göring immediately ordered that the division be rebuilt around those scattered – though numerous – components that remained in the Netherlands, Germany, Italy and France. Conrath assembled his headquarters staff at Mont de Marsan as Schmalz, now an integral part of the division, was finally transferred into the Luftwaffe as Commander of Special Purpose Grenadier Brigade of Panzer Division 'Hermann Göring' (Kommandeur der Brigade z.b.V. der Panzer Division 'Hermann Göring') at the beginning of May.

The number of men that the Luftwaffe had managed to accumulate beneath the umbrella of the 'Hermann Göring' Division and its ancillary formations appears to have been more than was required. Heinz Guderian had visited Conrath in early 1943 in his new role as Inspector General of Armoured Troops and was staggered at how many men Conrath controlled.

> On 22 March I discussed with the commander of the 'Hermann Göring' Parachute [*sic*] Division how his formation might best be reorganised; at that time this formation, which could produce only a single division for actual combat, was 34,000 men strong. The majority of this large number of men were leading a pleasant life in Holland. In view of our replacement problem this was intolerable, even in 1943.[4]

Nonetheless, given Göring's privileged position in the Third Reich hierarchy, he continued to jealously protect men in Luftwaffe uniform from transfer to the Heer and once again the Luftwaffe manpower pool was thoroughly combed for volunteers. At least one veteran, Adolf Scheckenbach, later recalled that he answered the call for volunteers to escape the tedium of barracks life to which he had been consigned as a trained electrician. He had desired action since the war's beginning and, with the division still in combat in North Africa at the time, the very name of that continent sounded evocative and alluring.

> After the war started, I volunteered with three friends for the Waffen-SS . . . We were enthusiastic about what was happening in Poland and wanted to take part in it . . . Like all my contemporaries, I was in the Jungvolk, later the Hitler Youth, then the NSKK [National Socialist Motor Corps], and, from the age of 18, also in the Party. With many others, I thought it was right. In 1933 I was not yet 12 years old, my father was back to work, roads and railway lines were being rebuilt . . . The war against Poland started on 1 September 1939, that was on a Friday. On 3 September, the following Sunday at 2:00 p.m., the ultimatum of England and France expired, so we were at war with these two countries. My confirmation sponsor, whom I was visiting in hospital that day in Aub, said to me, 'My boy, there is no way we can win this war.' I had a different opinion but kept it to myself.
>
> From 1936, I had been working as an electrician for the firm Nestmaier in Aub. At the end of August 1939, the owner of the firm and his BMW motorcycle were drafted, along with his journeyman. With Karl, the young son of the owner, I was the electrician responsible for all the electrical plant for the town of Aub. I suspect that the council pulled a few strings to ensure that I was exempted from the six months' community service preceding the usual military service. In February 1941 I was drafted into an armoured regiment at Erlangen. At inspection we were able to state where we wished to be posted and where possible our wishes were granted. The deciding factor for us was the reputation of the Panzers. The successes of Generals Rommel and Guderian thrilled and impressed me and my peers to the point where we wanted to be in on the action like in Poland and France. The tank soldiers, with their black uniforms, the short boots and the beret finalised the matter and we decided to join the armoured divisions. The propaganda and the media of the time

had convinced all the young people that we could win the war. We wanted to be there so that we could tell the story afterwards. Of the four of us from Baldershiem who, in 1939, had wanted to join the SS, only one was accepted and shortly thereafter, drafted in.

From February 1941 I was at Erlangen for quite a while. While I was there, I was kept busy as an electrician, assembling and installing lighting for air-raid shelters, although at the time, I didn't know what they were for. The fighting in Denmark, Norway, in the Yugoslavia of the time and Greece confirmed most of my comrades and my own opinions that we Germans could win the war. Wounded Panzer men came back to Erlangen from Yugoslavia and Greece. Our discussions with them only served to confirm our belief that we were right. Then came 22 June 1941 and with it war with Russia. Then, a week later, came the first special bulletins and further confirmation for us that our beliefs were correct. At this time we had beautiful summer weather while we drilled in the barracks, I have only just remembered that after all these years. In North Africa, Rommel had made it to El Alamein and many were dreaming of his triumphant entry into Cairo and Alexandria. But, as so often in war, you cannot always predict the outcome. I enlisted in the Afrika Korps because I wanted to get out of the barracks and be where the action was.

We discovered a new division was being established, named after Hermann Göring. It [later] had a sonorous and splendid sounding title: Fallschirm-Panzer-Division 'Hermann Göring'. This unit was being assembled from superfluous Luftwaffe units, particularly signals troops, and soldiers from the Panzerwaffe reserve and replacement units.

We were all sent to the Reinickendorf Barracks at Heiligensee just outside Berlin. More and more men arrived from all over Germany in the next little while. We were issued the distinctive Luftwaffe eagle for our uniforms and 'Hermann Göring' cuff titles, which we proudly sewed onto the right sleeves of our battledress.

A couple of days later we were all loaded onto a train and sent to the Münsingen training grounds where we were quartered in the Herzog Albrecht Kaserne [Duke Albert Barracks]. Münsingen is in the Schwabian Alps . . . The area was known as the Schwabian Siberia because it was very cold in winter and there everyone worked

> very hard – practising battle manoeuvres. Initially we weren't very good but we learned quickly. It was here that we were formed into the 7th Company, 2nd Battalion, 'Hermann Göring' Panzer Regiment. Oberleutnant [Alfred] Dreher – a Schwabian who was quite a bit older than us – was assigned as our company chief. I think he had come to us on a promotion from Russia where, in mid-1941, he had been a troop commander in 9th Company of 3rd Battalion of 21st Panzer Regiment. Over Christmas we were all given leave. The battle training was hard and we didn't like it but we could see its value.[5]

The bulk of the Panzer Regiment that had not been transferred to Tunisia had continued working up in the Swabian training ground at Münsingen. However, it had proved to be a contentious period as certain officers failed to harmonise with one another in their duties. The commander of 1st Battalion, Panzer Regiment 'HG', Major Preuss, sent a personal letter to company commander Karl Rossmann on 2 January 1943 that hints at disharmony within the ranks, perhaps exacerbated by the arrival of men from the Heer.

> I thank you for your letters and the other ongoing communications that you love to send me. You can be assured that your concerns are also ours and that we are following the development of the Panzer Regiment with vivid interest, especially the 2nd and 3rd Panzer Companies.
>
> The information that you passed to the Division 'Hermann Göring', has not gone unnoticed or been unsuccessful and the intention is to replace the regiment adjutant and to order Hauptmann Hahm to report here.
>
> If you keep in mind what fantastic officers there are in the Panzerwaffe and how unhappy we are with what we were provided, one can really get annoyed.
>
> I still hope that after this normal period of friction, the entire officer corps of the Panzer regiment can unite, and training in Münsingen takes the desired shape and achieve results.
>
> Do not hang your head, instead continue work as before with idealism for the great task we all face. Stronk [Battalion Adjutant] and the rest of the gentlemen send their greetings; I am in comradely solidarity.[6]

Exactly what Rossmann – soon to replace Preuss as battalion commander – found objectionable about men in the Panzer Regiment, and whether Hahm was one of those attracting his ire, remains uncertain and Hahm's subsequent dazzling career in the division does nothing to indicate any disfavour from his superior officers.

Certainly, there was a high level of political indoctrination in the 'Hermann Göring' units, particularly among those men who had been early recruits, subject to both the heady atmosphere of National Socialist principles bombarding Germany's civilian youth and subsequent ideological training by officers influenced by Göring's highly politicised instruction. This was not unique to the division, nor was it atypical of recruits from the time, from former Freikorps members to younger men such as Adolf Scheckenbach whose adolescence had been rigorously bombarded with nationalist propaganda. Indeed, political belief is not a prerequisite for the nationalism that recruiters sought to exploit with the promise of belonging to a military force among Germany's elite. However, if present, it does appear to have been highly valued in Göring's formation and was even included in guidelines for officer recruitment. Officers and those who aspired to be officers, were required to demonstrate that they possessed 'knowledge of National Socialism' and 'could spread National Socialist thought' among their subordinates.[7] As an example, in a highly favourable assessment dated 23 February 1943 of the Panzer-Jäger Company commander, Oblt. Norbert Stiller, Preuss included the line: 'His National Socialist attitude is flawless.' Shortly thereafter, Stiller was transferred from the Panzer-Jäger to become company commander of 4th Company, Guard Regiment 'HG' and promoted to *Hauptmann*. Of course, this potential politicisation of soldiery was not confined to the 'Hermann Göring' units, but it does reflect Göring's original belief that he had a well-indoctrinated arm of service under his control.

The urgency of rebuilding forces in Sicily and southern Italy was apparent and Kesselring hurriedly gathered key commanders at Gerbini to discuss plans for defence against the inevitable Allied offensive. He intended to create a new Panzergrenadier division from survivors of 15th Panzer Division who had avoided the surrender in Tunis. Those men, either hospitalised at the time of the Tunisian collapse or a minority that escaped to Europe, had been gathered in the so-called Division Sizilien and despite their Panzergrenadier status, by July possessed only two-thirds of their planned combat strength; many were in effect untrained and with a scarcity of transport that rendered their effectiveness as a mobile formation as barely 50 per cent.

The staff of XIV Panzer Corps – the name revived after the original formation's destruction in Stalingrad – reached Italy on 19 May commanded by General der Panzertruppe Hans-Valentin Hube, who had himself narrowly escaped capture in the Stalingrad pocket. He would ultimately create and command Gruppe 'Hube' in the coming battle for Sicily in which the 'Hermann Göring' units would play an integral part.

Conrath's reconstructed division was shaped along similar lines as previously planned, the most obvious organisational difference being adherence to a newly established Wehrmacht Panzer Division structure which required removal of the Sturmgeschütz Battalion from the Artillery Regiment and its renumbering as 3rd Battalion (StuG), Panzer Regiment 'HG'. The other battalions of the Panzer Regiment contained the original mixture of Panzer III and IV vehicles, these being the mainstay medium Panzers of the Wehrmacht. Contrary to popular belief, there was no integral heavy tank unit in the division; external Army Tiger units were later attached as the situation required.

As the division rebuilt, Reichsmarschall Göring officially endorsed redesignation of Conrath's formation as Panzer Division 'Hermann Göring' on 1 June 1943; flak reinforcements were received and integrated five days later.

The shape of the division is outlined here, though operational readiness was staggered dependent on the training state of the constituent personnel and availability of equipment from beleaguered Heer stores already in competition with the Waffen-SS.

Panzer Division 'Hermann Göring'	***Generalleutnant Conrath***	
Staff	*Ia: Oberstleutnant von Bergengruen*	
	Ib: Oberstleutnant (W) Bobrowski	
	II. Major Beinhofer	
	III. Oberkriegsgerichtsrat Dr Jagow	
	IVa: Oberfeldzahlmeister Klöpfel	
	IVb: Oberfeldarzt	
	V: Maj. Schmudlach	
Panzergrenadier-Regiment 1 'HG'		
'Grille' Platoon		self-propelled 15-cm sIG 33 on Panzer 38(*t*) Ausf. H chassis
1st Battalion (SPW)		SPW armoured personnel carriers
1st–4th Companies		

2nd Battalion (mot.)	*Hptm. Reichel*	later Hptm. Josef-August Fitz
5th Company	*Hptm. Langer*	
6th Company	*Hptm. Fuchs*	
7th Company	*Oblt. Flemming*	
Panzergrenadier-Regiment 2 'HG'	*Maj. Kluge*	
'Grille' Platoon		
1st Battalion		
1st–4th Companies		SPW armoured personnel carriers
2nd Battalion		
5th–8th Companies		motorised
3rd Battalion	*Hptm. Weber*	from 7 April
9th Company	*Oblt. Schwarz (Heer)*	from 10 May
10th Company		15cm siG 33
11th Company	*Oblt. Kramer*	Oblt. Wiedemann (Heer) from 10 May; Marder II Panzerjäger
12th Company		
13th Company		
14th Company		
Panzer-Regiment 'HG'	*Obstlt. Hans Urban*	
Panzer Workshop Company		
1st Battalion	*Hptm. Rossmann*	Panzer IV
Staff Company	*Oblt. Groll*	
1st Company	*Oblt. Nischelsky*	
2nd Company	*Lt. Tschierschwitz*	
3rd Company	*Oblt. Joachim Renz*	
4th Company		still forming
2nd Battalion		Panzer III
5th–8th Companies		
3rd (Sturmgeschütz) Battalion	*Hptm. Schmock*	
Staff Battery		
9th Battery	*Oblt. Wilmskötter*	
10th Battery	*Oblt. Heidrich*	
11th Battery	*Oblt. Hagemann*	
Armoured Reconnaissance Btn.	*Maj. Preuss*	from 26 May
1st (Armoured Car) Company		
2nd (Motorcycle) Company		
3rd (Grenadier) Company		SPW armoured personnel carriers

Unit	Commander	Equipment
Panzer-Artillerie-Regiment 'HG'		
Staff		
1st Battalion		
1st Battery, 2nd Battery		both 4 x 105-mm howitzers
3rd Battery		
2nd Battalion		
4th Battery, 5th Battery		both 4 x 105-mm howitzers
6th Battery		4 x 100-mm cannon
3rd Battalion		
7th Battery, 8th Battery		both 4 x 105-mm howitzers
9th Battery		4 x 100-mm cannon
Flak-Regiment 'HG'	*Maj. Friedrich Meyer*	
1st Battalion		
1st–3rd Batteries		each of 4 x 88-mm Flak
4th–5th Batteries		each of 6 x 20-mm Flak
2nd Battalion		
6th–9th Batteries		each of 6 x 20-mm Flak
10th–12th Batteries		each of 6 x 20-mm Flak Vierling
Armoured Engineer Battalion 'HG'		
1st–3rd Companies		
Armoured Signals Battalion 'HG'		
Armoured Supply Troop 'HG'; Medical Troop 'HG'; Administrative Troop 'HG'; Military Police Troop 'HG'		

The newly created Panzer units formed at Münsingen, from where the trainees were moved to France. Among them was volunteer Adolf Scheckenbach:

> Then we were put on a train and sent to southern France for large-scale battle training. We arrived at Mont-de-Marsan, in a rural area between Bordeaux and the Spanish border, in the middle of February 1943. It was there that the mayor of the village we were billeted in, told Oberleutnant [Alfred] Dreher that this was the first time in France's history that German soldiers had occupied the village – but French soldiers had occupied Berlin starting in 1806.
>
> There were many, many of us there, all belonging to our new division. We did Panzer and field battle training in the area, with our Panzers and Panzergrenadiers getting to know how to work

together as a unit – like Münsingen this involved a lot of hardship for all of us. Because I had a licence for a small motorcycle, I was made a despatch rider and issued with a BMW 750 cc machine. It was a lovely thing – my dream machine of a few years before! When I wasn't taking despatches around I was fixing any electrical problems that arose on our vehicles. We were there until the last part of May 1943. As training came to a close we were issued with tropical uniforms, so we knew were heading south and not to Russia.

Next thing we knew, a large number of brand-new Panzer IVs with the long-barrelled 75-mm gun arrived. They were painted in tropical colours, so we really knew this time we were headed to Italy. In the first week of June 1943, we loaded up and the trains took us down Italy's Mediterranean coast to Cancello e Arnone which is about 35 km north of Naples. We de-trained and drove the few kilometres to the Italian troop training grounds at Castel Volturno on the Tyrrhenian Sea. In the middle of June we did a big exercise there and at the end of that we cleaned ourselves up and were inspected by the Italian Crown Prince Umberto. Immediately afterwards we were sent to Sicily.

The division began its transfer to Sicily with 1st Battalion, Flak Regiment moving from the Naples area to occupy barracks in Matera, Altamura, and Spinazzola in Puglia and Basilicata between 16 and 19 June. From there they travelled via Reggio di Calabria by ferry across the Strait of Messina, light flak units moving onwards to the area around Caltagirone and Grammichele, the first 'Hermann Göring' troops to take up station on Sicily. Their task was to provide anti-aircraft protection for the remainder of the division which was scheduled to begin crossing immediately as anti-invasion alert Stage 3 was declared. Ferrying of mechanised transport across the Straits of Messina began on 19 June despite USAAF Ninth Air Force B-24 bombers launching raids on ferry and railway yards at Villa San Giovanni, ferries in the Straits of Messina, and the harbour of Reggio di Calabria that same day.

The tempo of Allied bombing on southern Italian and Sicilian targets had intensified greatly and directly impacted the arduous transport of troops across the Straits on 21 June when forty-three B-24s of 98th and 376th Bomb Groups again attacked the ferry terminal and surrounding areas at Villa San Giovanni, and the harbour area and the railway yards at Reggio di

Calabria, with RAF heavy bombers mounting follow-up raids on the same targets as the Allies attempted to prevent reinforcement of Sicily.

The Panzer Regiment successfully crossed, making their first overnight camp in Sicily near Messina before moving south along the coastal road past Mount Etna to Catania where they turned west to Caltigirone and Grammichele. Conrath told his men to move at speed low enough to avoid the creation of large dust clouds, avoiding attention from roving Allied fighter-bombers as defensive Luftwaffe air power had suffered grievous losses following intense Allied bombing of Sicilian and southern Italian airfields, being reduced to little more than reconnaissance missions over the western Mediterranean. Many aircraft had been posted east; Hitler's attention was focussed elsewhere on the ambitious Operation 'Zitadelle' near Kursk which absorbed large numbers of ground-attack aircraft in support of the cream of Germany's armoured forces. Sicily would be defended by whatever units Kesselring could muster. Once his troops had settled into their Sicilian billets, Conrath ordered further exercises that gradually expanded to entire divisional manoeuvres wherever possible to try and hone largely inexperienced troops into effective combined-arms fighters. Time was against him as Allied planners prepared their first invasion of European soil.

Chapter Six

Sicily

'War is a series of local emergency measures.'
Major-General J. F. C. Fuller

Since it was Italian territory, Generale d'Armata Alfredo Guzzoni's Sixth Army was in charge of all Sicilian operations. His force was subdivided into two corps: XII Corps in the western part of the island and XVI Corps to the east. Italian combat strength amounted to six coastal divisions (one of which was barely a skeleton contingent) and four held in reserve in the island's interior. The coastal divisions were predominantly Sicilian and composed of older men, inexperienced in combat, poorly trained and equipped with obsolete weaponry.

As the Italian Army had refused to accommodate a German corps headquarters on Sicily, both the 15th Panzergrenadier and 'Hermann Göring' Divisions were under Guzzoni's tactical control, though administrative command was exercised by Wehrmacht Generalleutnant Fridolin von Senger und Etterlin, attached to the Italian Sixth Army as German liaison. Senger maintained direct radio communication with subordinate German units, although effective cooperation with Guzzoni's headquarters remained difficult due to a general Italian unwillingness to provide insight into operational plans or even knowledge of the effective strength of local forces.

In mid-June, as the division was due to leave mainland Italy, Schmalz travelled in advance to Italian Sixth Army headquarters to discuss the planned conduct of operations against expected enemy landings as well as arranging provisional billeting for the incoming division. He was extremely disappointed with the proposed Italian battle plan. Existing coastal defences amounted to only isolated strongpoints, minefields, roadblocks and artillery observation posts, lacking strength in depth. With an equally weak Italian island garrison, according to Schmalz, Guzzoni intended to withdraw all combat troops to a defensive triangle in the island's interior, leaving the coast uncontested as the enemy landed. Instead, Italian troops would then launch a series of counter-attacks from positions inland.

Schmalz vehemently disagreed with this passive strategy and immediately suggested that instead of abandoning the coast without giving battle, both inbound German divisions would assemble at probable landing sites near Syracuse and Gela for immediate commitment to action; divisional artillery would be deployed for instant use and other troops quartered locally. In the event of landings elsewhere, they would relocate and counter-attack without delay. However, this proposal was rejected, and German troops were ordered to fight according to the Italian plan. Schmalz contacted Kesselring to plead with him to call a conference with Guzzoni despite Kesselring having no jurisdiction over Italian forces as these answered directly to Rome. Kesselring later related that, although he always found Guzzoni 'obliging and understanding', he was a 'weak' leader, the real control resting in the hands of General Mario Roatta, Chief of Staff of the Italian Army.[1] Kesselring was appalled that Guzzoni intended to evacuate the coastal areas without giving battle.

> The coast was the main line of resistance. Consequently, the German and Italian units had to counter-attack immediately to win this battle for the possession of the coast . . . During a subsequent personal conference with Guzzoni I was able to convince him again of the necessity of adhering to the conduct of operations [previously] proposed by me. However, the Italian formations were not notified about this change of tactics, and I am inclined to attribute this omission to interference by higher headquarters, since I don't believe Guzzoni capable of such a flagrant negligence.[2]

Kesselring and Guzzoni also appear to have disagreed on the most likely area in which the enemy would strike. The Italian believed the southeastern part of the island most probable, particularly between Catania and Gela. Correspondingly, he planned to assemble one Italian mobile division each in the region west of Catania and north of Gela while both German divisions would be held near Caltanossetta. Kesselring, on the other hand, believed that the western part of the island, though perhaps not a likely landing zone, was also vulnerable, persuading Guzzoni to station elements of 15th Panzergrenadier Division and two Italian divisions to the west near Marsalla while the 'Hermann Göring' Panzer Division was divided into two *Kampfgruppen* covering Catania and Gela.

Bonin, who was present at the conference, recalled:

> His idea was motivated by the desire to repel the enemy through immediate employment of reserves as long as landing operations were still in progress. Field Marshal Kesselring was also afraid that large-scale movements of motorised troops would inevitably result in great losses and delays because of the expected air supremacy of the enemy, especially since the roads in Sicily were very narrow and partly steep and therefore did not permit deployment on either side of the road.[3]

The 'HG' Division was assigned to Italian XVI General Reserve Corps East, alongside the Italian 4th Infantry 'Livorno' and 54th Infantry 'Napoli' Divisions. These units covered four areas considered most likely as an enemy landing ground: Gela and east of the city, its terrain considered most suitable for a major amphibious landing; south of Comiso; the region between Syracuse and Augusta; and Catania. To cover such a broad potential attack, Conrath divided his division. He controlled the bulk – alongside remaining elements of the already weak 15th Panzergrenadier Division – which transferred from the area around Catania to the region of Caltagirone to cover the first two expected danger areas. Schmalz then took charge of a brigade-size *Kampfgruppe* to cover the other two alongside an Italian division around Syracuse–Augusta–Catania. The division of both main German formations was also thought necessary in order to bolster Italian morale; the Germans did not count on energetic and determined resistance by their Italian colleagues.

At its inception Kampfgruppe 'Schmalz' consisted of Brigade Staff of the 'Hermann Göring' Panzer Division; 3rd (StuG) Battalion, Panzer-Regiment 'HG' (with 20 Sturmgeschütz III and 9 Sturmhaubitz 42 howitzers); 1st Battalion, Panzergrenadier Regiment 2 'HG'; 1st Battalion, Armoured Reconnassaince Battalion 'HG'; 1st Company, Armoured Engineer Battalion 'HG'; 3rd Battalion, Panzer Artillery Regiment 'HG' (150-mm sFH howitzers); 382nd Panzergrenadier Regiment (Oberst Wolgang Maucke) composed of former Afrika Korps soldiers returned from leave or hospitalisation; and one Italian light tank battalion.

The bulk of the division remained with Conrath and he mustered an impressive force: Divisional headquarters and the Signals Battalion; Panzer-grenadier Regt. 1 'HG'; Panzer Engineer Battalion (less one company); 2nd–4th Companies, Armoured Reconnaissance Battalion; 1st, 2nd and

4th Battalions, Panzer Artillery Regiment (105-mm leFH, 150-mm sFH, 100-mm schwere Kanone 18s respectively); Panzer Regiment (1st and 2nd Battalions, each of one company of Panzer IVs and two of Panzer IIIs); 1st Battalion, Flak Regiment (88-mm and 20-mm guns); 2nd Company, Heavy Panzer Battalion 504 (one company of Tiger I tanks); Construction Battalion 'Messina'.

The Army Tigers were a welcome addition to the 'Hermann Göring' firepower despite the disadvantages of using such heavy vehicles in Sicily's rugged terrain. The battalion had been formed in January 1943 and had already converted to tropical use for planned deployment in North Africa. Comprising two companies, the battalion was equipped with both Panzer IIIs and Tiger Is; only its 1st Company had been sent to Tunisia where it surrendered at Cape Bon with the Axis collapse. While 2nd Company had remained in Sicily, it was initially placed under the Army's 215th Panzer Battalion before being transferred to Conrath's command, leaving its Panzer IIIs with the Army unit though the seventeen Tigers on strength were passed over to Conrath. The relationship between the Tiger unit and its new parent formation was, however, immediately contentious. The highly experienced commander of 215th Panzer Battalion, Maj. Kurt Gierga, later recalled in a report to the Generalinspekteur der Panzertruppen on 28 August 1943 exchanges between himself and the commander of the 'HG' Panzer Regiment:

> Before the transfer, I proposed to the commander, Oberstleutnant Urban, as well as the division supply and technical officers, to give them a complete Workshop Platoon that was already entrusted with repair of Tigers along with elements of the Bergezug [Recovery Platoon] in exchange for one of their Workshop Platoons. Successful recovery and repair of the new Tigers would be questionable without this exchange. The proposal was rejected by Panzer Division 'Hermann Göring' with the excuse that an exchange was out of question; instead, only transfers from my battalion were to occur. I reported this to my division commander. After telephone calls between General Rodt and General von Senger, I was ordered to give up the ten special mechanics, all of the special tools, all replacement parts, as well as the portal crane along with the seventeen Tigers. Because of transport difficulties, Panzer-Regiment 'Hermann Göring' did not pick up all these replacement

> parts, so that some of them (rubber tyres, roadwheels and more) in addition to about eighty tons of 8.8 cm ammunition were left behind and fell into enemy hands.[4]

To compound the difficulties that faced German commanders, they found Italian signals communication to be consistently poor; the 'HG' Division subsequently received not a single tactical communication directly from Guzzoni's headquarters either before, during or after the Allied landings. Instead, after the arrival of the 'HG' combat units, Conrath authorised the continuous use of armoured reconnaissance vehicles at six locations along the southern coast between Gela and Augusta with direct radio links to divisional headquarters. From 25 June, experienced Army artillery and General Staff officer Oberstleutnant Hellmut Bergengruen was appointed Chief of Staff to the 'HG' Division and recalled communication issues between the two separate 'Hermann Göring' formations.

> At the beginning of operations, Gruppe Catania [Schmalz] remained under the command of Panzer Division 'Hermann Göring'. However, the latter was not able to issue direct commands because of the great distance between these two units. With the exception of the first combat mission (Augusta), Gruppe Catania received only instructions by radio and reports by liaison officers during the initial days of combat. In every respect, Gruppe Catania had to make its own decisions independently.[5]

Kesselring met with both Sicilian-based German divisional headquarters and emphasised the necessity of advancing immediately to meet any Allied attack, regardless of whether orders were received from Sixth Army. Conrath's reply must have heartened the Oberbefehlshaber Süd: 'Field Marshal, when I see the enemy I charge; that is my forte.'[6] Kesselring inspected assembled men of the 'Hermann Göring' Panzer Regiment on 8 July and delivered what he hoped was an encouraging speech about the impending battle.

A series of false alarms for the expected invasion were issued in early July, but strong winds sweeping across Sicily on the night of 9–10 July lulled defenders into a false sense of security after these repeated scares. Bombing continued unrelentingly and, during 9 July, Gen. Alfred Bülowius's II. Fliegerkorps forward headquarters at Taormina was attacked three times, destroying the central regional Luftwaffe telephone exchange. Nonetheless,

Luftwaffe aircraft repeatedly sighted strong landing formations approaching the island and recognition of an imminent landing became clear at Luftflotte 2 headquarters. Destruction of both the telephone connections and II. Fliegerkorps headquarters complicated matters, hampering German ability to form a coherent picture of the developing situation. Nonetheless, Bülowius's staff issued clearly worded reports of an imminent and extensive Sicilian invasion to Kesselring via the Kriegsmarine command in Italy. As Kesselring remained frustrated by the fog of war, Allied paratroopers began landing a little before midnight despite the difficult weather and so Operation 'Husky' began.

Within the 'Hermann Göring' Panzer Division's sector, men of the American 505th Infantry Regiment (82nd Airborne Division) were badly scattered by high winds and navigation errors. Their objective had been the highlands of the Piano Lupo 11 km northeast of Gela on which lay a strategic junction of coastal and inland roads. At 2200 hrs the headquarters of the 'HG' Artillery Regiment telephoned divisional headquarters to report paratroopers landing nearby; five Americans were killed in a brief firefight and nine captured before the rest melted away into the darkness. Within twenty minutes, the gunners received permission to open fire on enemy transport aircraft. At 2230 the codeword for Alarm Level 1 – Silberstreif – was received by all 'Hermann Göring' units; this was raised to Alarm Level 2 within thirty minutes and they swiftly mobilised. The War Diary of 2nd Battalion, Panzer Regiment 'Hermann Göring' records:

> 10 July 1943. 8 kilometres south of Niscemi.
> 2nd Battalion ready to move at 0100 hrs.
> 0310 hrs, Alarm Level 3 was passed along.
> The Division reports parachute drops on the San Pietro airfield.
> 0500 hrs: Panzers began to move to close up with 2nd Battalion. 1st Battalion ordered to reconnoitre to the west and establish contact with the Armoured Engineer Battalion east of Gela airfield. Oberstleutnant Urban is commanding the Regiment. Hauptmann Müller commanding 2nd Battalion. Several enemy parachute troops are taken prisoner and infantry weapons captured.[7]

In early morning darkness, landing craft carrying men of Lieutenant General George S. Patton's U.S. Seventh Army approached beaches in the southwestern Gulf of Gela, while General Bernard Montgomery's British Eighth Army landed to the southeast within the Gulf of Noto. Despite a strong offshore wind, both landings were successful against demoralised Italian defenders in disarray after intense bombardment. Not until the half-light before dawn did aircraft of the Luftwaffe and Regia Aeronautica respond. Their strongest attacks were against the western American landing areas though these never seriously troubled the overall invasion effort. The success or failure of Operation 'Husky' would be decided on the ground.

The middle of the American invasion sector was codenamed 'Dime' and centred on the fishing town of Gela. After his scout cars reported the Allied landing and still before dawn, Conrath ordered an attack, dividing his troops into two *Kampfgruppen*: the Panzer Regiment (four companies), Armoured Reconnaissance Battalion, two medium battalions of the Artillery Regiment, all but one company of the Armoured Engineer Battalion to the right on the edge of the Gela Plain; and Panzergrenadier Regiment 1, one light artillery battalion and the seventeen attached Tiger tanks of Heavy Panzer Battalion 504 to the left southeast of Caltigirone. As they tried to hasten to position themselves, the armoured vehicles were greatly slowed by narrow mountain roads and village streets. Alongside fighter-bomber harassment that began with daylight, scattered Allied paratroopers erected hasty makeshift road-blocks and sniped at passing vehicles, causing further delay, confusion and a trickle of casualties. The deficiencies and inexperience of the 'Hermann Göring' Panzer officers were beginning to show. Adolf Scheckenbach was involved in this first abortive attack.

> By now, the Americans had taken the area around Gela for five or six kilometres and it was our job to bundle them back into the sea. Because the terrain was very difficult, the attack, scheduled to start at 1400 hrs began late and got disorganised. We stopped when the American Navy began shelling us and we pulled back by about 1600. It was a shambles.

Conrath personally led his tanks into action, heading for the eastern edge of the Gela beachhead as subordinate elements of 15th Panzer-grenadier Division advanced from Ponte Dirillo, attempting to envelop the American paratroopers on the Piano Lupo. His tardiness in reaching the battlefield and complete absence of communication with the Italian 'Livorno' Division resulted in the Italians already having launched a three-pronged counter-attack with tanks and infantry from between Butera and Niscemi to recapture Gela. Unlike the majority of Italian units on Sicily, the 'Livorno' Division's morale was relatively high, despite most men being as yet untested in battle. They too suffered from a lack of communication from Guzzoni's headquarters, which was unaware of Italian, German or the enemy's locations. Naval gunfire caused heavy casualties among the Italians although a small number of Renault R35 tanks belonging to the attached 'Mobile Group E' entered the town of Gela while supporting infantry were forced to seek shelter from the heavy guns. Three tanks were destroyed by American Rangers before the remaining seven retreated. Although unable to retake Gela, the Italian 34th Infantry Regiment retired with a considerable number of American prisoners from the 26th Infantry Regiment. On the Piano Lupo, Italian troops from Niscemi breached a U.S. airborne 505th Regiment roadblock and secured the valuable road junction until USS *Boise* opened fire at 0910 hrs, soon joined by another cruiser, the USS *Savannah*, and the British monitor HMS *Abercrombie*. Stunned by the high explosive deluge, the Italians' advance on Gela was stalled and then forced to withdraw under pressure from arriving troops of the U.S. 16th Infantry.

Later that afternoon the 'Hermann Göring' attack made its belated start, supported by Fw 190 and Bf 110 fighter bombers, which struck the Gela beachhead. The 'Hermann Göring' troops approached the Piano Lupo from Niscemi while 15th Panzergrenadiers advanced from the Acate River. The unwieldy Tiger tanks encountered difficulty manoeuvring through acres of olive groves but Panzergrenadiers overran an American battalion before being stopped in their tracks by units of the U.S. 45th Division. Conrath pushed the 'Hermann Göring' troops through the American 16th Infantry Regiment on the Piano Lupo but was then battered by intense naval gunfire when attempting to move off the high ground towards the beachhead, in full view of enemy artillery observers. With all three advance routes stalled, Conrath's troops encountered fresh soldiers of the U.S. II Corps reserve, some of the 'Hermann Göring' troops on the left flank finally breaking under the pressure and panicking as Italian troops passed them retreating northwards. Admitting failure, Conrath withdrew to regroup as dusk approached and reserve forces of the U.S. 2nd Armored Division and 18th Infantry Regiment began landing to reinforce their beachhead.

> The division marched into the staging area on 10 July; leading elements around 0400 hrs with the bulk around 0500. Failure and breakdowns of the two *Kampfgruppen* described in the report of

> Oberst Bergengruen (of 31 December 1950) were – to re-emphasise – due to the inexperience of the troops, inadequate training, a lack of combined arms interaction and the unsuitability of the regimental commanders of both the Panzer and Grenadier Regiments. By personal intervention of the divisional commander with the right-hand group and Chief of Staff Obstlt. Bergengruen in the left-hand combat group, major calamities were averted despite being unable to get the attack going. However, it remains that the young soldiers of the division fought fiercely and that individual formations led by skilled officers did an outstanding job. The Artillery Regiment acquitted itself particularly well.[8]

To the northeast, Kampfgruppe 'Schmalz' had immediately gone on the offensive against enemy landings reported by their own reconnaissance vehicles near Syracuse. Schmalz notified divisional command of his immediate counter-attack – the last contact between Panzer Division 'Hermann Göring' and Kampfgruppe 'Schmalz' for several days – and launched his troops forward.

From the north the armoured personnel carriers of 1st Battalion, 2nd Panzergrenadier Regiment 'HG', 3rd (StuG) Battalion, Panzer Regiment 'HG' and 3rd Battalion, Panzer Artillery Regiment 'HG' attacked via Catania–Lentini in the direction of Syracuse. From the westerly direction of Sortino–Floridia Schmalz despatched the attached Italian light tank battalion with armoured cars of 1st Company, Armoured Reconnaissance Battalion 'HG'. Schmalz also intended the Italian 'Napoli' Division to advance along the same westerly axis, the German reconnaissance vehicles being included along the route both to support the Italian attack and to report its progress to him. The results were discouraging.

> These reconnaissance troops, which were driving ahead of the armoured battalion, engaged the enemy at Floridia, kept in contact with him [the enemy] and continuously reported the enemy's movements to me. In the course of the entire Sicilian campaign no further trace was found of either the Italian division which was supposed to attack along the road, or the Italian light armoured battalion. They were missing. Italian officers who came to see me on several occasions in order to establish contact were not able to give me any information as to the fate or the location of these units.[9]

Despite Schmalz's assertion, a battalion of R35 Renault tanks with supporting infantry from the 'Napoli' Division attacked and broke through the lines of the British Wiltshire Regiment, being stopped only by intense anti-tank and artillery fire in the outer suburbs of Syracuse and forced to retire.

Kampfgruppe 'Schmalz' locked horns with British troops at Floridia and Priolo as Italian coastal units between Syracuse and Augusta destroyed their guns and fled the battlefield. The *Sturmgeschütze* of 11th Company claimed six British tanks and four ammunition carriers destroyed, but once again naval gunfire proved decisive as intense bombardment against Schmalz's open flank forced the advance to halt. The position taken by 'HG' troops at Priolo was judged too exposed to the devastating naval gunfire and untenable, so Kampfgruppe 'Schmalz' concentrated instead on the defence of Melilli which was occupied during the night of 10–11 July.

The assumption on which both Schmalz and Conrath had based their combat plans – counter-attacks against confined beachheads – had been completely demolished during the first twenty-four hours of the 'Husky' landings. Italian troops had not defended the coast. With the Axis reserves disintegrating either through Allied action or desertion, the invaders were able to advance rapidly inland. Schmalz's planned powerful counter-thrust against the British landing area could now only be executed by a small number of German units, with no viable chance of success.

Schmalz's *Kampfgruppe* appeared dangerously isolated at this point with exposed flanks and rear and he identified the need to consolidate a position which could be adequately defended while allowing fragmented German units to re-establish contact with each other. The Catania plain was ideal, and its possession considered essential to the continued existence of Axis forces on Sicily. If it could not be held then the way to Messina would be open and all Axis troops cut off from potential evacuation to mainland Italy. Unaware of the success or failure of Conrath to the south, Schmalz fortified Lentini with newly arrived reinforcements despatched by Kesselring (382nd Panzergrenadier Regiment) while he combined his 'Hermann Göring' infantry and artillery in a defensive group on the line stretching from Monte Pancali towards the coast to fight a delaying action which would allow fortification work to be completed.

The following morning, knowledge of the Allied dispositions in Gela had improved and Conrath met with Generale di Divisione Domenico Chirieleison to coordinate in person a counter-attack towards the beachhead. The bulk of the 'Livorno' Division had now arrived and Conrath's forces would join them for a synchronised attack in three columns. Beginning at 0600, after a planned ten-minute Italian and German artillery barrage, the 'Hermann Göring' Division (with attached 15th Panzergrenadier units) would form the left wing, the virtually intact 33rd Infantry Regiment of the 'Livorno' Division would advance from the northwest, while the centre would be the 3rd Battalion of the Livorno's 34th Infantry Regiment.

The approach was extremely hazardous, over predominantly open ground with little shelter, the coastal corn fields having been reaped only days before. To compound their problems, the expected artillery support for the Italian advance was late; the 1st Battalion, 28th Artillery Group was not yet in position at 0550 when the first shells should have been fired. Following an absurdly melodramatic message from Göring to his namesake division – 'Victory or death!' – the slightly delayed attack commenced, without the promised bombardment for the 'Livorno' troops lest the Italians fall out of step with their German opposites. Adolf Scheckenbach remembered:

> At 0615 the next morning we attacked again, with the Italians of the 'Livorno' Division on our right. We pushed forward with our Panzer battalions approaching from the northeast while our Panzergrenadiers and our attached Tigers went in from the east. Our Panzers actually overran their infantry positions and pushed most of them back but some of the Americans had hidden in their foxholes and popped up after the Panzers had rolled over. They used their radios to call in naval gunfire. It was one of these big shells which struck one of our Panzer VIs and killed one of the crew. He was Oberleutnant Dreher's batman and the first man killed in our company.
>
> Around the same time one of our Panzers became immobilised because of a mechanical problem during a battle with American Sherman tanks. The driver could not move it forward, so they were sitting ducks. Oberleutnant Dreher personally ran over to the machine under fire and got his soldiers out and away.
>
> In another incident, during this period of attack, Oberleutnant Dreher, his Adjutant, a *Feldwebel* whose name I no longer remember, and I came under American shellfire as we observed the battle and prepared orders. We scuttled into cover and escaped unscathed.

The battalions, led by our 1st Company, got to within 1,000 metres of the landing beach and were firing at their landing craft and supply dumps but because we didn't have enough infantry and no way to silence the naval bombardment, we were forced back again. From what I have read of the battle, it seems that the 'Livorno' Italian Infantry Division, who were scheduled to meet us, had been literally shredded by naval gunfire. If they had survived, we could probably have pushed the Americans back into their landing craft.

This first action was where we took our first dead and wounded, of which I was one. Oberleutnant Dreher and I were constantly on the road and we were strafed by a Jabo and I suffered a minor wound.

I found out much later that the Gela counter-attack against the Americans failed badly. The commander of 1st Battalion was relieved of his command and after that we did much better as a combat unit. But because of poor leadership we lost many good soldiers, most of our Panzers as well as the monster Tigers which had come under the control of 'HG' just before the invasion.

It was not until three weeks later on 30 July when we had slowly pulled back to almost the lower slopes of Mount Etna that I was wounded. My company was supporting our Engineer Company holding a small town named Regalbuto against the British. The Britishers were fierce and fired mortars and artillery as the infantry attacked. I was about one kilometre to the east of the town on the main road when some mortar rounds landed close to us. I was hit by shrapnel in my right thigh and foot and, as I could no longer ride my motor bike, I was evacuated.

I was sent back to Livorno on the Italian mainland by hospital ship and then by hospital-train to Schwandorf which is to the north of Regensburg. On the trip I had my first malaria attack. In Germany I was taken to a specialised hospital which treated infectious diseases and over the next couple of weeks I was shunted from one hospital to another as they didn't seem to know what to do with me.[10]

Despite the momentary resurgence of supporting Italian and German aircraft, the attack was ultimately catastrophic. The 'Hermann Göring' Panzers were plainly visible under churning dust clouds as they thundered across the Gela plain towards the enemy, Conrath's staff car accompanying the spearhead advance. Both Panzer battalions mounted a frontal attack, pushing against the right flank of the American 1st Infantry Division. They had reached within 700 metres of the supply dumps for the 26th Infantry Regiment, when freshly disembarked American howitzers began pounding the advancing Germans over open sights and the first four Sherman tanks came ashore to join the battle. Several of Conrath's Panzers were close enough to fire at Allied shipping off the beachhead. The supply ship SS *Nicholas Gilman* was among those shelled; one of its naval Armed Guard was wounded. American shore parties were thrown into the defensive line and at first Conrath believed that they were beginning to evacuate, misinterpreting glimpses of reinforcements being unloaded. Seemingly within grasp of their objective the German attack faltered at which point USS *Boise* opened fire; its 6-inch shells sowed carnage among the 'Hermann Göring' troops, many of whom broke and ran. At 1400 Conrath called off the attack. Hauptmann Müller and Oberleutnant von Bomhard of 2nd Panzer Battalion were both wounded when their command tank was hit by an American anti-tank shell, the vehicle written off and abandoned. However, the battalion's losses as a whole were relatively light: a single Panzer IV was blown up by naval gunfire; three Panzer IIIs were destroyed along with the command tank and one further disabled Panzer III was blown up to prevent capture as the Germans retreated.

The 'Livorno' troops fared little better, though they forced American troops to retreat to the outskirts of Gela itself, capturing a quantity of American prisoners and weapons before naval gunfire battered the exhausted but triumphant attackers. As the Italians reached American roadblocks erected outside Gela the naval guns opened fire, killing most of the Italian officers and leaving only 400 men still capable of fighting. Urgent requests for ammunition, fuel and reinforcements resulted in a single mortar company being sent to assist the division and, as night fell and word of the failed German attack reached Italian survivors, they retreated, pursued by small groups of American troops that demonstrated their excellence at night fighting to the demoralised Italians.

Conrath's Panzers withdrew in relatively good order, taking defensive positions on the reverse slopes of the high ground. Allied aircraft harassed the retreating Panzers throughout the day, however. Casualties included Oblt. Schönhess of 2nd Battalion who was severely wounded. Elsewhere, after taking heavy losses, battered 'Hermann Göring' troops withdrew in disarray, prompting a sharply worded rebuke from Conrath the following morning.

> During the past few days, I have had the bitter experience of watching scenes which are not worthy of a German soldier, particularly not of a soldier of the 'Hermann Göring' Division.
>
> Men came running to the rear, hysterically crying because they had heard the detonation of a single shot fired somewhere in the distance. Others, deceived by false rumours, moved whole columns to the rear. In one instance, supplies were senselessly distributed to soldiers and civilians by a supply unit which had fallen victim to a rumour. I wish to state that not only the younger soldiers, but also NCOs and warrant officers, were guilty of panic-stricken behaviour.
>
> Panic, 'Panzer fear', and the spreading of rumours are to be eliminated by the strongest possible measures. Cowardice and withdrawal without orders are to be punished on the spot, and, if necessary, by the use of weapons. I shall apply the severest measures of court-martial against such saboteurs of the fight to free our nation, and I shall not hesitate to pronounce death sentences in serious cases. I expect all officers to use their influence in suppressing this undignified attitude throughout the 'Hermann Göring' Division.

The attachment of the potentially deadly Tigers to Conrath's division had also ended in dismal failure. Though a number had remained in action for much of the fighting, by the campaign's end only a single Tiger would be successfully evacuated from Sicily. Major Gierga's August report to the Generalinspekteur der Panzertruppen angrily blamed 'Hermann Göring' incompetence for the debacle.

> Based on the after-action report from the Tiger Company and the report from Leutnant Goldschmidt, the last commander of the Tiger Company . . . the Panzergrenadiers interfered with the employment of the Tiger Company and the terrain was insufficiently scouted, so that several Tigers became bogged in the mud. The Tigers became separated from our own infantry, so they were cut off, making recovery or repair impossible. Ten Tigers had already been lost during the first three days when they were blown up to prevent capture. Of the remaining seven Tigers, three more were lost by 20 July when they caught fire or were blown up to prevent

> capture. The excess Tiger crews were employed as infantry at the Gerbini airfield despite the strongest arguments from the Tiger Company commander. During the further retreat employed as rearguard, three of the last four Tigers broke down and were blown up to prevent capture. The last Tiger was transported across the straits to the mainland. Based on statements made by Leutnant Goldschmidt, a large portion of the Tigers could have been repaired and saved by well-prepared recovery and maintenance work if they had been guarded by adequate infantry support. In no way were the Werkstatt and the recovery service of Panzer Regiment 'Hermann Göring' up to this task. In addition, during the retreat the portal crane, so important for repairing Tigers, was blown up by the Workshop Company.

Facing the British, Schmalz's two 'Hermann Göring' battalions had taken up their defensive positions, withdrawing from Priolo which was bombed immediately afterward by thirty-six P-40 Kittyhawk aircraft. All three *Sturmgeschütz* companies were now in action, claiming between them six tanks of the 3rd County of London Yeomanry and twenty trucks destroyed, though Lt. Wirtz of 9th Company was posted missing in action. Kesselring returned to Sicily from Frascati on 12 July, visiting Guzzoni at Enna and then Brigade 'Schmalz'. Kesselring remained highly impressed with both Schmalz's combat leadership and his concise reporting of all combat measures undertaken. It was apparent, despite imminent reinforcements promised by the parachute drop of leading elements of the 1st Fallschirmjäger Division (formerly the 7th Flieger Division) on the Catania plain and allocation of all remaining mobile reserves of the 'Hermann Göring' Division, that serious counter-attacks against the British beachhead could no longer be carried out with any likelihood of success with the limited artillery and armour available.

In spite of Senger's best efforts, there were incessant communications failures so that liaison with the limited Italian leadership was insufficient for the smooth operation of German troops on Sicily and the establishment of a German corps command could be delayed no longer. To that end, with belated agreement from Mussolini, the XIV Panzer Corps command was committed to Sicily under General der Panzertruppe Hube. Kesselring also formed the slightly misguided impression that German forces were fighting virtually single-handedly. In fact, both the 'Livorno' and 'Napoli'

Divisions and some scattered Italian units had effectively covered the flanks of the 'Hermann Göring' troops' retreat. Regardless, the decision was taken to abandon western Sicily and withdraw all forces to form a strong main battle line from Stefano on the northern coast, through Nicosia and Agira to Cantenanuova and on to the eastern coast south of Catania.

In conference with Kesselring, Schmalz learned of Conrath's failure at Gela and received official approval of his decision to refrain from further offensive operations and thereafter conduct a defensive battle. Corresponding action was required from Conrath, and though Schmalz did not regain communications with him until 13 July, both officers had already reached the same conclusion. Conrath intended to retreat to the Catania Plain, thereby shortening their defensive front and reuniting the division, planning to meet Schmalz's troops at the plain's northern edge.

At dusk the first elements of 1st Fallschirmjäger Division began dropping near Catania airfield; the three battalions of the 3rd Regiment, arriving without heavy weapons, were collected, and trucked immediately to the front lines by 'Hermann Göring' vehicles. Conrath positioned two battalions east of his Panzergrenadier Regiment; the third was combined with one of his three available artillery batteries and moved to hold Francoforte where his reconnaissance troops were beginning to buckle under enemy pressure. Over the next three days, more *Fallschirmjäger* either dropped or were airlanded at Catania, including two battalions from 4th Regiment, a machine-gun battalion and some light artillery pieces.

For the next three days Kampfgruppe 'Schmalz' pivoted away from the coast under severe pressure from British forces as Conrath mounted a fighting retreat to close the gap between the two formations. In fierce combat on 13 and 14 July, the Sturmgeschütz Battalion claimed a total of sixteen tanks, numerous machine-gun and anti-tank positions destroyed, took sixty-six prisoners and fired at landing craft approaching Augusta as well as their three covering British destroyers. On the debit side, 11th Company commander Oblt. Hagemann was wounded on the first day and posted missing the next; a second company commander was also lost on 16 July when Oblt. Friedrich Wilmskötter and his crew were killed in action. During this period, Oblt. Jekosch, Battalion Adjutant, deputised for Schmock, who was hospitalised with malaria

During 13 July 2nd Battalion of the Panzer Regiment moved alongside the main body of Kampfgruppe 'Hahm' on reverse slopes southwest of Grammichele, while a newly consolidated Kompanie 'Hän', established from elements of 5th and 6th Panzer Companies along with four surviving Tigers, formed a defensive line before Height 398 south of the Caltagirone Carabinieri barracks. One Panzer III was destroyed in combat with American Shermans and a second blown up by its crew to prevent capture. Two Panzer IVs were lost the following day to anti-tank guns during a counter-attack launched by 7th Company Panzers with accompanying infantry. This threw American troops back from Height 398 and claimed twelve Lee and Sherman tanks destroyed during the fighting as well as three armoured cars, two anti-tank guns and a number of trucks. In return, alongside other casualties, and the loss of the two Panzers, Oblt. Hän was wounded and Lt. Götze posted missing in action

Conrath's men broke contact on 16 July, moving north in three main *Kampfgruppen* named after their commanders – Oberst Hans Oehring (commander Panzer Artillery Regt. 'HG' at Caltagirone), Hptm. Konstantin Hahm (Grammichele) and Hptm. Robert Rebholz (commander Armoured Reconnaissance Battalion 'HG' at Vizzini). Oblt. Dreher of 7th Company, Panzer Regiment took charge of a small rearguard *Kampfgruppe* to cover the retreat. Dreher blocked narrow defiles, blew up bridges and maintained harassing fire on pursuing American troops, who always appeared to take cover immediately after the first German shots and call up pummelling artillery support to dislodge the Germans. The Panzer Regiment was no longer commanded by ex-bomber pilot Hans Urban, who was replaced by the experienced Heer Panzer officer and holder of the 'Blood Order' Oberstleutnant Georg-Henning von Heydeback transferred into the Luftwaffe directly from OKH's Führerreserve.

Schmalz's withdrawal was complicated by British paratroops landing near the bridge over the Simeto River on the Catania–Lentini road. Though the Fallschirmjäger machine-gun battalion destroyed the British force, scattered remnants briefly prevented 'Hermann Göring' use of that single road, though it did not affect the overall German plan. Finally, the two 'Hermann Göring' components were reunited on the Catania Plain, forming a new main defensive line along the Leonforte–Catenanuova–Gerbini–Catania axis with the various *Kampfgruppen* distributed east to west as Kampfgruppe 'Schmalz', 'Rebholz', 'Hahm' and 'Oehring'. Conrath resumed overall command of the division once more, though Schmalz's brigade headquarters maintained immediate control over the Gerbini–Catania sector. Holding the western edge of the German line was the 15th Panzergrenadier Division, though contact between it and the 'Hermann

Göring' Division remained sporadic and the Panzergrenadiers were being severely pressed by Patton's troops. Reinforcements from 29th Panzergrenadier Division were beginning to cross the Straits of Messina to take part in the Sicilian battle, but if the line could not be held from coast to coast then disaster could still overtake all German troops on the island.

Kesselring urged the 'Hermann Göring' main battle line be relocated further forward at the Simeto River until Schmalz pointed out the fallacy of moving infantry to occupy the middle of the Catania Plain, with supporting artillery being necessarily moved to positions on flat ground that offered no cover at all. By maintaining the main battle line on the mountain slope the enemy was instead forced to cross the open ground under full view of German troops and artillery. Schmalz was subsequently proved correct as Allied troops failed to pierce the Axis line until the German and Italian troops voluntarily retreated during the night of 5–6 August following days of intense enemy pressure.

However, Allied intelligence misjudged Hube's strategic rationale. Though identifying with some accuracy the position and composition of the German defensive line, they anticipated an organised build-up of forces by which vigorous counter-attacks could be launched from a static defensive position. They were mistaken as Hube envisioned, rather than a 'final defensive line', the entire northeastern area occupied by the 'Hermann Göring' *Kampfgruppen* as ground on which he could establish a succession of strongpoints, almost, but not quite, in lateral isolation from one another. The terrain itself denied much freedom of manoeuvre, allowing concentrated defensive points that could hold almost independently before planned withdrawal along prepared roads to the next designated defensive position. The Allies failed to appreciate the imperative that was being placed on evacuation; the defensive battle being waged was perfect for the tried and tested *Auftragstaktik* principle.

Between 15 and 20 July a complicated reshuffling of *Kampfgruppen* and their constituent units was undertaken. To bolster the frontline heavy weaponry, one battery each of the flak battalion was designated 'for special use' (*zur besonderen Verwendung, z.b.V.*) to be put under the command of three different *Kampfgruppen* to assist in anti-tank and aircraft defence in the forward combat area; their use as anti-aircraft guns on rear communication lines was strictly forbidden. Furthermore, Conrath ordered that troops from both Panzer battalions who lacked vehicles be formed into two infantry 'Alarm companies'. The following breakdown provided for Conrath by

Oberstleutnant Bergengruen on 21 July showing the integration of organic divisional components with other German and Italian units.

Kampfgruppe 'von Carnap' *Obstlt. Gerhard von Carnap* Carnap was Adjutant, 1. Fallschirmjäger Division

1st Battalion, Fallschirmjäger Regiment 3; 13th Battery and mixed units of 4th Battalion, Panzer Artillery Regiment 'HG'; 923rd Fortress Battalion; 5th Company, Flak Bataillon z.b.V. 'HG'

Kampfgruppe 'Preuss'

Staff, Panzer Regiment 'HG'; 2nd Battalion, Panzer Regiment 'HG'; Gerbini Flak batteries

a. Kampfgruppe 'Kluge'

Regimental Staff and 1st Battalion, Panzergrenadier Regiment 2 'HG'; 1st Battalion, Panzer Artillery Regiment 'HG'; Panzergrenadier Battalion 'Oria'; 10th Company, Flak Bataillon z.b.V. 'HG'; 1 Italian infantry battalion; 1 Italian artillery battalion; remains of 1st Battalion, Panzergrenadier Regiment 1 'HG'

b. Kampfgruppe 'Rebholz'

Armoured Reconnaissance Battalion 'HG'; 2nd Battalion, Panzer Artillery Regiment 'HG'; Panzergrenadier Battalion 'Reggio' (formerly 69. Marsch Bataillon); 9th Company, Flak Bataillon z.b.V. 'HG'; remains of 2nd Battalion, Panzergrenadier Regiment 2 'HG'

Kampfgruppe 'Schmalz'

Brigade Staff z.b.V. 'HG'; Panzergrenadier Regiment 115 (without *Körner*) (15th Panzergrenadier Division); 1st Battalion, Panzer Artillery Regiment 'HG'; 3rd (Sturmgeschütz) Battalion, Panzer Regiment 'HG' (*Hptm. Schmock, wounded on 19 July*); Battalion 'Schachtleben'; Fallschirmjäger Regiment 4 (*Oberst Erich Walther*); Catania Flak Batteries; 1 Italian artillery battalion; 1 Italian infantry battalion; 2nd Battalion, 382nd Panzergrenadier Regiment; 904th Fortress Battalion

Division Reserve

1st Battalion, Panzer Regiment 'HG'; Fallschirmjäger Regiment 3 (minus one battalion, *Oberst Ludwig Heilmann*); Armoured Engineer Battalion 'HG' (moved to occupy a strongpoint at that time); 1st Battalion, Flak Regiment 'HG'

However, that was not the end of the reorganisation. An order issued on 20 July contained the following extension of the reshuffle and the amalgamation of formations that had been mauled in combat:

> To restore coherence among the units, the following changes will be carried out: 1st Battalion, Panzergrenadier Regiment 1 will

be dissolved and personnel, weapons and motor transport will be taken over by 1st Battalion, Panzergrenadier Regiment 2. In the same way, regimental headquarters, Panzergrenadier Regiment 2, will be taken over by 1st Battalion, Panzergrenadier Regiment 2. 2nd Battalion, Panzergrenadier Regiment 2 will be dissolved and incorporated into the Armoured Reconnaissance Battalion 'HG' which will use its new details to form a fourth (rifle) company, replenish the 3rd Company, and enrol specialists in the 5th and 6th Companies.

> The Headquarters personnel of the dissolved units will be formed into 'organisational staffs', strength up to 15, with three motor trucks each, under command of an officer. These staffs will include all personnel necessary for winding up the affairs of the units – clerks, specialist NCOs, armourers etc.[11]

However, the lack of training and diligence amongst some elements of the division was sharply pointed out by Oberst Hans Oehring after an inspection of batteries from his artillery regiment. He had noted the lack of protective fire trenches surrounding prepared positions, insufficiently dug-in guns, too few foxholes for crewmen in the event of counter-battery fire, a lack of 'track discipline' – the camouflaging of deep conspicuous vehicle tracks leading to camouflaged positions – and insufficient mobility in the event of being forced to move to an alternative position. In an order issued on 23 July, he lambasted his men for their negligence.

> We are in danger of suffering great damage by fire, not only because of incendiary bombs, but because of the carelessness of our own soldiers. I notice that, despite my repeated written and oral warnings, the requisite measures for protection against damage by fire have not been put into effect. I shall hold the commanding officers of units responsible if adequate measures are not at once ordered and carried out . . .
>
> To sum up, units containing elements which are still inexperienced or stupid or apathetic must be taken in hand, and energetically taught and controlled by the officers in command of these units. If this is done, the heavy casualties that we have been incurring up to the present time may be avoided in the future. In particular, the most careful measures are to be undertaken everywhere for the organization of an air-raid warning system. Each unit commander

> will see to it that the system operates smoothly and that any man who fails to perform his duty is punished ruthlessly. I have repeatedly stressed the principles contained in this order. Only when they are adhered to by everyone will the artillery avoid heavy casualties and, by maintaining its strength, be able to carry out its task.[12]

On 25 July events in Rome impacted on the battle for Sicily when Mussolini was dismissed by King Victor Emmanuel II as head of the government and replaced by Marshal Pietro Badoglio. Italy's war effort had been in steep decline with increased Allied bombing, food shortages and significant labour strikes for the first time since 1925. The country had held no great appetite for the war even in 1940 and with Italian forces in Sicily on the brink of collapse despite the staunch German defence of the island, the fall of Mussolini was guaranteed. He was subsequently arrested and spirited away to incarceration at Campo Imperatore in Abruzzo. While Badoglio maintained public support for the alliance with Germany, he dissolved the Italian fascist party and initiated covert peace talks with the Allies.

In Berlin, the Germans decided to cease reinforcement of Sicily immediately and instead set about preparing contingency plans for evacuating German troops from Sicily, Sardinia and Corsica. Kesselring assured the Führer that the evacuation of Sicily could be accomplished within three days. While Hitler vacillated over whether or not to evacuate Sicily, Kesselring, fearful of a repeat of the Tunisian disaster, took it upon himself to prepare the evacuation. To prevent any possibility of Italian discovery of his decision Kesselring called a conference on 27 July to brief commanders of the German formations on Sicily. In the event of Italian defection from the Axis, XIV Panzer Corps was ordered to disengage from the enemy forthwith and evacuate all troops from Sicily. Hube in turn directed Oberst Ernst-Günther Baade, commandant of troops guarding Messina, and the Kriegsmarine's Seetransportführer Messina-Straße (Transport Commander, Messina Strait), Fregattenkapitän Gustav von Liebenstein, to begin preparations for the evacuation. Hube also officially informed Guzzoni that German forces would no longer execute a 'stubborn defence' of Sicily.

Two further operations were hurriedly prepared: 'Eiche', the rescue of the incarcerated Mussolini by German troops, and 'Student', the planned occupation of Rome and restoration of Italian fascism by Army Group B, hurriedly formed in northern Italy under the command of Erwin Rommel.

Badoglio's assurances of Italy's commitment to the Axis had been justifiably treated with great suspicion by Hitler's government and in the event of an Italian armistice with the Allies, operations 'Achse' and 'Schwarz' would also be carried out; the capture of the Italian Fleet and seizure of key Italian military positions on land.

The task of the 'Hermann Göring' units now became one of a delaying action as troops were withdrawn. This noticeably boosted the men's morale as they were no longer fighting a battle that they stood no chance of winning. Despite being unable to reach agreement with Guzzoni's fractured command, Hube independently authorised the evacuation to commence, detailed plans naming the 15th Panzergrenadier Division first to be withdrawn, followed by the 29th and then the 'Hermann Göring' units. Local German counter-attacks continued to frustrate Allied pursuit. One such attack was mounted in the early morning hours of the last day of July when Leutnant Dreher led an armoured assault that reoccupied positions at Regalbuto which had been abandoned the previous day. However, at first light, Dreher could see that his flanks were dangerously exposed and a renewed Allied attack threw supporting German infantry back from the village, though the 'Hermann Göring' Panzers continued to fight at close range between the houses.

Despite stringent medical practices, malaria had also kept taking a steady toll on Conrath's troops and on 2 August disease-weakened soldiers broke off enemy contact as pressure mounted on their right flank and retired to prepared positions closer to Messina. Two Knight's Crosses were awarded that day for *Kampfgruppe* leaders Maj. Waldemar Kluge and Hptm. Robert Rebholz. Later that afternoon Conrath received the following instruction regarding the withdrawal and planned evacuation of his division, forwarding the information to his officers:

> Enclosure to 'Hermann Göring' Div. Order No. 31/43, 2 August 43: Directive for Future Moves and Battle Actions in Sicily
>
> 1. No demolition and no road blocks are to be manned by Italian personnel. Officers in charge of battle groups are responsible for the enforcement of this order.
> 2. Every German soldier who is forced to take to the mainland must be in possession of infantry weapons. Apart from revolver and bayonet he will carry a rifle, sub-machine gun, pistol or LMG, with ammunition. In the case of squads, one heavy MG or mortar. These

weapons are tickets for the ferry. Without those mentioned, soldiers will ruthlessly be prevented from crossing.

3. No Italian, whether civilian or soldier, may interfere in any way with the movement of the German armed forces. All Italian motor vehicles and heavy weapons will be ruthlessly removed from the roads. This does not apply to units which, as part of the division, have proved their worth in battle, and carry on the fight.

4. Isolated remnants of formations, platoons, and squads of any description are to be put under the command of local units. They will be made to form part of the current movement. Out-of-date orders are no longer valid.

5. Any motor transport, weapons or equipment that cannot be transported across to the mainland are to be completely demolished. Destruction by fire is strictly forbidden, since fires and traces of burning are liable to attract the attention of enemy aircraft, both by day and by night. Blowing-up is the most effective method of destruction and will be applied to weapons as a matter of principle. Motor vehicles will be destroyed so as to put them out of action for a long time at least. (They will be blown up, magnetos removed, tires slashed, the engine smashed, or the whole vehicle run over a cliff.)

6. The most rigid discipline is the main condition for the success of all future moves. Anyone not co-operating will be shot. Examples of individuals always work wonders.

7. All traffic control regulations come under direct orders of Division HQ. Whoever does not comply with regulations is subject to disciplinary action; see paragraph 6.

8. Roads which because of enemy action have been blocked (bomb craters or demolished houses) must be made passable as quickly as possible, or diversions created and flagged (attention drawn to them) by drawing on the civil population and prisoners of war.

9. All personnel will carry haversack rations for 24 hours as well as iron rations.[13]

Forward combat posts of the main battle line were withdrawn under Allied artillery fire that daily increased in intensity. Local Allied attacks and counter-attacks continued as fresh reinforcements were fed into the line. However, despite creeping advances, at each point the Germans successfully withdrew before catastrophic penetration of their lines occurred, strong rearguards covering each retirement. Naval bombardment caused limited casualties to the flank of Kampfgruppe 'Schmalz' and a reinforcing battery of 170-mm artillery pieces was put to use for counter-fire. On the right flank, 15th Panzergrenadier Division was being progressively forced back and Conrath's various *Kampfgruppen* began to pivot carefully as they withdrew to a shorter defensive line hinged on the inhospitable and easily defended terrain around Mount Etna, the main transport moves taking place at night as Allied aerial superiority ruled out wholesale movement in daylight.

On 29 July the new Kampfgruppe 'Paulus' was briefly formed to cover the Fiumefreddo coastal area opposite Mount Etna and counter possible enemy landings behind the German main battle line. Led by the company commander of 1st Company, Armoured Reconnaissance Battalion 'HG', Hptm. Helmut Paulus, this emergency unit comprised: 1st Company, Armoured Reconnaissance Battalion 'HG'; one battery, 33rd Artillery Regiment (170-mm guns); 9th Company, Panzergrenadier Regiment 1 'HG'; Alarm Company, 1st Battalion, Panzer Regiment 'HG' – comprised of dismounted Panzer crews employed as an infantry reserve; one company, 1st Battalion, Panzer Regiment 'HG' (eight Panzer III and IV tanks); a special composite company assigned by divisional headquarters; one battery of 88-mm flak weapons.

Although a trickle of troops had already been lifted from the island, on 6 August, Hube issued the official order for evacuation – Operation 'Lehrgang' – as British XIII Corps hammered at 'Hermann Göring' defences on the coastal strada statale 114 that would open the path to Messina. The original plan was for the evacuation to take place over five consecutive nights and, whenever the situation in the air permitted, by day as long as the massing of troops remained uncontested by the enemy. Specific approach roads and assembly areas were allocated to each division

Despite continuing to suffer heavy casualties, the 'Hermann Göring' troops maintained a cohesive defence as they withdrew towards Messina. Each division had been given its own assembly areas designated by Baade and one of five routes by which seaborne evacuation would take place; the 'Hermann Göring' Division and attached units were to take Route 4, departing Sicily from embarkation stages a mile north of Messina. At each staggered defensive line designated by Hube at XIV Corps headquarters, the line was sufficiently shortened to allow Conrath to release for evacuation up to two-thirds of the men holding the previous positions. Logistical troops were the first to begin crossing to Calabria, followed by Schmalz's

Brigade Staff z.b.V. 'HG' which subsequently prepared reception in Calabria of the remaining 'Hermann Göring' combat units that were transported in good order with virtually all of their equipment to the Italian mainland. The Kriegsmarine now sent additional Siebel ferries, ferry barges and R-boats to the straits as German artillery pieces, particularly flak units, were brought into position on both shores. Though some ancillary units had already been withdrawn, full-scale evacuation only got going on 11 August. By skilful withdrawal of defensive lines and extremely effective Kriegsmarine transport services under the protection of a heavy concentration of artillery and flak units, the Wehrmacht managed to extricate its troops successfully from the lost battle for Sicily, in daylight with minimal interference from Allied air or naval forces, and redeploy them in Calabria. The masterfully undertaken evacuation was completed by 17 August with 52,000 German troops (including 4,444 wounded), 14,105 vehicles, 47 tanks, 94 guns, 1,100 tons of ammunition, and about 20,700 tons of equipment and stores being taken off the island. Hube himself was among the last German soldiers to leave, during the early morning of the final day. The War Diary of 2nd Battalion, Panzer Regiment 'HG':

> 16 August 1943: The last defenders by Messina pulled back during the evening. The enemy laid artillery fire on the city.
> 17 August 1943 – At Messina: The last three Panzers of the 2nd Battalion under the command of Leutnant Thatenhorst were transported across the straits to the mainland. The campaign in Sicily has ended.
> 18 August 1943: The 2nd Battalion assembled in the Gambati area. For the first time it could be observed just how weak the individual companies were. Most of the losses were caused by illness. The cooler climate in the mountains was noticeably more pleasant. We were astounded that the Panzers could drive so high into the mountains.

From a planned armoured complement of 200 Panzers and assault guns, the 'Hermann Göring' Panzer Division had entered Sicily with an understrength armoured regiment of 43 Panzer IIIs (50-mm anti-tank gun), 3 Panzer IIINs (infantry support tank with short-barrelled 75-mm gun), 32 Panzer IVs and 7 command tanks, as well as 20 Sturmgeschütz IIIs and 9 Sturmgeschütz IVs. They had lost 28 Panzer IIIs, 21 Panzer IVs, 4 command tanks, 4 Sturmgeschütz IIIs and 3 of the howitzer Sturmgeschütz IVs: over half of their original armoured strength and half of all German Panzers and assault guns lost on Sicily. Furthermore, as we have already seen, only a single Tiger of 2nd Company, Heavy Panzer Battalion 504 was evacuated; it was immediately detached from the division and the battalion sent to the Netherlands to re-form before further service in Italy.

For their part, the demoralised Italians had been a secondary consideration for the Wehrmacht-masterminded withdrawal, operating their own four ferry routes. Though the Italian ferries were mostly incapable of carrying heavy equipment, Hube volunteered space as and when available so that in total the Italians recovered 62,182 men, 41 guns and 227 vehicles with the loss of only one of their own motor rafts and the train ferry *Carridi*, which was scuttled when Allied troops entered Messina. Sicily officially fell to the Allies the following day. The evacuation has been described by some as a 'miniature Dunkirk' but in essence it was far more successful as the troops that returned to Calabria did so in excellent fighting order after a highly skilful defensive battle against overwhelming odds. Many of Hube's staff marvelled at the good fortune provided by the Allied inability or unwillingness to seize and hold Messina at the Sicilian campaign's outset, as well as a subsequent lethargy in pursuit of the retreating Germans when the Allies held overwhelming material superiority over their enemy.

Though the battle of Sicily was now over, recriminations continued over the performance of the 'Hermann Göring' Panzer Division and its commander. Although undoubtedly courageous and militarily aggressive by nature, Conrath's and some of his immediate subordinates' deficiencies as armoured division commanders were arguably all too well illustrated in Sicily. The fatal flaw in the Wehrmacht's *Auftragstaktik* principle was exposed by such shortcomings and Kesselring, for one, was displeased, as he later expressed in a post-war report written for the U.S. Army regarding Conrath's entrance to battle in Sicily on the first day of invasion.

> The choice of General Conrath as commander of the Division 'Hermann Göring' was not a happy one. At that time I sharply criticised the following shortcomings:
>
> 1. Belated departure;
>
> 2. Use of roads which were not very suitable for the movement of tanks. It is part of the most primitive preparations to reconnoitre the roads, to repair them so as to be suitable for troop movements, and to instruct the troops properly. Nevertheless, this was not the

> main reason for the delays. These delays were further caused by harassing attacks of the enemy parachute troops which had been dispersed by the wind. These attacks were twice as unpleasant because:
> 3. The march units did not observe proper marching sequence. From the point of view of armoured tactics it is wrong to separate on the march the Panzer elements from their infantry, as was done in this case. Had they observed a proper marching sequence, the Panzergrenadiers could have quickly wiped out the snipers in trees, etc.[14]

Perhaps stung by Kesselring's criticism, Conrath – awarded the Oak Leaves to his Knight's Cross on 21 August for his performance in Sicily – strenuously denied these accusations in a postwar account and shifted blame for the loss of the Tigers elsewhere with allegations that appear unworthy of him. He also somewhat unfairly tarred all of his erstwhile Italian allies with the same brush, including those who had indeed fought better than expected in the first twenty-four hours of the Husky landings.

> No Italian fought during or after the landing; no Italian formation – apart from the four batteries in the Catania area – resisted. Also, the 'Livorno' Division did not fight either. Different reports, which Generalfeldmarschall Kesselring mentions, are wrong . . . The use of the streets was necessary for reasons dictated by the surroundings; the road had been thoroughly explored; it was easy for all vehicles to traverse and the troops had been carefully instructed.
>
> The Division had not considered it appropriate to tear either the Panzer or Grenadier Regiments apart. After a successful push to the coast, the Anti-aircraft and Engineer Battalions would have stood in the front right, the two Grenadier Battalions in front left. The Panzer Regiment would then have been used according to the situation.
>
> The Heer Tiger Company, which was already in the area of the Grenadier Regiment on 5 July, was left with the left (Grenadier Regiment) combat force. The Tigers could have worked well with the grenadiers, despite the olive groves. However, the commander of the Grenadier Regiment did not understand how to position the Tigers correctly and the leader of the Tiger company failed to bring his tanks to bear on his own initiative.[15]

Chapter Seven

Italy, 1943

'The allies we gain by victory will turn against us upon the bare whisper of our defeat.'
Napoleon Bonaparte

The Sicilian climate had taken its own toll on the 'Hermann Göring' Panzer Division, multiple cases of malaria swelling divisional sick rolls, though they never reached epidemic proportions thanks to rigorous enforcement of the consumption of anti-malarial medication. Despite suffering heavy combat casualties during the month of fighting in Sicily, OKW still rated the division highly and once it was ashore in Calabria the attached *Fallschirmjäger* were released, remaining there while Conrath's men withdrew to Santa Maria to begin immediate refitting.

To that point all German corps and divisional headquarters in Italy remained subordinate to the Italian Seventh Army that had been charged with the defence of southern Italy and answered directly to Comando Supremo. Now, aware of the likelihood of Italian defection from the Axis, the Wehrmacht established the Tenth Army on 15 August under Generaloberst Heinrich von Vietinghoff, which officially took control of all German forces in southern Italy seven days later. This new headquarters, however, was immediately plagued by the lack of an organic signals unit and complex messages were frequently laboriously encrypted before broadcast from Army headquarters, offering Allied intelligence invaluable information thanks to broken Enigma codes and adding tedious decryption delays. Furthermore, Vietinghoff possessed no dedicated quartermaster staff capable of handling difficult logistics; fuel supplies available to the mobile units near Salerno were already critically low, with no immediate re-supply in sight.

Hube's XIV Corps was one of two corps-level headquarters subordinate to Vietinghoff, and established itself in the area of Caserta. Hube continued to exercise operational control over the 15th Panzergrenadier Division, 16th Panzer Division (re-formed during March after destruction in Stalingrad) and Panzer Division 'Hermann Göring'. After its losses in Sicily, Conrath still mustered a strong artillery presence but only two Panzergrenadier battalions (one formed of recruits from Utrecht), a single weak Panzer battalion of around thirty serviceable vehicles, the Armoured Engineer Battalion, Armoured Reconnaissance Battalion and the remains of the Sturmgeschütz Battalion.

Expecting fresh Allied landings, and prompted by the doubtful attitude of his Italian allies, Conrath posted signals detachments at Capri, Naples, Cuma and in the Volturno estuary to monitor the coast for any enemy action alongside similar elements from 16th Panzer Division which was the single most powerful local German unit. Though not quite at full strength it mustered 17,000 men – many with no combat experience, however – more than 100 tanks, 36 assault guns and three artillery battalions. Of its four infantry battalions, one was equipped with half-tracks and despite the overall inexperience, morale was high.

On 3 September, British troops crossed the Strait of Messina and landed on the toe of Italy at Reggio Calabria in Operation 'Baytown'. Kesselring declined to oppose the British landings strongly, correctly deducing them to be a diversion and the main Allied effort likely to be directed either at Salerno or, more worryingly, closer to Rome, perhaps at Anzio. Correspondingly, troops of 19th Panzergrenadier and 26th Panzer Divisions mounted a fighting withdrawal before the British advance, demolishing bridges and blocking roads, allowing the inhospitable terrain to take care of slowing British progress.

On the day of the landings Pietro Badoglio's government signed an armistice with the Allies, which became public knowledge five days later. In Berlin OKW had already become increasingly concerned about the fidelity of their Italian allies and contingency plans had been discreetly drawn up in the event of Italian surrender. Originally named Operation 'Alaric' but later renamed 'Achse', they involved the immediate transfer of troops from the Eastern Front and Balkans to Italy, rapid disarming of Italian units and occupation of previously Italian-held positions. Though some fascist Italian troops would remain with the Axis and a soon-to-be rescued Mussolini's puppet government, most either simply 'became neutral' or actively assisted the Allies, and German retaliation was swift. With previously manned defensive installations now abandoned, mainland Italy and Sardinia were occupied as were former Italian possessions in the Balkans and southern France. Though the 'Hermann Göring' Division appears to have played little part in the disarming of locally based Italian troops, it would later be involved in the round-up of men for transport to Germany for labour.

Shortly before the announcement of Italy's surrender, Luftwaffe reconnaissance aircraft reported a mass of ships moving north into the Tyrrhenian Sea, the information reaching Conrath's headquarters on 7 September. The projected course of the enemy shipping led to Naples, and the Gulf of Salerno was considered the most likely landing ground. Though placed on high alert, 'Hermann Göring' troops did not leave their billets until 9 September as the first Allied troops began storming ashore.

Despite the removal of Italian military control, German forces in Italy continued to operate under a divided command structure with Rommel's Army Group B responsible for northern Italy and Kesselring's Oberbefehlshaber Süd handling the south, the demarcation line between the two being Pisa–Arezzo–Ancona. Kesselring requested clarification from Hitler regarding the actual chain of command in Italy and received, on 12 September, the reply that Rommel was not yet authorised to issue directives to Kesselring; these could only be issued by Hitler himself should units under the jurisdiction of Oberbefehlshaber Süd come close to Army Group B territory. This disjointed arrangement was not the only hindrance to a swift response to the Allied landing at Salerno. The two commanders were fundamentally opposed to each other's defensive strategy. Rommel, mindful of the depredations of Allied air power after his North African experiences, believed that southern Italy could not be defended, therefore advocated a line held in the northern Apennine Mountains or possibly even further north. Kesselring, however, believed that, given sufficient strength, he could capitalise on Italy's mountainous terrain, holding a defensive line south of Rome and conducting, if need be, a slow fighting retreat northward. Unfortunately for Kesselring, Hitler initially backed Rommel's stance and there would be no reinforcements for the battle at Salerno other than what Kesselring already controlled. A mistaken belief that the Balkans remained the real target for a further Allied invasion – planted by a skilful misinformation campaign run by Allied intelligence – did little to support the concept of holding southern or even central Italy.

Operation 'Avalanche' involved the Anglo-American U.S. Fifth Army under Lieutenant General Mark W. Clark landing in the Gulf of Salerno, their objective the seizure of the port of Naples and dissection of Italy from the Tyrrhenian to Adriatic Sea, potentially trapping Kesselring's southernmost troops. While 'Avalanche' unfolded, the 1st British Airborne Division landed by sea at Taranto in Operation 'Slapstick', securing the southern arch of the Italian heel, capturing the port and nearby airfields, and acting as a diversion for Salerno. Eventually the two forces were planned to meet at Foggia, capturing its strategically important airbase.

Clark had taken the baffling decision not to bombard the American invasion beaches despite all strategic surprise having obviously been lost to effective Luftwaffe reconnaissance. Though a target list had been compiled totalling 275 locations suitable for preliminary bombardment, Clark denied the request, citing the element of surprise and concern over potential civilian casualties and destruction of non-military structures. The fallacy in Clark's reasoning was soon exposed: the landscape clearly favoured infantry and artillery defence if any was available. Fortunately for Clark, it was only at the last minute that the sparse abandoned Italian strongpoints were occupied by German troops.

The 16th Panzer Division was first on the scene and deployed its strength in four combat teams, each comprising an infantry battalion with supporting Panzers and artillery. Three were positioned three or four kilometres from the coast in preparation for counter-attacks against landing zones, while one was held in division reserve. Nearer the shoreline, eight strongpoints were established between Salerno and Agropoli, each manned by a platoon of infantry supported by heavy machine guns, mortars, anti-tank and anti-aircraft pieces. German troops occupied six abandoned Italian coastal batteries, but there was no continuous defensive system stretching along the Salerno beaches. Suddenly deprived of Italian support and holding an excessive length of coastline, the division was at a disadvantage. Defences at the landing sites were disorganised with no properly laid minefields, scant barbed wire obstacles and only a scattering of trip wires. A few heavy machine guns covered the most likely landing spots with some artillery pieces inland covering the plain, beaches and water approaches.

Vietinghoff judged Salerno to be the primary Allied landing, thereby requiring little reserve to be held against a second effort nearer Rome. He ordered XIV Panzer Corps to make a 'ruthless concentration of all forces at Salerno'; the corps was now commanded by the gifted tactician Generalleutnant Hermann Balck, who was holding the post in Hube's stead, the latter on leave after Sicily's exertions. However, Balck was severely handicapped by a lack of telephone communication with either Tenth Army headquarters or Kesselring, only able to make tenuous and occasional radio contact. He lacked firm intelligence on enemy dispositions and was therefore hesitant to fling everything at the beaches. Instead he ordered 15th Panzergrenadier Division to assemble a regimental *Kampfgruppe* to occupy both sides of the Volturno River and be prepared to take action against any landings at the river mouth or further south in the zone held by 'Hermann Göring' troops. When rumours of a landing at Castellammare reached him, Balck hesitated to alter his dispositions, instead sending the 'Hermann Göring' Armoured Reconnaissance Battalion to Nocera to discern what was happening. Due to this rare tactical misjudgement Generalmajor Rudolf Sieckenius's 16th Panzer Division fought alone during the crucial first hours.

All six Italian coastal batteries were soon silenced by naval gunnery as German forces launched piecemeal local attacks against the landing grounds, the unfavourable terrain for armoured vehicles causing excessive caution on behalf of the inexperienced Panzer crews. Although they held the high ground, all attacks were made downhill in full view of Allied artillery and naval gunfire and by the end of the first day only thirty-five of Sieckenius's Panzers remained operational. Aided by effective spotters on the ground and in the air, the U.S. Navy set a new standard for naval gunfire support, swinging into action on the morning of the landing despite the presence of unswept mines and poor communications with troops ashore. On that day alone, gunnery support ships bombarded at least 132 targets, with 53 per cent accuracy. General der Kavallerie Siegfried Westphal, Kesselring's Chief of Staff, later concluded that, 'The greatest distress suffered by the [German] troops was caused by the fire of ships' guns of heavy calibre, from which they could find no protection in the rocky soil.'

The Armoured Reconnaissance Battalion 'HG' was the first of Conrath's units to be thrown into action, initially operating under Sieckenius's direction until Conrath could establish his front-line headquarters. The 'Hermann Göring' troops moved from Caserta via Nocera, skirting Vesuvius and aiming to reach the coast at Vietri sul Mare. Contact with reconnaissance units of 16th Panzer Division, which had been pushed back from the coast, was made at Nocera and they reported the coastline from Salerno to Vietri occupied by enemy troops and large groups of enemy vessels in the gulf offshore. The main body of the 16th Armoured Reconnaissance Battalion was in action on the northern outskirts of Salerno and as 'Hermann Göring' arrived they were pushed along the road to Vietri to block the Allied advance in preparation for counter-attack. Spearheads of 2nd Battalion, Panzergrenadier Regt. 1 'HG' reached the area north of Cava de Tirreni by the evening and occupied the hillsides to left and right of the road. Their progress was impeded by destruction and casualties caused by naval artillery fire as the British had ignored Clark's example and allowed a 'softening up' bombardment, followed by well-directed naval support throughout the day. The advancing Germans soon encountered British troops of No. 2 Commando who had been charged with taking and holding the Molina Pass on strada statale 18. Panzergrenadiers launched an attack on the mountainous slopes south of Montalbino while parts of the Reconnaissance Battalion moved along the narrow winding road stretching from Pagani to Maiori, where American Rangers had come ashore and raced to occupy the 2,600 foot high Chiunzi Pass supported by the guns of HMS *Ledbury*. The 'Hermann Göring' troops lost the race and were stopped by Rangers in a clash at Campinola; American self-propelled guns were soon positioned with a perfect view over the plain of Naples and German troop concentrations.

Elements of the 1st Fallschirmjäger Division that had been in Naples were immediately sent to Salerno and distributed among the various divisions; 3rd Battalion, Fallschirmjäger Regiment 1 constituting the major part of Kampfgruppe 'Becker', led by Major Karl-Heinz Becker, a pre-war officer in Regiment 'General Göring'. Attached to the *Fallschirmjäger* was 11th Company (StuG), Panzer Regt. 'HG' and Becker's group was placed under Conrath's command, fighting Americans holding the Chiunzi Pass who stubbornly refused to give ground.

The following day 'Hermann Göring' elements launched attacks that reached the southern edge of Cava but stalled in the face of staunch British resistance. The division's Panzers could not be adequately deployed in the defilade of the narrow valley and the Germans instead relied on mixed composition *Kampfgruppen* to battle with their enemy. In the Cava valley heavy fighting broke out as 'HG' troops attempted to establish artillery observation posts by which fire could be directed against the landing zones into which reinforcements were disembarking. However, German strength was weak and British troops infiltrated their patchy front line. Individual 'Hermann Göring' defending companies launched local raids to attempt to establish some form of continuous main battle line, although unified control of operations was extremely difficult amidst the confusion exacerbated by a lack of communications equipment and heavy, well-directed naval gunfire. British defences of Dragonea Hill – held initially by 41 Royal Marine Commando and then No. 2 Commando – survived repeated probing attacks though they underwent a more strenuous assault under cover of early morning mist on Monday 13 September when Kampfgruppe 'Fitz' of the 'HG' Panzer Division attempted to dislodge them with artillery and armoured support. Austrian Knight's Cross holder Hptm. Josef August Fitz, known affectionately by his men as 'Gustl', had only recently transferred from the Heer and was now commanding 1st Battalion, Panzergrenadier Regiment 1 'HG'.[1] Fitz was renowned for his aggressive leadership and almost reckless courage under fire, leading his men from the road below in a spirited assault on Dragonea Hill. Within an hour they had taken the crest and driven the defenders of No. 2 Commando, with Brigadier Laycock's headquarters staff, back as far as Vietri. There they combined with 41 Commando and checked the German advance, holding a re-formed line on the fishing village's northern outskirts as heavy Allied naval and land artillery fire rained down on Fitz's exhausted grenadiers. Covered by smoke laid by an American chemical mortar unit, the commandos then counter-attacked and reclaimed Dragonea Hill within two and a half hours, albeit with heavy casualties.

There was no tangible improvement in the situation faced by the 'Hermann Göring' Panzer Division, though the Allies were unable to force a way past them. On 13 September, LXXVI Panzer Corps that had been fighting its planned retreat before Montgomery's Eight Army launched a major assault on American positions, briefly panicking Clark, who believed he might be forced to abandon the beachhead, before naval gunnery broke up the attacking Germans. That day XIV Corps called a conference with Conrath and his senior officers to discuss a proposed major assault on the town of Salerno itself by the 'Hermann Göring' troops in conjunction with a concerted effort by 16th Panzer Division, 29th Panzergrenadier Division and elements of 15th Panzergrenadier Division against Paestum at the southern edge of the American beachhead. The 'Hermann Göring' *Sturmgeschütze* were detached and given over to Kampfgruppe 'Stroh' of the 15th Panzer-grenadier Division for its fight against the Americans,[2] which was scheduled to commence in three days time. Reinforcements from 3rd Panzergrenadier Division were brought up to the front line of the Salerno–Avellino road, making contact with the enemy and relieving troops needed for the assault, scheduled for the night of 15–16 September.

The 'Hermann Göring' infantry planned a surprise attack during the hours of darkness and without any tell-tale artillery preparation to take the heights south of Sordina – known to the British as 'White House Hill' – and attempt to force their way to the sea, driving a wedge between the

British and American beachheads. At dawn, the division's armour would then attack in a southeasterly direction from San Mango and attempt to reach the sea at Arechi. There, they would reunite with the infantry and make a concerted attack against Salerno itself, driving northwest along the coastal landing ground.

During the afternoon of 15 September German troops forced 5th Hampshires to abandon positions at the western end of the ridge, capturing the hamlet of Piegollele lying south of a dominant conical hill known to British troops as 'The Pimple'. However, intense artillery fire and a strong British counter-attack spearheaded by commandos forced a halt. At that moment two German battalion headquarters were knocked out during close-quarter fighting, the ensuing confusion amongst leaderless troops bringing the assault to a complete standstill. Meanwhile, the Panzer-grenadiers operating in support of the armoured thrust were sent into action prematurely due to the unexpected intervention of a senior German officer and advanced without support, the attack breaking down in the region of Alfani.

One of the *Kampfgruppen* taking part in the attack was that headed by Hauptmann Hans Sandrock. Sandrock was an experienced Panzer commander who had been commissioned into the Wehrmacht's Panzer Regiment 5 in 1936. After taking part in the Polish and Western campaigns he had served with distinction as part of the Afrika Korps until severely wounded in the fighting around El Alamein in November 1942. After being hospitalised in Germany, he was transferred to the Luftwaffe and Conrath's division in July 1943, serving with the 3rd (StuG) Battalion, which he would rise to command in July 1944.

The following report of isolated pockets of close-quarter fighting on 15 September was filed by a Panzergrenadier named Huhn of the anti-tank section, 8th Company, part of Kampfgruppe 'Sandrock'. Huhn had been part of a small troop of one NCO and five men led by Oblt. Hohlbein, ordered by the Kampfgruppe command post to take food to Reconnaissance Troop 'Onken' on Monte Sant Angelo (Height 1130).

> At 2305 hrs the Hohlbein supply team reached the agreed meeting point and shot two white flares shortly afterward. The Onken group at the summit answered with two white flares, which Oblt. Hohlbein observed. We tried to call the Onken group but were unsuccessful. Even after I had descended 300 metres with another

> comrade, we received no answer to our shouting and whistling. Efforts by the rest to find the Onken squad were also unsuccessful. Oberleutnant Hohlbein then ordered defensive positions taken so that the rest of our squad could get some sleep. Oberleutnant Hohlbein woke us at dawn and we climbed to the summit to explore further. We discovered a telephone cable which we followed and around 0700 hrs I saw a freshly dug mound of earth through field glasses. Oberleutnant Hohlbein advised us again to exercise extreme caution and ordered three men to form a firing line and follow him. The rest of the squad stayed behind to cover them. He reached the mound and found the position unoccupied. After further searching we saw about 200 metres to the right a similar mound near a boulder and the figures of two people. We couldn't make out if they were German or British, but in response to our call 'Halt! Who's there?!' we came under rifle and machine-gun fire and recognised several other British soldiers. Oberleutnant Hohlbein ordered the machine-gunner to his side, who was already under enemy fire. I watched the British begin sneaking towards us and fired several shots at them. When I got up a little from my cover, I suddenly felt a pain immediately under my left eye and I virtually couldn't say or hear anything any more. I called Oblt. Hohlbein, but couldn't see or hear anything from him, even though he was very close to me. I decided to leave the summit and head to the main Kampfgruppe area. On the lower slope of the mountain during my return march I saw about eight to ten British soldiers 200 metres in front of me (long trousers, blue shirt, flat helmets) talking loudly. I took cover behind a boulder and let them pass me before continuing on my way. At the first houses I found I renewed my bandage, drank some water, and asked an Italian – because everything kept going black before my eyes – to accompany me to the Kampfgruppe area.[3]

Though the Germans had certainly gained ground, they had failed to split the two Allied forces and held territory that proved highly disadvantageous, vulnerable to intense enemy bombardment. With little by way of reserves, and British troops of Montgomery's Eighth Army slowly approaching from Calabria, Vietinghoff had to issue orders for the German withdrawal to begin at 1700 on 17 September. The 'Hermann Göring' Panzer Division was instructed to hold its hilltop positions south of Sordina as long as possible while the valuable port of Naples was prepared for demolition and Tenth Army established a new stop-gap defensive line along the Volturno River. The division's own withdrawal was handled by sectors as delaying actions were mounted, reminiscent of the Sicilian battle. New defence lines were scouted by advance parties that established light defences into which troops fell back during the hours of darkness, protected by strong rearguards. These latter troops were instructed only to fall back once enemy pressure reached crisis point, theoretically covered during their withdrawal by artillery fire.

The defensive 'Hermann Göring' line swung northwards on the hinge provided by strong positions held in the Molina Pass and assaults by British X Corps met stubborn resistance; Cava was not taken until 25 September by an advance spearheaded by 46th Infantry Division on the Vietri–Nocera road. Conrath's division suffered relatively few casualties in two days of intense fighting, and even after the village fell to the British the new occupiers found that isolated groups of 'Hermann Göring' troops dominated much of the surrounding mountainous country and Cava remained under strong sniper fire. The British advance was slowed and not until nightfall did it reach the village of San Lucia while fighting still raged for the terraced hill of San Martino and the church perched on top.

On 27 September, Conrath's men retreated to a battle line running from Camerelle to Baronissi, newly landed elements of the British 7th Armoured Division launching probing attacks towards Nocera and American Rangers finally pushing inland from the mountain pass to the west. That evening the German units were ordered to fall back to the Volturno Line and, fortunately for the 'Hermann Göring' troops, pursuit – particularly by the Americans – was slow and cautious; narrow winding roads hindering the deployment of Allied artillery which was always used vigorously before each attack. So effective was the German withdrawal that the Allies remained ignorant of it for nearly twelve hours whereupon, rather than apply greater pressure at that crucial moment, Clark lingered at Salerno. This breathing space allowed German defences to be strengthened and engineers to block or demolish roadways and bridges. Ironically, one bridge still in use by the retreating Germans was destroyed by a lightning strike during a violent storm and was hurriedly rebuilt before being demolished once more. The delay 'caused some excitement', as Schmalz recollected, though the slow Allied advance failed to capitalise on the Germans' brief discomfiture.

Despite having lost the battle, the Germans had forced their enemies to pay a costly price for victory. The Allies lost approximately 12,560 men killed, while the Germans lost between 3,500 and 4,000. Furthermore, the successful defensive retreat convinced Kesselring to push OKW to rethink its initial plan to withdraw to the Apennines and hold the Allies there. Instead, Kesselring advocated holding central Italy along the general axis of Garigliano–Cassino–Maiell massif–Sangro River. This would become the 'Winter Line' and, with Hitler revising his earlier decision, OKW endorsed the request and appointed Kesselring as Oberbefehlshaber Südwest as of 21 November, moving Rommel's Army Group B command to France. Kesselring's new post superseded Oberbefehlshaber Süd and also served as commanding element of the newly established Army Group C, controlling the Tenth and Fourteenth Armies.

Vietinghoff's Tenth Army War Diary summarised the fighting at Salerno that had contributed to Kesselring's enthusiasm for his ongoing defensive strategy:

> Though victory was denied, the Tenth Army and its divisions had registered a defensive success under difficult conditions, with almost no air support and under fire of a strong fleet and a powerful air force. The enemy had hoped that German resistance would quickly collapse . . . Instead he was forced to fight a tough opponent for every yard of territory and use up valuable troops in a minor theatre of war.

Schmalz later elaborated on the German performance:

> The defenders [against coastal landing] cannot expect success unless they have strongly manned and fortified positions or strong land and air forces can brought up to counter-attack. The defence could not fulfil these preliminary conditions either on Sicily or at Salerno. On Sicily the Italians holding the coast fled from their positions the moment the landing was made and they had only just deserted their allies when the Salerno landing took place. The only replacements along the whole coastal sector were German signals detachments, whilst Salerno itself was held by one German company with six field guns. German counter-measures could not be put into effect until troops had been brought up to the enemy beachhead. Owing to the urgent nature of the situation, these movements had to be made by day and were exposed to enemy air operations . . . The 'Hermann Göring' Division, for example, could only use two narrow mountain roads to make an immediate counter attack, and these were covered

> by the enemy air force and naval artillery. High ground had to be taken from the enemy before German artillery observation positions could be established. The enemy used the time thus lost to make further landings and bring up reinforcements. Fire from heavy naval artillery was particularly troublesome . . . A battery of 17-cm guns which was at our disposal on Sicily was used with good effect against British warships. There was no such artillery at Salerno. The enemy air force did not have a decisive influence on the ground fighting in the mountainous terrain around Salerno, but had a marked effect on supply routes.[4]

The 'Hermann Göring' Panzer Division – rear echelon elements were forced finally to evacuate the barracks at Santa Maria – offered strong resistance across the head of the Sorrento Peninsula which marked the right wing and pivot point of the defending German line, the boundary between XIV Panzer Corps and its eastern neighbour LXXVI Panzer Corps running between Avellino and Avezzano.[5] The main battle line then crossed the country to the Ofanto River which drained into the Adriatic Sea. Sharp but brief local counter-attacks were made to dissuade close pursuit and delay the Allied advance long enough to allow German engineers to demolish Naples' port district and destroy roads and railways. Indeed, the pursuing Allied forces of British 7th Armoured Division appeared wary of the 'Hermann Göring' rearguard and were scathingly referred to by Conrath as obviously either unable or unwilling to press home an attack against his men. Kesselring hoped that the destruction in and around Naples would prevent the Allies from quickly driving deep into the plains of Campania and it was entirely in line with instructions from the Führer and OKW that the withdrawal to the north was to be made in a scorched-earth manner. Feldmarschall Keitel at OKW had specified that:

> The commanders in charge, of all ranks, are expected to conduct the evacuation and destruction with the utmost energy, giving no quarter and showing no regard, in view of the unparalleled nature of the betrayal and the German troops lost as a result of that betrayal. Inflicting damage on the enemy must outweigh all human considerations.[6]

It appears that only elements of 2nd Battalion, Artillery Regiment 'HG' were actually in Naples at the time of the wholesale destruction of parts of the city, though divisional engineers were also provided and specific instructions passed through divisional engineering officer Maj. Artur Jacobi. He was directed to destroy bridges, stations, water, gas and electricity works, factories and mills as well as mine roads, houses and the entrances to villages. Defensive lines were constantly updated, as designated by corps command, including the minimum time each line was to be held; the Volturno positions were the most rigid before the heavier defences of the 'Winter Line', planned not to be evacuated before 15 October. Concurrently, 'Hermann Göring' elements were involved in the forced removal of able-bodied men to Germany for labour. A curiously worded report by the Chief of Staff of XIV Panzer Corps on 23 September, recorded that the division reported '3,000 slaves' captured by 23 September.[7] Within the division records, a 'gripping action' (*Greifaktion*) against eligible Italians was carried out; approximately '7,000 prisoners' tallied by the same date.[8]

Naples and the coastal area around Vesuvius were already occupied by two battalions of the 1st Fallschirmjäger Division, who were ordered to contact the 'Hermann Göring' Division, to whom they would be temporarily attached. This marked the first of the main rearguard positions held by 'Hermann Göring' troops on the night of 28–29 September on Vesuvius, the western coastal slopes of the volcano being held by attached Fallschirmjäger at Torre del Greco. The following day both units fell back to the Regi Lagni on either side of Acerra, a 300-year-old set of man-made canals designed for flood prevention and land reclamation covering a vast area in the provinces of Caserta, Avellino, Benevento and the Metropolitan City of Naples.

Following the Italian armistice, Naples, which had suffered greatly under heavy Allied bombing, descended into a state of near anarchy after both Italian generals charged with military responsibility for the city fled in civilian clothes. A decree was instead published handing liability for Naples to the Germans, banning all civilian gatherings, and providing military forces full authorisation to open fire on openly disobedient civilians. Armed rebellion against occupying German troops began flaring sporadically within the city, with heavy handed responses involving summary executions and deportations under the control of the newly appointed senior Wehrmacht officer in Naples, Oberst Walter Schöll. Finally, growing insurrection ignited what has become known as 'The Four Days of Naples', a semi-organised armed revolt that began on 27 September and prevented complete German demolition of Naples's infrastructure, though the strategically important port was comprehensively damaged and the culturally priceless Library of Naples was partially burnt.

Very few men of the 'Hermann Göring' Panzer Division appear to have been directly involved in fighting against the Neapolitan insurrectionists, though they had already suffered their first casualties to Italian partisans when a grenade attack from a rooftop in Nola wounded Oblt. Erich Drotbohm, commander of 8th Company, Panzergrenadier Regt. 1 'HG'. Drotbohm's lower left leg was subsequently amputated, the young officer being moved to the Utrecht training units shortly afterwards and promoted to *Hauptmann* in the New Year. On 1 October, as the last German troops left Naples with Allied forces immediately entering the city behind them, guns of 2nd Battalion, Panzer Artillery Regiment 'HG' conducted a punitive bombardment, opening fire on the city from the Capodimonte heights. This is thought to have killed at least ninety-three civilians. This appears to have been the first major skirmish causing significant innocent civilian deaths in which the 'Hermann Göring' Panzer Division was involved.

The German retreat to the Volturno Line was a carefully timed multi-stage withdrawal, enabled by an increasingly obvious Allied unwillingness to launch aggressive pursuit. Following the Italian surrender, harassment by small, largely disorganised, partisan bands had begun to plague the retreating Germans. Indeed, it would not be too far a stretch to suggest that the general perception of the German troops towards their former allies was one of contempt, bordering on a potentially dangerous antipathy for a nation that they believed – regardless of whether this was justified or not – had repeatedly performed poorly during the years of fighting and then deserted them at their most perilous hour.

During the first day of October, German troops of an unspecified unit carried out a major raid on the town of Acerra northeast of Naples to collect able-bodied men for labour, rounding up and transporting away approximately 200 men. During the night that followed younger residents of the town began erecting barricades to prevent German transit through the town itself, potentially interfering with the orderly withdrawal. The situation escalated rapidly with daylight when a small number of armed civilians opened rifle fire on passing German vehicles, hitting at least one man of the 'Hermann Göring' rearguard, men and vehicles predominantly of 1st Battalion, Panzer Regiment 'HG' and 1st Battalion, Panzergrenadier Regt. 2 'HG'. In response, a reported seven Panzers and accompanying Panzergrenadiers approached the town, smashing through the makeshift barricades and opening fire indiscriminately. By eyewitness Italian reckoning, approximately 50 men under the leadership of 23-year-old Lt. Gerhard Tschierschwitz (2nd Company, 1st Panzer Battalion 'HG') killed a total of 84 people including women and children. The 'Hermann Göring' war diary records on that date: 'Clash with Italian gangs in Acerra. The location is completely destroyed and the inhabitants annihilated.' Among the personal accounts of the massacre are the words of the widow of Michele Terracciano:

> On 2 October 1943, during the revolt of Acerra, I was hidden with my husband in our home located in Corso V.E. III 65. Five armed Germans appeared, broke through the door and devastated the house, taking my husband while they forced me to leave. Subsequently, I returning to find my home burned and my husband murdered on the side of the street.

While many such tragic scenes were repeated throughout the town, a number of those killed were also undoubtedly in the process of erecting barricades in front of the advancing Panzers, some carrying weapons though many remained unarmed. Over the same period nine recognised partisans were killed in the general area, two while attempting to set fire to Luftwaffe fuel stocks at a small airfield, another killed by shell splinters while attempting to remove German demolition charges from a bridge.

Such barbarity as in Acerra reflects German hostility towards the Italian populace, which had undoubtedly increased since the armistice, and their propensity for retaliation against civilians who might or might not have given aid to – or even been numbered among – partisan bands. Even considering the vicious nature of anti-partisan warfare, waged against an enemy frequently difficult to identify, this was a clear war crime as the leash was slipped off aggressive, young and angry soldiers. Ultimately, many people innocent of any transgression against the Germans were undoubtedly killed indiscriminately.

The Sturmgeschütz Battalion was also instrumental to the 'Hermann Göring' rear-guard, attached to Abteilung 'Rossmann' and on 2 October deployed near Cardito alongside infantry of 9th and 10th Fallschirmjäger Companies and a group of pioneers led by Feldwebel Kuter. Hauptmann Lübke of the Armoured Reconnaissance Battalion exercised local control, dividing the available troops into two small groups. Two *Sturmgeschütze* commanded by Wachtmeister Kurt Börner were positioned as a forward observation post at the junction of the Cardito–Afragola–Casavia road; Stabsfeldwebel Schulze-Oswald's platoon was deployed with two *Sturmgeschütze* at the southern entrance to Cardito; Lt. Wallhäusser's platoon held the ground 2 km southeast of the town. At 1745, enemy tanks were reported from Afragola and within fifteen minutes Oblt. Jekosch and Lt. Adolf Röbig of 11th Company both mounted a BMW motorcycle sidecar combination driven by Gefrieter Rabitsch to establish contact with Börner who was in danger of becoming cut off by the Allied advance. Nearing the two *Sturmgeschütze*, the heavily laden motorcycle came under fire and Röbig was shot in the head and died instantly. Jekosch and Rabitsch were both wounded by the flurry of gunfire from a concealed Sherman of the British 23rd Armoured Brigade. Alarmed by the proximity of the enemy, Börner opted to break out of potential encirclement and head to Cardito, engaging and hitting two Sherman tanks during the escape, destroying two trucks and scattering enemy infantry abandoning the burning vehicles. Schulze-Oswald also withdrew, after destroying the Sherman that had killed Röbig, assuming command of the *Sturmgeschütze* positioned at the southern exit of Cardito as company commander Jekosch was taken to an aid station.

Track and engine noise of enemy armour was heard between 1900 and 2330, the defenders estimating at least 25–30 enemy tanks advancing into their area. Two reconnaissance patrols despatched by Schulze-Oswald on the request of Hptm. Lübke failed to find the enemy location, as did two further patrols led by Schulze-Oswald himself. At 2000, Lübke transmitted a brief message to the men under his command signalling a general withdrawal: 'Password Vesuvius. Sturmgeschütze will remain until the last infantrymen have pulled out of position.'

Two tanks of 1st Battalion, Panzer Regt. 'HG' passed near Schulze-Oswald's Platoon, moving swiftly to take up their own defensive positions while 10th Fallschirmjäger Company immediately retired without reporting its withdrawal. Dangerously unsupported, Schulze-Oswald refused to remain in his allocated position without infantry and Oblt. Berger of the 9th Fallschirmjäger Company took over infantry protection for the assault guns, as heavy rain began to fall during the pitch-black night.

The following day the first enemy tank was sighted by Karl-Heinz Wallhäusser's group of three *Sturmgeschütze* and a single howitzer armed *Sturmhaubitz* at 1000. After a brief exchange of fire the enemy tank was destroyed with only Wachtmeister Börner lightly wounded in the head by a shell splinter. Within a quarter of an hour an enemy armoured car was also sighted and destroyed, but heavy artillery fire began to fall around the stationary assault guns. As a full-scale British attack developed, Lt. Wallhäusser received orders from Lübke to lead his platoon of three *Sturmgeschütze* against enemy armour advancing from Cardito to Caivano, engaging a column of Sherman tanks at 150 metres as they approached the main bend in the road. His after-action report was filed four days later:

> After strong enemy infantry and tank forces broke through our positions near Cardito at 1600 hrs, I met the leader of the Armoured Reconnaissance Battalion, Hauptmann Lübke. He gave the order to launch a counter-attack with my available *Sturmgeschütze*. I manned two assault guns, whose crew had been relieved after being wounded, with the crew of a *Sturmhaubitz* whose vehicle had a jammed gun breach. I decided to lead the counter-attack with my own and the other two *Sturmgeschütze* and asked for infantry support. Hauptmann Lübke answered me: 'Find all the available people along the way and use them to stop the attack.'
>
> I rolled slowly forward through the village with my gun, securing both sides as ordered and reached the southern exit of Caivano. On the way I had accumulated about thirty infantry, under command of a *Leutnant* from 3rd Company. To him I explained that I had received an order from Hptm. Lübke that all available men were to accompany my gun and form a defensive line at the southern village boundary. We arrived together and the infantry took position. The enemy opened a heavy mortar bombardment. After ten minutes, the 3rd Company *Leutnant* informed me that Hptm. Lübke had ordered a withdrawal to the village centre. I retreated for some 200 m to the ordered point.
>
> A short time later, Lübke joined us and ordered us to proceed with the counter-attack, he leading in front. As we approached an S-shaped bend in the road to Cardito at the southern edge of Caivano, our view ahead was completely blocked by a two-metre high stone wall. I informed Lübke that any further advance was impossible, since our line of fire was totally obstructed. I stopped 10 metres before the second curve and ordered the infantry forward to scout the road and they soon reported several Sherman tanks stationary ahead. Hauptmann Lübke gave orders to immediately cross a field in a right-hand direction and open fire on the enemy

> tanks. I argued that this position was very unfavourable. I said to Hptm. Lübke that this was an impossible position, as we were less than 200 metres from the enemy and would show them our flank as we moved to a suitable firing position. Hauptmann Lübke replied, 'Move up, there is no alternative, it's either you or the Shermans.'
>
> I proceeded to the ordered position, but due to the muddy ground my vehicle moved very slowly. It took some 5 minutes to move into the right position. Although the engines of the enemy tanks were not running, their guns tracked our advance exactly and were directly aimed at us. Despite this I fired my first round. A second later, I received the first hit and our engine stalled. I tried to fire a smoke canister but received a second hit which struck the left slope above the driver's visor. The impact lifted off the roof plate over my gunner and hit and damaged the cupola, then slowly fell into the fighting compartment and struck my shoulder and hand. I immediately shouted 'Out!' In the blink of an eye a third shot hit us and I was catapulted out by the shockwave.
>
> When I regained consciousness, I was lying in a roadside ditch some 40 metres from my vehicle. I became aware of two infantry-men dressing my wounds. How I came to be in the ditch I don't remember. A short time later a second *Sturmgeschütz* moved up, but also received a direct hit, though still able to move under its own power. I was able to return with this assault gun.[9]

One *Unteroffizier* of 'Panzer Abteilung Rossmann' was killed, another posted missing after this combat, which left five men wounded as well as Wallhäusser who was taken to Teano field hospital with an injured hand and burns. One vehicle was destroyed, another seriously damaged after suffering two direct hits and the third able to be repaired within two weeks.

The StuG Battalion commander endorsed Wallhäusser's report, with the following reprimand to Lübke:

> To Panzer Division 'Hermann Göring'.
> Attached to this letter is an after-action report of 11th (StuG) Company, Panzer Regt. 'HG' describing the total loss of a *Sturmhaubitze*, the temporary failure of a further *Sturmgeschütz* and considerable loss of life.

> All losses were caused by the completely inappropriate commitment of the *Sturmgeschütze*, ordered by Hauptmann Lübke. It is absolutely impossible to commit *Sturmgeschütze* in such combat situations – especially in darkness – without determined infantry support.
>
> A StuG cannot defend itself at night. At 1645 hrs, the order was given to move into an absolutely inappropriate position to combat the enemy tanks. The leader of 11th Battery rejected the order due to the onset of darkness, but this was overruled and he continued the deployment.
>
> The battalion considers that by ignoring the legitimate objections of a battery leader, we regard the actions of this officer, who lacked experience and any knowledge of the tactical commitment of Sturmgeschütz, as intolerable. With his exclamation 'you or the Shermans', the loss of men and equipment was recklessly accepted. If the *Sturmgeschütze* had been deployed correctly, we could have inflicted serious damage on the enemy without any loss of personnel. The battalion hereby issues a reprimand to Hauptmann Lübke for his poor judgement.

The positions flanking Acerra were evacuated on 3 October, bridge and road demolition preventing a close pursuit. The final halt before the river was made on Marcianise Hill to allow troops to cross a temporary bridge southwest of Caiazzo, completed by 4 October as the last German troops traversed the Volturno, the *Sturmgeschütze* among the last to reach the northern bank.

Reconnaissance units of British 7th Armoured Division entered a shattered Naples on 1 October, reaching the Volturno Line held by the Germans four days later after negotiating the myriad mines and obstacles sown by the Germans along their route of retreat. This interim defensive line stretched from Termoli on the eastern Adriatic coast, along the Biferno River through the Apennine Mountains to the Volturno River that drained into the Tyrrhenian Sea only 10 km north of Naples. When this was inevitably breached, the Germans would be forced to fall back to the 'Barbara Line' at the Trigno River, south of the stronger 'Winter Line' – in fact the primary 'Gustav Line', augmented by two subsidiary separate defensive lines ('Bernhardt' and 'Hitler'), under construction by workers of the Organisation Todt and centred on the formidable obstacle of Monte

Cassino.[10] Kesselring had already begun preparations to withdraw to the 'Barbara Line' after troops of No. 3 Commando, No. 40 (Royal Marine) Commando, and elements of the 2nd Special Service Brigade landed at Termoli on the Adriatic coast in the rear of the 'Volturno' Line. After they were swiftly reinforced by two brigades of the 78th Infantry Division, Operation 'Devon', launched on 3 October, was designed to turn the left flank of the German line.

Kesselring quickly sent elements of 16th Panzer Division to counter-attack. Frantic Allied engineers erected bridging that allowed armoured reinforcements to counter the 16th Panzer Division's thrust, which had made initial headway toward Termoli. The Volturno Line was therefore scheduled to be abandoned, but not yet as time still needed to be bought for German construction on the Winter Line. Once the river was crossed in strength and had lost its strategic importance, the withdrawal would take place as planned.

It is difficult to discern the exact strength of an extremely fractured 'Hermann Göring' Panzer Division by mid-October, though a G-2 Intelligence Summary was issued by the headquarters of the U.S. 82nd Airborne Division, compiled by information provided by higher command and local prisoner of war interrogations.

> ***Strength of German units: 'Hermann Göring' Division***
>
> Reconnaissance unit: Only three companies, the 1st, 3rd and 5th now exist, the 2nd, 4th and 6th companies having been dissolved. The total strength of the Recon unit was estimated at 21 Officers and 503 enlisted men on 20 September and at 300 Officers and enlisted men on 29 September. Status of the three remaining companies is estimated as follows:
>
> 1st Co. Armored Car Company. Not more than nine armored cars remaining.
>
> 3rd Co. A rifle company.
>
> 5th Co. Heavy Company, composed of infantry-gun platoon, heavy MG platoon and heavy mortar platoon.
>
> HG Tank Regiment: Has not been identified since Sicily. Believed to have 40 tanks and an assault gun battalion of 30 SP 75-mm guns on a Mark III chassis.
>
> HG PGR I: Only HQ Co of 250 men and 2nd battalion of this Panzergrenadier Regiment seem to still exist. Probable strength:

5th Co – 100 Officers and enlisted men; 6th Co – 60 Officers and enlisted men; 7th Co – very weak, strength not known; 8th Co – 100 Officers and enlisted men; 10th Co – 100 Officers and enlisted men.

HG PGR II: Only one or possibly two battalions exist. 1st Battalion near full stength.

115 PGR: Attached to 'HG' Div from 15th Div. Only 1st and 3rd Battalions exist. 1st Battalion averages approximately 150 officers and enlisted men per company. 3rd Battalion is weaker than 1st.

HG Artillery Regiment: Has approximately ten 4-gun batteries, of which two are 88-mm gun batteries.

HG Engineer Battalion: probably still has four companies and is believed to be almost up to full strength.[11]

'Hermann Göring' occupied the coastal plain of vineyards, olive groves, and carefully tilled fields stretching from Grazzanise to the Triflisco ridgeline and as far east as Caiazzo at the foot of the first mountains; the division was flanked to the west and east by the 15th and 3rd Panzergrenadier Divisions respectively. The boundary between the right wing of Kampfgruppe 'Corvin' (1,930 men of 2nd Battalion, Panzergrenadier Regt. 1 'HG', 1st Battalion, Panzergrenadier Regt. 2 'HG' and Lt. Wibbelt's 11th (StuG) Company, all under the command of Oberst Lothar von Corvin-Wiebersbitzki, commander of Panzergrenadier Regt. 1 'HG') and the left wing of 15th Panzergrenadier's extra third regiment, Kampfgruppe 'Haase' (previously 'Maucke', of 1st and 2nd Battalions, Panzergrenadier Regt. 115, and again temporarily attached to 'Hermann Göring' control), was marked by the last house of the southern exit from the town of Bellona, occupied by 'Hermann Göring' troops. To the east, Corvin's troops bordered 1st Battalion, Panzergrenadier Regt. 2 'HG' at the road intersection 1,500 metres south of the town of Villa. The main Allied thrust was expected to be made on both sides of the road that led from Capua, via Cassino, to Rome and it was here – and at Cassino – that engineers and Organisation Todt workers concentrated their construction of defensive positions.

Though a natural obstacle, the Volturno was not an ideal defensive location, hence the position's planned temporary nature. Though the wide river was in a state of semi-flood as the autumn rains had begun, its bed had been cut away in places by erosion, resulting in dead ground for some of the German guns on the southern bank, providing cover for the enemy. Furthermore, the southern bank was frequently higher than the northern, putting defenders at a distinct observational and artillery range disadvantage, and forcing many positions to be created well back from the riverbank. Hills east of Route 6 (Via Capua) and north of the river also impeded artillery observation. Though the mountainous area north of the river favoured defence, no positions had been prepared and they offered no firm defensive barrier. Conrath issued instructions to his division that, due to the imperfections of the main battle line, one third of all heavy weapons were to be deployed in close proximity to the front line for direct fire support.

After delays caused by heavy rain, not until the night of 12 October did Clark order the Fifth Army to cross the Volturno; the British 7th Armoured and 56th Infantry Divisions and U.S. 3rd Infantry Division advancing against the 'Hermann Göring' troops that were deployed in *Kampfgruppen* formations organised as befitted their topographical location.

Allied reconnaissance patrols had established that, though swiftly moving and cold, the river barrier was frequently no more than chest high. These patrols also recorded many strong positions on the far bank that possessed clear fields of fire; not a single patrol returned to Allied lines unscathed by machine-gun and rifle fire. The U.S. Army subsequently published its own assessment of the German defence of the Volturno Line in its periodical *Tactical and Technical Trends*:

> Contact with advanced Allied elements was maintained by patrols after the enemy's main body had crossed the river. The function was observation rather than delay and they disengaged as the Allies approached. These patrols withdrew over the railway bridges at Cancello, Capua and Triflisco which were destroyed last. Removal of the railway tracks had enabled these bridges to be used by motor transport after the road bridges had been destroyed. It is presumed that the decision to demolish rail bridges last was on account of their greater strength and smaller vulnerability to bombing attacks. The enemy succeeded in timing the destruction of the three railway bridges so that his patrols were able to cross but before the bridges could be seized by the Allies . . .
>
> From his positions on the flood levée and from observation points in buildings and trees the enemy was able to observe very closely all Allied movement and our own patrols on the river line and on

> the lateral road were at all times subjected to heavy small-arms and mortar fire. Any major movement south of the river drew heavy fire not only from the river bank but also from the commanding enemy artillery positions. Unobserved assembly within five or six miles of the river was almost impossible owing to the open nature of the country.
>
> East of Capua the hilly and wooded nature of the terrain dictated a different form of defense and made the holding of a continuous river-line impracticable.
>
> Observation of Allied movements was only possible to a limited extent and was obtained from commanding features overlooking the southern bank of the river. No attempt was made to cover the whole river-line. An estimate had been made of the most probable crossing points and the approaches and exits to these were mined, covered by antitank and artillery fire and supported by mixed counterattack forces. The enemy's defensive scheme consisted of a series of battle group positions organized in depth in order to counter and seal off penetration in the event crossings were effected.[12]

Facing the 'Hermann Göring' troops, the 7th Armoured Division advanced at Grazzanise, assault troops reaching the river just after dark on the night of 12 October. Spearhead troops strung a cable across the river but were forced back by counter-attacks, though the cable remained intact. A second attempt made by pulling boats across using the cable was defeated by air-burst artillery fire and not until a third attempt at crossing the river was a small foothold established on the northern bank in the deep river bend. This the Germans could not dislodge and from here the 7th Armoured Division would exploit its gain during 14 October by advancing 1,000 yards to the north.

On their right flank, the 56th Infantry Division attempted to cross at Capua but was comprehensively beaten back. A secondary attack at Triflisco managed to cross the Volturno and form a small enclave until forced to evacuate by counter-attacking Panzergrenadiers.

However, to left and right, the Allies had made significant gains. The first major breach was made by U.S. 3rd Infantry Division, the troops successfully fording the Volturno River in the darkness at a hairpin bend south of the imposing Monte Majulo. Accurate German artillery and small-arms fire took a considerable toll on the attackers, the light of dawn bringing five

American tank destroyers of the 601st Tank Destroyer Battalion into the fray. Dug-in in the valley below Monte San Leucio, they added their deadly high-velocity shells. At 0815 hrs *Sturmgeschütze* of 11th Company under the command of Wachtmeister Kurt Börner and Stabsfeldwebel Schulze-Oswald were ordered to reconnoitre a potential path for the company to advance towards American infantry sighted crossing the river. After only one and half kilometres, they clashed with enemy infantry climbing toward the mountainous Height 502 to the right of their path. Fresh instructions to break the enemy troops' line of advance and establish contact with other elements of 3rd Battalion were received at 0845 hrs, though they were blocked one kilometre further by a freshly laid American mine barrier. As StuG crewmen dismounted to clear a path, they came under violent small-arms and mortar fire from nearby, Schulze-Ostwald's vehicle suffering track damage and the engine of Börner's StuG being disabled. His vehicle immobilised and under fire, Börner was killed. Unteroffizier Lohse struggled back on foot to the company command post to request another *Sturmgeschütz* be despatched to assist. Oberfeldwebel Kreft immediately took his StuG to the scene, coming under fire as he negotiated the narrow road. The crew struggled through and recovered four severely and two lightly wounded men as American troops were driven off, though Börner's body could not be retrieved.

The Germans did not immediately retreat and not until 1830 hrs did Unteroffizier Lohse, who had returned to the stranded *Sturmgeschütz*, report to the company commander the possibility of recovering the assault guns under cover of darkness. An infantry group and 10th Battery *Sturmgeschütze* were sent to assist and the damaged vehicles successfully taken to Liberi.

After offering brief resistance, 'Hermann Göring' armour withdrew to the north, using the cover of sunken dirt roads that led into the mountains. Behind them, elements of the British 56th Division were directed to follow the American path and reinforce their success by holding the Americans' western flank.

To the west, facing 15th Panzergrenadier Division, British troops of 46th Infantry Division, with naval artillery support, penetrated the defensive line, assisted by two squadrons of Sherman tanks amphibiously landed north of the river mouth. By the end of that first day, despite a local counter-attack retaking the area west of Cancello, the 139th Brigade had managed to reach the Agnena Canal three miles north of the Volturno River. By 14 October, the bridgehead was secured, minefields were being systematically cleared and counter-attacks successfully repulsed. At 1630 hrs that day Conrath's Chief of Staff issued Divisional Order Number 60/43:

> The enemy has, in his left divisional area, forced a breakthrough to the west and taken the highlands on both sides of Peak 292 north of Triflisco. Counter-attacks from the north by elements of Battalion 'Oehme' [Hptm. Horst Oehme of the divisional staff] still in progress. There is a risk of the enemy outflanking the right wing of the 15th Panzergrenadier Division at the Volturno mouth.
>
> Panzer Division 'HG' triggered the keyword 'Oktoberweise' at 1410 hrs this afternoon and, beginning at 2000 hrs, will leave strong combat outposts in the previous main battle line at position Z1.[13]

'Oktoberweise' signified the beginning of a series of counter-attacks against Allied bridgeheads over the Volturno. 'Hermann Göring' Panzer-grenadiers were ordered to form a solid defensive line from the junction with 1st Battalion, Panzergrenadier Regt. 115 at Bellona via Point 367 (Monte Grande) to the northeast where they intersected with the Panzer Artillery Bataillon 'HG' situated to prevent any enemy approach from east of Monte Grande. Hauptmann Georg Ilius controlled a battalion-strength *Kampfgruppe* that included six *Sturmgeschütze*, ordered to cooperate with the armoured company attached to Kampfgruppe 'Oehme'. Ilius was positioned in the centre of the 'Hermann Göring' front line to provide immediate infantry support and prevent enemy infantry or armoured breakthroughs while anti-aircraft *Kampfgruppen* east of the Capua–Rome road were redeployed to their rear as a final backstop position.

The Panzer Regiment, of approximately 1,400 men, was divided into two main components: the first comprising the Regimental Staff with signals units and a single light platoon of five Panzer IIs for security of the regimental command post; the second, two battalions, each of staff, signals and light armoured reconnaissance detachments, one medium Panzer company (Panzer IV), three light Panzer Companies (Panzer III) and associated workshops and supply columns.

Heavy fighting followed over the next few days and a number of reports generated by the 'Hermann Göring' Panzer Division for forwarding to radio and press outlets have survived in the divisional records, all of them related to events on 16 October. The first was written by the company commander, Oblt. Bellinger, of 9th (StuG) Company, Panzer Regt. 'HG':

> The 9th Sturmgeschütz Company of Panzer Division 'Hermann Göring' was deployed in the Capua area to cover the approach roads. The *Sturmgeschütze* had been in position for many hours without a single Englishman showing up, until the afternoon hours when the tank alarm was suddenly given. Finally, facing the armoured enemy of the Grenadiers, the crews prepared for battle. Tank noise was soon heard. When the four tanks came closer, a German group went into the attack. Splitting the bushes behind which it had been standing, the *Sturmgeschütz* drove forward, but enemy gunfire tried to put a curtain of steel and iron in front of it, blocking its firing position. However, one shell after the other soon left the gun barrel. The first tank burned with the second shot. The second was hit and disabled, so that the crew escaped. The third Sherman was able to retreat with two hits, while the fourth had already tried to get away after the first shot. Angry about the unsuccessful attack, English artillery dropped hundreds of shells into the square where the *Sturmgeschütze* had been standing for about an hour without, however, doing any damage.[14]

A second transcript, dated 20 October, was written by Hptm. Heinz Freygang of the divisional staff, forwarded to XIV Corps.

> For report to the press and radio at home about combat operations on the Italian front, short reports of exemplary conduct of individual soldiers or units were requested by Oberkommando Panzerarmee 10. Militarily correct and accurate combat reports of this kind best come from the troops themselves. This is the only way to ensure that the troops' achievements are recognised correctly and quickly.
>
> Examples of such short reports:
>
> 1. In the area before Capua, ten heavy Sherman-type English tanks were sighted by an advanced outpost of a 'Hermann Göring' *Kampfgruppe*. This single anti-tank gun destroyed three of the attacking tanks, the third of them at a range of only 30 metres, the others breaking off their attack. The gun leader of the successful anti-tank gun thus destroyed his fifteenth tank.
>
> 2. With a shock troop in the mountains near Caiazza, a small group of 'Hermann Göring' Panzergrenadiers managed to overpower two well-developed American fighting positions by surprise attack.

> After a short, hard, man-to-man fight, four Americans, three machine guns and two mortars were captured, and the strongpoints blown up. Our assault team returned to their own lines with the captured weapons and prisoners.[15]

Allied troops on both flanks of the 'Hermann Göring' position continued to push forward, particularly those of the American VI Corps, and after a stubborn fighting retreat with wholesale demolition to slow the enemy advance, permission was granted on 16 October for the XIV Panzer Corps to withdraw its entire front; one day after the planned timetable to hold the Volturno Line. The retreat to the Bernhardt Line was to be made with the most economical use of troops, as little by way of reinforcement could be expected. The aim was to inflict heavy losses on the enemy, while not risking large infantry engagements. Therefore, it became warfare dominated by artillery and engineering units; infantry were used sparingly in isolated strongpoints before making a 'leap-frogging' retreat to allow the other two services to complete their missions. The terrain favoured this tactical use of troops with mountainous country providing good artillery observation, cut through by narrow roads, bridges, watercourses and ridgelines. Fog, rain and mud helped the German defenders as they mined and demolished roads and bridges; in Venafro alone – captured by the U.S. 157th Infantry Regiment on 7 November – American engineers removed over 2,000 pounds of explosives from mined buildings.

At the beginning of November, the Sturmgeschütz Battalion was battling for the heights west of Presenzan; 9th Company supported by Panzergrenadiers of Kampfgruppe 'Reimnitz' fighting American troops and taking one officer and twelve men prisoner as well as capturing a quantity of weapons that included two anti-tank guns and ammunition. By 3 November they were fighting for the main road between Rome and Naples, Oblt. Bellinger leading two *Sturmgeschütze* into a bold attack that delayed the enemy in time for Hptm. Ilius to bring infantry reinforcements into action, though the German main battle line was still pushed 2 km backwards. A single *Unteroffizier* StuG commander was wounded in the action and successfully evacuated to a field hospital.

With the strong autumn rains, XIV Corps, now under the command of Generalleutnant von Senger und Etterlin, withdrew its mobile divisions as quickly as possible and replaced them with infantry units more suitable to static defense. The majority of the 'Hermann Göring' units were therefore taken out of the line to go into Army reserve near the Lepini mountains in the Frosinone province southeast of Rome. The remains of 2nd Battalion, Panzergrenadier Regt. 1 'HG' then travelled to Utrecht and the divisional training grounds, beginning their journey on 18 November via Rome, Innsbruck and Cologne. There the veteran troops would provide the nucleus for a re-established Panzergrenadier Regt. 1 'HG' under the command of Oberstleutnant Kluge. As other elements left the front, the division's flak and Panzer artillery regiments were taken from Conrath for temporary attachment to other formations holding the line, continuing to provide invaluable support for the heavy fighting that raged into the new year.

During this period there occurred what remains a controversial episode within the divisional history. As the fighting moved north from Salerno, the German authorities' somewhat ironically titled Kunstschutz (Art Protection Commission) had undertaken to move priceless works of art or relics of great cultural significance from areas in which they were threatened with damage or destruction to safer locations. Two 'Hermann Göring' Panzer Division officers – Oberstleutnant Julius Schlegel, commander of the Motor Transport Repair Battalion (Kfz. Instandsetzungs Abteilung) and medical officer Hauptmann Dr Maximilian Becker – arrived separately at Monte Cassino abbey on 14 October 1943. Each man's motivations appear to have been completely different. While Schlegel is often hailed as the instigator of what appears an altruistic act, Becker later countered the accepted course of events with his own recollections made public post-war. Becker understood fully that the impending battle for the 'Gustav' Line would hinge on Cassino, the abbey dominating the future battlefield and likely to appear centre stage amid any protracted struggle. An art enthusiast, Becker fully appreciated the cultural value of material stored inside the abbey which had been declared a sacred site and intellectual centre from its establishment in AD 529. Within its walls were a library of 70,000 volumes, 1,200 precious manuscripts (including of the works of Cicero, Horace, Virgil, Ovid and Seneca), 80,000 documents, objects of worship in precious metal, the Treasure of San Gennaro, the relics of San Benedetto da Norcia, of Santa Scolastica, of Santa Legno and precious paintings, from Naples's Museum of Capodimonte that had been brought to Monte Cassino for security reasons. Among these were works by Leonardo da Vinci, Tintoretto, Domenico Ghirlandaio, Pieter Bruegel the Elder, Titian and Raphael.

According to Becker's recollection, he developed a plan whereby the treasures would be evacuated from the abbey and moved to safekeeping. In an account quoted by author Robert M. Edsel, Becker then conferred with a divisional transport and supply officer to obtain trucks for such an ambitious plan. He names this officer as Obstlt. Siegfried Jacobi – probably actually Obstlt. Artur Jacobi, although Jacobi did not become Verbindungsoffizier of the division until 1 May 1944. During October 1943 Jacobi, recently promoted from *Major*, is understood to have been commander of the Wach Regiment 'HG'. Regardless of this apparent name discrepancy, Becker was alarmed by Jacobi's cooperation hinging on the proviso that 'a couple of paintings' should be kept by the German authorities.

During the following day, Becker arrived for his first meeting with the 78-year-old Abbot Gregorio Diamare to find Schlegel already present and negotiating the removal of the abbey's treasures. Schlegel was a 48-year-old Austrian who had owned a transport firm before the outbreak of war and subsequently commanded Luftwaffe vehicle maintenance units, transferring to the 'Hermann Göring' Panzer Division during May.

Diamare was reportedly initially sceptical of the motivations of the German officers, their Reichsmarschall commander-in-chief being well known as a 'collector' of artworks from countries conquered by Germany. Questions regarding the destination of the transported items were initially answered with sketchy assurances that they would be taken 'north'. By the next day, however, Diamare had acquiesced to the arrangement. Monks would accompany trucks carrying items belonging to the abbey to Villa Colle-Ferreto near Spoleto, which had been requisitioned by the 'Hermann Göring' Panzer Division as a supply depot while negotiations were conducted with the Vatican for reception of the treasures. To safeguard the material during transit, wood and nails were removed from a Cassino bottling factory and 'Hermann Göring' troops began the creation of suitable crates. Each evening, trucks left the abbey and made their way to Spoleto. Minor transport problems were encountered as Italian officials pushed for daylight haulage in trucks marked by the Red Cross, which Kesselring denied. The decision was made to move by night, Italian officials expressing concern to Baron Bernhard von Tieschowitz, director of the Italian branch of the Kunstschutz, regarding the state of material held at Spoleto after having been denied inspection access, but they were assured that everything was in good condition. Tieschowitz certified that all contents were correctly stored and accounted for in Spoleto, and at this stage it is unlikely if he was aware of any potential wrongdoing. The U.S. Army later classified Tieschowitz as having 'opposed vigorously organised confiscation proceedings in France and Italy and was consistently conscientious in his efforts to protect the art treasures of the occupied countries from destruction and looting'.[16]

After Becker and Schlegel received official endorsement from Conrath to continue the removal, the 'Hermann Göring' Panzer Division again provided transport from Spoleto to two Benedictine monasteries in Rome – the Papal Basilica of Saint Paul Outside the Walls, owned by the Vatican (though not within the Vatican City State) and Sant'Anselmo all'Aventino on the Aventine Hill.

Tieschowitz met Italian officials in Rome on 22 November to announce that the 'Hermann Göring' trucks would begin transferring the abbey's stored contents to Rome within a week, though he would no longer be there to oversee the operation. Instead, Major Professor Hans Gerhard Evers was to take his position and would supervise after Tieschowitz was transferred to France on 29 November. Evers met Michelle De Tomasso, officer responsible for the protection of valuable Italian art, on 6 December to discuss the impending arrival of Cassino's treasures, refusing further requests for Italian officials to inspect the stored items. Following the evacuation of the material from the abbey, Allied propaganda made great mileage of the 'theft' of 187 'cases' of material, though there were in fact over 600 crates of material transported; the discrepancy no doubt being a distinction between crates containing fine art and the total number, which included the abbey's extensive library. The fact that the 'Hermann Göring' unit – considered with justification to be 'politically powerful and somewhat independent' by Allied intelligence – had taken it upon itself to remove the treasure and refused inspectors permission to assess it with the answer that the 'division alone was responsible for the safety of the objects', led to an obvious conclusion that their intention was to take their spoils to Berlin.

Only two officers of the German Archaeological Institute in Rome were permitted to examine the items in Spoleto, while Professor Evers negotiated their return. Eventually, after the explanation of fuel and transport shortages was given to justify the extended delay in moving the items from Spoleto, Evers was able to inform De Tomasso that an initial shipment would reach the Italian capital in December, arriving at Castel Sant'Angelo on the 8th for delivery to Vatican authorities with due ceremony. The remainder would finally be transported to Rome in early January.

> Evers thinks [the transfer to Rome] should be done with a certain solemnity because it has profound political significance as result of

> radio reports. The German command thinks it necessary to place all these things in safety so as to show how solicitous they are to save manuscripts and works of art from the dangers of battle. Therefore the trucks with the precious material will enter Castel Sant'Angelo with solemnity at noon next Wednesday after the convoy has stopped at the Colosseum and been shown to members of the press and to those of the Administration who are interested. There may be a movie taken for propaganda purposes. I tell Evers that the Administration will have no difficulty in giving public recognition to the German military for the partial evacuation of the material at Monte Cassino, but that the evacuation should include as soon as possible the works of art belonging to the state which are stored there too.[17]

Despite difficulty procuring fuel for this non-military transport, Evers promised forty 'Hermann Göring' trucks would arrive on 3 January with approximately 600 cases from Monte Cassino. With a window of less than four hours in which the vehicles were required to begin their return to divisional duties, Italian workmen were to be on hand for the unloading after a brief ceremonial presentation by Schlegel to Generalleutnant Reiner Stahel, German military commander of Rome, in the Piazza Venezia. The cases would then be kept in the Palazzo Venezia rather than Castel Sant'Angelo, awaiting later transfer to the Vatican.

On 4 January the trucks arrived as planned at the Palazzo Venezia, a final cargo load of 772 separately crated items being safely received and verified by Italian officials. However, they were dismayed to learn that according to 'Hermann Göring' officers, two trucks carrying some of the Neapolitan treasures had been delayed by enemy machine-gun fire, the Luftwaffe officers advising Italian guards to remain in position and await their arrival. Not until the following day were the Italian guards told to leave the site, assured that all trucks had arrived; the crates were moved to the safety of the Vatican. After the fall of Rome, U.S. Army officials inspected the stored cases in the presence of Italian authorities and discovered that several had been repackaged with items from their manifest missing, while other cases were simply not there.

In the meantime, Becker's subsequent enquiries regarding the 'lost' trucks, according to his own account, resulted in his presentation of a memorandum from Göring's chief adjutant, Obstlt. Bernhardt von Brauchitsch, that the sixteen crates from the two trucks that had been sent to Spoleto would comprise a gift to Göring in time for his January birthday celebrations. Evers also later claimed under American interrogation that he first discovered the cases were missing from a British radio broadcast following the Allied occupation of Rome. He explained that he had no authority to question the orders of the 'Hermann Göring' Division and his enquiries established simply that the missing crates were temporarily at Kesselring's headquarters at Monte Sorace, but that he had been bluntly told that it was 'no business of his'.[18]

Ultimately, seventeen paintings, four cases of large bronze statues, two cases of gold and silver objects from Pompeii and Herculaneum and a suit of armour that had belonged by Emperor Charles V were presented to Göring at his Carinhall residence at Christmas 1943; two other 'Hermann Göring' officers – Obstlt. Ulrich Bobrowski and Maj. Günther Rahls – were later implicated by U.S. Army investigations in the removal of the items to Germany. Göring placed the items on temporary display at Carinhall before being instructed by Hitler to move them immediately to the safety of the bunker complex at Kurfürst, Luftwaffe headquarters outside Berlin. The Führer intended them to become displays at his planned Führermuseum in Linz, Austria, following Germany's ultimate military triumph. Instead, after the war's end, they were found amidst other looted material in an Austrian salt mine by American troops; their return to Italy was supervised by Lt. Col. Ernest T. DeWald.

Schlegel's account of the removal of the abbey's treasures is notably different, of course, and post-war the two men conducted their arguments about whose initiative had saved the relics from destruction via the press in the public domain. Regardless of the initial motivations of the 'Hermann Göring' officers, Schlegel and his men received communion at a Mass celebrated by Diamare on 1 November 1943, the Oberstleutnant then being presented with a parchment manuscript of thanks for saving the monks and possessions of the holy monastery of Monte Cassino.[19]

Away from this contentious issue, the machinery of reinforcement continued and the division received a constant stream of replacements. Among them was eighteen-year-old Hermann Lohmann.

> In 1942 I had registered as a volunteer for the Panzer Division 'Hermann Göring' . . . my professional goal being the Höhere Forstdienst [Higher Forestry Service] for which service in an elite

Wehrmacht unit was a prerequisite. For members of the division of Reichsforstmeister Göring, the chances of acceptance in the highly coveted forestry profession were particularly favourable. In 1942 I had to take an intelligence and courage test in Hamburg-Rissen to join the 'Hermann Göring' from which only those who passed with at least 'good' were accepted. My acceptance certificate for the 'Hermann Göring' Division also prevented me from being forced while still in the Reich Labour Service by a recruiting commission of the Waffen-SS to go 'voluntarily' to the Waffen-SS, like many of my comrades . . . I was drafted in Hamburg after my time in the Labour Service in 1943. From there, the recruit transport went by rail directly to Holland. On 26 August 1943, I arrived in Utrecht in civilian clothes . . . Together with three sons of forestry officers, I requested *Fallschirmjäger* when I was asked which type of unit I would like to serve in. How stupid and blind you are when you are a teenager. Luckily for me, there was no *Fallschirmjäger* unit in the 'Hermann Göring' Division in Utrecht. I was assigned z.b.V.: 'for special use'. I was happy because I was a little wiser when I was assigned to the artillery, and I then served in the Parachute Panzer Artillery Regiment 'Hermann Göring' until the end of the war.

The basic training (standing, walking and learning to walk) took place in the Hoyel barracks in Utrecht, while still in civilian clothes . . . On the parade ground the Band was playing 'Alte Kameraden' and I thought: 'Well, it has started well, it can only get better.' The basic training was hard. The physical performance demanded of us brought us to the limit of physical exhaustion. We often had to pull ourselves up on the banisters in the barracks to get to our dormitories on the upper floors. We were systematically toughened up and made fit for warfare at the front.

On 19 September 1943, we were transferred to the Krumhout barracks, and training began on the leFH 18, the 105-mm light field howitzer. In between, marches took place in the vicinity of Utrecht for the purpose of infantry exercises and also at the Hilversum military training area.

We young soldiers had no problems with the Dutch population. On the contrary, we received help. I can remember that we once had a field exercise in an orchard where apples lay fallen under the trees. We politely asked the fruit growers whether we could get the apples

> and they said 'of course'. It was strictly forbidden for Wehrmacht members, even abroad, to take anything away from the civilian population. Each soldier had in his paybook on the penultimate cover page the 10 commandments for the warfare of the German soldier. The 7th commandment included: 'The civilian population is inviolable. The soldier must not plunder or deliberately destroy.' I do not know whether these instructions were always followed, but I personally experienced no attacks by my comrades. I am also not aware of attacks by other units.[20]

Lohmann was attached to the Observation Battery (Beobachtungsbatterie) after arriving in Italy in mid-November.

We were temporarily accommodated behind the front in a Catholic chapel for one or two days, in order to then be assigned to the individual front line units as replacements . . . The tasks of the Beobachtungsbatterie 'HG' were:

> 1.) The location of enemy artillery positions through either flash spotting or sound measurement. Using a light and sound measurement method, the firing flash or firing bang of enemy guns was observed and measured from four or five measuring points distributed along the front. By analysis of results, the location of the enemy artillery was determined on the map based on the different directions of observation or the arrival of the sound at the individual sound measuring points at different times.
> 2.) Provision of weather data for the artillery and flak departments of the division to eliminate ballistic influences on the shellfire. Weather data was essential for developing exact firing orders for the artillery to be able to target enemy gun emplacements in a precise and effective manner. In particular, wind direction and wind speed on the ground and at higher altitudes were important because of the deflection of the projectiles in the air. The measurement was carried out using red weather balloons filled with hydrogen, the buoyancy of which had previously been balanced by means of attached weights. With the help of a theodolite (an instrument for the precise measurement of horizontal angles), the red balloon and the measurement of the wind direction and wind speed could be determined. The observations, including the measured temperatures,

> were summarised in a weather report, the so-called 'Barbara report', and transmitted by telephone to the ArKo [Artilleriekommando, artillery command], which created the fire orders.
> 3.) Production and procurement of maps for the staff and troops. For this purpose, a printing and surveying team was available, which had to explore and print maps of the respective front areas for the division.[21]

Lohmann and men of his observation unit shared a semi-detached house with an Italian family at St Apollinare, Cassino. After weeks of intense Allied bombardments, Christmas and New Year were relatively quiet in Cassino and he remained there until 31 January when he and his comrades were abruptly moved to Albano-Genzano near Castel Gandolfo, the Pope's summer residence. By this time a fresh crisis had overtaken the Wehrmacht in Italy as the Allies attempted to outflank the Gustav Line by landing at Anzio.

Chapter Eight

Anzio

'We are so outnumbered there's only one thing to do. We must attack.' ***Admiral Andrew Cunningham***

Kesselring was fully aware that, with the requirements of the Eastern Front draining the Wehrmacht dry, he possessed barely enough troops to hold the Winter Line and strengthen rear area forces as well. During November 1943 the situation regarding Italian partisans had already deteriorated to the point that numerous men travelling individually or in small groups through Italy had gone missing, leading Kesselring to issue instructions that road travel was only to be undertaken by day and with arms at the ready. Couriers carrying important documents were to travel in convoy only, and German intelligence would constantly re-evaluate the guerrilla situation in areas traversed by courier routes. The horrors of anti-partisan warfare would soon come to Italy, with the 'Hermann Göring' troops periodically in its vanguard.

With Allied forces stalled against the Winter Line, the likelihood of an amphibious landing in the German rear increased with each passing week. In Berlin OKW formulated arrangements at the end of 1943 by which adjacent theatres would despatch reinforcements to Italy in the event of such a landing. Kesselring himself also prepared five contingency plans for such an event: Case 'Richard' for a landing near Rome; Case 'Ludwig' near Livorno; Case 'Gustav' near Genoa; Case 'Victor' for the Rimini–Venice area; and Case 'Ida' against Istria. His inclination favoured 'Case Richard' as the most likely scenario and he spent considerable time creating a viable mobile reserve to counter such a landing, while also drafting movement orders for elements of the Tenth and Fourteenth Armies, XI. Fliegerkorps and the Waffen-SS.

Kesselring had learned the lessons of Sicily and Salerno and understood that any landing had to be defeated on the beachhead within twenty-four hours before overwhelming Allied material strength could be brought ashore. Italian coastal fortifications were sparse and there remained no time to create new strongpoints. With few troops, and those stretched between several potential landing areas, Kesselring allocated 29th and 90th Panzergrenadier Divisions of I. Fallschirmjägerkorps to the defence of the Rome area in the event of Case 'Richard', Conrath's resting 'Hermann Göring' troops forming a mobile reserve located mid-way between the Winter Line and Italian capital.

The respite for some units was to be brief. The three companies of the Sturmgeschütz Battalion had taken part in the defensive battle culminating at the Garigliano River while 1st and 2nd Battalions of Panzergrenadier Regiment 2 'HG' had been thrown into the line during December after British troops pushed the 15th Panzergrenadier Division from its Bernhardt Line positions in the Camino peaks south of the Mignano Gap, the pass leading to the Liri River valley through which trailed the road from Caserta to Rome. Operation 'Raincoat' had been launched by Lieutenant General Omar N. Bradley's U.S. II Corps and Lieutenant-General R. L. McCreery's British X Corps, being sardonically well named as the battlefield was deluged by Italian winter downpours in the course of weeks of grinding mountain warfare. During the savage fighting for Monte La Remetanea (Hill 907), which was assaulted by commandos of the American/Canadian 1st Special Service Force – colourfully known thanks to Hollywood's post-war output as 'The Devil's Brigade' – Leutnant Walter Knaf, platoon leader of 8th Company, Panzergrenadier Regiment 2 'HG' was killed by intense supporting shellfire, buried in a mass grave after the Germans were forced to retreat and posthumously awarded the Knight's Cross on 5 April 1944. Nonetheless, the stubborn defence of the 'Hermann Göring' troops helped check the Allied advance at the Garigliano River and 'Raincoat' ended on 10 December.

The New Year in Italy dawned grey and wet. Mud clogged the battlefields, arguably of greater hindrance to the attacking Allies than German defenders, though both sides struggled to maintain effective logistic support for operations. Meanwhile exposure and frostbite began to claim as many Allied casualties as German defensive fire.

At the beginning of 1944, OKW notified Kesselring that he would be forced to relinquish several divisions for redeployment to the Western Front in anticipation of an Allied spring invasion as not only were troops in short supply on the Atlantic Wall, but few of those available were battle-tested. Among the formations designated for transfer was the 'Hermann Göring'

Panzer Division, scheduled to pass to the command of Oberbefehlshaber West from 20 January and be based near Rennes in Army reserve. Kesselring requested on 9 January that, in view of the situation on the ground facing XIV Corps, the division not be transported to France before the relieving 71st Infantry Division had arrived and been established within the corps area.

At that point a minor change was also afoot with the 'Hermann Göring' Panzer Division. In Divisional Order 64/44, dated 3 January 1944, Conrath commanded the wearing of the division's famous '*weisse Spiegel*' (white epaulettes) to end. The distinctive bright white insignia had hindered effective camouflage of troops in action and provided a handy aiming point for Allied soldiers. Henceforth, small metal wings denoting rank could be worn directly on a plain collar. Silver tresses for non-commissioned officers were also forbidden on field service tunics, and administrative elements of each battalion were instructed instead to source field-grey braid. Furthermore, for more obscure reasons, the wearing of grey-green caps with blue clothing was also prohibited.

The Allied drive towards the main defences of the Gustav Line continued into January, and II Corps attacked the commanding Monte Porchia position just south of Highway 6 at dawn on 6 January. The American 6th Armored Infantry attacked the high ground held by 5th Company, 134th Grenadier Regiment, taking heavy casualties but battering their way steadily forwards. Three 'Hermann Göring' Panzergrenadier companies launched a strong counter-attack at 2210 hrs from the northwest after being rushed to the front from reserve positions six miles west of Cassino. Despite these units hooking around the rear of American troops on Porchia and causing considerable confusion amongst their opponents, the hill fell to the Americans at the end of the following day after several vigorous counter-attacks were fended off. By 8 January, the Germans had lost their best positions for defending the approaches to the Liri valley and the Gustav Line.

Only Monte Trocchio remained before Cassino, a series of rough and barren hills near Le Pastinelle that again dominated Highway 6. German troops of 71st Panzergrenadier Division, with some supporting 'Hermann Göring' elements, holding Cervaro to the east had been pushed out by 11 January and 1st Battalion, Panzergrenadier Regt. 2 'HG' rushed to the front that night along the main road from Cassino and stumbled headlong into strong forces of the U.S. 168th Infantry Division, which unleashed a terrifying artillery bombardment, driving the grenadiers back. The 'Hermann

Göring' men converted many stone houses on a hilltop known as Point 189 into pillboxes and clung to their positions for three days before falling back to the Gustav Line proper and the formidable bastion of Monte Cassino.

To the west, the British X Corps had crossed the Garigliano River that marked the border between Campagna and Lazio on 18 January. The river was between 50 and 100 metres wide and swollen with seasonably bad winter rains, running strong and fast. After a fierce preparatory artillery bombardment, 46th Division troops found themselves unable to land due to the current and high banks in their sector, while the 56th (London) and 5th Divisions downriver forced a small bridgehead that by dawn the following day included the small town of San Lorenzo in the approaches to Castelforte. The relatively weak Wehrmacht 94th Infantry Division held this latter town, their only immediately available reserve was 7th Company of 'Hermann Göring' Panzers of Maj. Hahm's 2nd Battalion and 94th Division's replacement battalion. Castelforte lay northeast of the daunting obstacle of Monte Damiano, connected to the valley below by two nearly parallel roads that intersected a third trailing Damiano's lower edge at San Lorenzo. On its eastern flank, 15th Panzergrenadier Division with the attached 'Hermann Göring' Kampfgruppe 'Corvin' held the front stretching from the river east of Castelforte to the railway south of Cassino town. As 7th Company ran its Panzers immediately into action, veteran company commander Oblt. Alfred Dreher – who had been awarded the German Cross in Gold on 17 October – was killed in action.[1] Adolf Scheckenbach, still in convalescence after his wounds and malaria suffered in Sicily, later remembered the loss of his company commander:

> During the time I had been away wounded and training recruits, my Panzer regiment and the Division had opposed the Allied landings at Salerno and Nettuno [and] Oberleutnant Dreher was killed. I found out that his widow had written a very nice letter to the Company and told us that he had thought of us as his children. He was a good man. I was sorry he had been killed.[2]

Hauptmann Sandrock's 3rd (StuG) Battalion had also been moved in stages from its reserve position at Arce to the region of Castelforte, delayed by the virtual destruction of Pontecorvo by bombers aiming for the valuable bridge over the Liri River. They engaged the enemy near San Lorenzo on 21 January but were unable to dislodge the Allied bridgehead, and were forced back to Castelforte that night. Elements of Kampfgruppe 'Corvin',

'Hermann Göring' Armoured Reconnaissance and Engineer Battalions, were also thrown into the battle, bolstered by reinforcements from 29th and 90th Panzergrenadier Divisions and now controlled by the recently arrived I. Fallschirmkorps (General der Fallschirmtruppe Alfred Schlemm).[3] The counter-attack experienced some measure of success, hemming in the Allied bridgehead north of Minturo, partially retaking the high ground, and pushing the enemy back on both sides of Castelforte. However, after several days of fighting alongside Heer grenadiers and *Sturmgeschütze*, the 'Hermann Göring' Sturmgeschütz Battalion disengaged and retreated north on 26 January, still under enemy artillery fire as a fresh crisis had developed to the rear of the Gustav Line.

The attack across the Garigliano had been part of an attempt to draw German reserve formations from the north into action on the Gustav Line, and in this it had succeeded – Kesselring's swift reinforcement using mobile reserves was designed to crush the Garigliano crossings. A second hastily concocted assault across the Gari River before Monte Cassino resulted in disastrous failure and extreme losses for the U.S. 36th Infantry Division, decimated during the attempted crossing by well entrenched defenders of 15th Panzergrenadier Division. The pressure against the Gustav Line was thus only partially successful, though Kesselring's belief that no further amphibious landing would be made until an effective breakout from the Garigliano River was wrong.

The forces of Operation 'Shingle' had sailed overnight from Naples and began landing troops at 0200 hrs on 22 January around the ports of Anzio and Nettuno. They had arrived completely undetected by German intelligence or the severely diminished Luftwaffe reconnaissance capability after a preceding six-day air offensive against German communication lines and airfields. However, the attack was not without its immediate limitations.

Due to the gathering of landing craft in Britain preparatory to a cross-Channel invasion, the 'Shingle' force was relatively small; initial landings being made by just two infantry divisions – British 1st and U.S. 3rd – coordinated by the latter's senior officer Major General Lucian K. Truscott. More crucially perhaps, it was beset by confusion as to its actual goal. 'Shingle' was of British design, dreamt up by Churchill to enable the capture of Rome, only thirty miles distant, but commanded by U.S. Major General John P. Lucas who had little confidence in the plan and believed its purpose to be diversion of defensive strength from the Gustav Line, rather than its own independent invasion front.

Six miles north of the small port town of Anzio, British troops stormed ashore as part of Peter Force supported by light cruisers, destroyers and anti-aircraft/fighter-direction ships. An American Ranger Group was put ashore directly at Anzio's port from a single transport ship, while American infantry landed east of Nettuno as 'X-Ray' Force, supported by light cruisers, destroyers, destroyer escorts, minesweepers, subchasers and smaller units. Although heavy losses had been anticipated, the landings were virtually unopposed. The only German units in the entire Rome area were either battle-fatigued and refitting or undergoing training and of a strength suitable for little more than coastal observation; one nine-mile stretch of coastline was occupied only by a single company. Within the Rome–Albanese Mountain area there was only a single Panzer company, one Italian assault-gun company, one light anti-aircraft battery, units of the 4th Paratroop Division in training and 'Hermann Göring' replacement units. The 'Hermann Göring' units were the newly created divisional reserve unit under the command of Hptm. Fuchs and the Combat School (Divisionkampfschule) under the command of Oblt. Hans-Georg Lehmann. Neither they nor the *Fallschirmjäger* were completely up to strength nor trained.

By the end of Shingle's first day 36,000 Anglo-American troops were ashore having suffered thirteen casualties through accidents. Both Anzio's port and Nettuno were captured without difficulty and the 1st Division penetrated two miles inland on the first day, the 3rd reaching three miles from the beach; advance guards of the American 30th Infantry Regiment and 3rd Reconnaissance Troop seized all bridges over the Mussolini Canal, a feature vital to defence of the beachhead's right flank. Italian resistance leaders even offered to guide Allied troops through the Alban Hills towards Rome, but their proposal was refused.

Though the landing's exact time and place surprised Kesselring and his staff, he had long considered such an attempted outflanking manoeuvre likely, despite Abwehr assurances to the contrary. His reaction was made with customary speed and determination, using the tried and tested method of forming *Kampfgruppen* from available troops. Both his reaction time and the calibre of troops still available for deployment had been completely underestimated by Allied intelligence analysts. Kesselring learned of the landings three hours after the first Allied troops had set foot on the shoreline, and orders were immediately issued under the pre-prepared Case 'Richard'.

Guided by this plan, Army Group C alerted the 4th Paratroop Division and replacement units of the Panzer Division 'Hermann Göring' to block all roads leading to Rome and all roads leading from the south to the Albanese Mountains. General der Gebirgstruppe Hans Schlemmer, Commandant of Rome, was immediately placed at the head of an improvised staff to exercise tactical command over these forces until inbound General der Fallschirmtruppe Schlemm arrived with his I. Fallschirmkorps headquarters to take charge, beneath the umbrella of Generaloberst Eberhard von Mackensen's Fourteenth Army which became officially responsible for the Cicina sector at 1800 hrs on 25 January.

Case 'Richard' initiated a widespread re-allocation and re-distribution of troops within Italy, including troops transferred from France and the Balkans. However, because neither Oberbefehlshaber West or Südost could provide as many troops as desired for 'Richard' due to transfer of forces to the Russian Front, the newly raised 92nd Infantry Division was immediately activated in Italy.

Forces were despatched from the Replacement Army in Germany, including artillery and rocket demonstration units and 508. (schwere) Panzer Bataillon, equipped with Tiger tanks. At 0710 hrs on the first day of the landings Kesselring ordered Fourteenth Army to transfer all forces provided for in Case 'Richard' to the Anzio region, an hour and twenty minutes later signalling Tenth Army to move the headquarters of I. Fallschirmkorps and all combat troops that could be spared to the beachhead as quickly as possible; these included the 71st Infantry Division that had been en route to Istria and the bulk of 3rd Panzergrenadier Division, which had just withdrawn to the vicinity of Rome. The first elements of these divisions began arriving opposite the Anzio beachhead on the morning of 23 January. Despite continued heavy Allied attacks against Cassino, among the troops withdrawn from the Gustav Line was a reinforced regimental *Kampfgruppe* of the 'Hermann Göring' Panzer Division which included the Staff, Armoured Reconnaissance Battalion, one artillery battalion and an anti-aircraft battalion. When it rapidly became clear that the Anzio landing was a major operation, Army Group C suspended counter-attacks at the Garigliano River to free additional troops and a further three 'Hermann Göring' Panzergrenadier battalions and one artillery battalion were immediately transferred to the area of Conrath's headquarters near Cisterna.

The mobile forces disengaging from the Allied bridgehead over the Garigliano were able to do so without significant problem; Castelforte remained in German hands and the front line was relatively stable as local attacks continued against British troops holding Minturo. Two artillery batteries, one heavy Panzerjäger battalion, one battery of heavy artillery, two battalions of 1st Fallschirmjäger Division and the Armoured Reconnaissance Battalion of 26th Panzer Division were also hurriedly moved north and during the evening of 23 January, Conrath himself arrived near Anzio by Kubelwagen.

Schlemm divided his front into three sectors: Western, held by the still-forming 4th Fallschirmjäger Division, assigned to coastal defence between the Tiber and the Allied beachhead; Central, commanded by 3rd Panzergrenadier Division but comprising one regiment of 4th Fallschirmjäger, one of 3rd Panzergrenadier and one of 15th Panzergrenadier Division, straddling the strategically important Anzio–Albano road; and the Eastern sector under the command of the 'Hermann Göring' Panzer Division, comprising the bulk of the division plus two battalions of 1st Fallschirmjäger Division and the Armoured Reconnaissance Battalion of 29th Panzergrenadier Division. This sector also held the coastline as far as Terracina.

As troops of myriad formations streamed into the area, they were swiftly organised into the relevant *Kampfgruppen* as the Germans built their strength, the normal chains of command being suspended for expediency. Despite the emergency, strong reserves were still assembled after transferring from northern Italy and held to counter a feared second landing in the region of Civitavecchia, 100 kilometres from Anzio to the northwest of Rome. Nonetheless, as Lucas appeared content to build up strength within his beachhead rather than expand the territory he held, within three days the Allies ashore faced a solid defensive line.

As early as the first night following the Allied landing, 'Hermann Göring' troops rushed into position, attacked and retook the bridges held by American soldiers over the Mussolini Canal. They in turn came under counter-attack by the 30th Infantry Regiment with armoured support which, in sharp fighting, drove the Germans back across the bridges along the western canal branch. A 'Hermann Göring' assault with three Panzers and a half-track of the Engineer Battalion – Kampfgruppe 'Rossmann' – regained control over the bridge on the Cisterna road north of Conca, until, exhausted and low on ammunition, they were forced to withdraw once more by fresh American troops of the 504th Parachute Infantry, losing one man killed and twelve wounded.

While the depleted Luftwaffe mounted a strenuous effort against Allied ships off the Anzio beachhead over the days immediately following the landing, Allied troops showed little aggressive action. Despite Rome being virtually defenceless at the time of the landings, they had thus far achieved little due to Allied caution rather than German defence. Lucas, instead of striking aggressively toward Rome, chose to consolidate his beachhead, allowing the energetic Kesselring time to reinforce scant defences. Though it is doubtful that Lucas could have taken and held Rome with the forces available to him, he most certainly could have taken a larger area to hold and consolidate, thereby posing a greater threat to the rear of the Gustav Line.

The Anzio front swiftly bogged down. Some two miles beyond the Mussolini Canal, men of the U.S. 30th Infantry Regiment were fought to a standstill by a company of 'Hermann Göring' troops entrenched around the road junction halfway to Ponte Rotto. To their right the U.S. 15th Infantry Regiment gained 2 km up the Conca–Cisterna road before being stopped by machine guns concealed within farmhouses. An attempt to bring tanks and tank destroyers of the 751st Tank and 601st Tank Destroyer Battalions into action to destroy these strongpoints was foiled by 'Hermann Göring' troops who filtered along a sunken stream-bed and menaced the American infantry's flank, compelling them to withdraw. On the Conca–Cisterna road four Sherman tanks were destroyed by *Sturmgeschütze* of 3rd Battalion, blunting the American spearhead's advance.

Attempting to unbalance the 'Hermann Göring' troops, American paratroopers of the 504th Parachute Infantry launched a diversionary attack across the main canal toward Littoria, advancing behind a curtain of heavy artillery and naval gunfire. The attackers captured the villages of Borgo Sabotino, Borgo Piave, and Sessano on the east side of the canal until Company D was cut off beyond Borgo Piave by a surprise counter-attack of five 'Hermann Göring' tanks and eight *Flakwagen* which caused heavy casualties among the lightly armed paratroopers. The Americans went to ground and withdrew under cover of darkness, covered by strong defensive combat patrols.

A 'Hermann Göring' strength return to XIV Corps of 20 January, gives an accurate picture of the overall state of Conrath's somewhat depleted and disjointed combat division.

Assigned strength:	7,190 men
Effective strength:	3,380 men

Armour and weapons

Light field howitzers:	12
Medium field howitzers:	15

Self-propelled medium field howizers:	6
100-mm guns:	11
75-mm guns on tank chassis:	1
20-mm guns on tank chassis:	8
75-mm *Sturmgeschütze*:	24
105-mm *Sturmhaubitze*:	3
Panzer IV:	27
Panzer III:	35
Medium anti-tank guns:	24
Self-propelled anti-tank guns:	3
88-mm anti-aircraft guns:	36
37-mm anti-aircraft guns:	9
20-mm anti-aircraft guns:	88
Four-barrelled 20-mm anti-aircraft guns:	23

Order of battle and strength of units

Panzergrenadier Regiment 'Corvin'	1,930 men	I./Panzergrenadier Regt. 2 'HG' and II./Panzergrenadier Regt. 1 'HG'
Panzer Aufklärungs Abteilung	660 men	
Panzer Pioneer Bataillon	790 men[4]	

Not until 25 January did Allied troops take Aprilia to the north, while only making small advances towards Cisterna. American troops attacked the latter in battalion strength at 1545 hrs but were repelled by 'Hermann Göring' troops. Less than two hours later the American attack was resumed, though during the night small Allied penetrations were sealed off and destroyed. To Conrath's west, a combined American armoured and infantry attack was broken up by well-directed artillery fire. The following day an attack on the 'Hermann Göring' right flank was repulsed, while to Conrath's centre the enemy attacked in regimental strength, supported by ten tanks, and infiltrated past German outposts south of Isola Bella and 2.5 km northwest of Sessano, though the front line changed little.

By the month's end Allied strength in the crowded beachhead totalled 69,000 men, 508 guns and 208 tanks after the landing of the U.S. 45th Infantry and 1st Armored Divisions. There they consolidated positions under unrelenting bombardment from German artillery that, during February, included the famous 'Anzio Annie' and 'Anzio Express' Krupp K5 railway guns. To break the inertia, Lucas designed a two-pronged attack for 30 January: the right-hand American push by the 3rd Infantry Division reinforced by the 504th Parachute Infantry Regiment aimed to capture Cisterna, while the stronger left-hand attack by the British 1st Infantry and U.S. 1st Armored Divisions would advance northeast up the Via Anziate to take Campoleone in the Alban Hills. Both towns were considered key locations as they occupied important road and rail junctions that had been improved by Wehrmacht engineers as main lines of transport and communications. Operations within the region were complicated by the fact that the low ground was primarily reclaimed marshland, drained by Mussolini's government, and now deliberately flooded by the Germans, exacerbated by heavy winter rains. The few roads that had been resealed by Todt workers were therefore of even greater importance for tracked vehicle movement. Unfortunately for the American assault – spearheaded by the 1st and 3rd Ranger Battalions who would attempt to penetrate German lines before the main attack – their plan was based on faulty intelligence. While American analysts identified the main German defensive line to be some five miles beyond Cisterna, the town itself was heavily occupied and had been designated an assembly area for German troops preparing their own offensive, originally planned for 28 January, but postponed due to delay in expected reinforcements because of Allied bombing.

Schlemm had devised his own three-pronged attack against the beachhead. At the northern edge of the German line Gruppe 'Pfeifer' (led by the energetic Generalleutnant Helmuth Pfeifer, commander of 65th Infantry Division) was to attack with nine battalions of 65th Infantry and 4th Fallschirmjäger Divisions in a southerly direction against British positions. In the centre, Gruppe 'Gräser' (General der Panzertruppe Fritz-Hubert Gräser, commander of 3rd Panzergrenadier Division) would advance along both sides of the main road with 3rd Panzergrenadier and 26th Panzer Divisions in the vanguard, while 715th Infantry Division attacked further east. On the southern edge, Gruppe 'Conrath' would advance in a southwesterly direction with almost the full weight of the assembled 'Hermann Göring' Panzer Division and 114th Jäger Division. Its mission was to penetrate to the Astura creek from the area west of Cisterna and support would be provided by 32 heavy field howitzers (15-cm), 42 light field howitzers (10.5-cm), and three 10-cm guns.[5] This attack was intended to draw away the strongest possible enemy forces, particularly artillery fire, from the other two axes of attack. The assembly area for the 'Hermann Göring' troops was Cisterna – American reconnaissance units even detected

German troops digging in along the railway tracks west of the town. However, Allied intelligence continued to misinterpret and underestimate German intentions and strength.

> The enemy's attitude on our front is entirely defensive . . . His MLR [main line of resistance] will undoubtedly be found on true high ground both east and west of Velletri . . . The enemy's immediate situation with respect to tanks and artillery is not too good, [and their mission] is to prepare and man defenses on the MLR rather than to be used in a counter-attack against the beachhead . . . [Due to the low quality of non-German units in the area] our own actions, if carried through with particular vigour and firmness, whether in attacking or defending, may enable us to attain successes which would not have been possible against old-type, all-German formations.[6]

Harassing artillery fire from artillery batteries along the entire beachhead and naval forces offshore was directed against the right flank of the 'Hermann Göring' Panzer Division on 29 January, though answering German fire forced two cruisers and several MTBs to withdraw seaward. That night, the Allies attacked.

Heavy shelling preceded the main attacks for two hours, though U.S. Army Rangers had quietly crept past advanced German outposts before the Cisterna main battle line, departing their own positions at 0100 hrs. The 1st Ranger Battalion led the way, with 3rd behind, entering the west branch of the Mussolini canal and crossing into the Pantano Ditch which followed the Conca–Cisterna road. The Americans by-passed outposts, able to hear German gunners and sentries conversing in hushed tones. One hour later, 4th Ranger Battalion began to follow in marching formation, coming under heavy German machine-gun crossfire within an hour of departure, after being sighted by the outlying German positions. Lightly armed Rangers were soon involved in heavy fighting against troops under 'Hermann Göring' command, fighting their way through isolated strongpoints and encountering an improvised roadblock made of two damaged jeeps and an American truck.

Both 1st and 3rd Ranger Battalions were still in the Pantano ditch, advancing in a single column in the darkness, when the gunfire erupted to their rear. Radio communications between the 3rd Battalion and Ranger Force commander Colonel William O. Darby's headquarters in an isolated farmhouse just to the right of the Conca–Isola Bella–Cisterna road were almost non-existent after four of the battalion radio operators got lost in the darkness and returned to Darby's position. The two battalions also lost contact with one another half-way to their objective, while 1st Battalion became split in two, three companies advancing and three remaining in place. Captain Charles Shunstrom took command of the 1st Ranger Battalion's three rear stationary companies and sent a runner to find the 3rd Ranger Battalion to their rear. The runner then returned with news that Major Alvah Miller, the recently appointed 3rd Battalion commander, had been killed by a single round from a German tank but that his battalion was moving forward to attempt to link up; German defenders still appeared not to have raised a general alarm.

As morning approached, the covering depth of the Pantano ditch diminished and the Rangers crossed to the western edge of the road to exploit the cover offered by a deeper drainage ditch; valuable time was consumed by carefully crossing the exposed road and the subsequent re-forming of units. At 0610, Major Jack Dobson (commander 1st Ranger Battalion), still unable to establish radio contact with his headquarters, decided that, with dawn approaching, speed was now more important than stealth. His fast-moving leading elements were less than 800 metres from the outskirts of Cisterna, having raced through bivouacs of sleeping German outposts killing anybody inside. They were on a flat open plain hemmed in by the Ponte Rotta road to the north and the Conca road to the east when 'Hermann Göring' troops opened fire from covered positions within the town.

While the exposed Americans went to ground and dug in, Conrath's troops counter-attacked with Panzers and half-tracks to the fore. The two leading American battalions were soon surrounded while 4th Battalion failed to batter its way through to their position despite the attachment of tank destroyers and divisional reserve troops. The fighting was intense, Major Dobson knocking out one Panzer by shooting its commander with his pistol and dropping a white phosphorous grenade inside the hatch and Rangers capturing two more Panzer IVs, though these were later mistakenly destroyed by other Rangers with bazookas. Nonetheless, the lightly equipped Rangers' position was untenable and by early afternoon the last of them were overwhelmed and only six of the 767 men from the two-battalion infiltration force returned to Allied lines. In total, the 'Hermann Göring' Division took 680 American prisoners that day, losing 94 killed, 205 wounded, and 212 missing.

Strong American infantry attacks continued during the rest of the day. These were counter-attacked and fought to a standstill by the onset of darkness, though the defenders had been forced to yield some ground. The German defensive front line now ran from Isola Bella to benchmark 45 (3 km southeast along the Canale Mussolini) to north of benchmark 31 (6 km southeast of Isola Bella). Elements of 114th Jäger Division arrived at the front and were attached to 'Hermann Göring' as Kampfgruppe 'Berger', while elements of 26th Panzer Division were ordered to attack the 3rd Infantry Division's penetration south of Cisterna. In almost constant fighting the previous German main battle line was restored by 1 February despite stubborn resistance.

In the other two German sectors the fighting had been equally brutal, and equally destructive of Allied hopes. One British regiment, the Sherwood Foresters, that assaulted Campoleone was virtually annihilated by heavy German resistance, and nowhere was a decisive breakthrough achieved. Immediately, German thoughts turned to their own planned attack, which had been thrown off balance by the Allied assault. German commanders on the ground at Anzio now doubted their ability to drive the Allies back into the sea after suffering heavy losses and while they were uncertain of receiving the requisite ammunition supply following further transport chaos on road and rail networks due to Allied bombing. Nonetheless, orders to begin the planned offensive operations stood.

> The Fourteenth Army is to start a counter-offensive, if, in the course of the defence, a good opportunity presents itself. Assault groups are to be held in readiness, in order that such a possibility can be exploited at any given time. The entire Army coast artillery south of the Tiber has been put under the I. Fallschirmkorps, so as to achieve a greater concentration of forces. The artillery is to be emplaced near the coast, so that as many pieces as possible will be able to fire, from the flank, at enemy shipping at the beachhead. Since additional enemy landings appear likely, the Fourteenth Army has ordered the thorough demolition of the harbour of Civitavecchia.[7]

At Cassino, renewed Allied attacks made a requirement to reinforce German reserve units highly likely, and with landings still expected in the region northwest of Rome, the imperative to destroy the Anzio beachhead attained fresh urgency. However, despite his significant artillery strength, Generaloberst Mackensen indicated that such offensive operations would require extra stringent preparation due to numerical and training weaknesses in his available infantry. Only one such effort to launch a decisive stroke would be possible, after which his forces would probably possess insufficient strength to make a second attempt. Mackensen issued the following order to troops under his command:

> In the sectors where we are not able to attack for the time being, an intensive consolidation of positions must be started, such as the laying of mines, construction of trip wire entanglements, etc. Not a foot of soil will be given up. Enemy penetrations or breakthroughs must be prevented by a consolidation of the assigned main line of resistance and of the battle positions behind it. In addition, forces from the defensive sectors will be employed at the points of concentration in attacks. Foxholes will be converted into individual points of resistance and will be connected by trenches and connecting wire entanglements will be set up. The next priority is the construction of a secondary connecting trench system along the artillery entrenchments. The battle position will consist of a system of mutually supporting points of resistance, machine-gun nests, anti-tank gun and infantry howitzer positions, observation posts, artillery and mortar positions, shelters for reserves, distributing points, etc. They will all be consolidated as strongpoints, as soon as possible. The strongpoints assigned to the local reserves will be kept as near to the main line of resistance as the terrain and the missions will permit.
>
> In front of the main line of resistance as many anti-tank and anti-personnel mines as possible will be laid. Natural and artificial tank obstacles and anti-tank weapons of all kinds are to be supplemented by barriers of anti-personnel mines.
>
> Only a battle position based on the system of strongpoints and supplemented by a system of tank defence can break up a large-scale attack by the enemy. Penetrations cannot be avoided, but a breakthrough must be prevented.
>
> These constructions must not lower the offensive spirit of the troops. Entrenchment is a means of maintaining power for the offensive. Positions must be consolidated, even though the commanding officer is aware that he will no more than start this construction. Whatever he can do will be profitable for the reserves

> which follow. It is the task of all commanders, especially company commanders, to fight against indifference, and to force the men to entrench themselves.

Though they were likely not to have noticed any particular change, on 1 February Conrath's exhausted men received what would be the final alteration to their formation's designation: from that date forwards it was known as Fallschirm-Panzer-Division 'Hermann Göring'.

This change was actually more than just an arbitrary retitling. At the beginning of the following month, Generaloberst Kurt Student would be named head of the newly created 1. Fallschirm Armee, based in Nancy. Though 'Hermann Göring's move to France had been postponed it was still scheduled, and it was earmarked for Student's new army. The assignment to Student's new command was, however, tempered by a provision that the status of the 'Hermann Göring' volunteers remained unchanged; their tactical employment would still be handled by the Heer while the Fallschirm Armee exercised Luftwaffe supervision in matters of discipline, military justice, decorations and awards and promotions. There was a vague plan for the future training of 'Hermann Göring' as genuine *Fallschirmjäger* and to create a truly air-mobile division with heavy weapons transported by large aircraft. Schmalz – awarded the Oak Leaves to his Knight's Cross on 23 December for his performance in Sicily – was one of the most enthusiastic proponents of this ambitious plan:

> Once an airborne force has been landed, its operations are always handicapped by its lack of heavy weapons, especially tanks. An airborne army with an armoured command at its disposal is an operational force with enormous possibilities.[8]

The scheme was, however, stillborn both through a lack of suitable aircraft, fuel, and time required for training. In the meantime, fresh blood was brought into the division, a new 3rd Battalion, Flak Regiment 'HG' being created from what was formerly 1st Battalion, Flak-Regiment 49 (mot.).

Meanwhile at I. Fallschirmkorps headquarters, Schlemm requested permission to relocate the right wing of Conrath's division backwards as they and the neighbouring 71st Infantry Division had been greatly weakened by unrelenting Allied pressure, including a 'Hermann Göring' counter-attack repulsed with heavy losses after an advance of only one kilometre. Massive Allied artillery barrages temporarily demoralised the younger more inexperienced members of the division and rattled even the veterans. Schlemm needed to form reserves and the only way by which this could be achieved was by shortening his front. Reluctant to yield ground, Mackensen in this instance approved the request after a personal tour of the area and discussions with commanders including Conrath.

Kesselring had by this point grasped the very real danger of betrayal by the Italians, even among those Italian officers professing loyalty to Mussolini's rump fascist state. While the Allies benefited greatly from decrypted German radio traffic, they were also greatly assisted by on the spot intelligence gathered by Italian partisans, even directly from Kesselring's headquarters. Sent by OSS radio transmitters in Rome to Allied command at Caserta, this information frequently preceded even Ultra information and provided the opportunity to prepare against imminent German assaults. This intelligence leak led to Kesselring issuing orders individually; personnel receiving such orders were graded strictly on a 'need to know' basis. Attack times were henceforth not to be announced to troops until the last moment, and no previous notice at all was given to troops not taking direct part in an operation.

Kesselring also reshuffled his command structure, balancing the requirements of his hard-pressed troops at both Cassino and Anzio. The headquarters of General der Panzertruppe Traugott Herr's LXXVI. Panzerkorps was transferred from the Tenth to Fourteenth Army and took command of the main line of resistance at Anzio, headquartered at Giulianello. Herr subsequently disbanded Kampfgruppe 'Pfeifer' and reorganised his troops:

Kampfgruppe 'Gräser'
  3rd Panzergrenadier Division and 715th Motorised Infantry Division

Kampfgruppe 'Raapke' *Generalleutnant Wilhelm Raapke*
  Reinforced 71st Infantry Division

Kampfgruppe 'Conrath'
  Reinforced Fallschirm-Panzer-Division 'Hermann Göring' and 26th Panzer Division

I. Fallschirmkorps retained control of only 4th Fallschirmjäger and 65th Infantry Divisions, redirected to defend the main line of resistance between LXXVI. Panzerkorps at Aprilia and the coast, guarding the coastline to the mouth of the Tiber River and also taking control of the military Kommandanteur of Rome, including its SS security units.

Mackensen's view of the prevailing situation was far less optimistic than Kesselring's and twice during early February he tendered his resignation to OKW only to be refused both times. Regardless, he urged the constant delivering of 'blows against the enemy, at least with strong assault detachments' in a bid not only to gather prisoner intelligence but also to force dispersal of the Allied troops to defend every sector of the front. Assault detachments of 'Hermann Göring' units inflicted heavy losses on Allied engineers after attacking a bridge under construction northeast of Borgo Montello, though the ground captured was almost immediately given up again after an American counter-attack, preventing destruction of the bridge. Units of the Armoured Reconnaissance Battalion observed strong Allied occupation of further bridge-building points as 'HG' divisional artillery harassed the engineers and assembly areas for Allied reserves heading for the front line.

Kesselring finished planning his 'all-or-nothing' vigorous counter-attack, codenamed 'Fischfang' (fish trap), in which the Fourteenth Army was to open its attack on 15 February. A slight modification as the reckoning day approached pushed the launch one day later, concentrating its main effort between 1.5 km west of the Aprilia–Nettuno highway and the Fosso di Spaccasassi. To the north I. Fallschirmkorps was to attack from the sector west of Carroceto (Aprilia) in a southerly direction, covering the west flank of the entire attack as LXXVI. Panzerkorps smashed through enemy lines and advanced on Nettuno. This initial assault would be mounted by 3rd Panzergrenadier Division (less 103rd Armoured Reconnaissance Battalion), 114th Jäger Division, 715th Motorised Infantry Division and the Fallschirm-Panzer-Division 'Hermann Göring', temporarily less the bulk of the Panzer Regiment and staff of the Panzergrenadier Regiment. Additional Wehrmacht and Waffen-SS units would bolster these main units, distributed to the various divisional commands. By an increased use of artillery in the 'Hermann Göring' sector, it was hoped to persuade the Allies that this was the decisive location of the offensive, rather than the actual centre of German ambitions which lay further west. Once the enemy lines were broken, exploitation would be made by a second combat wave of the selected reserve of 26th Panzer and 29th Panzergrenadier Divisions.

Though the German offensive was largely predicted by Allied commanders, to attempt deception and cover the withdrawal of the reserve divisions from the line, Conrath was instructed to continue robust raiding activity within the 'Hermann Göring' sector. It was an almost redundant instruction as the division remained under constant pressure, Allied troops piercing the 'Hermann Göring' main line of resistance south of Borgo Podgora on 10 February and only being repulsed after fiercely aggressive counter-attacks with artillery support.

In the days immediately before 'Fischfang' the reinforced 956th Grenadier Regiment of the 362nd Infantry Division relieved 'Hermann Göring' troops in the line to free them for the attack, though Conrath's troops also in turn occupied positions vacated by 26th Panzer Division as it moved into corps reserve. During the night of 12–13 February two assault detachments of the 'Hermann Göring' and 4th Fallschirmjäger Divisions silenced three entrenched machine-gun positions and took prisoners as the Luftwaffe also bombed Anzio and Nettuno harbours.

At midnight on 15 February, Fallschirm-Panzer-Division 'Hermann Göring' was detached from LXXVI. Panzerkorps and placed under the immediate tactical command of Fourteenth Army. Conrath had at his disposal an eclectic mix of formations with two Panzergrenadier battalions, the Armoured Reconnaissance Battalion, Engineer Battalion, an 'Emergency Battalion' of the Divisionkampfschule and Divisionsreserve from the 'Hermann Göring' establishment. Other formations attached included 2nd Battalion, SS-Panzergrenadier Regt. 35 'Reichsführer SS', 2nd Battalion, SS-Panzergrenadier Regt. 36 'Reichsführer SS', Luftwaffe z.b.V. 7th Field Battalion, Heer Infantry Demonstration Regt., Heer Machine-gun Battalion, 129th Assault Gun Company, 362nd Füsilier Battalion and 956th Grenadier Regt. (362nd Infantry Division).

'Fischfang' opened before dawn the next morning, Conrath's troops attacking with supporting heavy artillery fire and gaining one kilometre of ground before the intense Allied artillery retaliation inflicted heavy casualties and forced the grenadiers to dig in. The bombardment was so devastating that Oblt. Lehmann's Divisionkampfschule was annihilated almost completely after suffering eighty casualties. The attached Heer Infantry Demonstration Regiment disengaged without orders after the loss of nearly all officers and NCOs and American troops recalled the advancing Germans were reacting 'like zombies as they were walking to us in a shell rain for about 45 minutes'.[9] Local ceasefires were arranged between the opposing sides as dusk approached, allowing 'Hermann Göring' troops to recover at least some of their wounded.

The terrain was difficult at best, the ground muddy after constant rain, yet not hardened by frost. Even where the ground was solid enough to allow passage by tracked vehicles, it was frequently broken by a tangled network of ravines and gullies. Infantry were the cutting edge, supported by every artillery piece that could fire. Mackensen urged the assault detachments to keep pressure on the enemy along their western flank, attempting to keep them off balance and unable to reinforce the most threatened part of the line nearer Aprilia. The first day ended with some measure of German success though any form of decisive breakthrough remained elusive despite gaps being pried open in the American front lines.

> Our heavy losses were due to insufficient training of troops, heavy enemy artillery fire, frequent fighter attacks, and enemy sniper activity. Because of tank losses, Fourteenth Army ordered that tanks are to operate only within our lines, and under no circumstances in front of them. Our artillery could not completely neutralise the enemy artillery due to lack of ammunition.[10]

The following day, the German advance was staggered by the heaviest Allied artillery fire and aerial bombardment since the Anzio landing had begun; German observers estimated that something in the region of 22,000 rounds were fired into a geographically small area. This fearsome naval and land bombardment was augmented by 730 sorties by the USAAF Twelfth Air Force as it mounted the heaviest ground-support raids of the war to that date. Additionally, carpet-bombing by 288 unescorted B-24 and B-17 bombers of the Fifteenth Air Force unloaded 1,100 tons of ordnance on the positions ahead of the U.S. Fifth Army's Anzio battle line. Thirteen Allied aircraft were claimed destroyed by 'Hermann Göring' anti-aircraft gunners and many American fighter-bombers were successfully decoyed to attack Tiger tank dummies assembled by Conrath's troops.

The 'Hermann Göring' attack was stopped after it had captured the road fork 250 m northeast of Colle del Pozzo, in the face of stubborn resistance from well-fortified positions supported by heavy weapons, tanks and constant sniping. Mackensen was aware of the perilous condition of Conrath's division and ordered them to anchor the enemy along their front line as he prepared to throw his two reserve divisions into action. At 0400 the following morning, the 'Hermann Göring' western flank resumed its advance in support of the reserve troops, which began their assault at dawn.

Once again a breach was torn in the Allied front, the U.S. 179th Infantry Regiment overrun and American troops pushed back to their 'Corps

Beachhead Line', a fortified position on the hill mass north of Anzio, the final defensive barrier before the Allied beachhead. Success must have appeared tantalisingly close to German commanders and a battalion of the 362nd Infantry Division that had been employed in a coast defence role at the mouth of the Tiber was attached to 'Hermann Göring' to allow formation of assault units in order to maintain pressure on the western flank of the advance. On 19 February, the 'Hermann Göring' division attacked Colle del Pozzo 2 km west of Cle Carano, but was stopped by intense defensive fire, and ended up digging in across two hills northeast of Colle del Pozzo. During the day the remainder of 362nd Infantry Division was transferred to replace the mauled 'Hermann Göring' men, relieving them at 1200. Conrath's troops were to be employed further west for offensive operations in the Spaccasassi sector, near Carano. The division was now reduced to Kampfgruppe 'Corvin': 1st Battalion, Panzergrenadier Regt. 2 'HG', 2nd Battalion, Panzergrenadier Regt. 1 'HG' and the Armoured Reconnaissance Battalion 'HG' – under a new commander, 28-year-old Rittmeister Christian Kurt von Loeben, since 17 February – all attached to the 715th Infantry Division.[11]

However, despite this reshuffle, by 21 February, 'Fischfang' was over. Though German forces had pushed steadily forward against all odds they had been devastated by stubborn defence backed by firepower that the Wehrmacht could no longer provide. With Allied artillery use increasing to almost 30,000 rounds per day, it had become extremely difficult to evacuate German wounded with ambulances, even armoured half-tracks, being destroyed by the shelling. Instead, men were carried to the rear in assault guns and Tiger tanks.

The Fourteenth Army appealed for reinforcements in the shape of one combat-ready infantry division and another of mountain troops for heavily wooded areas. Engineers, artillery and mortars were all in urgent demand as were additional portable radio sets of which Mackensen's army was 468 sets short. There were, however, no forces available. Mackensen planned to restructure his depleted units and attempt on or about 26 February to break through the line of the Mussolini Canal, with 'Hermann Göring' troops once more in the vanguard:

> By order of Hitler, tank assaults in small groups will be made prior to the attack from and south of the area of Borgo Podgora in the direction of the Mussolini Canal. The tanks of the Panzer Division

> 'Hermann Göring', used for this purpose, will return to their division shortly before the attack begins.[12]

At 0400 hrs on 29 February, LXXVI Panzer Corps launched its renewed attack against the beachhead with 114th Jäger Division, 362nd Infantry Division, 26th Panzer Division and Fallschirm-Panzer-Division 'Hermann Göring'. All formations experienced difficulty in bringing forces forward to their initial jumping-off points due to mud caused by the heavy rain and troops who were already exhausted by marching through the glutinous morass before the attack began. They made little headway as the American defensive line had been strengthened with minefields and barbed wire while U.S. engineers had cratered the roads leading towards the German lines. Heavily fortified strongpoints were doggedly defended and most Panzers were unable to join the initial attack, largely immobilised by the mud; the battle was instead carried forward by fatigued infantry. 'Hermann Göring' units reached a line stretching for a kilometre southeast of Isola Bella, the division's right flank making little progress due to strong enemy resistance though, at 1200 hrs, several 'Hermann Göring' Panzers reached the northern edge of Isola Bella, losing three vehicles to tank destroyers. Once again, in the face of devastating artillery fire, the offensive ground to a halt and an American counter-thrust pushed them back and regained all lost ground while capturing fifty-three exhausted 'Hermann Göring' troops.

Mackensen bluntly informed Kesselring that, despite the latter's assertion that 'Fischfang' had failed due to an 'overestimate of the enemy' and subsequent lack of aggressiveness, it simply was not possible to eliminate the Anzio beachhead with the available troops. Insufficiently trained replacements were unsuitable to meet the Allies in battle and every veteran formation was now but a shell of its former self. With Allied pushes from Anzio and against Cassino inevitably looming once better weather arrived, there was no alternative but to go over to the defensive, discontinuing all but minor offensive actions. As Army Group C Chief of Staff, General der Kavallerie Westphal, was later to note, 'the blanket has got too thin' and after five years of war the Wehrmacht was no longer capable of sustained attack in the face of such overwhelming material superiority.

Fresh fears emerged of a possible diversionary landing at Livorno or Genoa to distract from the expected Allied invasion of northern France and on 4 March Kesselring ordered 'Hermann Göring' to be withdrawn from Anzio and transferred to Armee Gruppe 'von Zangen' (General der

Infanterie Gustav-Adolf von Zangen) for employment in the area of Livorno. There they would remain in reserve until the still-scheduled transfer to France took place, remaining available to Kesselring in the meantime for deployment at the Italian front, though only with direct permission from OKW in Berlin. Within nine days the last elements of Fallschirm-Panzer-Division 'Hermann Göring' – consisting of anti-aircraft and Panzer regiments – were sent to Tuscany, to be based in the region surrounding Livorno, Pisa and Lucca.

Chapter Nine

Rebuilding and Counter-Insurgency, Italy 1944

'The one means that wins the easiest victory over reason: terror and force.' *Adolf Hitler*

The battered division was once again re-formed from reinforcements arriving from the training unit at Utrecht, though returning to anywhere near a full establishment of armour was noted as impossible owing to production difficulties in Germany. Among those responsible for turning fresh volunteers into combat troops in the Netherlands was Adolf Scheckenbach, now recovered from the wounds he had suffered in Sicily.

> The 'Hermann Göring' Division had a big training establishment in the area around Utrecht and I was posted into 2nd Battalion, which trained recruits in the use of artillery pieces, Panzers, *Sturmgeschütze* (StuGs) and *Sturmhaubitze* (StuHs), and *Panzer-abwehrkanone* (PAK: anti-tank guns). The battalion headquarters was at Amersfoort but we were actually billeted in the area between Amersfoort and Harderwijk in farmhouses, barns and stables. My new job was to train replacement crews for our Panzers and the StuGs and StuHs, as well as provide coastal protection at Harderwijk on the then southern shore of the Zuider Zee against any attacks that might be made by the Allies.
>
> Before we allowed newly conscripted recruits anywhere near the really noisy pieces of equipment, they had to be trained in the basics of soldiering. Once they were conscripted, these fellows had to remain in the barracks, even in civilian clothes. It was not safe for them to go out alone as the Dutch were not friendly and their Resistance movement had become quite bold . . . It was an odd situation for we had both raw recruits – who were just boys –

> and many ground-duty Luftwaffe personnel whose units had been disbanded because of lack of fuel and curtailed flying activity. Some of these Luftwaffe fellows were highly skilled mechanics and radio men and there were some who were highly decorated. I knew of some fighter pilots who were sent to us.
>
> These men and boys were divided up into groups along the lines of soldiers who had no idea of infantry skills and those with varying levels of combat and weapons skill. As in all armies, we taught our raw recruits both field and battle craft. They would need it. In the short time we had them, we took a lot of care in teaching them how to use their personal weapons. We first trained them on the Pistole 08 – the Luger, then the Karabiner 98k – our standard infantry rifle and lastly the MG42 – our standard machine gun and a very good weapon – which is still in use today. On parade we instructors were ruthless in making sure that a recruit's uniform, weapons and equipment were clean, tidy and functioning properly. They would need it all when they got into combat.
>
> Once the recruits were familiar and competent with those weapons, they had also completed their abbreviated infantry training and we put them to work learning how to use the cannons in our Panzers and how to drive and care for their vehicles, which were more skills which would help keep them alive at the *Hauptkampflinie* – the front – which was rapidly approaching from the east and the west. Even so, our recruits were rushed through training and simply didn't have the training that we had received earlier in the war.[1]

Unfortunately for the 'resting' 'Hermann Göring' troops in Tuscany, they were about to become embroiled in the war against Italian partisan units that had been intensifying since the armistice of September 1943. Many scattered guerrilla groups had sprung into existence after eligible men evaded the draft into Mussolini's Italian Social Republic (RSI) forces by going underground, opportunistically arming themselves with weapons cached by disbanded army units. Frequent skirmishes between guerrillas and fascist troops occurred over the months that followed. Since the Anzio landings and a series of national strikes within German-held regions of Italy, partisan activity had dramatically increased and become both more organised and effective. Largely, though not totally, Communist, the guerrilla bands were receiving greater levels of Allied support with OSS supply drops and agents provided to help streamline both logistics and training. The Allied supreme command had actively encouraged partisan operations behind German lines as it became clear that construction had begun of yet another new defensive line named the Gothic Line: a 16 km-deep belt of fortifications extending from just south of La Spezia to the Foglia Valley, through the natural defensive wall of the Apennines to the Adriatic Sea between Pesaro and Ravenna.

During December Kesselring issued orders that either Polizei or Army commanders would take control of local anti-partisan operations, though this instruction was largely circumvented by Waffen-SS, Polizei and Italian RSI security troops being placed under the control of the newly created SS und Polizeiführer (SSPF) Oberitalien-West on 23 January, responsible for all of Italy apart from the pre-Alpine and northern Adriatic coast. These latter areas were to be controlled by the Wehrmacht, Armee Gruppe 'von Zangen' deploying forces to secure the stretch of Italy from the Ligurian coastline through the northern Apennines.

For such highly mobile deployment against partisan bands, traditional army formations generally used their reconnaissance units and so it was that Rittmeister Christian Kurt von Loeben and Lt. von Poschinger received orders from Oberstleutnant Helmeth Dannehl of Bologna's Militär-kommandantur, to take the reinforced Armoured Reconnaissance Battalion 'HG' into action against 'bandits' in the Modena Apennines. At that time, the reconnaissance unit amounted to the following components:

Armoured Reconnaissance Btn. 'HG'	***Hptm. Christian Kurt Von Loeben***	
1st Armoured Car Company	*Lt. Gerhard Flechsig*	
4 x SdKfz 231 8-rad; 2 x SdKfz 263 8-rad radio cars; 4 x SdKfz 222; 1 x SdKfz 223; 1 x SdKfz 250/1 Befehlspanzer		
2nd Motorcycle Company	*Hptm. Richard Heiman*	4 platoons
3rd Schützenpanzerwagen Company	*Hptm. Walter Hartwig*	
4th VW-Schwimmwagen Company	*Hptm. Hans Vogel*	4 platoons
5th Heavy Company	*Hptm. Wolfgang Bach*	
Wespe Platoon		4 x 105-mm self propelled guns
Infantry Gun Platoon	*Fw. Willi Drews*	1 x 75-mm Infantry Gun
Engineer Platoon	*Lt. Ferdinand Osterhaus*	
Anti-tank Platoon	*Lt. Ferdinand Wirth*	2 x 75-mm Pak 40
KwK Platoon	*Lt. Helmut Barthel*	4 x SdKfz 251/9 with 75-mm L/24

An attempt on 8 March by the RSI to arrest young men who had dodged the draft into Mussolini's fascist forces had resulted in skirmishes with scattered guerrillas and ultimately a full-scale battle against a partisan group under the command of Giuseppe Barbolini on 15 March. Known as the battle of Cerrè Sologno, this was the first organised attack by partisans on German and RSI forces, Luftwaffe reservists of the Jagdkommando having been involved in the operation. German *Feldgendarmerie* were immediately sent to bolster Italian security forces of the Guardia Nazionale Repubblicana and two German officers and six soldiers were killed alongside fifteen Italian fascist troops in the subsequent fighting. A number of fascist Italian and German troops were taken prisoner by the partisans and, raising the stakes yet higher, Political Commissioner Eros Didimo Ferrari had six of them executed near Cerverolo. The fascist prefect of Montefiorino, Francesco Bocchi, and the commander of the Guardia Nazionale Repubblicana, Arturo Mori, appealed for more heavily armed Wehrmacht assistance and Loeben's reconnaissance unit, headquartered in a villa on the outskirts of Crespellano, departed for the upper Secchia valley on 17 March.

The following morning, while *Feldgendarmerie* guarded either flank of his chosen operational area, Loeben opened his action against three villages deemed likely to have actively supported the partisans: Monchio, Costrignano and Susano. Loeben positioned 88-mm guns of Hptm. Helmut Odenwald's 10th Anti-Aircraft Battery on high ground facing the walls of the fortress of Montefiorino and opened fire shortly before dawn across the Torrente Dragone against all three villages.

After this bombardment, the 'Hermann Göring' reconnaissance troops of 2nd and 4th Companies and a scattering of Italian security forces moved in and began burning homes and stables, Monchio alone seeing 150 houses go up in flames. Livestock and food were requisitioned as women and children were rounded up and separated from male villagers, who were subject to seemingly arbitrary summary executions. By the day's end 136 Italian civilians were dead: 71 in Monchio, 34 in Costrignano, 24 in Susano and 7 others who had been found in neighbouring fields. Among the dead were 6 children under the age of ten, 7 between eleven and sixteen, 7 pregnant women and 20 people over the age of 66. In his official report, Loeben listed 'about 300 bandits executed', familiar Wehrmacht parlance that described all civilian casualties as partisans.

Two days later, 3rd Company, Armoured Reconnaissance Battalion 'HG' under command of Oblt. Walter Hartwig and assisted by fascist GNR

(Guardia Nazionale Repubblicana) troops of Reggio Emilia also entered the villages of Cervarolo and Civago and gathered men in the village square where they were shot, twenty-four in the former and four in the latter. Both villages were then set ablaze, Loeben reporting: 'Cervarolo and Civago annihilated by fire. Seventy-eight men were shot.'

These were not the only such actions in which 'Hermann Göring' troops took part; in fact the division was heavily implicated in a number of such massacres in Italy comparable to those associated with the 16th SS Panzer-grenadier Division 'Reichsführer SS'.

It has been proposed that the ideological perspective of many 'Hermann Göring' officers was akin to that of the Waffen-SS, and perhaps this was so. At any rate, the very nature of partisan warfare guarantees civilian casualties, let alone in Italy which had been in a state of civil war since the armistice of 1943. Subsequent partisan reprisals against isolated German or Italian outposts fanned the flames of greater repression and increasing violence whipping around a largely innocent population. That, of course, does not excuse such actions as those undertaken by the 'Hermann Göring' units, or the apparent wanton cruelty with which they were frequently carried out.

By the beginning of April Oberstleutnant Georg-Henning von Heydebreck of the Panzer Regiment was ordered by General der Infanterie Anton Dostler (LXXV Corps) to 'clean up' the area of the Gothic Line by forcibly removing civilians and undertaking armed demonstrative measures to discourage support for Italian partisans. Heydebreck was specifically tasked with reclaiming territory between state road 71 of the Passo dei Mandrioli and state road 67 of the Passo del Muraglione, between Bibbiena, Verghereto, San Godenzo and Dicomano.

On 8 April 'Hermann Göring' officers conferred with Italian counterparts on the best way to achieve their mission. As a result three English-speaking men of the Armoured Reconnaissance Battalion – Lt. Heinz Domeyer, Oberfeldwebel Ewald Maasakkers (both platoon leaders from 2nd Company) and Feldwebel Christian Blomenkamp (4th Company) – were sent in civilian clothes to pose as escaped American prisoners of war to attempt infiltration of local resistance cells. They made contact with partisans of the Garibaldian brigade 'Faliero Pucci' but their identity was exposed and as they attempted to flee Domeyer and Maasakkers were shot and killed; Blomenkamp was wounded in the left arm by grenade splinters but successfully escaped.

Two days later, Loeben and his Reconnaissance Battalion arrived in Vallucciole along with 'shock groups' of the Panzer and Anti-Aircraft Regiments, where at 0300 hrs he ordered the civilian population of the valley rounded up and executed in reprisal, their villages burnt to the ground. The orgy of violence that followed included multiple instances of rape and ended with the deaths of 105 people.

Despite the fact that in these and other isolated incidents, men of the 'Hermann Göring' division killed at least 372 people during April, the anti-partisan measures largely failed, though seventeen confirmed partisans were shot against the cemetery wall in Stia on 17 April.[2] Furthermore, elements of Loeben's unit took part with other Wehrmacht and Italian troops numbering a total of more than 2,000 men to comb the area around and including the village of Mommio on 4 May. Following a brief clash with the partisans, the Germans captured a considerable quantity of airborne material, including parachute fabric in Mommio. Most of the village was burnt and twenty-two male villagers shot.

The weeks that followed saw little let up in the punitive expeditions carried out by German and Italian troops in the escalating partisan war. The complexities of the Italian civil war are beyond the scope of this work, but suffice it to say that the already disorganised RSI security apparatus virtually collapsed by June placing the onus more firmly on German shoulders to battle anti-fascist guerrillas. During June Carabinieri began defecting to guerrilla bands in large numbers, eventually leading to futile German attempts to disarm those who remained for potential use as anti-aircraft auxiliaries in Germany. Instead, the RSI disbanded what was left of them in German-controlled Italy. The GNR had also dramatically shrunk in size and combat effectiveness.

On 9 March 'Hermann Göring' Division Order Nr 32/44 had been issued for the creation of four Alarm units (*Alarmeinheiten*); 'Pauke', 'Alarich', 'Flamme' (each of three officers and 120 NCOs and men) and 'Vesuv' (commanded by Oberleutnant Siegfried Böttcher of two officers and 100 NCOs and men). These special mobile formations were designed for rapid deployment against either sea or air landings as well as the danger posed by Italian partisan attack.

Three alarm levels were established: Alarm Level 1 (codeword 'Osterspaziergang') in which case the entire division was to be mobilised to counter a major threat; Alarm Level 2 (codeword 'Pfingstrosse') in which case localised threat forced mobilisation of individual units; Alarm Level 3:

(codeword 'Kampfeinsatz') which would mobilise only rear-area units such as headquarters and supply troops. Both the 'Pauke' and 'Vesuv' Alarm units were implicated in further reprisal actions against villages during June and July.

Even as the remainder of the division headed back into conventional action against Allied advances in the south, executions of over 500 Italian civilians were carried out by 'Hermann Göring' elements during various anti-partisan drives. One of most notorious officers implicated was 29-year-old Hptm. Heinz Barz, commander of the division's Feldgendarmie Trupp (mot.) 1000. Barz had been a member of the National Socialist Party since December 1937 and was a former Ordnungspolizei officer.[3] He had been part of the notorious Reserve Police Battalion 101 in Poland before transferring to Police Battalion 305 during the invasion of the Soviet Union. Injured in Russia in 1943, he was promoted to *SS Hauptsturmführer* after having been a member of the SS since March of that year. It is unclear exactly when he transferred to the 'Hermann Göring' Division, but, together with the III. (StuG) Fallschirm-Panzer-Bataillon 'HG' and Alarmeinheiten 'Pauke' and 'Vesuv', Barz led an attack on Civitella Val di Chiana on 29 June. The Feldgendarmerie Trupp numbered approximately a hundred men, its headquarters element comprising Barz, his deputy, three to five *Unteroffizier* interpreters, and another three to five drivers and orderlies. Under his command were three platoons of military policemen and a support group of armourers, medical personnel, mechanics and drivers. Among them were many men of the Musikkorps which had become increasingly redundant by 1944 and its members largely absorbed into the Feldgendarmerie Trupp during the year. Civitella Val di Chiana was a small town of about 400 original inhabitants, 523 metres above the Chiana Valley, and following nearby skirmishes between German troops and partisans, nearly 200 residents had fled into the countryside for fear of reprisal, but gradually returned when nothing untoward occurred. It was then that Barz led his men and supporting troops to surround Civitella and storm the town from the north and south, torching homes and indiscriminately killing 150 men women and children. In nearby San Pancrazio 72 people were also killed, 60 of them lined up and shot in the wine cellar at Pierangeli Farm after refusing to betray the location of local partisan bands.[4]

In April alone, Armee Gruppe 'von Zangen' carried out 116 anti-partisan operations which killed approximately 4,300 people, captured a further 2,400 and led to the arrest of more than 3,000 civilians. These attacks on civilians have left a lasting legacy and stain on Wehrmacht history. Official Wehrmacht directives of the time frequently referred to Italian partisans as 'common traitors' and 'lawless bandits', helping create the air of contempt that appears to have been held by some German troops towards Italian citizens. Their partisan enemies were, after all, civilians with weapons. Suspicion appears to have been engendered towards the population of a country that the more politically or ideologically motivated troops within the Wehrmacht and Waffen-SS may well have seen as having betrayed them in September 1943.

Despite his postwar protestations to the contrary, Kesselring undoubtedly fanned the flames. There existed much animosity between Kesselring and SS-und Polizeiführer Italien, Obergruppenführer Karl Wolff, and after a convoluted and argumentative exchange between the SS and Kesselring, Oberbefehlshaber Südwest was ultimately given top-level direction of anti-partisan warfare in Italy with Wolff and the SS theoretically subordinate. Kesselring ordered implementation of the OKW's 'Directive for Combating the Partisan Movement' (*Richtlinien zur Bekämpfung der Partisanenbewegung*) and added his own instructions that: 'If attacked, shoot immediately, regardless' and that 'in the current situation, a too rigorous crackdown will never be grounds for punishment'.[5]

Away from the tumult of anti-partisan warfare change had come to Fallschirm-Panzer-Division 'Hermann Göring'. On 15 April, Oberst Schmalz was elevated to command, promoted to *Generalmajor* at the beginning of May. Paul Conrath, the unit's longest-serving commander, had been moved to staff duties, appointed Inspekteur der Luftlande und Fallschirmtruppen as part of the Luftwaffe General Staff and concurrently the training commander (Komm. Gen. der Ausbildungs und Ersatztruppen der Fallschirm Armee) in Student's 1. Fallschirm Armee based in Berlin-Reinickendorf. As such he retained overall control of both the Fallschirm Ausbildungs und Ersatz-Regiment 'Hermann Göring' and Escort Battalion 'Hermann Göring'.[6]

In the stagnant Anzio beachhead, Kesselring refused to authorise a reduction in pressure on Allied positions until the evening of 24 May. However, he had been already overtaken by events as Mackensen had been forced to restructure his defences that afternoon. A full-scale Allied offensive against the Gustav Line was launched on 11 May, Operation 'Diadem' crossing the Garigliano and Rapido rivers, drawing German reserves into the battle and thereby reducing pressure on the Anzio beachhead. By the 16th, Kesselring knew that Monte Cassino could hold no longer and authorised a withdrawal ten miles to the Hitler Line – renamed Dora Line as it too was not designed to be held for long. With Allied troops pouring into the Liri Valley, General Lucian Truscott, who had replaced Lucas at Anzio, launched the long-awaited breakout from the beachhead at 0545 hrs on 23 May with a bombardment by 1,500 artillery pieces. Kesselring urgently appealed to OKW in Berlin and was granted the release of the Fallschirm-Panzer-Division 'Hermann Göring' for its return to action at the Italian front.

Later that morning Mackensen's Chief of Staff, Generalmajor Westphal, called Schmalz and ordered the immediate departure of 'Hermann Göring' from Tuscany to an assembly area northwest of Valmontone near the front line south of Rome, the transfer being expected to take two days. Schmalz pointedly emphasised two significant problems with the abrupt movement order: the severe danger posed by enemy air attacks on any movement by daylight, and the fact that the division possessed only enough fuel for a march of 250–300 km which would place the lead elements in the region of Viterbo by the time supplies were exhausted. Though a fuel depot was located near Florence, it lay under Army Group control and Schmalz, as a Luftwaffe officer, possessed no authority to draw from it. Westphal did his best to allay Schmalz's fears, promising sufficient fuel in the area around Viterbo in time for the division's arrival. Orders to move were received between 1000 and 1100, though no further instructions about the commitment of the division to action once all elements had assembled near Valmontone were received. Schmalz strongly advocated movement only under cover of darkness but his objections were overruled. Despite Schmalz's strong reservations, there were no extended breaks in the planned travel time, the division being ordered to make a forced march by both day and night, with their first intended refuelling stop to be made from stocks positioned near Viterbo, to be arranged through normal Wehrmacht supply channels.

At 1130 hrs that day Rittmeister von Loeben's Armoured Reconnaissance Battalion moved out from its assembly point towards Viterbo as the division spearhead. Three routes had been hurriedly planned: Route A, following the coastal highway through Cecina, Grosseto, Tarquinia, Vetralla before cutting inland to Bracciano; Route B, the mountain route, via Poggibonsi, Siena, Acquapendente and Viterbo; and Route C, from Florence to Arezzo and Orvieto. The heavy anti-aircraft units of Oberst Meyer's Flak Regiment were divided and allocated to each route. It leapfrogged its batteries to provide constant heavy flak cover while the light batteries were incorporated in the moving groups. Route C was used by the division's reconnaissance battalion, followed by divisional headquarters, signals battalion and one anti-aircraft battalion. Route B was shared by both Panzergrenadier regiments, the engineer battalion and another anti-aircraft battalion, while Route A carried the bulk of the division's tracked vehicles; the Panzer Regiment, Panzer Artillery Regiment and the last anti-aircraft battalion.

Movement was regulated by a divisional timetable, control maintained, and orders issued through liaison officers attached to each column who reported events directly to Schmalz's headquarters through existing postal communications systems, message centres established at Viterbo, Oriolo and two other points along the various routes as radio silence was strictly maintained.

Inevitably, movements along both Routes A and B were discovered by Allied reconnaissance within hours of the transit march beginning. Relentless low-level air attack followed by both day and night that caused heavy losses, the aircraft operating as part of the devastatingly effective Operation 'Strangle' tasked with the interdiction of German supply and transport networks north of Rome. Compounding the division's misery was the fact that after reaching the Viterbo area, no fuel stocks had arrived. Only after intense pressure on Kesselring's chief quartermaster from the 'Hermann Göring' chief of staff and quartermaster was an ad hoc fuel supply achieved on the morning of 24 May. While some fuel was shipped to the division, the rest had to be picked up by the division's own fuel trucks from a Wehrmacht depot, causing considerable delay.

While the elements that had travelled by Route C reached the assembly area near Valmontone delayed by fuel problems but relatively intact, the same was not true of the remainder which straggled in piecemeal. Of Oberst von Heydebreck's Panzer Regiment's seventy-two tanks, only eleven reached the intended concentration area by the evening of 26 May. Stragglers that had been disabled but repaired by the division's mobile workshops increased the number to eighteen, of which only eight to ten would henceforth be operationally fit at any one time. The remainder had been destroyed by Allied air attacks. The headquarters company and parts of several different companies of Panzergrenadier Regiment 2 arrived during the course of the same day. The remainder were immobilised along the route, having had at least 30 per cent of their vehicles shot to pieces, the men later collected by empty vehicles returning for them over the course of the next two days. Furthermore, though they had suffered relatively few casualties, they had lost a great number of machine guns, mortars and rifles with the destroyed transport. The same was true of Panzergrenadier Regt. 1 and the Engineer Battalion which began straggling in twenty-four hours later. Of Oberst Oehring's Panzer Artillery Regiment, eighteen vehicles had been disabled by fighter-bombers during the forced march. Hermann Lohmann of the Beobachtungsbatterie was among the men whose transport was destroyed.

> Our division had been ordered to go to the front at Valmontone [and] because of the hurry, a daylight march was ordered – a fatal mistake in leadership. As a result of Allied air supremacy, the Fallschirm-Panzer-Artillerie Regiment suffered especially high losses to low-flying aircraft, particularly in terms of material. The loss of people was relatively small. Our weather car (Opel Blitz truck with closed box body for the equipment and crews) was set on fire on 23 May on Via Aurelia near Follonica opposite Elba. Fortunately, after a timely warning from our comrade sitting on the wing, we were able to jump out and get to safety in good time. We sought shelter in culvert pipes and behind stone walls on the slope from where we fired carbines at the low-flying aircraft with the success that one aircraft crashed in flames. There were four bottles of hydrogen gas, hand grenades, tracer ammunition and rifle ammunition in the car, which exploded after a short time. Fortunately, the bottles with the high explosive gas burned out. Because of the unpredictability of when and if things would explode, we could not leave cover in the immediate vicinity of the car.
>
> I can still remember that later that day after we were fed, two low-flying aircraft attacked me, firing all their weapons. With a sausage under my arm, I ran around a large pile of straw. Before the planes turned around, I quickly ran to the other side before they attacked from the side where I had been. Fortunately, the two aircraft never came up with the idea of attacking separately from both sides. As far as we could see, at least half of the vehicles in our observation battery had burned out. Because we were no longer operational, we returned to our old quarters in Perignano after a few days.[7]

Informed of the grievous state of the division, Kesselring maintained that such regrettable losses were justified by the urgency of the military situation at the front, though there were several heated discussions regarding the length of time the division took to reach the battle area. Schmalz was informed that Kesselring intended to commit the division to action as soon as possible, probably in an offensive operation designed to eliminate the Allied penetration east of Velletri, and possibly an extended advance as far as Anzio. Otherwise, the division would probably be used for a containing action, involving a more limited offensive objective. However, at that point, it remained unclear whether the division would receive orders directly from Kesselring's headquarters or be placed under the control of either the Fourteenth or Tenth Army. Schmalz, after a quick briefing by Kesselring at Monte Soratte, was instructed to familiarise himself with the situation at the front by reporting to Fourteenth Army headquarters along with Kesselring's operations officer, Oberst Baelitz, arriving at 1500 hrs to be briefed by Mackensen himself. By Baelitz being present Kesselring hoped that speedy directives for the division's deployment could be issued with immediate movement possible. While Mackensen was told by Kesselring that Armoured Reconnaissance Battalion 'HG' was being moved to the breakthrough sector and would remain under Fourteenth Army orders, the bulk of the division was intended to be held back for possible commitment with the Tenth Army.

Schmalz learned that, contrary to Kesselring's rather far-fetched ambitions, the situation at Valmontone was critical. Large portions of the defending 362nd and 715th Divisions had been annihilated; one further strong attack might prove capable of pushing the inner wings of the Fourteenth and Tenth Armies apart and allowing an exploitative breakthrough that could encircle I. Fallschirmkorps and drive a deep wedge into the flank of Tenth Army by fanning out both east and west. The gap torn in German lines at Valmontone needed to be sealed immediately and Schmalz established his command post at Oriolo and prepared contingency plans to stop any possible enemy attacks using all arriving elements as the division concentrated.

The troops that had taken the relatively unimpeded Route C began arriving at Monte Porcio, east of Frascati, during 25 May after delays caused by fuel shortages. Both the Armoured Reconnaissance Battalion and Anti-Aircraft Battalion were ordered that night to push through Valmontone immediately and seize the high ground south of Artena where they clashed with reconnaissance troops of the U.S. 3rd Division, advancing rapidly from the Anzio break-out, during the morning of 26 May. Though American pressure eased temporarily, a further push by the 'Hermann Göring' troops to gain the high ground failed due to a lack of artillery support and the following day a renewed American attack in strength forced the Germans back out of Artena.

The front line was so near that Schmalz was able to watch through binoculars from a forward headquarters the growing concentrations of tanks belonging to the U.S. 3rd Armored Division only two miles from Velletri. The urgency of establishing a blocking position across the Valmontone–Cisterna gap between I. Fallschirmkorps and LXXVI. Panzerkorps was paramount to Schmalz, though his forces remained perilously weak; only the already committed Reconnaissance Battalion, headquarters and miscellaneous elements of Oberst Hans Horst von Necker's Panzergrenadier Regiment 2 'HG', approximating a battalion in strength, as yet being available to him. Fragments of several artillery regiments of destroyed divisions reported to Schmalz's headquarters and were immediately placed under the command of Panzergrenadier Regiment 2 and thrown straight into the line next to the Reconnaissance Battalion.

> Despite the extremely open terrain and the weakness of this group, the division ordered it to seize the Lariano–Artena road during the night of 26–27 May and to hold it while maintaining contact with the adjacent Armoured Reconnaissance Battalion. The division planned to erect a blocking position across the Valmontone–Cisterna gap and to assemble newly arriving units behind this line for a later attack on Giulianello. So far, the only element of the Panzer Regiment which had arrived was headquarters.
>
> The force under HQ 2. Panzergrenadier Regt. reached the Lariano–Artena railway and was halted there by enemy artillery fire. C-in-C Southwest was evidently not in agreement with the measures taken, since a very sharp order from the *Feldmarschall*, which reached the division on the morning of 27 May, directed the halting of all attacks and the concentration of the division north of Valmontone. In the division's opinion C-in-C could have arrived at this decision only through ignorance of the actual situation. The commitment of the Armoured Reconnaissance Battalion had halted the enemy attack and thereby permitted the division's concentration for later offensive action. This was the reason for the commitment of the weak group of 2. Panzergrenadier Regiment. The execution of

> the C-in-C's order would have resulted in relinquishing the gained blocking position, would have invited the enemy to press further to the north towards Valmontone, and would have automatically forced the Fourteenth and Tenth Armies apart. Duc to this frontline evaluation, the division did not follow the order.[8]

The following day, the entire Fallschirm-Panzer-Division 'HG' was officially attached to Fourteenth Army, placed once again under General der Panzertruppe Traugott Herr's LXXVI. Panzerkorps control, and ordered to open an attack to the south by noon that day.

By that stage the frontline strength of the 'Hermann Göring' Division was organised by Schmalz as follows:

Gruppe Panzergrenadier Regt. 1 'HG' — *Obstlt. Waldemar Kluge*
concentrated southeast of Rocca Priora

Gruppe Panzergrenadier Regt. 2 'HG' — *Oberst Hans Horst von Necker*
Elements of Panzer Regiment 'HG' (eight tanks) under the command of Maj. Rossmann; Elements of Panzer Artillery Regiment 'HG' with attached Heer artillery fragments (Oberst Heine); Elements of Armoured Engineer Battalion 'HG', one anti-aircraft Abteilung, with heavy batteries employed in anti-tank role

Gruppe Commander Panzer Regiment 'HG' — *Oberst von Heydebreck*
Armoured Reconnaissance Battalion 'HG'; two battalions of 29th Panzergrenadier Division; one anti-aircraft battalion; divisional and other assorted artillery, approximating two battalions (Oberst Oehring)

There was small chance of success if any attack was launched in broad daylight over open terrain in the face of overwhelmingly superior Allied fire-power so the troops advanced at 1930 hrs on 27 May, initially successfully as the Lariano–Artena lateral road was captured until heavy artillery fire stopped the attack in its tracks. American patrols of 36th Division had already penetrated as far as the wooded slopes of Monte Artemisio, a four-mile-long ridge running from northeast to southwest and overlooking Velletri from about a mile to the north. Herr immediately ordered Schmalz to despatch trucks to the 'Hermann Göring' assembly area near Volmontone to bring two battalions to the Artemisio ridge. The battered remains of 715th Infantry Division were also dragged to the area to bolster Schmalz's slender forces.

That night 'Hermann Göring' was ordered by Herr to continue the attack south of Valmontone the following day, aiming to reach the line Giulianello–Roccamassima where the division's right wing should be able to establish contact with the decimated 362nd Infantry Division occupying the left wing of I. Fallschirmkorps in the area of the small hamlet of Menta southwest of Lariano. Gruppe 'Kluge' had assembled north of Lariano on the southern slopes of Monte Artemisio, Kluge being ordered to commit one half-tracked battalion on the right and carry the main battle line towards the southeast to link with Gruppe 'von Necker' and then attack in tandem towards Giulianello supported by Oberst Heine's artillery.

While Kluge was a pre-war veteran of the 'Hermann Göring', forty-year-old Necker had been in Army Reserve since being wounded in Russia with the 9th Panzer Division. Transferred to the 'Hermann Göring' Division as a training officer, he had returned to Russia as Chief of Staff of the Sixteenth Army before being named commander of Fallschirm-Panzergrenadier-Regiment 2 'HG' in March 1944.

The attack began as planned but soon was forced to a halt in Necker's area by extremely heavy defensive fire. Kluge's half-tracked battalion passed the main battle line north of Lariano and advanced one further kilometre to the southeast before being stopped by previously sown German defensive minefields. Unable to clear the mines during the hours of daylight, the battalion was swiftly withdrawn to positions in the main battle line. His second battalion achieved partial success, reaching the corps boundary at Menta after encountering only minor American patrols of the 36th Infantry Division. An officer and a few troops were stationed in the small cluster of houses and thereafter reported to both the Fourteenth Army Chief of Staff and Schmalz daily by telephone of the situation on the ground.

Pushing further, strong flanking fire was encountered along the Lariano–Velletri Road and the advance stalled with the 'Hermann Göring' front line stretched perilously thin. German patrols reached Velletri and established contact with 362nd Infantry Division at the road fork northeast of the town. This left a three-mile gap between the two corps and Schmalz was able to observe enemy troops penetrating that gap, immediately ordering his final reserves, a platoon of engineers, to occupy the Castello d'Ariano, a medieval ruin located on Monte Artemisio's crest 5 km north of Velletri and 2½ km west of Lariano.

The 'Hermann Göring' troops had taken heavy casualties and the front line was growing weaker hourly. Prisoner of war interrogations by Allied intelligence officers had begun to note the presence of rear-echelon troops – bakers, clerks, supply troops – among those captured as every available man was thrown into action. Only with the most strenuous efforts were relentless

American attacks repulsed and, in an attempt to close the gap and make up for the deficit of numbers, both Necker and Heydebreck committed heavy and light flak units to ground fire; the sole reinforcements received by the division during that period were the rocket launchers of Werfer Brigade 5 under the command of Oberst Andrae.

Schmalz had repeatedly warned Mackensen's staff of the huge gap in the German line but not until the afternoon of 29 May after a brief visit to the forward area of I. Fallschirmkorps did Kesselring learn of it and immediately issue orders for it to be closed. However, Mackensen laboured under the impression that it was satisfactorily held and during the night of 29/30 May, men of the U.S. 36th Infantry Division began climbing Monte Artemisio. By 0635 hrs the leading American units had reached the summit, capturing three German artillery observers, one of whom was in the bath at the time. Not a shot was fired until German observers spotted the American troops during the following afternoon and opened a harassing artillery barrage. For the Americans, the only artillery support required was to blast the 'Hermann Göring' engineers from the Castello d'Ariano. By the onset of darkness the entire ridge was in American hands as other units mounted assaults against the German main battle line. The gap was broken open, Velletri successfully outflanked and a 200-degree field of vision now given to American artillery observers who beheld a glut of tempting targets.

Mackensen remained convinced that Allied troops would never have been able to capture the Artemisio Ridge if the 'Hermann Göring' division had been immediately placed at his disposal on its arrival. Instead, by his reckoning, he had been ordered to place them in the rear, and though two battalions had taken over the foremost German positions, they were subsequently withdrawn without Mackensen's knowledge. Kesselring, for his part, was enraged by the American success and, after Mackensen asked, for the third time since February, that he be relieved of his command, the request was now accepted. Within a few days Mackensen departed for retirement in Germany, replaced by General der Panzertruppe Joachim Lemelsen.

In the interim, the American push of 30 May inflicted severe losses on Gruppe 'von Necker' and pushed it back to the railway northwest of Artena. Gruppe 'von Heydebreck' was also forced to retreat, while fresh orders to counter-attack arrived at Schmalz's forward command post. Almost two-thirds of his infantry had been lost during the fighting and only six Panzers remained operational. Clearly a daylight attack was impossible, particularly with the newly established excellent American artillery observation posts and so Schmalz planned a thrust by Gruppe 'von Heydebreck' with accompanying Panzers from the southern outskirts of Valmontone towards Stazione di Artena. Predictably, the exhausted German forces failed and in subsequent strong American counter-attacks, the gap between the 'Hermann Göring' troops of LXXVI. Panzerkorps and I. Fallschirmkorps was widened. The commanders of each 'Hermann Göring' *Gruppe* had received firm instructions to keep tight control over their troops and defend every inch of ground, but they were eventually overrun and suffered debilitating casualties. Gruppe 'von Necker' – Panzergrenadier Regiment 2 'HG' – practically ceased to exist by the end of the first day of June, stragglers fighting their way back to German lines in small groups or individually; Necker was awarded the Knight's Cross on 24 June for valour in action. Oberstleutnant von Heydebreck and two of his battalion commanders were seriously injured that same day, leaving his *Gruppe* without leadership until the commander of the Armoured Reconnaissance Battalion assumed control over the remnants near Valmontone.[9] By then the *Gruppe* amounted to Panzer Regiment headquarters, one battalion headquarters of the Panzer Regiment, four Panzer IVs, the Armoured Reconnaissance Battalion, elements of the attached 1066th Grenadier Regiment, one medium battalion of the Panzer Artillery Regiment and one anti-aircraft battalion. In total, on the final day of May the division reported twenty Panzers and seven assault guns still combat ready.

During the course of the day's fighting, telephone communications were interrupted, and Schmalz lost direct control over his fragmented division, able to lead only by personal contact, radio communications or liaison officers, if they could find the relevant command posts in action.

> The division was overrun on 1 June 1944. It is significant for the high fighting morale of the young volunteers of the Panzer Division 'HG' that no man surrendered, but all held their positions until they fell or were taken prisoner after being wounded. This was the day of the destruction of the 2nd Panzergrenadier Regiment. There survived the regimental and two battalion headquarters with parts of their signal platoons and runners. These headquarters fought the defensive actions on 2 and 3 June 1944 in small dispersed groups. A couple of days later the British Army Radio Station brought the news:

> 'The "HG" Division fighting heroically succumbed for the third time near Valmontone.'
>
> Gruppe 'Kluge' could still be considered a fighting unit that same night (1 June) although having suffered heavy losses. It was broken through on 2 June and finally destroyed during the fighting on both sides of Colonna on 3 June 1944. From 2 June on, the division was merely in a position to fight delaying actions in small strongpoints.[10]

Schmalz personally intervened in the fighting at Colonna, to provide direct fire instructions for artillery batteries still in action. Bereft of commands from above, he authorised the remnants of the division to pull back to the area of Cervara behind the Aniene River on the eastern outskirts of Rome. Crossing the river near Lunghezza and Tivoli, the shattered remnants of the division successfully withdrew under enemy fire, Schmalz moving his headquarters to Mentana at 1800 hrs that day. Ironically, the magnetic attraction of occupying Rome itself lessened pressure on the retreating German troops and LXXVI. Panzerkorps directed 'Hermann Göring's remnants to pull back once more and occupy the defensive line Tiber–Monte Rotondo–Mentana–S. Angelo, as the 15th Panzergrenadier Division moved to cover Schmalz's left flank. A long-delayed Panzergrenadier battalion, stalled at Sutri 32 km north of Rome during the move south due to a lack of fuel, was finally reunited with the division as welcome reinforcement.

Though German forces were now in disarray and at their lowest ebb, the victorious Allies then missed their opportunity to shatter Kesselring's defences once and for all. Instead of full-blooded pursuit Clark instead opted for the prestige of capturing an open city from which the German occupiers had long departed. His glory was short-lived. After entering Rome on 5 June, his coveted newspaper headlines were lost the following day to the opening of Operation 'Overlord' and the long-awaited Allied landings in Normandy.

Chapter Ten

From South to East, and East to West

'The place of all commanders of armour up to the divisional level is on the battlefield.' *Generalmajor Hasso von Manteuffel*

Italy had virtually destroyed the Fallschirm-Panzer-Division 'Hermann Göring'. During May alone, the division lost 62 officers and 2,485 men to death, injury, sickness or missing in action. During the month that followed a further 45 officers and 1,331 men were killed or missing, 57 officers and 1,942 men wounded or ill. In return 18 officers arrived from Utrecht training, along with 247 men, and 4 officers and 171 men returned to action after convalescing. On 9 June, the combat strength of the division had fallen to 977 men and only by rigorously combing the divisional rear echelon units and staffs did Schmalz estimate that it could be raised to 3,124 men within ten days. Of those, though, it was unsure how many were suitably prepared for front-line action. Losses in equipment and armour had been equally serious and of the permitted complement of 31 *Sturmgeschütze* and 98 Panzer IV tanks, only 12 Panzer IVs were serviceable on the first day of July 1944.

To Kesselring the loss of ground was of less importance than the necessity of rebuilding shattered units and, despite Hitler's direct orders to stand and fight, he maintained his steady withdrawal towards the Gothic Line, fighting the grinding defensive war that vexed Allied pursuit and allowed the weeks required to finish defensive installations under construction to the north.[1] 'Hermann Göring' had moved out of the line to regroup, though as the Germans were pushed progressively north, Schmalz's division returned to the Tenth Army's right flank north of Orvieto opposite the British XIII Corps, defending the Maggiore Monte area. There they occupied field fortifications of the temporary Trasimene Line under unrelenting pressure but acquitted themselves well in combat as they retreated gradually into the Arno Valley. Rittmeister Röther, commander of the Armoured Reconnaissance Battalion since 4 July, was seriously wounded on 16 July, Oblt. Bach taking command as they withdrew from the line.

The division's time in Italy was finally ending – it was relieved by the light infantry of the 715th Jäger Division with the transfer completed by 18 July. The campaign culminated in diminished fighting power that Kesselring would later lament. Nonetheless, the Fallschirm-Panzer-Division 'Hermann Göring' was to be refitted and redeployed to the Eastern Front, one of five divisions promised by Hitler to the newly appointed commander of the shattered Army Group Centre, Generalfeldmarschall Walter Model, for a proposed counter-strike against the devastatingly effective Soviet Operation 'Bagration' that had brought the Red Army to the gates of Warsaw. General der Panzertruppe Nikolaus von Vormann's Ninth Army had been shattered by the Soviet onslaught, its remnants constituted as Gruppe 'von Vormann' and placed under command of the Second Army until reconstitution during August thanks to an influx of new troops. However, Vormann faced a herculean task as he tried to halt the tidal wave of Soviet power.

On 25 July when Vormann's Ninth Army staff was activated once more, not a single German division was located in the area between Puławy and Siedlce and the road to Warsaw from the southeast was open for the Red Army. Fallschirm-Panzer-Division 'Hermann Göring' had been immediately earmarked to hold this ground, alongside the 17th and 73rd Infantry Divisions frantically being shuttled from the Balkans and Norway as well as the 174th Reserve Division (soon absorbed into the 26th Infantry Division). In Warsaw itself the tension was palpable with the Red Army seemingly poised to throw bridgeheads across the Vistula to the south of city. Operation 'Tempest' – the Polish rising against German occupation by General Tadeusz 'Bór' Komorowski's Polish Home Army (Armia Krajowa, or 'AK') had already begun as early as March in other regions which the Red Army had neared, so a similar uprising was considered almost inevitable in Warsaw. A partial evacuation of the city had been ordered by the German military governor, SA Gruppenführer Ludwig Fischer, on 22 July.

As the Eastern Front collapsed under the weight of the Red Army steamroller, Göring had personally requested the return of his division from Italy. In Prussia on 13 July 1944, the Guard Regiment, commanded by Obstlt. Eric Bertram, was renamed Escort [Begleit] Regiment 'Hermann Göring' and assigned to protect the hunting lodge and Ob.d.L. Staff train from both air and ground attack. Protection of the train required an

The 'Hermann Meyer' peaked cap, used only by Luftwaffe tropical troops, is worn here by a 'Hermann Göring' man, along with standard Heer Panzer insignia on his lapels.

Adolf Scheckenbach, wearing the white-backed Panzer insignia peculiar to 'Hermann Göring' troops. (*Alan Scheckenbach*)

Sturmgeschütz IIIB used for training at Harderwijk in 1944; Adolf Scheckenbach at far left. (*Alan Scheckenbach*)

Above: A new Panzer IV delivered to the 'Hermann Göring' Division in Germany. (*Alan Scheckenbach*)

Left: Oberst Wilhelm Schmalz.

Right: A 'Hermann Göring' Panzer IV commander.

Clearly relieved: 'Hermann Göring' men being evacuated on a Red Cross vessel from Sicily. (*Alan Scheckenbach*)

Top left: A 'Hermann Göring' *Sturmgeschütz* on the move.

Left: The exposed Sicilian ground on which 'Hermann Göring' Panzers were concentrated before being hammered by Allied naval gunfire. (*Alan Scheckenbach*)

Komm zu uns!
DIVISION
HERMANN GÖRING
stellt Freiwillige ein!
Auskunft und Meldung bei allen Wehrbezirks-Kommandos

Above: Hermann Göring inspecting reinforcements for his namesake division in Germany, 1943.
Left: The cover of a 'Hermann Göring' Division recruiting pamphlet, published in 1943.

An 88 mm cannon belonging to 2. Batterie, I./Flak-Regiment 'Hermann Göring' ready for action in Italy.

Above: The awesome power of naval gunfire: the remains of a Panzer IV near Salerno.

Above right: 'Hermann Göring' Panzergrenadier prisoners of war escorted to the rear by PFC Ira O. Creed of the U.S. Army after the fierce fighting on Mount Porchia during January 1944's battles before the 'Gustav Line'.

Left: Gerhard Tschierschwitz, photographed here after the award of his Knight's Cross on 6 December 1944 for action in East Prussia.

Right: 'Hermann Göring' troops in action in Italy, 1944.

'Hermann Göring' troops unloading trucks carrying the treasures of Monte Cassino Abbey at the Palazzo Venezia, Rome, 1944.

Bringing fresh water to the front lines, past a wrecked American Sherman tank, Italy, 1944.

Above: Training of fresh Panzer recruits near Utrecht, 1944. (*Alan Scheckenbach*)

Right: Highly decorated Oberst Georg-Henning von Heydebreck. Among his awards are the Knight's Cross, German Cross in Gold, Iron Cross First Class, Panzer Assault Badge, ribbon for Iron Cross Second Class, and four- and twelve-year service bars. On his right pocket is the ribbon of the political 'Blood Order'; one of the most prestigious decorations of the Nazi Party commemorating the November 1923 attempted Putsch.

A local woman examining the wreckage left behind by the 'Hermann Göring' Division after a reprisal action against San Pancrazio, July 1944. (*Canadian National Archives*)

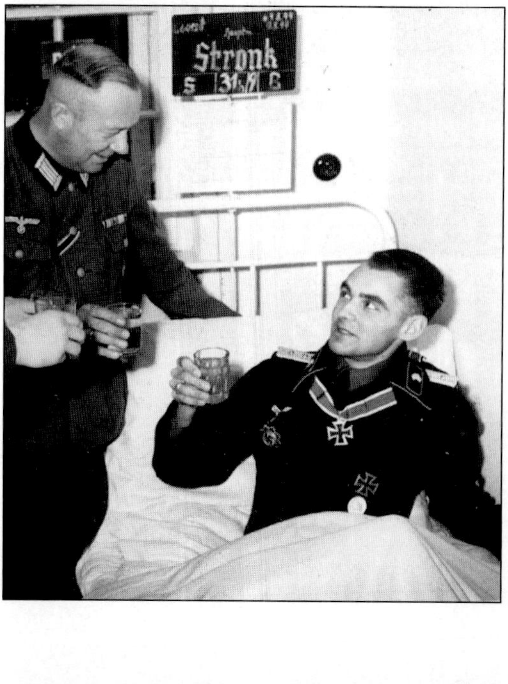

Above: Generalmajor Schmalz confers with SS-Gruppenführer Heinz Reinefarth during the fighting in Warsaw, 1944.

Far left: Hauptmann Wolfram Stronk receives his Knight's Cross while recovering in hospital following the loss of his right leg in the battles near Warsaw.

Left: Major Hans Briegel also received the Knight's Cross for his role in the Warsaw area battles.

Top left: Oberst Hans Horst von Necker, final commander of Fallschirm-Panzer-Division 1 'Hermann Göring'.

Left: Franz Lürbke. (*Franz Lürbke*)

Right: Generalmajor Erich Walther, commander of Fallschirm-Panzergrenadier-Division 2 'Hermann Göring'.

Far right: Karl Rossmann (*left*) with Gerhard Tschierschwitz atop Rossmann's Panther tank, 1945.

Knight's Cross award ceremony, East Prussia, December 1944. *Left to right:* Hptm. Werner Stuchlik, Oblt. Gerhard Tschierschwitz, Oblt. Rupert Kraus, Lt. Karl-Heinz Wallhausser, Uffz. Werner Grunhold, Gef. Konrad Steets, Gef. Albert Plapper, Ofw. Fritz Bowitz (awarded German Cross in Gold).

Hermann Göring inspects the men of his Wachregiment near his Reichsjägerhof on the Rominte Heath as the Eastern Front draws closer.

additional rifle battalion, while Bertram's original regiment numbered seven companies, six Panzergrenadier and one cavalry, plus 2nd (Flak) Battalion (formed from Flak Battalion 194), stationed in Tollmingkehmen and Gross Rominten. Bertram's regimental headquarters was located in the Hotel zum Hirschen in Gross Rominten, 2 km by road to the southeast beside the Rominte River. Three large barracks had been constructed by mid-1942 in a horseshoe configuration south of the junction of Wehrkircher and Nassawer Strasse, 750 metres from regimental headquarters and here, Hptm. Adolf Zillmann's 1. Wachkompanie was permanently based as the fighting in the east drew inexorably closer.

The day following the attempted assassination of Adolf Hitler by Oberst Claus von Stauffenberg, Göring delivered a bellicose speech to men of his Begleit Regiment in Prussia, decrying the approaching enemy and extolling the virtues of his namesake troops and their ability to defeat the enemy using Panzerfaust anti-tank weapons.

> You should see what a rabble the Russian infantry is! For brave men even tanks hold no fears, because now a staunch man can defend himself even at close quarters against tanks.
>
> Any soldier who throws away his arms, even a pistol, in order to retreat faster, puts himself beyond the pale of honour and obligation: each and every one of you, whether NCO or soldier, has the duty to shoot cowards like that on the spot. Just as the British and Americans in Italy now speak of your division with awe, the Russians must learn to fear you too . . . Comrades, you must make this pledge: You may give ground in Russia – that is not decisive – but never in Germany. Not one German woman or German child must fall into their bestial hands. And if fate should be against us, if the Russians should come into this province, then that must only be possible when no soldiers of the Hermann Göring Division are left alive.[2]

Bertram's Escort Regiment 'HG' was briefly attached to General der Infanterie Gerhard Matzky's XXVI Army Corps in the Baltic States during August 1944 as the Soviets pushed German forces back. It was attached to Fallschirmjäger Regiment 16 and constituted Kampfgruppe 'Oberst Schirmer' (Oberst Gerhart Schirmer), stationed first on the East Prussian border and then in Lithuania. In heavy fighting near Vilnius the *Kampfgruppe* suffered severe casualties, before both Bertram's men and the

Fallschirmjäger regiment were withdrawn and swept up in a reorganisation of the 'Hermann Göring' formations during September. From Bertram's regiment, two companies were detached along with 12th Battery of the 2nd (Flak) Battalion, these three units forming the Begleit Bataillon 'Reichsmarschall' under the command of Hptm. Siegfried Kühn. By January 1945 this battalion had expanded to seven companies: 1st Grenadier Company; 2nd Flak Battery; 3rd Grenadier Training Company; 4th Grenadier Training Company; 5th Driver Training Company; 6th Driver Training Company and 7th Convalescent Company.

Meanwhile, the battered remnants of the division still in Italy marched over the Arno River at San Giovanni and headed north to Bologna. The journey was fraught with danger as recalled by Hermann Lohmann:

> I still remember our trip over the Apennine Mountains somewhat unpleasantly. We drove at night; during the day was not possible due to the Allied low-flyers, with a truck through the sometimes very steep mountains. I was sitting with several comrades in the loading area, on which all kinds of war equipment lay. The journey went on a dark night with very little light over steep switchbacks up to the Futa Pass, which is almost 1,000 m high. For reasons of darkening due to the risk of air raids, the headlights were taped down to a small transverse slot, through which only a little light fell on the road. When we got to the top of the pass, the brakes unexpectedly locked. The driver was forced to drain the brake fluid to release the brake pads. We suddenly got gunfire from the right side, probably from partisans. We shot back into the night, roughly in the direction of the muzzle flashes, and this was enough to create calm. The partisans were probably more afraid than we were.
>
> The journey from the Futa Pass down to the plain near Bologna then became a risky adventure. I'm still surprised today that we didn't fall into a canyon somewhere. The truck driver only had the engine brake for the steep, winding and serpentine descent. But everything went well. The clutch and gearbox endured the steep descent.[3]

Once in Bologna, the division boarded seventy-two passenger and freight cars which travelled in two groups via the Brenner Pass towards the Eastern Front. The troops finally began disembarking at the West Warsaw freight station, considered far enough from the front to escape Soviet aerial bombardment and protected by Warsaw's heavy anti-aircraft units and local air superiority. However, because of Soviet bombing, large portions of the division were forced to off-load in Pruszków and Piastów, before reaching the freight yards, and reassemble in Warsaw's western suburbs. Both en route and in Warsaw they received fresh armoured vehicles for the depleted Panzer Regiment.

A reorganisation of the division had been planned since May: the Panzer Regiment's 2nd Battalion was to consist of four Panzer companies, each with seventeen Panzer IVs and with an attached platoon of eight FlakPanzer 38(*t*) vehicles. The 1st Battalion was to be converted from Panzer IVs to Panthers in July but the division had already sent men to Berlin for training on the new tanks on 4 March. The 3rd Battalion was to become a Panzerjäger unit, equipped with twenty-one Jagdpanzer IV tank destroyers while 3rd Company, Panzerjäger Battalion, was to be outfitted with towed 75-mm Pak 40s. Thirteen of the Jagdpanzers were successfully collected in transit from the Breslau Heereszeugamtes on 22 July.

The division was ordered to march as small units in battle order through Warsaw, cross the Vistula and assemble in the Rembertów–Praga area for an expected counter-attack towards the southeast. While divisional headquarters was established in Warsaw's eastern railway station, the supply train would remain in western Warsaw, and as fresh units arrived at the freight station they were to be unloaded as rapidly as possible, separated into small groups and camouflaged against air attack for the journey. The march itself was also designed to intimidate the population of this potential trouble spot as Soviet propaganda broadcasts repeatedly urged city-wide rebellion against the German occupation. Schmalz issued strict instructions on 25 July that troops were to be prepared for a quick march to the south or east, ready for deployment within two hours at the latest. In the region around Rembertów defences were to be created covering all access roads from the east and southeast. Alongside potential ground attacks and airborne landings, 'bandit activity' (*Bandentätigkeit*) was considered inevitable and hedgehog positions offering all-round defence were to be established as quickly as possible. All available heavy weapons were to be utilised, camouflaged carefully from the air as the troops had grown accustomed to doing in Italy; all available anti-aircraft weapons were cleared for use, including machine guns. Motor vehicles were to be dug in and foxholes and slit trenches immediately created for all combat teams.

The first units arrived in Warsaw on schedule, the Armoured Reconnaissance Battalion and part of the Flak Regiment unloading and marching straight for the front across the Vistula bridges while they were being wired for demolition by Wehrmacht engineers. Praga's southeastern suburbs had come under threat from the Soviet 2nd Tank Army which had already taken the area around Garowlin. Only Generalleutnant Friedrich Franek's 73rd Infantry Division faced them and, combined with the leading 'Hermann Göring' elements, Kampfgruppe 'Franek' was allocated the task of slowing down the Soviet advance along Warsaw's eastern approaches, taking such heavy losses – including the capture of Franek – that his division retreated in tatters across the Vistula. Isolated and vulnerable, the Armoured Reconnaissance Battalion retreated to Praga where it was reunited with the majority of the Fallschirm-Flak and Fallschirm-Panzer-Artillerie regiments and Engineer Battalion on 30 July. The Fallschirm-Panzer-Regiment 'Hermann Göring' and both Panzergrenadier regiments experienced some dislocation in their march to the front as they arrived from Italy at staggered times and in different locations.

Schmalz's division was attached to General der Panzertruppe Dietrich von Saucken's XXXIX Panzer Corps as the German front finally began to stabilise. The 'Magnushev Bridgehead' to the south, created by amphibious armoured units of General Chuikov's 8th Guards Army, had been contained and no further breakthroughs were achieved by the exhausted Soviet front-line troops. 'Hermann Göring' units were thrown into action immediately they arrived, fighting against Marshal Konstantin Rokossovsky's 2nd Guards Tank Army which had been ordered to seize Praga.

Caught in the fierce action was Oblt. Heinz Göring – nephew of the Reichsmarschall – scheduled to take command of 10th (StuG) Company, Panzer Regt. 'HG' after Oblt. Wallhäusser had moved to a different company of Jagdpanzer IVs. Göring's *Sturmgeschütz* was badly hit by splinters from shellfire exploding in treetops above and the young officer was killed in action on 29 July, only one day after arriving by train at the Warsaw front.

Rokossovsky redirected his main thrust north from the Magnushev Bridgehead and ran headlong into 'Hermann Göring' units and remnants of the 73rd Infantry Division, fighting erupting on 30 July. By this stage 'Hermann Göring' mustered thirty-five serviceable Panzers of 2nd Battalion in the main defensive line and had consolidated positions outside Marki with Panzergrenadier Regiment 1 'HG'. That same day XXXIX Panzer Corps launched a counter-offensive before Warsaw. Augmented with tanks and artillery, a *Kampfgruppe* from Fallschirm-Panzergrenadier Regt. 1 'HG' attacked in the direction of Wołomin from Marki.

These two German units withstood the worst of the initial Soviet assaults. However, the 3rd SS Panzer Division 'Totenkopf', 5th SS Panzer Division 'Wiking', 4th and 19th Panzer Divisions were already beginning to arrive in the line east of Warsaw, Model orchestrating his own swift counter-attack using these understrength formations. Major-General Nikolai Vedeneev's 3rd Tank Corps thrust northwest through Okuniew and Wołomin to reach Radzymin, 10 km from central Warsaw and only five from the strategic bridge over the Narew River at Zegrze. On 31 July, tanks of the 60th and 58th Armoured Brigades (8th Guards Armoured Corps) attacked Okuniew and seized the town by early afternoon, though their further advance towards Ossów was halted by fierce defence mounted by 'Hermann Göring' Panzergrenadiers who used the swamps, forests and two rivers – the Długa Struga and the Czarna Struga – that separated both towns to their advantage. In the Praga area, concerted counter-attacks on 1 August by elements of 19th Panzer Division and Panzergrenadier Regiment 1 'HG' recaptured Aleksandrów and Okuniew where the Germans dug in to await the appearance of Waffen-SS reinforcements.

Schmalz's division had continued to arrive by rail and on 1 August the last twenty-two Panzer IVs of the Panzer Regiment's 5th and 7th Companies were unloaded in Pruszków and Piastów, driving to Ulrych Gardens between Prince Janusz and Gorczewska streets, north of the freight yards in Warsaw's Wola district. There they played an important albeit unwitting role in the subsequent uprising as they stood between approximately 1,500 Polish fighters of the Home Army poised to rise up against the Germans, and their arms caches hidden in the neighbourhood.

Across the Vistula Model formed Kampfgruppe 'von Saucken' from elements of 'Hermann Göring', 'Wiking' and 19th Panzer Divisions and intensified his armoured attacks on the weakened spearhead corps of the 2nd Guards Tank Army over the following three days near Wołomin. By 3 August the other German Panzer divisions had joined the battle and with strong artillery support forced the 103rd Armoured Brigade to retreat in disarray, abandoning much equipment on the battlefield as Radzymin was retaken, reopening the Warsaw and Wyszków road and reconnecting the wings of the German Ninth and Second Armies. Vedeneev's encircled corps was badly mauled. Near Pogorzelka, the Panzerjäger IVs of 3rd Battalion, Panzer Regiment 'HG' alongside Panthers of 1st Battalion, 27th

Panzer Regiment (19th Panzer Division) successfully fought to prevent the armoured units of 8th Guards Armoured Corps from breaking through to the encircled Soviet troops, inflicting heavy casualties; on 3 August Hptm. Hans-Joachim Bellinger's 9th Company, Panzer Regiment 'HG' alone reported the destruction of thirty-six enemy tanks, for which Bellinger received the Knight's Cross on 30 September.

Hauptmann Wolfram Stronk, who had been awarded the German Cross in Gold on 10 January 1944 in Italy, was in the thick of the action at the head of 6th Company, Panzer Regt. 'HG', his tanks instrumental in halting the Soviet advance. Stronk's troops were finally granted a reprieve on 4 August after fighting died out during the night. Exhausted, the young *Hauptmann* took the opportunity to get out of his vehicle and relax in the shade of a tree when unexpected shellfire landed nearby, splinters severing his right leg. With no medical assistance at hand and any attempt to save him by taking him to a field hospital considered futile, the unconscious and bloody officer was thrown on a heap of bodies collected for identification and burial at a nearby church. It was there that his deputy, Dr Herbert Burgert, found him and transported him to an aid station, thereby saving his life. Stronk was awarded the Knight's Cross on 18 October as he convalesced in hospital.[4]

On the morning of 4 August General der Panzertruppe Nikolaus von Vormann, commander of the Ninth Army, reported to Model the destruction of the 3rd Tank Corps, though it had not in fact been completely annihilated. Kampfgruppe 'von Saucken' was subsequently divided in half and elements of 19th Panzer Division and the 'Hermann Göring' Division were ordered back across the Vistula at Pilica to shore up defences against the Magnushev Bridgehead to the south of Warsaw. The Waffen-SS would remain to hold the line before Praga. The final assault mounted by 'Hermann Göring' troops before their relocation took place that day alongside *Kampfgruppen* from both 19th and 4th Panzer Divisions near Wołomin, though the same terrain that previously favoured their defence now inhibited the attack along both banks of the Długa River. The assault stalled with heavy losses, despite managing to destroy a reported seventy-six Soviet tanks. The following day an attack by Soviet 47th Army forced both SS Panzer divisions to withdraw, leaving the defence to the 'Hermann Göring' and 4th Panzer Division troops. Though German spoiling attacks were blunted, the Soviet advance was successfully brought to a halt and by 8 August the Red Army assumed a defensive posture as the front line reached stalemate. Between 20 July and 8 August, the 2nd Tank Army had lost 155 T-34/85s, 48 M4A2 Shermans,

4 IS-2 heavy tanks, 3 Mk 9 Valentines, 18 SU-85s and 15 SU-76s destroyed in the fighting.

Behind the German front line the dramatic Warsaw Rising had begun during the afternoon of 1 August. General 'Bór' Komorowski launched the long-planned Warsaw battle as part of the culmination of Operation 'Tempest'. Approximately 800 'Hermann Göring' troops were involved in the first few days of confused fighting in Warsaw, particularly within the Wola district. The twenty-two Panzer IVs of 2nd Battalion, Panzer Regiment as well as parts of 3rd Battalion, Panzergrenadier Regiment 2 and 4th Battalion, Fallschirm-Panzer-Artillery Regiment took part in the fighting. Their primary concern was breaking through hastily erected, though effective, barricades that hindered the supply routes from the freight yards through the city to troops over the Vistula.

Commander of Panzergrenadier Regiment 2 'Hermann Göring', Oberst Hans von Necker, led his grenadiers (and 14th Company of Marder tank destroyers) supported by four Panzer IVs of 7th Company, Fallschirm-Panzer Regt. 'HG' against barricades built with trams from the local depot at the intersection of Młynarska and Wolska streets. Once these were breached, Necker avoided pockets of heavy fighting in the city and led his troops to Zawisza Square and onwards to Grójecka Street and the southern city outskirts. His objective lay in the front line facing the Red Army rather than the Polish Home Army. Two 'Hermann Göring' men were lost during these sharp engagements: Unteroffizier Franz Eitt and Gefreiter Erich Gieth. Major Hans Briegel, later named regimental commander after Necker's departure, was awarded the Knight's Cross on 14 January after distinguishing himself in battle on the outskirts of Warsaw and subsequently in action against the Magnushev bridgehead. As Necker fought his way south, five Panzer IVs of 6th Company, Fallschirm-Panzer Regt. 'HG' under the command of Oberfähnrich Wilke and supported by FlakPanzer 38(*t*)s of the anti-aircraft platoon were in Praga as the uprising began, returning briefly to the west to support German troops of the central garrison. During a single day of combat Wilke reported seven resistance positions destroyed and between fifty and sixty insurgents killed.

German repair depots for armoured vehicles were also located in Warsaw as well as important communications and supply conduits. One of the primary repair stations was in ex-ammunition factory No. 1. in the Wola district and a nearby warehouse in Bem's Fort. A single Jagdpanzer IV of 10th Company, Panzer Regt. 'HG', commanded by Unteroffizier Bruno

Kanhert, was proceeding to this depot for repairs to a damaged main gun when the Rising began. Informed of the fighting when he reached Kierbedź Bridge, Kanhert opted to continue his journey despite the fresh dangers as he also wanted to deliver a gravely wounded crewman to field hospital. His damaged vehicle remained the sole 'Hermann Göring' *Panzerjäger* in Warsaw during the uprising. However, the presence of other strong 'Hermann Göring' units, as well as elements of the SS 'Totenkopf' Division, had a hugely detrimental effect on the Polish Home Army, the concentration of German forces in Praga also making it impossible to make any but the briefest attempts to attack German troops on the Vistula's eastern bank. Nonetheless, the uprising severely hindered the transit of troops through central Warsaw as the Wehrmacht and Waffen-SS in action against the Red Army hurriedly moved their mobile units from one threatened sector to the next.

To that end, swift suppression of the Warsaw uprising was to be handled by SS Obergruppenführer Erich von dem Bach-Zelewski who formed Korpsgruppe 'Bach', which in turn commanded two *Kampfgruppen*. Of these, Kampfgruppe 'Reinefarth', commanded by SS Gruppenführer Heinz Reinefarth, was the stronger, albeit composed of some of the most unsavoury elements ever to serve in the German armed forces. Unfortunately for the history of the 'Hermann Göring' Division, a reserve battalion of 'Hermann Göring' troops was attached to Reinefarth's group alongside formations including Kaminski's RONA Brigade of White Russians and Dirlewanger's SS Brigade of convicts and murderers. All these opened a full-scale assault on Warsaw's western suburbs on 4 August. It is unknown in which part of the fighting – if any – the Luftwaffe troops were used, but Kampfgruppe 'Reinefarth' was responsible for some of the most heinous atrocities committed by any troops during the Second World War as it raped, looted and murdered its way through the civilian population that Hitler himself had ordered exterminated without pity.

Away from the hideous events unfolding in the city, Schmalz had been ordered to move his division to face the Magnushev Bridgehead, the final trains carrying men from Italy being redirected to Radom to unload, from where the 'Hermann Göring' Division would launch its counter-attack. Unfortunately for Schmalz, the shortest route for the remainder of his division disengaging in the north to reach their new battle area was through Warsaw and the lengthy bypassing of the embattled city allowed the Soviet 8th Guards Army time to strengthen its forces in the bridgehead.

Nonetheless, by 6 August, 'Hermann Göring' reported fifty-one operational armoured fighting vehicles, and 2nd Battalion, Fallschirm-Panzer Regt. 'HG' went into action the following day against the Polish 1st Warsaw Armoured Brigade near Magnushev, now under the control of General von Lüttwitz's XLVI Panzer Corps. Schmalz established his headquarters inside a house in the forested area east of Glowaczow as the division mounted repeated counter-attacks that failed to dislodge the Soviets. On 9 August, Oblt. Wallhäusser excelled himself with his Jagdpanzer IV unit as he repelled repeated Russian assaults and launched his own spoiling attacks. Near Studziansk, he captured a small village from Russian control, destroying six tanks as well as several anti-tank and infantry positions; two of the destroyed tanks were hit by rounds fired by Wallhäusser himself after his gunner was wounded and incapacitated. Feldwebel Karl Kulp, leader of 13th Company, Fallschirm-Panzergrenadier Regt. 1 'HG' also distinguished himself in combat against the Soviet/Polish enclave and was awarded the Knight's Cross on 5 September. Oberfähnrich Fritz Birnbaum, Sturmgeschütz Platoon leader in 8th Company, Panzer Regiment 'HG' also received his Knight's Cross in East Prussia on 19 October.

Once again, the battle reached a stalemate, the Soviet/Polish bridgehead holding firm, but being contained for the time being. Model considered this his most threatened sector after the lull in activity northeast of Warsaw, and armoured reserves and reinforcements were allocated accordingly. However, on 16 August Model was moved west to take charge of the retreating Wehrmacht forces in France, replaced by Generaloberst Georg Hans Reinhardt who inherited a battlefield seeing fresh Soviet assaults as remorseless pressure against the thinly spread Waffen-SS units northeast of Warsaw pushed them back towards the Polish capital. On 13 September, German defenders were finally driven out of Praga to Żerań, blowing up the steel Kierbedź Bridge and the railway bridge at Cytadela as Polish and Soviet troops reached the Vistula in Warsaw.

'Bór' Komorowski had hoped that the Warsaw uprising would need to last only forty-eight hours before the arrival of the Red Army would complete the German defeat. At most, the Home Army considered it possible to hold out for six days. Over six weeks later, on 13 September, Necker's Fallschirm-Panzergrenadier Regt. 2 'HG' was brought to the western bank of the Vistula, intended to oppose any attempted crossings by enemy troops. There, in company with a *Kampfgruppe* of 25th Panzer Division, and a company from 2nd Battalion, SS-Panzer Regt. 3, they reported a combined total of eighteen serviceable Panzer IVs, sixteen Jagdpanzer IVs and four Marder IIIs. Technically, they remained under the control of Korpsgruppe 'Bach', though he was judged not only to lack front-line competency, but was focused on the destruction of Home Army pockets of resistance. Instead, Lüttwitz's XLVI Panzer Corps took command of the Vistula defensive line between Młociny and Góra Kalwaria, though Vormann sent an alarming message from his Ninth Army headquarters to Reinhardt claiming that:

> Only Division 'Hermann Göring' can be said to be fully adequate with regard to combat strength and battle-competence. The hard tested SS-divisions 'Totenkopf' and 'Wiking' – as well as the Ninth Army – have, during the past several weeks of combat, become so decimated that at this present juncture they are only equivalent to a very mediocre fighting force.

Within days Vormann was sacked, replaced with Lüttwitz as commander of the Ninth Army as Major-General Zygmunt Berling's 1st Polish Army attempted to cross the Vistula in central Warsaw. The crossing was a disaster; isolated pockets established on the western bank were decimated by German troops now familiar with urban fighting. Elements of the 8th Polish Regiment were cut to pieces by 'Hermann Göring' machine gunners aboard SdKfz 251 halftracks and accompanying Marder artillery fire. Those troops already landed were driven back into the river, though anti-tank fire forced the German vehicles to retire; the two Polish battalions that had attempted the crossing in the 'Hermann Göring' sector lost 370 men killed, 300 taken prisoner and only scattered troops linked up with the hard-pressed Home Army. It was the only Soviet/Polish effort to assist the uprising and cost the 1st Polish Army a total 1,987 dead or missing and 627 evacuated, of whom 289 were wounded.

North of Praga, SS-Obergruppenführer Herbert Gille's two battered divisions of the IV SS Panzer Corps were exhausted and unlikely to withstand further Soviet attacks. In consequence, with the fighting around the Magnushev Bridgehead at a standstill, Fallschirm-Panzer-Division 'Hermann Göring' – with the exception of its 2nd Panzergrenadier Regiment – was transferred to Gille's corps, boarding trains to Modlin and Włochy, though delayed by Soviet air attacks on the railway bridge near Warka. Towards the end of September Schmalz's men arrived to reinforce the exhausted SS men taking part in Operation 'Meteor' against Polish insurgents based in the Kampinos Forest. Three battalions of 'Hermann

Göring', 'Totenkopf' and 'Wiking' troops swept the area; all villages which were thought to have provided shelter for insurgents were burned, all male villagers shot. By 30 September the Kampinos Group of Polish insurgents had been largely eliminated.

The division's tenure with IV SS Panzer Corps was, however, to be brief. On 6 October orders were received from OKW for the division to be immediately removed and entrained once again, this time bound for Instersburg in East Prussia. There it was to be reinforced and thrown into action against the Soviet Third Belorussian Front, which had breached the German border and was pushing into Prussia. Amidst this tumult, Schmalz's force was also now to be expanded to become one of two divisions that would form the Fallschirm-Panzer-Korps 'Hermann Göring'.

The Netherlands

While the bulk of the division had been deploying in and around Warsaw, the Fallschirm-Panzer Ersatz und Ausbildung Regiment (Reserve and Training Regiment) 'Hermann Göring' was engaged in routine drill while also handling coastal defence duties in the West. It occupied part of what was known as the 'Land front', a secondary defensive line which, dependent on topography, lay three to eight kilometres from the 'Sea front' fringing the coastline itself.[5] Unit commander Obstlt. Robert Schulz moved to take command of Fallschirm-Panzergrenadier Regt. 1 'Hermann Göring' during August 1944, replaced by Oberst Fritz Fullriede. A veteran of the First World War, 49-year old Fullriede had distinguished himself in Tunisia as commander of the Grenadier-Regimentstab z.b.V. 165 in April 1943, winning the Knight's Cross in action against the British 6th Armoured Division. After a period in command of Fallschirm-Panzergrenadier Regt. 1 'HG', to which the Army Personnel Office first assigned him, he took control of the training regiment at Schmalz's personal request.

During December 1943 Franz Lürbke had enlisted in the 'Hermann Göring' Division after completion of his time in the Reich Labour Service.

> On the fourth day, after the morning roll call, we were to be assigned to training units. When asked who wanted to join the Panzer-grenadiers or Engineers, hardly anyone answered, almost everyone wanted to join the Panzers, including me. So, there was an individual selection in which it quickly became apparent that one's profession played a part. Because I claimed to be a car mechanic, I was accepted

and transferred to the 6th Panzer Company in Harderwijk with thirty other recruits who had also indicated a technical profession. My 196 cm height obviously didn't bother the instructors, although I often later felt that I was too tall for Panzers. I always experienced special difficulties when I had to get out of the driver's seat during exercises. We were trained on Panzer IIIs and Panzer IVs with 75-mm short-barrel cannon, or, as we called it, the '7.5 stub'.

At the end of January, the *Hauptfeldwebel* asked at morning roll call if anyone would like to be trained as an accountant. I volunteered and then in the afternoon I was sitting warm and dry in the office of the accounting officer, Obergefreiter Fally, a grumpy Innsbruck man with a heart, while my friends continued to drill outside.

Before the invasion began, in early June 44, the entire *Abteilung* was moved to the coast, the 6th Panzer Company to Castricum. I stayed in Harderwijk for about four weeks, initially for a few days with a small detachment as Duty NCOs from our company block. Then I was given further training by the staff company accounting officer, a calm, somewhat older *Feldwebel* with whom I got on really well. There was not much to do in the fairly empty barracks, it was a pleasant week. The radio was on all day in the office. When we were alone, we switched on the British 'Wehrmachtsender Calais' which had some interesting news, but also hair-raising propaganda reports that we cheerfully smiled at. Somehow this confirmed to us that, despite their success, the Allies could not be so remarkable if they believed they had to tell us such fairy tales. The most important thing for us was the great music, especially when the Andrews Sisters were played in between bulletins.

At the beginning of July the battalion commander, Hauptmann Müller, asked all those still in the barracks area the purpose of their presence. When it was my turn, he considered me to be completely superfluous in my training position in Harderwijk and sent me back to my company. The next day, it was a beautiful Sunday, I climbed onto the truck with comrades who were also headed to their units, driving in an arc around Amsterdam and taking us to the individual locations of our battalion's area on the coast. Such trips were extremely unpopular during daylight due to the constant risk of *Jabo* [fighter-bomber] attacks and we all kept watching the sky, but nothing happened.

The company in Castricum were quartered in houses on a side street, secured with barriers and barbed wire . . . At the end of August, two operational companies were formed by the battalion and immediately set off on bikes. I was assigned to the so-called 'A Company' as accounting officer. Through several changes of location, I travelled across Holland with this unit: Bloemendaal, Delft, Oosterbeek, Kasterlee in northern Belgium, s'Hertogenbosch, Tilburg, Roosendaal. In Bloemendaal we had the most beautiful quarters: a sanatorium with double rooms and white, real beds in which you could sleep wonderfully. Unfortunately, we were only able to enjoy it for one night, because shortly after waking up we received a new marching order.

After a short stay in Delft, we went on to Oosterbeek near Arnhem. There I got the order to go to Bloemendaal again by train and pick up our company's personnel documents. They had been forwarded to us by the battalion but had not reached us in Bloemendaal because of our sudden departure for Delft . . . When we returned to Oosterbeek on the evening of the second day after completing our task, our company was no longer there. Members of an SS division who had taken over our quarters could only confirm that it had moved but didn't know to where. The next morning we drove to the Luftwaffe reception point in Nijmegen. From there they wanted to send us to an alleged division collection point in Osnabrück. We didn't want to go to Germany, but to our company . . . I therefore suggested that I be allowed to try again at the Heer reception centre in Arnhem, which we were then allowed to do.

Of course, our unit's location was not known in Arnhem either . . . We also tried and asked around the barracks. On 16 September finally two soldiers who had just arrived told us that they had seen a unit with the 'Hermann Göring' cuff in Eindhoven. I immediately went to the office, claimed to know the location of our unit and left, again . . . the three of us now issued with the required marching orders. The *Kettenhunde* who checked us on the platform found this incomprehensible ('. . . aren't the Americans already there?') but let us on the train anyway.

We didn't meet our company in Eindhoven, but we found the right place to stay: Kasterlee in northern Belgium. Equipped with bicycles and marching supplies, we set off the next morning, as it

> turned out just in time, and in the afternoon we found our unit in the main battle line on the Prince Albert Canal. On the way we were able to observe the gigantic approach of the Allied air fleets to their destinations in Eindhoven, Nijmegen and Arnhem.[6]

It is surprisingly difficult to ascertain exactly which units comprised the Fallschirm-Panzer Ersatz und Ausbildung Regiment by September 1944 in the face of conflicting information. The most likely composition appears to have been that the regiment was divided into four main *Abteilungen* based in the Netherlands:

Unit	Commander	Equipment
1st Battalion	*Major Johann Wimmer*	
HQ Company		
1st–5th Motorised Grenadier Companies		
2nd Battalion	*Hptm. Willi Müller*	
HQ Company		
6th Panzer Company	*Lt. Sommer*	1 x Panzer III and 2 x Panzer IV
7th Motorised Panzergrenadier Coy	*Oblt. Minn*	
8th Bicycle Grenadier Company	*Oblt. Hagenmüller*	
9th Bicycle Grenadier Company	*Oblt. Esterer*	
10th Armoured Reconnaissance Coy	*Lt. Vetter*	
11th (Sturmgeschütz) Company		
12th (Panzerjäger) Company.		
3rd Battalion	*Maj. Werner Krahmer*	
13th Battery		20-mm and 37-mm flak
14th Battery		2 x 105-mm lFH, 2 x 150-mm sFH
15th Battery		150-mm sFH
16th Battery		6 x 88-mm Flak
4th (Combat Engineer) Battalion		
17th–19th Companies		
29th Unterführer-Lehrkommando		[NCO school)]
Rekrutenbataillon		[Recruit depot]

Furthermore, a motor-transport training battalion was based in Berlin and under direct divisional control, alongside the Signals Battalion that doubled as liaison between active 'Hermann Göring' units and recruiting offices, office for dependency benefits, procurement agencies for weapons and equipment and other ancillary Berlin units.

At the beginning of September, Student's 1. Fallschirm Armee, which had hitherto largely been a training formation, took control over a hastily assembled group of units facing the Allied advance into Belgium as the Wehrmacht lines in the west had ollapsed following the disaster in Normandy. Generalleutnant Kurt Chill, commander of 85th Infantry Division, had been ordered to take the remains of his command, which had suffered heavily at Falaise, to Germany for refitting and reinforcement but instead opted on his own initiative to create reception centres at the bridgeheads of the Albert Canal in northern Belgium. There, stragglers from France were gathered together to form a hasty defensive line to face the inevitable Allied thrust into Belgium. To this end Kampfgruppe 'Chill' came into being, a motley assortment of units from all three Wehrmacht service arms that were then hurriedly entrenched along the Albert Canal. The panic that had permeated the German retreat from France began to subside and the once virtually open Belgian border began to harden. An attempt by British 11th Armoured Division to cross the Albert Canal at Merksem was repulsed by troops of LXXXVIII Corps that had also been rapidly assembling outside Antwerp and to which Kampfgruppe 'Chill' was attached on 5 September.

Fullriede's Fallschirm-Panzer Ersatz und Ausbildung Regiment was among those committed piecemeal to the front line. On 2 September Hptm. Willi Müller's 2nd Battalion was ordered from Haderwyk towards Eindhoven, travelling onwards into Belgium and the Maas–Scheldt Canal at De Kolonie. Müller positioned his recruits in Locht, a small hamlet on the edge of the forest north of Hechtel. This latter town – a key settlement on the road leading to Eindhoven – had been almost completely taken by British Guards units of XXX Corps after they successfully seized a bridge over the Albert Canal at Beringen on 6 September, advancing on Hechtel where heavy fighting raged for three days against *Fallschirmjäger* of 3rd Regiment.

Müller's men were to be attached to Kampfgruppe 'Chill' and received orders to advance west to establish contact with German troops in Leopoldsburg while also mounting a counter-attack against Hechtel. Müller divided his force into four columns but the armoured vehicles under the command of Oblt. Otto Minn soon straggled behind the marching grenadiers because of the close nature of the surrounding countryside. When the advance was only 300 metres from Hechtel's outlying buildings, concealed British Guards opened fire, splitting the advancing troops in half. Two companies veered west, ran headlong into tanks of the Irish Guards and were beaten back. The remaining troops reached the outskirts of Hechtel where fighting continued throughout the day, the 'Hermann Göring' men reinforcing the last survivors of Oblt. Günther Plaumann's *Fallschirmjäger.*

During the following day, Müller concentrated his armour in a wooded area named Kamert north of Hechtel from where they could cover the eastern approaches and as dawn arrived tanks and infantry of the Irish Guards emerged from the morning mist, intent on cutting the road leading to Eindhoven and completely surrounding the troops still holding out in Hechtel. Battle erupted, with both sides taking casualties as the Guards battered their way towards their objective. British reinforcements from 11th Armoured Division arriving from the east at last broke the deadlock and after intense hand-to-hand fighting Hechtel was finally surrounded, though Müller and Plaumann's surviving troops continued to resist. Müller had established his command post in the village tavern but was wounded by shrapnel from direct artillery fire at 1500 hrs on 11 September; he had to be carried into the building basement while Plaumann directed the remaining defenders. Two 'Hermann Göring' *Stumrgeschütze* forced bombarding M10 Achilles vehicles to retreat and the town blazed as what was now designated Kampfgruppe 'Müller' continued to resist despite having lost contact with any other German commands. A patrol despatched by Chill to ascertain the situation in Hechtel reported the defenders surrounded, though his subsequent requests to grant permission to any survivors to withdraw were rejected by both Student and Reinhard.

The following day, 12 September, all British troops in Hechtel were pulled back and the town suffered a forty-five minute artillery barrage after which infantry and tanks once again battered their way into the shattered village. The final point of resistance – the Rijkswacht (National Police) building in the northeast of Hechtel – was held by Oblt. Minn and his surviving troops until 1400 hrs when they were finally forced to surrender. Approximately 400 men from the 'Hermann Göring' Battalion and 1st Battalion, Fallschirmjäger Regt. 20 were taken into captivity, including the wounded Müller. Only scattered troops successfully escaped and returned to German lines. A Leutnant Sommer was among them and the depleted survivors were grouped together as Abteilung 'Sommer', gathered in Bakel and assigned security duty on the eastern approach roads to Eindhoven.

Both 1st and 3rd Battalions were also subsequently attached to Kampfgruppe 'Chill'. Wimmer's 1st Battalion was in Loon op Zand and Krahmer's 3rd Battalion in Udenhout when they were ordered to the front with all possible speed. Krahmer was instructed to establish artillery positions around Retie, while Wimmer's grenadiers were rapidly transported in civilian buses towards Tenaard and thrown into battle against 8th Royal Scots who had crossed the Maas–Scheldt Canal in assault boats to capture a small bridgehead on the north bank. All bridges at Tenaard had been destroyed and the fighting became a confusing melee as both sides dug in throughout the town. Only when Krahmer's artillery began bombarding the British enclave did the 'Hermann Göring' troops withdraw, lest they receive casualties from their own shellfire. Fighting for the town raged unabated as British artillery fire then pulverised Wimmer's men attacking from the direction of Kasterlee. By the end of 16 September, most officers and NCOs had been killed or wounded and the young trainees became incapable of mounting serious attacks against the British who continued to receive reinforcements ferried across the canal.

The following day Fullriede, whose staff relocated from Utrecht to a castle near Hoevelaken, inspected his troops. He arrived in Krahmer's headquarters at Pomfort during early afternoon as 88-mm guns of 16th Battery engaged an airborne armada sweeping overhead. That day the Allies had launched Operation 'Market-Garden'; an ambitious plan for the First Allied Airborne Army to seize bridges in the Netherlands that would create a salient leading directly into Germany. The final objective – the bridge at Arnhem – crossed the formidable natural barrier of the Rhine River and, with all crossings captured, would open a clear invasion route into northern Germany. While airborne troops of U.S. 101st and 82nd and British 1st Airborne Divisions would take and hold the river crossings, British XXX Corps of the British Second Army would drive along the single road linking all crossings to consolidate the Allied hold over the corridor. However, events soon showed all too clearly that the plan was fatally flawed.

As Allied aircraft droned overhead, Fullriede drove to Kasterlee to discuss the situation at Tenaard with Wimmer before travelling to Bakel to meet the bedraggled survivors of 2nd Battalion. He had been appalled at the pitiful state of his troops who were being bled white in a battle at Tenaard that had now lost its importance following the start of 'Market-Garden' and the shift of focus to the east and the narrow road to Eindhoven. As Fullriede returned to his headquarters he once again came across the survivors of Abteilung 'Sommer' and changed their orders, directing them to begin the journey back to Germany via Utrecht rather than remain as security troops.

On 20 September, Wimmer was severely wounded, his place taken by Hptm. Westphal. It proved the final straw for the 'Hermann Göring' unit and Chill withdrew the remains of the battalion from Tenaard where it had lost eleven officers and two-thirds of its men as casualties. Ironically, the British had also suffered crippling casualties and withdrew, abandoning the contested bridgehead and evacuating troops by boat under cover of darkness. Though British commanders were unaware of it at the time, the loss of this bridgehead would unexpectedly exert unwelcome influence 'Market-Garden' as XII Corps no longer possessed a launch pad across the canal from which it could effectively cover the western flank of XXX Corps' advance into the Netherlands.

The battle for the major bridges was already well under way. The 101st Airborne seized four of its assigned bridges in and around Eindhoven on the first day, though that over the canal at Son was destroyed by the German garrison before capture, forcing a delay while a Bailey bridge was constructed by XXX Corps. However, the Waal bridges proved more difficult for the 82nd Airborne, which had not expected veteran troops as opposition. SS-Gruppenführer Willi Bittrich's II. SS Panzerkorps, headquartered in Doetinchem, had been detected by Allied intelligence but largely ignored in the lead-up to 'Market-Garden'. Bittrich realised that the retention of the Waal bridges was essential to containing the Allied advance, allowing supply of men both north and south of the river and the eventual isolation and destruction of the XXX Corps spearheads. He entrusted the defence of Nijmegen and its environs to SS-Brigadeführer Heinz Harmel's 10th SS Panzer Division 'Frundsberg'.

While the Nijmegen garrison commander, Hptm. Hagemeister, had fled across the Waal to Elst, Oberst Fritz Hencke of a *Fallschirmjäger* training unit gathered an ad hoc collection of troops and organised defence of the Waal bridges. Kampfgruppe 'Hencke' was, in addition to its own staff, composed of three companies of Ersatz-Bataillon 6 – elderly troops, reservists and convalescing wounded – a company of *Ordnungspolizei* and Hptm. Max Runge's company of 'Hermann Göring' trainee NCOs (Unteroffiziere Ausbildungs Kompanie) from 21. Unterführer-Lehrkommando. Supported by scattered flak units, Hencke's men were swiftly reinforced by SS troops from the direction of Nijmegen and three *Kampfgruppen* were soon formed, two of them comprised largely of 'Frundsberg' men while the 'Hermann Göring' trainees formed Kampfgruppe 'Runge', guarding the main Nijmegen bridges.

SS-Sturmbannführer Leo Reinhold, commander of 2nd Battalion, SS Panzer Regt. 10, arrived to take charge of Nijmegen's defence and under his energetic leadership the 'Hermann Göring' troops became embroiled in heavy fighting against the American paratroopers, who had been dropped south of the Waal, and advancing elements of XXX Corps. The bridge across the Meuse at Grave was soon lost by the Germans and the battle moved north into the streets of Nijmegen. Fierce attacks and counter-attacks took place, so that by dawn on 19 September Kampfgruppe 'Runge' was mainly involved in defending Nijmegen road bridge. That day Fullriede recorded the destruction of a British tank on the Nijmegen road bridge by a Gefreiter Casper armed with a Panzerfaust, the young NCO being hit by enemy machine-gun fire as the British tank burned.

In an audacious assault, men of the 82nd Airborne mounted a daylight crossing of the Waal to rush the stubbornly defended bridge from both ends simultaneously. Many of the 'Hermann Göring' men positioned themselves among the girder work but, despite their efforts, they were unable to prevent the bridge's capture by the paratroopers. Escaping Nijmegen, the shattered remnants of Kampfgruppe 'Runge' filtered back to the German lines near Arnhem, Fullriede later noting that some men from the NCO training company had swum the Maas to reach German territory and had reported the unconfirmed sight of American troops killing a number of prisoners and – improbably – throwing wounded men into the river.

Fighting against the 1st British Airborne Division at Arnhem were the men of the 'Wossowski Battalion' from 3rd Company, Fallschirm-Panzer-Ersatz und Ausbildung Regiment under the command of 26-year-old Oblt. Artur Wossowski, a former flak artillery officer with little infantry training and no experience in ground combat. The 'battalion' appears to have originated as a single company from Wimmer's battalion, detached on orders from Student on 18 September from its coastal duty at Katwijk aan Zee and directed towards Arnhem. Bereft of transport, 'Battalion Wossowski' – which is listed as numbering nearly 600 men by the time of its commitment to action – travelled by commandeered bicycles, initially at night for fear of Allied air attack, but later forced to proceed by day as well as night in all possible haste to the front.

Wossowski was placed under the command of a grandiosely titled battle group, 'Division von Tettau', and spent the night of 19 September on the Ede–Arnhem Road preparing for action against isolated pockets of British paratroopers reported in woods near Ginkel Heath. However, they found nothing during the following day except the detritus of previous fighting. Wossowski then led his men to Wolfheze under the control of the 9th SS Panzer Division 'Hohenstaufen'. SS-Oberführer Walter Harzer ordered Wossowski to take part in a concerted attack against British troops on the Westerbouwing Heights overlooking the Driel Ferry near Oosterbeek, scheduled to begin at 0800 hrs on 21 September. The attacking force was a conglomeration of several improvised units, thrown into action without knowing exactly what their objective was or indeed where the enemy were.

The 'Hermann Göring' troops followed their company commander's car on bicycles and were unaware of the presence of enemy troops when, near the Westerbouwing Inn, they suddenly came under machine-gun fire from B Company, 1st Borders, who defended the Heights. Taking casualties, the troops scattered before Wossowski marshalled his men to attack. Four formerly French Renault tanks from Panzer Company 224, with their main guns replaced by flamethrowers, supported the 'Wossowski Battalion' as it stormed the heights; no heavy artillery support was provided as the Heer officer in overall command, Oberst Schramm, forbade its use for fear of 'friendly fire' casualties.

The lack of supporting fire was hugely detrimental to the attackers and, although they eventually forced the British troops out of Westerbouwing, nearly every officer – except a single *Leutnant* – and half of 'Battalion Wossowski' were casualties and all four Renault tanks lost. A counter-attack by survivors of B Company was defeated and the British company commander, Major T. W. W. Armstrong, wounded and captured. His company sergeant-major and two platoon commanders were killed as B Company was decimated. Wossowski's troops regrouped and continued their advance towards Oosterbeek, taking further casualties from snipers and well-directed British automatic weapons fire. By noon Wossowski himself was dead and his men, scattered and thoroughly demoralised, were pulled back from the line shortly thereafter.

Fullriede was outraged at Oberst Schramm's decision to withhold artillery support; Schramm was relieved of duty two days later. Furthermore, Fullriede was scathing about the general lack of leadership among officers of Kampfgruppe 'von Tettau' at every level, including the flawed management by General der Infanterie Hans von Tettau. Later informed that the 'Hermann Göring' Recruiting Battalion would also soon be deployed in action, Fullriede replied that such an action would constitute 'infanticide' and immediately applied for rail transport to carry the recruits back to Germany. Angrily reminded that a direct order from the Führer had forbade the removal of troops from the Netherlands, he instead sent the young recruits and their officers to Student's depot in Emsland by foot.

Though fighting along the length of the 'Market-Garden' corridor continued – Maj. Werner Krahmer of 3rd Battalion was killed on 26 September at Schyndel (succeeded by Hptm. Pauls) and Hptm. Westphal of 1st Battalion captured – the brief and tenuous British hold on Arnhem was lost and the last pockets of resistance surrendered after nine days' battle. To the south the main German line of resistance occupied by Kampfgruppe 'Chill' to the west of the Allied corridor remained relatively static following roughly the canal line from s'Hertogenbosch to Veghel. However, the two 'Hermann Göring' units attached had been virtually annihilated and Fullriede withdrew them to Oosterbeek, the remains of 1st Battalion only numbering two officers (Leutnant Niedermeyer commanding) and a handful of men who were deployed as infantry before being re-formed under the command of Maj. Horst Pohl of Füsilier Battalion 85.

Absurdly, given the fact that British and Polish troops south of the Rhine had taken heavy casualties in a failed bid to cross into Arnhem by boat, Kampfgruppe 'von Tettau' launched its own attempted crossing to establish a bridgehead on the Rhine's southern bank. The unlucky SS Hauptsturmführer Heinrich Oelkers was given the task, forming a *Kampfgruppe* that included SS NCO trainees from the Arnhem school, a company from the Labour Service, one of Kriegsmarine troops, another of Luftwaffe personnel plus the remains of Wossowski's 'Hermann Göring' company.

After suffering terrible casualties crossing the river near Doorwerth Castle, SS troops stormed a brick works 200 metres from the water's edge on the southern bank and dug in, 'Hermann Göring' troops making the same crossing the following day, 2 October, with similar results; survivors reinforced the slim SS bridgehead that still clung to the brickworks. For ten days they held out, unsupplied and unsupported, as planned armoured attacks by troops near Nijmegen failed to break through. Oelkers repeatedly asked permission to withdraw and was denied each time until he made the decision himself. The *Haupsturmführer* was the last man to leave the small enclave on the night of 10 October.[7]

The failure of 'Market-Garden' heralded harsh times for Dutch citizens still in occupied territory. Men from Fullriede's Fallschirm-Panzer Ersatz und Ausbildung Regiment 'Hermann Göring' were involved in a reprisal action against the civilians of Putten at the beginning of October. On the night of 30 September seven Dutch resistance men and Sgt. Keith 'Tex' Banwell – an escaped British paratrooper from the Arnhem debacle – ambushed a staff car near the Oldenaller bridge, between Nijkerk and Putten. The car contained Oblt. Eggert, Lt. Otto Sommer and Obergefreite Hedrich and Hüttebreuker of the 2nd Battalion, travelling from Utrecht to re-join the remainder of the badly mauled regiment in Harderwijk.

The Dutch group was led by a former military policeman, thirty-year-old Ab Witvoet, and had originally intended to blind occupants of an oncoming German military vehicle using the headlights of a flatbed truck the resistance men had positioned at the roadside. Discrepancies exist in recollections regarding the rationale behind the attack, ranging from the capture of a German officer in order to extract information on troop positions to a strike ordered against an officer carrying V-2 secrets. Likewise, the post-war accounts given by Banwell of the attack and diary entries by Fullriede regarding its outcome vary considerably. What is certain is that, as the car approached, Banwell opened fire with a Bren gun that briefly jammed creating momentary confusion among the attackers. Automatic weapons were used to bring the car to a halt and as it swerved into a telephone pole its occupants returned fire and wounded resistance man Frans Slotboom, shot in the liver. In return, both German NCOs escaped (though Banwell claimed they were killed) as did Lt. Sommer, who had been badly wounded in the abdomen. The Dutch captured Eggert, who had been shot in the knee and was in considerable pain as the resistance men fled the scene with their captive.

> The officer was taken back to our headquarters and interrogated. He was badly wounded in the knee and afterwards they were at a loss what to do with him. So, I said, 'Well, the best thing is, I'll shoot him.' They said, 'Oh no, you can't do that.' So, I said, 'Well, if one of you were to be captured, you would suffer severe torture.' So again, I offered to shoot him. They said, 'No. We'll take him back to the old bridge [which was where we laid the ambush near Putten] and we'll leave him alongside the road.' I had already said, prior to leaving the area, that we should have pushed the German vehicle into the woods, picked up our empty rounds of ammunition, which could be identified as British, and left the place clear. But they wouldn't do this. So, they took him back and laid him alongside the road. In the

> morning [of Monday 2 October], of course, the first vehicle along had to be German.[8]

While Eggert was spirited away by his captors, the badly wounded Sommer made his way to a nearby farmhouse where the Dutch farmer and his wife tended to his wounds. The pair of *Obergefreite* had become separated from the *Leutnant* and raised the alarm at the first Wehrmacht post they found, while the Dutch farmer managed to flag down a passing German truck and pass Sommer over to their care; they transported him to a field hospital in Harderwijk where he died on 2 October. The unfortunate twenty-year-old Slotboom also died from his wounds and was hurriedly buried in a garden in Voorthuizen near where the resistance cell had its headquarters.

The morning following the raid, with Eggert still missing, the German response was predictably harsh. The Wehrmacht military commander in the Netherlands, General der Flieger Friedrich Christiansen, was incensed after receiving news of the attack near Putten, and is reputed to have exclaimed: 'That entire nest needs to be burnt down and everybody put up against a wall!' His chief of staff, Generalleutnant Heinz-Hellmuth von Wühlisch, issued immediate orders for Fullriede to encircle the village and men of the 'Hermann Göring' training regiment's Engineer Battalion duly surrounded it during the early morning of Sunday 1 October. Local farmers attempting to collect and milk their cows were arrested and their buildings searched for any trace of Eggert. Nearby forests were combed by 'Hermann Göring' troops to find a possible trace of the culprits who had launched the attack or of Eggert.

Meanwhile the majority of Putten villagers attended their customary church service, after which those who lived in the neighbouring countryside were forbidden to leave to return home. Several attempted to flee the net and seven people were shot. With the assistance of a small number of men from the fascist Dutch NSB (Nationaal-Socialistische Beweging in Nederland) a list of thirty prominent Putten residents was compiled, to be held hostage until the missing officer and perpetrators of the attack were found. These hostages were placed under armed guard against the wall of a garage and the local café, while the remaining men of the village were held in the local school, and the women and children placed under guard in the old church. Further instructions from Christiansen soon followed: the culprits were to be shot; all men aged between eighteen and fifty removed and transported to Germany for forced labour; Putten and neighbouring farmsteads were to be burned to the ground, with the exception of the house belonging to those who had aided Sommer and those belonging to confirmed pro-German citizens and NSB members.

Fullriede was unhappy with the orders that he had received. While he fully agreed with some form of reprisal, he believed that Christiansen's orders were too harsh. He was in no position to shoot the culprits as they had not yet been found; therefore it was likely that he would be punishing the innocent.

> That seemed completely pointless to me because it only achieved the opposite. I forbade the incumbent SD to participate in the campaign and, in order to avoid further reprisals, let only a few less valuable buildings burn down. The SD removed the prisoners.[9]

With the threat made public, Eggert was released by his captors that night and soon found beside a road by German troops. Nonetheless, during the morning of 2 October, Fullriede carried out his orders, later claiming during the post-war Dutch trial of Christiansen that he had not been informed of Eggert's return. A total of 659 men were handed over to a detachment from SS Wachbataillon Nordwest and marched to the train station, while women and children were ordered out of Putten within two hours before buildings began to be set alight by the 'Hermann Göring' troops.[10] Eighty-seven houses in Putten were burned down. Of the men deported, fifty-eight were released from the transit camp at Amersfoot which had been their first stop. The remaining 601 men were transported to Neuengamme concentration camp near Hamburg where 540 of them died before the war's end. In total, only 48 of those evacuated returned to Putten after the war.[11]

Of the German officers involved in the raid on Putten, both Christiansen and Fullriede were put on trial in Arnhem after the war. Christiansen was sentenced to twelve years' imprisonment in 1948 but was released in December 1951. Fullriede received two and a half years while Wühlisch committed suicide in his prison cell on the night of 20 September 1947.

For Fullriede this inglorious chapter marked the end of his tenure with the division's training regiment. He was posted during early October to Army Reserve in Hirschberg where he was to take a divisional commander's training course. However, declared ill during preliminary interviews, he spent until January 1945 in hospital, before returning to the Eastern Front in various divisional command roles, including as the last commander of Festung Kolberg. He ended the war commanding naval infantry in Kampfgruppe 'Fullriede'.

Before the fighting in the Netherlands had begun, elements of the Fallschirm-Panzer Ersatz und Ausbildung Regiment 'HG' had been transported to Ruppin, West Prussia, to join the four companies of the field training unit (Fallschirm-Panzer Feldersatzbataillon 'HG') that had formed the nucleus of Oberst Major Georg Ilius's new Fallschirm-Ausbildungs-und Ersatz-Brigade 'Hermann Göring' . Originally, the entire regiment was to have been transferred by 27 September but fighting against British forces in Belgium and the Market-Garden offensive overtook those troops remaining in the Netherlands.

Franz Lürbke had narrowly escaped potential harm after departing his battalion's Willemskaserne barracks in Arnhem on 16 September, the day before its destruction by Mosquito fighter-bombers.

> At the end of September, in the meantime, we had been withdrawn from the main fighting line and moved to Tilburg, I was promoted to *Gefreiter* prematurely because of 'my loyalty to the company'. Shortly thereafter we took up changing positions in the Rosendaal area. Although the front was already very close, it was initially pretty quiet for us in October. We moved quite freely in the company staff and occasionally visited restaurants in Rosendaal. One evening we went to a nice bar for a couple of drinks. My comrade was a *Gefreiter* and a good guy. But he was constantly complaining about what he thought was overdue promotion to non-commissioned officer. His father would surely change that during an occasional dinner with Hermann Göring, after all, the two were friends from the First World War.
>
> When we entered the restaurant, the conversations of any Dutch who were present immediately stopped. As always on such occasions, an absolutely hostile mood was obvious. Only the landlord, who had no other choice, had to talk to us about our order. At our kind request, he hesitantly pushed out a deck of cards and my *Gefreiter* immediately started performing card tricks. He was really good at it and even managed to involve the other guests. One by one they came closer and watched. Finally came the trick of blowing the top card out of an open stack. He brought his mouth close to the card, inflated his cheeks fully and blew vigorously and

> suddenly laying there in all their splendour were his false teeth. He quickly tried to put them back in his mouth with trembling hands, but of course that didn't work out immediately in all the excitement.
>
> Suddenly the spell was broken; something very human had happened and with roaring laughter all those present tapped each other on the shoulders and wanted to see this entertaining 'magic trick' again. When we parted ways with the Dutch guests after a few hours of lively entertainment, we were even sent on our way with best wishes for our personal future well-being.
>
> At the end of October our company practically went under in the fighting at Wouw, near Rosendaal. The new company commander, Oberleutnant Gerhard Glaeske, paid with his life when he tried to lead his men in an attack on Canadian troops facing us. I don't know what the number of casualties was, but there were only fifteen people left in our company after the unsuccessful battle. We were pulled out of the front line, loaded onto a truck and first transported to Utrecht for delousing and then to Harderwijk. From there, our group was sent to Rippin in West Prussia on the Eastern Front.[12]

The dislocation of the training regiment resulted in those parts left behind in the Netherlands being redesignated Fallschirmjäger Regiment 31 in February 1945, under the command of Oberst Pinzer, who had replaced Fullriede, and attached to Armee-Abteilung Straub that ended the war as occupants of the *Festung* established in the Hook of Holland. The majority of Pinzer's command at this time comprised men combed from defunct parts of the Luftwaffe, with little infantry experience. It has also been written that strong elements of the training regiment that had remained in the west were redesignated Sturmregiment z.b.v. 'Hermann Göring' and retreated into Germany where they would later surrender to American forces after becoming trapped in the Ruhr pocket around Bonn-Bad Godesberg. However, there remain barely any recorded references to this unit.

In Rippin Oberst Friedrich Meyer, former commander of the Flak Regiment, was given command of the newly established Fallschirm-Ersatz-und-Ausbildungs-Brigade 'Hermann Göring', after the hospitalisation of Major Ilius through illness. The new brigade was composed of two separate regiments: Fallschirm-Panzer Ersatz-und-Ausbildungs-Regiment 1 'Hermann

Göring' (Hptm. Günther Findeis), concerned with the training of Panzergrenadiers and Engineers, and Fallschirm-Panzer-Artillerie Ersatz-und-Ausbildungs-Regiment 2 'Hermann Göring' (Maj. Hans Beinhofer), handling the training of flak and artillery personnel with a small Panzergrenadier element.

The increase in size of the divisional training unit from regiment to brigade was predicated upon the fact that Schmalz had been instructed to expand his forces from a single armoured division to an armoured corps, along lines that he had already proposed to OKL.

Indeed, during 1944, Schmalz had been asked to examine the possibility of creating a genuine airborne army, and his conclusions – supported by the experience of the British 1st Airborne Division at Arnhem – are worth quoting verbatim from a historical report that he prepared for the U.S. Army after the war's end.

> In a major strategic commitment of parachute and air landing troops, it is essential that the airborne forces, once landed, be able to hold their own and to retain some freedom of action. Typical objectives of such major operations are oil fields, centres of war industry, main lines of communication etc.
>
> Whether the airborne force is defending or attacking, enemy reaction will become progressively stronger from day to day; the enemy will employ all possible weapons, including tanks. The amount of time required for the link-up between the ground front and the airhead varies with the size of the operation. The forces in the airhead, however, must not be left to fight a hopeless battle until the link-up occurs. In modern warfare, however, it is impracticable to hold out without tanks and aggressive strategic action without them is unthinkable.
>
> Obviously, air superiority and a sufficient number of transport aircraft are prerequisites for a large airborne operation. I consider it extremely important to also mention that the supply of ammunition and rations must be continuous after the initial commitment. The standardisation of ammunition is important. Thus, there should be no calibre variations in infantry ammunition and no fluctuations in calibre among the tanks, rocket projectors, mortars and anti-aircraft artillery. Despite standardisation, there will inevitably be plenty of different types of ammunition.

> I had established the following landing schedule for the commitment of an airborne Panzer division:
>
> First Wave: All nine parachute battalions, accompanied by their machine guns, mortars and engineers. The division's operations staff (parachutists).
>
> Second Wave: The armoured battalions of the three regiments. Armoured vehicles mount 20-mm anti-aircraft guns which are usable against both ground and aerial targets. The signals battalion and the remainder of the divisional staff.
>
> Third Wave: The Panzers, which provide both active and passive anti-tank defence, as well as the armoured artillery.
>
> Fourth Wave: Antiaircraft artillery.
>
> Fifth Wave: Field artillery.
>
> Sixth Wave: Engineer battalion and medical battalion.
>
> The first wave is a parachute wave; all others are airlanding waves. The second through sixth waves include supplies of ammunition . . . When all elements of the division have landed, the division commander will reorganise his forces for the main effort on the basis of the general situation, form a reserve, and – above all – endeavour to retain command control of his Panzer regiment. The well-known cry of the infantry for Panzers should not cause the division command to relent, and dissipate the shock, defensive, and fighting power of its most important weapon. The tactical deployment of the Panzer regiment must be constantly under divisional control.[13]

In reality the aerial Luftwaffe was at no point during 1944–5 anywhere near capable of supporting such an ambitious programme, regardless of its military validity. Instead, Schmalz was ordered during October to expand his command, a task he undertook under extremely difficult circumstances in Prussia where 'Hermann Göring' troops remained under sustained Soviet pressure.

Chapter Eleven

Panzer Corps

'More is not better, better is better.'
General George R. Sullivan

Schmalz's initial proposition to create two Panzer divisions for the new corps was impracticable due to a shortage of available armour. Instead the compromise of one Panzer and one Panzergrenadier division was reached, which would, in turn, present its own difficulties. Sourcing a pool of additional manpower was the first obstacle to be overcome and two battalions of Fallschirmjäger Regiment 16 (2nd and 3rd Jäger Battalions, staff, engineer, heavy infantry gun and Panzerjäger companies) were quickly reinforced and redesignated Fallschirm-Panzergrenadier-Regiment 3 'Hermann Göring' for the new division. The 1st Battalion, Fallschirmjäger Regt. 16 was detached to become Fallschirm-Panzer-Füsilier-Bataillon 2 'HG'.[1] Personnel were also transferred from the aerial Luftwaffe (including two entire signals battalions) and an Army medium artillery battalion taken on strength. Furthermore, Göring's security regiment – Oberst Karl-Eric Bertram's Begleit Regiment 'Hermann Göring' – was disbanded on 24 September, its 1st Battalion and Staff becoming part of Fallschirm-Panzergrenadier-Regiment 1 'Hermann Göring' while 2nd (Flak) Battalion became 4th Battalion, Fallschirm-Flak-Regiment 'Hermann Göring'.

Obviously, expansion required a complex reshuffling of men and material as the original division supplied cadres for the new regiments, with the corps staff, two divisional staffs and new regimental staffs all formed from nuclei of existing staff units. To enable the change, each divisional staff became smaller, allowing greater flexibility. Schmalz detached the entire supply organisation from both divisions and placed it directly under corps control, allowing divisional staffs instead to focus completely on tactical management of their units. Divisional supply officers routed requisitions directly to the corps quartermaster *Abteilung*, which handled all facets of supply with its own integrated transport system.

Although plans to increase each Panzergrenadier regiment from two to three battalions never reached fruition, the corps maintained control over its own 'Storm' and Engineer battalions, for independent deployment where required, with no corresponding weakening of divisional assets. The Storm Battalion – formed from the Sturm-Bataillon der Division-Kampfschule 'Hermann Göring' – was organised along the lines of a reinforced Panzergrenadier battalion with integral *Sturmgeschütze* and was trained for raids and surprise thrusts in cooperation with armoured formations. The corps pioneers were originally intended to possess heavy bridging equipment, though this never materialised. Instead, they were to complete tasks begun by divisional engineers, freeing the latter to continue supporting leading divisional elements. Furthermore, the anti-aircraft regiment was expanded to four battalions and placed directly under corps command.

A planned Panzer battalion of heavy Tiger Is was supposed to be created immediately under corps command and available for commitment at the point of main effort, but it appears that production and transport difficulties nullified Schmalz's intentions. Four medical battalions were created under direction from the Corps Chief Medical Officer; one battalion was assigned to each division in action, one engaged in establishing a stationary field hospital with specialists of every kind and the last held in reserve.

Each division was allocated a Panzer fusilier battalion, a heavily armed unit envisaged for use as a mobile reserve capable of either reconnaissance in force, assault or static defence and frequently required in full commitment to the line. Leutnant Karl Koblauch was an experienced navigator from a reconnaissance Staffel of Aufklärungs Gruppe 14 who had been severely wounded after being shot down by Soviet fighter aircraft over Vyazma on 2 September 1943. In August the following year he was discharged as fit for duty, though, as a result of his injuries his flying days were now behind him. Instead, he volunteered to join the 'Hermann Göring' division, reporting on 18 October in East Prussia.

> Presentation to the Corps. The officer replacement roster has begun and commanding general GenMaj. Schmalz enters the scene. After his greeting, the 'commanding officer' thinks he has to say that it is finally time for us to appear on the front lines. The accusation could not be clearer. I suppress my rising anger.
>
> The adjutant steps forward, picks up an extensive list, and reads the officers' assignments to individual units. Among other

things, I hear: 'Leutnant Knoblauch – Corps Sturm Bataillon. The commander is here now; he will take you with him!'

I go over to the other side of the staff accommodation and report to the leader of the Sturm Bataillon, Oberleutnant Lehmann. He greets me with a handshake, looks at me and then asks about the silver wound badge on my field jacket: 'What type of wound do you have? Has it disabled you in any way?'

'I have lost the sight in my left eye.'

Lehmann tells me that, under these circumstances, there is no question of joining the Sturm Bataillon. He goes back to the adjutant with me and explains the situation. He scans his list and decides quickly: Leutnant Knoblauch, you will be transferred to the Füsilier Battalion of the 2nd Division, which means you should first register with the 1st Battalion, Fallschirmjäger Regiment 16; its commander is Hauptmann Teusen. When the reorganisation around the 2nd Division has ended, I./16 will operate as Fallschirm-Panzer-Füsilier Battalion 2 'HG'![2]

Knoblauch joined Fallschirmjäger Regiment 16 while it was entrenched around Wolfseck, south of the large town of Gumbinnen, his battalion being redesignated as fusiliers at the beginning of November, passing into the command of Maj. Arnold with a strength of approximately 400 men.

The accomplishment of this expansion was made exceedingly difficult during the period October–November 1944: the division saw action in Poland near Tilsit and near Gumbinnen in East Prussia (where it engaged in an offensive). By the time these battles were concluded in November 1944, final accomplishment of the project seemed questionable because of the heavy casualties incurred during the fighting. Replacement personnel and equipment arrived slowly. Transferred Luftwaffe officers, non-commissioned officers and troops, who had no previous experience in ground warfare, received practical combat training either in their own units or in training schools in the Fallschirm Armee area. Despite all the handicaps encountered, both divisions were ready for action at the outset of the Russian offensive in January 1945.[3]

Schmalz had been elevated to corps commander, his place at the head of the redesignated Fallschirm-Panzer-Division 1 'Hermann Göring' being taken by Oberst von Necker, in turn replaced as regimental commander by Maj. Hans Briegel. As acting commander of the newly created Panzergrenadier Division, Oberst. Erich Walther was transferred from the Netherlands. Walther was one of the original officers of Regiment 'General Göring', who had subsequently led an illustrious career in the Fallschirmjäger (attached to Kampfgruppe 'Schmalz' in Sicily) and most recently as commander of a *Kampfgruppe* in the fighting against 'Market-Garden'. During June 1944 Walther had also been appointed NS-Führungsoffizier to 1. Fallschirm Armee in the Netherlands, fulfilling the prerequisite for political zeal that Göring had long wanted for his officers.

Fallschirm-Panzerkorps 'Hermann Göring' ***Generalmajor Wilhelm Schmalz***

Chief of Staff — Maj. Heinz-Herbert Schweim
Quartermaster — Maj. Werner Grün
Ordnance Officer — Lt. Franz-Josef Kleine-Sextro
Staff
Staff Company; Artillery Commander; Feldgendarmerietrupp; Aerial Coordination Officer; War Correspondent Troop

Korpstruppen

Sturm-Bataillon Fallschirm-Panzerkorps 'HG'	*Oblt. Hans-Georg Lehmann*	7 companies
Fallschirm-Panzerkorps Panzerjäger Btn. 'HG'	*Maj. Hans Sandrock*	
Fallschirm-Panzerkorps Signals Btn. 'HG'	*Hptm. August Wolf*	3 companies
Fallschirm-Panzerkorps Engineer Btn. 'HG'		5 companies
Fallschirm-Panzerkorps Flak-Regiment 'HG'	*Oberst Friedrich Meyer*	

1st Battalion
1st–4th Batteries (Heavy) 5th–6th Batteries (Light)

2nd Battalion
7th–9th Batteries (Heavy) 10th–12th batteries (Light)

3rd Battalion
13th–15th Batteries (Heavy) 16th–18th Batteries (Light)

4th Battalion
19th–22nd Batteries (Heavy) 23rd–24th Batteries (Light)

Unit	Strength
Corps Supply Troop 'HG'	
Supply Regiment (later Battalion) 'HG'	7 companies
Maintenance Battalion 'HG'	8 detachments
Administrative and Supply Battalion 'HG'	4 detachments

Medical Battalion 'HG'		5 emergency medical detachments; 1 decontamination & 5 ambulance platoons
Corps Field Post Office 'HG'		
Fallschirm-Pz.-Div. 1 'Hermann Göring'	***Oberst Hans Horst von Necker***	
Division Staff; Staff Company; Feldgendarmerietrupp; Field Post Office.		
Fallschirm-Panzer-Füsilier Btn. 'HG'	*Hptm. Sachs*	
1st–4th Companies		
Fallschirm Panzer Signals Btn. 'HG'		2 companies
Fallschirm-Panzergrenadier-Regiment 1 'HG'	*Oberst Erich Bertram*	
Staff Company		
1st Battalion		half-track
1st–3rd Panzergrenadier Companies		
4th (Heavy) Company		
2nd Battalion		motorised
5th–7th Panzergrenadier Companies		
8th (Heavy) Company		
9th Sturmgeschütz Company		
10th Mechanised Engineering Company		
11th (Heavy) Self-propelled Gun Battery		
Fallschirm-Panzergrenadier-Regiment 2 'HG'	*Maj. Hans Briegel*	
[Composition as above]		
Fallschirm-Panzer-Regiment 'HG'	*Maj. Karl Rossmann*	
1st Battalion	*Hptm. Joachim Renz*	Panzer V Panther
2nd Battalion		Panzer IV
Fallschirm Sturmgeschütz Battalion 1 'HG'		
Fallschirm Panzer Artillery Regiment 'HG'		
1st Battalion (1st–3rd Batteries)		
2nd Battalion (4th–6th Batteries)		
3rd Battalion (7th–9th Batteries)		
Fallschirm Panzer Reconnaissance Btn. 'HG'	*Oblt. Gerhard Kruse*	
1st–4th Companies		
Fallschirm Armoured Engineer Battalion 'HG'		
1st–5th Companies		
Field Replacement [Feldersatz] Battalion 'HG'		
1st–4th Companies		

Fallschirm-Pz.-Gren.-Div. 2 'Hermann Göring' ***Oberst Erich Walther***

Division Staff; Staff Company (*Hptm. Kirchhofer*); Feldgendarmerietrupp (*Hptm. Theiss*); Feldpostamt (*Feldpostmeister Maar*)

Fallschirm Panzer Signals Btn. 2 'HG'	*Maj. H. Kunze*	
Fallschirm Panzer Füsilier Btn. 2 'HG'	*Maj. Arnold*	Arnold hospitalised 18 Nov., replaced by Hptm. August Wolf
1st Company	*Fw. Tischler*	
2nd Company	*Oberfähnrich Rapp*	
3rd Company	*Oblt. Kalff*	
4th Company	*Oberfähnrich Staguhn*	
5th Supply Company	*Hptm. Werner Klingbeil*	
Fallschirm-Panzergrenadier-Regt. 3 'HG'	*Oberst Gerhard Schirmer*	
Staff Company		
1st Battalion		
2nd Battalion		
3rd Battalion		
9th Sturmgeschütz Company		
10th Mechanised Engineer Company		
11th (Heavy) Self-propelled Gun Battery		
Fallschirm-Panzergrenadier-Regt. 4 'HG'	*Oberst Waldemar Kluge*	soon replaced by Maj. Stauch
1st Battalion		
2nd Battalion		
Fallschirm Sturmgeschütz Btn. 2 'HG'	*Maj. Hans Sandrock*	
Fallschirm Panzer-Artillery Regt. 2 'HG'	*Obstlt. Henning von Kahlden*	
1st Battalion (1st–3rd Batteries)		
2nd Battalion (4th–6th Batteries)		
3rd Battalion (7th–9th Batteries)		
Fallschirm Armoured Recce. Btn. 2 'HG'	*Hptm. Ernst Springorum*	
1st Company		armoured cars
2nd Company		armoured recce. company
3rd Company		armoured recce. company
4th Company		heavy company
Engineer platoon SPW, infantry-gun platoon 2 x light guns, flak platoon 4 x 20-mm, two PaK platoons with 3 x 75-mm Pak 40, 6 x 75-mm Pak 40		
5th Company		supply company

Fallschirm Panzer Engineer Btn. 2 'HG'	*Hptm. Heinrich Böttcher*	
1st–3rd Companies		
Fallschirm Panzer Feldersatz Bataillon 2 'HG'		
1st–4th Companies		

Other 'Hermann Göring' units:

Heimatstab Fallschirm Panzer Korps 'HG'	*Gen. Paul Conrath*	Kommandierender General der Ausbildungs und Ersatztruppen der Fallschirm Armee; Berlin-Reinickendorf
Fallschirm-Ersatz-und-Ausbildungs-Brigade 'HG'	*Oberst Friedrich Meyer*	
Staff Company	*Lt. Güldner*	
Signals Company	*Oblt. Blumenhagen*	
Medical Company	*Stabsarzt Dr. Renken*	
Infantry Gun Company	*Lt. Drews*	2 x 150-mm sIG 33, 4 x 75-mm lIG
Ausbildungs und Umschulungs Btn. 'HG'	*Hptm. Helmut Friebe*	Retraining battalion
Offizieranwärter Lehrgang	*Oblt. Krauß*	Officer Training Detachment (later 1./A. und U. Btn. 'HG')
Unteroffizieranwärter Lehrgang	*Lt. Giesemann*	NCO Training Detachment (later 2./A.und U. Btn. 'HG')
Umschulungs Lehrgang	*Lt. Freytag*	Retraining Detachment (later 3./A. und U. Btn. 'HG')
Fallschirm-Panzer-Ersatz- und Ausbildungs-Regiment 1 'HG'	*Hptm. Günther Findeis*	
I. Bataillon	*Hptm. Fuchs*	
1. Kompanie	*Oblt. May*	Panzergrenadiers
2. Kompanie	*Oblt. Hahn*	Panzergrenadiers
3. Kompanie	*Lt. Selzer*	Panzergrenadiers
4. Kompanie	*Oblt. Arnheiter*	Panzergrenadiers
II. Bataillon	*Hptm. Wolfgang Bach*	
5. Kompanie	*Lt. Schneider*	Sniper company
6. Kompanie	*Lt. Ellwanger*	Panzergrenadiers
7. Kompanie	*Lt. Alf*	Panzergrenadiers
8. Kompanie	*Oblt. Stürcken*	Panzergrenadiers
III. Bataillon	*Hptm. Mack*	
9. Kompanie	*Hptm. Mönkmeyer*	Panzergrenadiers
10. Kompanie	*Lt. Wolf*	Panzergrenadiers

11. Kompanie	*Oblt. Fasshauer*	Panzergrenadiers
12. Kompanie	*Hptm. Schäfers*	Panzergrenadiers
Fallschirm Pionier Ersatz und Ausbildung Bataillon 1 'HG'	*Oblt. Breig*	
1st–3rd Companies		
Fallschirm-Panzer-Artillerie Ersatz- und Ausbildungs-Regiment 2 'HG'	*Maj. Hans Beinhofer*	superseded by Maj. Rudolf Graf
1st Battalion	*Hptm. Josef Matthias Edmund Francois*	
1st (Heavy) Company	*Hptm. Schrader*	4 x 88-mm flak batteries
2nd (Heavy) Company	*Lt. Müller*	2 x 88-mm flak batteries
4. (Light) Company	*Hptm. Vollmer*	6 x 20-mm Flak 36
5. (Light) Company	*Hptm. Odenwald*	2 x 20-mm flak batteries
2nd Artillery Battalion	*Hptm. Walter Eggeman*	added in Feb. 1945 from Paratroop Artillery Btn. 4, previously of 4th Paratroop Div.
Fallschirm-Panzer Ersatz und Ausbildung Regiment 'HG' (Netherlands)		
Escort Battalion 'Reichsmarschall'	*Hptm. Siegfried Kühn*	
Führer Flak Regiment	*Maj. Fritz Roth*	attached Apr.–Oct. 1944
Fire Fighting Company		Führer Headquarters
1st Battalion	*Hptm. Lücke*	
1st Battery	*Oblt. Kropf*	6 x 88-mm motorised
2nd Battery	*Oblt. Pachmeyer*	6 x 105-mm motorised
3rd Battery	*Oblt. Springstein*	6 x 105-mm motorised
4th Battery	*Oblt. Günther*	6 x 105-mm motorised
5th Battery	*Oblt. Wilk*	12 x 37-mm motorised
6th Battery	*Oblt. Mittag*	12 x 20-mm motorised
2nd Battalion	*Hptm. Dentzer*	
7th Battery	*Oblt. La Grange*	12 x 20-mm Vierling motorised
8th Schützen Company		
9th Battery		9 x 20-mm, 3 x Vierling motorised
10th Battery		9 x 20-mm, 3 x Vierling motorised
11th Battery		6 x 105-mm
12th Battery		6 x 105-mm
13th Battery		6 x 105-mm
14th Battery		6 x 105-mm

Leichtkranken Lazarette (Erholungsheime) [Rest Home], (Oberau & Reit im Winkel)

The ambitious restructuring of a Panzer division to a corps was vastly complicated by the Soviet Baltic Offensive – an overall strategic plan comprised of multiple subsidiary geographically separate offensive actions – which had opened on 14 September with over one and a half million troops, some 17,500 artillery pieces and 3,080 armoured vehicles falling on German defensive lines. After the success of the Memel Offensive which pushed the Third Panzer Army back to the East Prussian border, encircled Memel and cut off the escape route of Army Group North from the northern Baltic states, Soviet troops now stood on the shore of the Curonian Lagoon. Moscow then ordered General Ivan Chernyakhovsky to push his Third Belorussian Front (one air and five land armies) directly into East Prussia through Gumbinnen and Insterburg with the final objective of Königsberg.

Aided by terrain criss-crossed with numerous waterways that frequently limited mobility, German defences were particularly strong along this axis of advance. In Berlin OKW had predicted the attack, despite Hitler's initial reluctance to designate East Prussia a military operational zone and thereby be compelled to pass control from his devoted Party functionaries to the Wehrmacht. The first elements of Necker's Fallschirm-Panzer-Division 1 'Hermann Göring' detrained and went immediately into action to bolster a small German bridgehead held on the northern bank of the Neman River at Tilsit which was under intense Soviet pressure. Alongside the 65th Panzer Division, 'Hermann Göring' troops helped halt the Soviet attacks, though the urgent need to transfer armoured forces south to the area of Gumbinnen soon necessitated the evacuation of the Tilsit bridgehead, completed in a relatively orderly fashion by 22 October.

As the first 'Hermann Göring' units deployed south of Gumbinnen on the western banks of the Rominte River, Chernyakhovsky's offensive opened with powerful aerial and artillery bombardment on 16 October. Subordinated to General der Infanterie Friedrich Hossbach's Fourth Army, Fallschirm-Panzerkorps 'Hermann Göring' elements went immediately into action, crashing headlong into the northern flank of the Soviet 11th Guards Army between Angerapp and Nemmersdorf. The Soviet advance had been slowed by Volkssturm units, Hitler having ordered the entire male population of East Prussia between the ages of 16 and 60 mobilised, many equipped with nothing more than Panzerfaust anti-tank projectiles and antiquated Russian or Italian rifles,though given crucial support by heavy flak weapons of the 18th Flak Division.

The 'Hermann Göring' armour was key to halting the Soviet advance, among it Hans Sandrock's Jagdpanzer IV tank destroyers of Fallschirm-Sturmgeschütz Battalion 2 'Hermann Göring'. During the heavy fighting in East Prussia, Sandrock's unit tallied a total of 123 enemy tanks and armoured vehicles destroyed. Sandrock was promoted to *Major* on 18 October and awarded the Knight's Cross that same day; the medal – and a Luftwaffe Honour plate (*Erhenschale*) which had been awarded on 29 September – were both presented to Sandrock by General der Artillerie Weidling, commander of XLI Panzer Corps.[4]

Both 'Hermann Göring' divisions and the 5th Panzer Division drove desperately into the Soviet northern flank aiming for Grosswaltersdorf, while from the south and the direction of the Rominte Heath, the still forming armoured Führer Grenadier Brigade from Hitler's escort unit pushed north in fierce close-quarter combat. The ferocity of the fighting is evidenced by Feldwebel Fritz Bowitz of the Panzer Regiment's 4th Company who destroyed thirteen Soviet tanks with his Panther during a single day. On 21 October, Soviet troops captured an intact concrete bridge over the steep-sided Angerapp River and seized Nemmersdorf, fighting raging for hours before the Soviets were slowly forced back in confusion after violent German counter-attacks, spearheaded by 'Hermann Göring' Panzers. In the devastated town German troops discovered the grisly remains of raped and murdered civilians, providing a macabre boost to Goebbels's propaganda machine as it announced the fate awaiting German civilians at the hands of a vengeful Red Army.

The two German pincers from north and south established contact on 23 October near Gross Tellrode. For nearly fourteen days the Wehrmacht battled Chernyakhovsky's troops who stubbornly tried to continue their frontal westward advance before being halted and repulsed. During the first four days of fighting, Fallschirm-Panzer-Division 1 'Hermann Göring' alone recorded the destruction of 99 tanks and 43 Soviet anti-tank units. However, it too suffered considerable casualties, including the commander of 1st Battalion, Fallschirm-Panzer Regt. 'HG', Hptm. Joachim Renz, killed on 23 October as his tanks moved up to engage the enemy.

Oberleutnant Gerhard Tschierschwitz's 2nd Company of Panthers continued the assault despite their battalion commander's death and broke through the flank of advancing Red Army forces and reached the village of Jägershagen, 7 km southwest of Trakehnen. There he surprised a Red Army command post and troop assembly area, before continuing a roaming attack behind the Soviet front line, without any infantry support, and destroying 16 tanks, 16 anti-tank guns, 6 artillery pieces and 13 machine guns as well as killing an estimated 300 Soviet soldiers. Finally, after a circuitous route allowed his unit to re-establish contact with German infantry, the company withdrew; Tschierschwitz received the Knight's Cross for this action on 6 December.[5]

Three days later, Wallhäusser's tank destroyers locked horns with a major Russian tank force and were able to drive it back to its starting line, collecting German stragglers along the way to provide infantry cover to his armoured vehicles. When a neighbouring unit was forced to retreat, Wallhäusser attacked the Russians' flank, recapturing the position and inflicting heavy casualties, destroying several tanks and self-propelled guns and blunting the attempted Soviet advance on Gumbinnen. Wallhäuser was also later awarded the Knight's Cross for this action on 30 November; one of six such awards granted that same day.

In another sector of the 'Hermann Göing' advance, a diminutive eighteen-year-old, Gefreiter Albert Plapper, squad leader in 4th Company, Fallschirm-Panzergrenadier Regt. 2 'HG' commandeered a captured Russian machine gun and opened fire on enemy troops, managing to stop an infantry attack in its tracks. When T-34 tanks were called up for support, Plapper attacked and destroyed five of them using a Panzerschreck before gathering his men and counter-attacking to stabilise the German line. He too was awarded the Knight's Cross.

To bolster its anti-tank capability, the formidable Tiger II tanks of schwere Bataillon 505 were attached to the Fallschirm-Panzerkorps on 28 October and ordered to assemble south of Altkrug. At the beginning of November they were briefly reassigned, this time to Fallschirm-Panzer-grenadier-Division 2 'Hermann Göring', before moving on once more to the control of the Führer Begleit Brigade.

Göring himself visited the division during this period, dressed in the uniform of a ground force commander and meeting Schmalz at his head-quarters at Gut Austinshof near Nemmersdorf. Around this period, while attending conferences at the nearby 'Wolfsschanze' Führer headquarters, Göring took the opportunity to stay at his Reichsjägerhof, hunting on the Rominte Heath for one last time. Following his departure, on 20 October the codeword 'Johannisfeuer' was sent to the guard detachment. To prevent the lodge falling intact into enemy hands, thirteen fires were set at pre-determined locations within the main and outbuildings and the grand hunting lodge was destroyed; its guard detachment returned to the main body of the 'Hermann Göring' Corps.

Defeated by the German defence, the Red Army pulled back to rest and refit for fresh offensives in the new year. Losses on both sides had been extremely heavy, for example the Sturm Bataillon Fallschirm-Panzerkorps 'HG' which had started the battle with a strength of 974 men had lost 11 officers, 107 NCOs and 488 enlisted men between 10 September and 31 December 1944, including commander Hans-Georg Lehmann, posted missing in action. While Necker's division was pulled back into XXXV Army Corps reserve to refit, Walther's Fallschirm-Panzergrenadier-Division 2 'Hermann Göring' remained in the front line, dug-in in extensive trench networks reminiscent of the First World War as snipers prowled both sides of the line. Each trench was dug to a depth of between two and two and a half metres, with a maximum width of one and a half metres. At intervals in the trench walls, holes were dug for up to three men to sleep and shelter from the winter rains that turned the battlefield and no-man's land between German and Soviet positions into a quagmire of mud before solidifying as the first snow of winter 1944/45 fell in East Prussia.

On 23 December Schmalz submitted a corps status report to OKW:

Fallschirm-Panzer Division 1 'Hermann Göring'

Three full battalions
Two half-strength battalions
Reconnaissance, Engineer Battalions both half-strength
8 complete batteries
14 heavy anti-tank weapons
30 Panzer IVs
45 Panthers
25 *Sturmgeschütze*
Mobility 60%

Fallschirm-Panzergrenadier Division 2 'Hermann Göring'

One full Panzergrenadier battalion
Three half-strength Panzergrenadier battalions
Full reconnaissance Battalion
7 batteries
19 heavy anti-tank
32 *Sturmgeschütze*
Mobility 50%[6]

Gefreiter Karl-Heinz Schmeelke was a member of Fallschirm-Panzergrenadier-Regiment 4 'Hermann Göring' – also one of its *Kriegsberichter* [War Correspondent] photographers – dug in along the front line, and wrote extensively about his experiences, later published on a website. He recounted an unofficial ceasefire agreed locally with Russian troops in equally miserable trenches opposite them.

> 'Just an hour of peace, then everyone can go back to their positions!' Our company commander H. Lütz did not think long, agreed and therefore was later punished and lost his rank as an officer in the Zinten area, relieved of his command and demoted to a simple soldier! . . . It is true that the meetings didn't take place along the entire front, but only in the Hochfließ–Grünweiden area. Nevertheless, on 25 December 1944, I wrote in my diary: 'Things happen in war that you simply don't believe and I wouldn't have believed it if I hadn't seen it myself. At eight o'clock in the morning the Russians are holding up a white scarf and bawling in Russian? Then the Russians left their trenches, unarmed, led by two officers.'
>
> Our Feldwebel H. Völke admonished us not to talk to anyone about this story, even within the company we shouldn't talk to any other soldiers about it. (Feldwebel Völke fell, twenty-one years old, on 12 January 1945 by a bullet in the stomach before Grünweiden). We had strict orders to remain silent; but not everyone adhered to them. Three days after the festival, all the photographs that I had taken with the Russian soldiers were confiscated to prevent the unwanted fraternisation from becoming known. Silence, above all, because the common soldiers in the main battle line had more in common with their opponents than with their commanders from 4th Company, Fallschirm-Panzergrenadier Regt. 'HG'. They belonged to a certain class. We soldiers to another and we were treated accordingly. Here we had the slogan: 'Every officer is your enemy!'
>
> The same men who had done everything a few hours ago to kill each other now stood together, laughing, chatting, smoking. After that, we buried all the dead, who had first had their pay books and wallets removed with photos and addresses of their families. The belongings of the fallen were handed over to the division pastor and divisional grave registration officer. The ceasefire was also very

> convenient for us not just because the many bodies in no-man's land that had been bad for our fighting morale were finally gone, but also we were able to repair the front trenches with wood and wicker available at supply points, without being fired at by snipers . . .
>
> As a precaution, the spontaneously agreed ceasefire had not even been reported to the respective commanders, in order not to receive any of their usual orders. We built on our luck and, if necessary, pretended that the war was taking place. When the Commanding General of the Fallschirm-Panzerkorps, Generalmajor Schmalz with Generalmajor [*sic*] Walther and Major Stauch [regimental commander] came to the front lines for inspection on 27 December, everything seemed to be as normal in war. But there was an explanation for that: the field phone from Hochfließ [battalion headquarters] to the main battle line was operational and the advance warning worked. There was enough time to get everything in order. The guards were in the eight-watch position and were looking grimly at a rotten turnip on a stick that had previously been mistaken for a Russian shooting over the trench parapet.
>
> But we had made a crucial mistake: a single Russian was just over there with a spade and was busily working. We hadn't told him, but now he had to guess, because the general who had just arrived ordered a soldier to shoot down this apparently insane Russian. That was the order. Courageous Obergefreiter Erwin Roock shot just past him and the commander reprimanded him for shooting 'in the dirt'. However, when the Russian also waved his spade before he went from the parapet into his trench, the general no longer believed it to be a coincidence. The company commander had no choice but to inform his superiors. He reported that the only thing they had agreed with the enemy was to repair the trenches and not shoot at each other during this time and that from tomorrow it would be all the better to go back to war again. This white lie was pretty good and sounded convincing.[7]

A flurry of changes to the divisional command took place at the end of 1944 and in the early months of 1945. Acting commander Walther departed the division during November after being wounded, briefly replaced by Oberst Wilhelm Söth, a Heer officer, until January when Söth moved on to command the 3rd Panzer Division. In his place came a second Heer officer,

Oberst Georg Seegers, who took charge between 6 February and 24 March when Erich Walther was fit to return.

In thickening snow and sub-zero temperatures, German defensive preparations continued in anticipation of a January Soviet offensive, Schmalz stating on 11 January in a circular to officers of his divisions that: 'According to a captured Russian officer, the expected Soviet offensive against East Prussia is due on 13 January 1945.' However, Hitler's preoccupation with the aftermath of the Ardennes Offensive in the west and an abortive attack to relieve German forces encircled in Budapest negated any attempt to form a substantial reserve force for the front in East Prussia.

Therefore, while Schmalz kept his Panzergrenadier Division dug in southeast of Gumbinnen and placed on high alert on the eve of the expected onslaught, Necker's Panzer Division was situated to the west of the town, 15 km behind the front as an operational reserve with approximately 80 combat-ready tanks and 65 others in the workshops. At the beginning of January Necker had received his final promotion to the rank of *Generalmajor*.

As expected, the Soviet attack on East Prussia began anew on 13 January, Söth's Panzergrenadiers suffering sustained bombardment before combined Soviet infantry and armoured advances focussed on the area between Grunweiden and Hochfleiss, though here they were hemmed in by swampy terrain and taken under accurate fire by heavy flak guns. By the end of the first day's fighting, the 'Hermann Göring' troops had held their line, anti-tank guns and 88-mm flak guns having destroyed forty-four Red Army tanks, though losses among the high-silhouette '88' crews had also been severe.

However, the main Soviet assault against the German lines in East Prussia had yet to begin in its full intensity and at that moment, despite strong protests from Heinz Guderian in his role as OKH Chief of Staff, Hitler personally intervened in the dispositions of the slender forces available in the east. On 15 January he ordered Fallschirm-Panzer-Division 1 'Hermann Göring' transferred as part of General der Panzertruppe Dietrich von Saucken's Panzerkorps 'Großdeutschland' (alongside Panzergrenadier Division 'Brandenburg') from East Prussia to Kielce in Poland to block the potential Soviet break-through towards Posen. Somewhat absurdly, the Panzergrenadier Division 'Großdeutschland' was then detached from Saucken's command and placed under Schmalz's corps control, remaining in East Prussia. Guderian was aghast at the idea as, although the situation on the Vistula was critical, a similar threat posed by vast Soviet superiority in men and materiel now hung directly over East Prussia. Across the days that followed Necker's powerful division was entrained and headed south at exactly the moment that it could have been most useful remaining as part of Fallschirm-Panzerkorps 'Hermann Göring'.

The move was as disastrous as Guderian had feared. Crucial days were spent in railway sidings as Guderian and Hitler wrangled over where the divisions should go, until they were finally shipped south and forced to detrain under Soviet air attack and shellfire at Litzmannstadt (Łódź), 50 km short of the intended destination. Necker, his chief of staff and headquarters staff were among the first to arrive, disembarking amidst a swirling mass of German refugees all attempting to flee the advance of the Red Army. He established divisional headquarters to the southeast in the village of Kalino for a few days before moving west to Ruda Pabianicka as staff officers attempted to organise the incoming division which had been entrained haphazardly out of planned sequence and arrived in dribs and drabs. Not until the afternoon of 21 January was the division in relative order, but by this point Soviet forces had punched through German lines around Warsaw and the Wehrmacht's Ninth Army was in full retreat.

The two divisions of Panzerkorps 'Großdeutschland' covered the withdrawal to the west, heavily engaged against overwhelming enemy forces. Though the 'Hermann Göring' Panzers and grenadiers acquitted themselves well against the advancing Red Army – several Knight's Crosses were awarded during this period – they could not stem the enemy's advance and barely escaped encirclement and destruction as they and the Panzergrenadier Division 'Brandenburg' formed a 'wandering hedgehog' mobile defensive formation. On 27 January 'Hermann Göring' troops reached the old border with Germany at Waffendorf and three days later were on the western bank of the Oder in Lower Silesia, Necker establishing his headquarters in Alexanderhof, north of Köben. Rossmann's Panzers had performed particularly well in the bitter fighting and were instrumental in the successful withdrawal of Panzerkorps 'Großdeutschland' and on 1 February he was awarded the Oak Leaves to his Knight's Cross. One month later he would be promoted to *Oberstleutnant*.

The often-chaotic German retreat to the Oder had cut off a recently redesignated Army Group North, isolating the Fourth Army, including Fallschirm-Panzerkorps 'Hermann Göring', in East Prussia. The elements of the Third Panzer Army that had been under siege in Memel were evacuated by the Kriegsmarine on 28 January and what scattered parts remained in East Prussia were then placed under the command of the Fourth Army and encircled in a pocket around Königsberg. To the south, the bulk of the Fourth Army was encircled in what became known as the 'Kessel von Heiligenbeil' ('Cauldron of Heiligenbeil'). Separated from the Fallschirm-Panzerkorps, Oberst August Meyer's relatively powerful Fallschirm-Ersatz-und-Ausbildungs-Brigade 'Hermann Göring' had been ordered to move southeast from Rippin into XXIII Army Corps reserve and establish a defensive line near Skrwa. Hauptmann Mack's 3rd Battalion was in action near Insterburg and Gumbinnen as 'Bataillon Hauptmann Mack', leaving room for a new 3rd Battalion to be formed from an influx of fresh recruits, arriving under the command of Hptm. Erich Drotbohm from Utrecht. These were both volunteers and conscripts as the previous acceptance requirements had been completely abandoned by this stage of the war. The brigade had been undertaking a three-day field exercise when the movement orders were received. Attached to the 83rd Infantry Division, Meyer's first act as his brigade occupied its 35-km defensive line along the Skrwa River was to communicate directly with Reichsmarschall Göring regarding a dangerous shortage of ammunition for his men. Göring assured Meyer that twenty-six rail wagons loaded with munitions would be arriving shortly at Hohensalza station west of the Vistula; Mayer's concerns were alleviated – until the entire load was found to be missing the required fuses.

Soviet troops of Rokossovsky's Second Belorussian Front hurled their full force at the German lines of Army Group Centre and reached Sichelberg on 19 January, near Meyer's positions. Once again, the brigade commander contacted Göring, requesting permission to return to Germany nearly 1,000 troops who had received virtually no training other than in how to march in step. His request was granted and Hptm. Drotbohm – who had replaced Mack as commander of 3rd Battalion, Fallschirm-Panzer-Ersatz-und-Ausbildungs-Regiment 1 'Hermann Göring' – led the inexperienced recruits back to Berlin to begin training at the flak barracks in Veltin. The day following Meyer's call to his Reichsmarschall, the first Soviet tanks were sighted before his brigade's lines.

Possessing no armour-piercing ammunition, the 'Hermann Göring' troops became embroiled in difficult fighting against the advancing Soviets and were forced steadily back. Aware that his troops faced potential encirclement if they attempted to hold their ground, Meyer opted instead for a fighting withdrawal, covered where possible by his own artillery. Nevertheless, Soviet troops broke through the brigade's lines and penetrated the rear where they captured a number of prisoners. On the evening of 20 January Meyer authorised a general withdrawal towards Strasburg on the Druwenz River, a tributary of the Vistula. Artillery under the command of Hptm. Oberländer battered a Soviet armoured spearhead in a narrow defile on the Okalewo–Rippin road and gained a brief, though valuable, respite for the retreating troops. During the withdrawal, before the town of Hohenkirchen on 21 January, Maj. Rudolf Graf – Knight's Cross holder, earned with the regiment during the French campaign – was killed in action along with his adjutant.[8] Newly promoted Maj. Josef Matthias Edmund Francois took command of 2nd Regiment, Hptm. Weigert in turn taking charge of the artillery battalion.

By the end of January, under merciless pressure, Meyer had withdrawn his brigade to Graudenz as part of the general German retreat. Despite the mauling that the Soviets had given the Second Army, the withdrawal had followed the original plan more closely than any German officer had dared hope though roads were clogged with military convoys and refugees streaming westwards in freezing cold temperatures; bridges across the Vistula were reserved for Wehrmacht transport and the refugees had to cross the thick river ice.

The Second and Ninth Armies were combined into Army Group Vistula and placed under the completely inadequate command of Reichsführer-SS Heinrich Himmler in his first military role, while the defence of Graudenz and its valuable combined road and rail bridge over the Vistula was assigned to XXVII Corps. Knowing that the city would soon be swamped by the advancing Red Army, Generaloberst Walter Weiß, commander of the Second Army, requested permission to abandon the city but was curtly refused by Himmler who spouted the now familiar fantasy of 'last man and last bullet' to hold the city and enable it to be used as a springboard for 'future offensive operations'. On 25 January Soviet troops were sighted approaching Graudenz from the south and the Wehrmacht's 190th Sturmgeschütz Brigade advanced to disperse this weak thrust. By 1500 hrs Soviet troops had reached the Culm–Graudenz rail line and units of Meyer's training brigade that had already entered Graudenz were ordered to occupy outposts in the outer fortress ring. This outer ring of defensive positions was backed by an inner perimeter composed of twelve independent forts lying in a semi-circle around the modernised eighteenth-century citadel on the eastern bank of the Vistula in the northern part of the city; this was known to the Germans as Feste Courbiere (Fort Strzemięcin). The entire fortress area – and troops therein – was briefly subordinated to the commander of the 83rd Infantry Division, GenLt. Wilhelm Heun.

> The Vistula River was for the most part frozen over and, when the ice had strengthened, was passable for heavy vehicles. The expansive, snow-covered, open terrain and the dam on the west bank provided an excellent defensive position. Fortress Graudenz was well-constructed and improved. This new position, therefore, could afford the troops a much needed rest and an opportunity to reorganise the units and even to rehabilitate them. The fortress was inadequately manned, but had an ample supply of ammunition, food and fuel.[9]

The following day the 252nd Infantry Division crossed the Vistula and elements of other units that had been attached during the preceding days were reassigned to Meyer's brigade in the southern part of the outer fortress defences, guarding approaches to the outlying town of Rudnik. On 2 February, as the last rearguard elements of Hptm. Bach's battalion entered Graudenz, the combined road–rail bridge over the Vistula was destroyed after Russian shellfire detonated demolition charges prepared by Wehrmacht engineers. One week later the city was completely encircled and officially declared a 'Fortress' by OKW, Meyer establishing his brigade headquarters in the expansive villa belonging to civil engineer August Ventzki.

Repeated strong Soviet attacks were repelled, while Red Army engineers reinforced the Vistula ice to bear the weight of armour and began shuttling forces into an expanding bridgehead established on the western bank. Heun returned control of Feste Courbiere to Festung Graudenz's Wehrmacht Commandant, GenMaj. Ludwig Fricke, and aware of what would surely happen shortly, on 14 February Fricke ordered all remaining residents to evacuate the city and head for Dragaß, though few complied.

Fighting edged into the suburbs of Graudenz and on the night of 17 February, Heun began an attempted break-out towards Danzig of his 83rd Infantry Division, Hptm. Findeis's Fallschirm-Panzer-Ersatz-und-Ausbildungs-Regiment 1 'Hermann Göring' being commandeered by Heun despite Meyer's protests. While Obstlt. Staedke's Grenadier Regt. 257 of 83rd Infantry Division was ordered to remain in Festung Graudenz, Hptm. Walter Eggemann's 1st Battalion, Fallschirm Artillery Regiment 4 was added to the 'Hermann Göring' order of battle for the break-out, together with two engineer companies from Oblt. Brieg's Fallschirm-Pionier-Ersatz-und-Ausbildung Bataillon 1 'HG'.

The battered training brigade was restructured between 10 and 13 February with each company downsized to roughly the strength of a platoon, enabling the organisation of three new companies. Meyer's battalions were now dissolved as they were severely understrength; Findeis's 'regiment' now numbered only three grenadier companies with attached engineers and artillery. Heun's planned break-out over a pontoon bridge across the Vistula took Findeis's men north along the western bank of the Vistula. They fought off a major Soviet flank attack near Neuenburg as well as suffering severe casualties in the defence of the Klempiner Berg, the final high ground 20 km from Danzig. The last of Findeis's unit thereafter retreated to Gotenhafen and were transported by sea to the Hela peninsula where, on 9 May, the last forty survivors surrendered to Red Army troops.

In Graudenz, the remainder of Meyer's brigade fought a vicious urban battle over the weeks that followed, 2. Regiment now renamed 'Kampfgruppe Francois' and containing all of the artillery troops, the remaining training units from Friebe's battalion and pioneers of Fallschirm Engineer Battalion 21 z.b.V. 'HG' under the command of Hptm. Borgis, attached to the 'Hermann Göring' units since 25 January.

Before the end, both Friebe and Bach were promoted to *Major* and Bach awarded the German Cross in Gold. As the street fighting was constricted into a shrinking German enclave, Meyer authorised Francois to plan a break-out to the northeast with whatever volunteers he could muster from his *Kampfgruppe*. However, on learning of the plans being prepared by Francois' regimental staff, Fricke ordered both Meyer and his chief of staff Maj. Rebholz to report in person to him and berated them as 'traitors' for preparing a secret escape from the *Festung*; the Führer's very declaration that Graudenz was a fortress city meant that it must be defended to the last man. Fortunately for Meyer and Rebholz, Fricke was not in a position to instigate any form of military punishment as by this stage of the war summary executions for perceived lack of fighting spirit had become all too commonplace.

On 6 March the OKW War Diary recorded:

> The start of a large-scale attack against Graudenz. The garrison is crowded in a narrow space, in the Courbieres fortress. The end of resistance is imminent.

The final 'Hermann Göring' break-out attempt had taken place during the previous night, the majority filtering out from the northern gates of the citadel. This desperate group of men successfully crossed the bridge over the Ossa River at Burg Belchau, overwhelming the small number of Soviet guards. However, in wooded country to the north they ran into enemy infantry and were scattered; very few straggling survivors later reached German lines to continue the retreat to the Baltic. Francois was not among them; he was killed in action on 7 March south of the city after it had fallen, Graudenz having been finally overwhelmed on 6 March. Fricke signed the capitulation, leaving 117 officers and about 5,000 soldiers – including Meyer and all survivors of his brigade still in the city – to be taken into Soviet captivity over the course of next two days. At 2100 hrs in Moscow, 224 guns fired a salute to celebrate the capture of this Prussian city.

With the destruction of the Fallschirm-Panzer-Ersatz-und Ausbildungs Brigade 'Hermann Göring', a second unit of the same name was established in Velten and Joachimsthal from those men that had returned to Germany with Hptm. Drotbohm. Major Konstantin Hahm had already taken command of the four companies of the Rekruten Ausbildungs Bataillon 'Hermann Göring' during January 1945 in Berlin-Reinickendorf, and this formation morphed into the Fallschirm-Panzer-Ersatz-und-Ausbildungs Regiment 3 'Hermann Göring', forming half of the new brigade. Major Georg Ilius was then placed in command of Fallschirm-Panzer-Ersatz-und-Ausbildungs Regiment 4 'Hermann Göring' established on 14 March, at Velten; the new brigade was placed under the command of Oberst Breuer, transferred from the Heer.

Franz Lürbke had been posted to Germany from the Netherlands, expecting to transfer straight to West Prussia but instead being diverted to Berlin and then onward to Panzer training.

> I was back on the train and went with twenty-four comrades to Erlangen, where we were trained for the Panzer V 'Panther' for six weeks. In special training I belonged to the group of radio operators. Unfortunately, there were only two examples of the fast and agile tank in Erlangen, so the practical briefing was a little short . . .
>
> On 5 February, I arrived again in the flak barracks camp in Velten amidst a troop alarm. From my marching company and other units, companies were put together for the Oder front. Suddenly and unexpectedly, I found myself among many strange faces in the new group as 'Machine Gun Sagittarius One', with an antique MG 15 on my shoulder. Unfortunately, my friends Werner and Walter

were not among them; they had been transferred to a tank company beforehand. Only on 28 April would I see them again, under special circumstances.

When dusk set in, we drove east on trucks. I no longer remember the place name of our first accommodation in a village school. In any case, in mid-March we were relocated to the Crussow area near Angermünde, got a modern MG 42 and, with pioneer support, built and moved trenches and bunkers in the second front line, the so-called 'Wotan position'. We had a lot of trouble with the new machine guns as they jammed while loading far too often.

At this time, the Fallschirm-Panzer-Ersatz-und-Ausbildungs Brigade 2 'HG' with Regiments 3 and 4 was set up in the Joachimsthal area between Angermünde and Eberswalde. Since the beginning of March it was clear that the 1st Brigade with Regiments 1 and 2 had perished in the fighting on the Vistula, the last parts as a fortress garrison in Graudenz. With our company we belonged to the 3. Regiment. The brigade was also assigned to the Fallschirmjäger-Ersatz-und-Ausbildungs Regiment 1, named after its Austrian commander 'Regiment Kratzert'. It was north of us between Angermünde and Schwedt. I covered the way to Angermünde on foot several times . . .

Finally, one day I had to fulfil a special order with my MG squad at Angermünde train station: we were supposed to protect an important cargo against enemy aircraft. There we three soldiers stood with our MG 42 mounted on a tripod on an embankment at the train station, directly in front of us the residential barracks of the railway staff, but there was no sign of any special transport. In the late morning, a Russian Po-2 aircraft caused a brief alarm, based on the characteristic whirring of the 110-horsepower 5-cylinder radial engine. In regional jargon we called it either the 'sewing machine' or 'coffee grinder'. However, the pilot only made one lap above the train station and then flew on again.

It was ridiculously stupid and foolish, but we suddenly felt extremely strong, wanted to be heroes and so I sent a volley from our machine gun behind the slowly moving machine, quite short because of the usual jam, but long enough. Luckily, the pilot hadn't noticed anything of our furious gunfire, but numerous Reichsbähner rushed out of the barracks, shouting excitedly that we 'shouldn't provoke an

> attack for God's sake!' We actually had no further opportunity to do that, as everything stayed calm until evening when we marched back to our position.
>
> Somehow they remembered my course as a radio operator in the Panzer V. I got the 'field radio telephone' that was newly assigned to our company and was transferred to the company group. I never used the device once.[10]

The new brigade remained largely in situ until April by which time the front line rested on the Oder and the final Soviet assault on Berlin had begun.

In the meantime, the Fallschirm-Panzerkorps 'Hermann Göring' isolated in East Prussia had undergone a relentless pounding from the Soviet offensive. With the loss of the Panzer Division to the Vistula front, Schmalz's Panzergrenadier Division had become trapped in the Kessel von Heiligenbeil by the combined weight of seven Soviet armies. The HG component units were handled skilfully and had been repeatedly reorganised and merged to maintain at least some form of combat readiness. In recognition, at the beginning of February, Oberst Erich Walther was decorated with the Swords to his Oak Leaves and Knight's Cross, the only 'Hermann Göring' soldier to receive the award. Later that month, Fallschirm-Panzerkorps Chief of Staff, Oberstleutnant Bern von Baer, was decorated with the Oak Leaves. In the interim, on 9 February, the divisional War Diary recorded that:

> The losses are great. In total, the 4th Regiment has 180 casualties, both dead and wounded, over four days. In view of these casualties and the lack of officers in the main line of combat, the regiment orders the immediate merging of both battalions under the command of Major Stauch with the later goal to completely dissolve the 2nd Battalion. The new position occupied on 8 February south of Globuhnen runs through confusing heights, which enables the Russians to sneak in almost unnoticed as well as to filter behind our positions and attack from behind, necessitating another change of position in the area of Reichsstrasse 126.

That same day Gefreiter Lothar Schirner distinguished himself in action against the persistent Soviet armoured attacks. An account published by the central German press office during early April described his achievement and the subsequent awarding of the Knight's Cross.

> The Führer has at the recommendation of the Supreme Commander of the Luftwaffe, Reichsmarschall Göring, awarded the Knight's Cross of the Iron Cross to Gefreiter Schirner, gunner in the Fallschirm-Flak-Regiment 'Hermann Göring'. Gefreiter Lothar Schirner, born on 20 October 1916 in Militsch, has distinguished himself through exemplary intrepidity and bravery in the fierce battles around Kreuzburg. During a massive Soviet assault on 9 February 1945 Schirner would show no quarter to the enemy. As a result of the misty, rainy weather the enemy tanks were forced to come close to his firing position. Then, over the course of five hours and despite the lack of ammunition, Schirner succeeded in destroying fourteen T-34 tanks. In doing so he contributed significantly to the frustration of the enemy attempts to force a breakthrough in this area.[11]

On 19 March, Schirner was killed in action near Heiligenbeil. By this stage the Fallschirm-Panzerkorps contained three 'divisions' and held the northern end of the Prussian pocket with Panzergrenadier Division 'Großdeutschland', 562nd Volksgrenadier Division and the Fallschirm-Panzergrenadier-Division 2 'HG' before Plössen. To their right was the 50th Infantry Division of the neighbouring XLI Panzer Corps. The Sturm Bataillon, now under the command of Maj. Hans Ostermeier, narrowly escaped destruction after being temporarily isolated behind advancing Soviet Guards regiments north of Zinten. With bridges over the Stradick River blown by German engineers, Ostermeier's troops were located by Soviet scouts covering engineers constructing new crossings. Breaking out towards the northeast, Ostermeier led his men across the iced river to the rail line leading southwest towards Düsterwalde manor. Divisional headquarters had been established at the nearby Gasthäus Dösen – previously Schmalz's corps headquarters – which came under attack on 8 March as Soviet tanks attempted to break through the 'Hermann Göring' left flank, only to be engaged by the Füsilier Battalion supported by Tiger and Panther tanks of the 'Großdeutschland' Division.

Schmalz personally directed the counter-attack, throwing 2nd Company, Fallschirm-Panzergrenadier-Regiment 4 'HG' into the fray as well as Ostermeier's Sturm Bataillon. Rolling into action in half tracks, the grenadiers dismounted and engaged Soviet armour with Panzerfaust and Panzerschreck rocket launchers, destroying seven T-34s and two Josef

Stalin tanks on top of the fourteen destroyed by 'Großdeutschland' Panzers, which lost four of their own. Two Russian tankers were captured near Gr. Klingbeck, while twelve Russians taken prisoner by the Sturm Bataillon were released by Ostermeier to run back to their lines as the German retreat continued.[12]

Though defending German forces exacted a high price from the Soviets, it was an attritional war that they could never win. The frozen Vistula Lagoon became the route for refugees and the evacuation of wounded from Balga towards the Vistula spit, Pillau, or Kahlberg where Kriegsmarine evacuation shipping gathered. On 23 January Grossadmiral Karl Dönitz had launched Operation 'Hannibal' to evacuate by sea German troops and civilians from Courland, East Prussia and the Polish Corridor, an operation that continued until the final days of the war. Luftwaffe transport aircraft landed at Putzig airfield near Gotenhafen until the end of February when heavy losses from enemy fighter aircraft forced all flights to be cancelled. Amidst the chaos, the heavy handed Feldgendarmerie, including those of the 'Hermann Göring' Corps, monitored traffic and hunted for any possible signs of desertion.

> Soldiers separated from their units who could not show any marching orders were [frequently] sentenced to death and shot by the military police without due process. A Grenadier, 19 years old, and an *Oberfähnrich*, 24 years old, both from our company, were executed on 21 March, 1945 in a ravine near Gr. Hoppenbruch. What we heard was so outrageous that we didn't want to believe it at first. Hauptmann Theiss from Magdeburg, from 4th Company Fallschirm-Panzergrenadier. Regt. 'HG' had ordered the court to sentence both soldiers to death . . . The signs on their chests said: 'Traitor! Coward!'
>
> We just couldn't believe it; it was murder of our own comrades! The Oberfähnrich had never been particularly nervous. He wore five tank destruction badges on his sleeve – each representing one tank destroyed in close combat – and the wound badge in silver! And the man who initiated this procedure was Hptm. Theiss of all people, who had always been in the background during difficult combat situations. I don't think anybody ever liked him. He was considered sneaky and unpredictable . . . In the military Ordnungsdienst, Feldgendarmes on patrol duties monitored the

> correct behaviour of the front-line soldiers whenever they were out of sight of their immediate superiors. They searched for soldiers who had been separated in defensive battles and had not returned within a short time. They interpreted this as desertion and Hptm. Theiss's firing squads were active . . . Unfortunately, it must also be mentioned that at that time on the high and steep banks of the lagoon east of Rosenberg and to Balga thousands of people who had been scattered, cowards, officers and also soldiers – allegedly wounded and sick – had entrenched themselves. That was genuine unauthorised departure from combat; it was a desertion! Everywhere on the lagoon they marauded and tried to reach the spit somehow to save their own lives. Here the German Feldgendarmes weren't looking for soldiers who had left their units on their own initiative. Two thousand of those mentioned (deserters) had settled on the banks of the Lagoon and on 29 March 1945, the Russians' offensive of extermination pushed us into the Lagoon.[13]

Schmalz had established his corps headquarters in Fischhausen at the northern end of the Vistula Lagoon as German troops were forced from Balga. On 27 March Maj. Walter Straub was killed in action 6 km south of the town, his adjutant Oblt. Hans Schink already having fallen a week before. At the end of March, Schmalz's chief of staff, Maj. Schweim, reported that only 1,923 men of Fallschirm-Panzergrenadier-Division 2 'HG' remained in and around Pillau, with whatever weapons they had managed to bring over the ice from Balga. Heavy vehicles such as the surviving Jagdpanzer IVs had been destroyed, and approximately 200 men had been stranded in Balga when the Russians entered the port town. Pillau was under constant heavy artillery and aerial bombardment and the streets were overflowing with panicking civilians, soldiers and the corpses of those killed in the inferno. The most organised core of the bedraggled 'Hermann Göring' troops were quartered in Elkenkrug and marched to Pillau on the last day of the month, sheltering in the Kurfürsten Kaserne, the division's first troops finally being evacuated amidst crowds of other soldiers and refugees. By 9 April, the last 'Hermann Göring' troops – including Schmalz and his staff – were lifted from Pillau and sailed to Swinemünde and Kiel. From the combined strength of 24,000 Corps and Panzergrenadier Division troops that had been in East Prussia at the beginning of the Soviet January offensive, only around 6,000 survived to be returned to Germany. Once returned, they were transported immediately by rail on convoluted and exhausting journeys, complicated by Allied bombing, to Berlin-Reinickendorf or Velten to reorganise and refit. The remains of Walther's division were shortly to be shipped first to Saxony and then reunited with the Panzer Division engaged in heavy defensive fighting in Upper Silesia.

Chapter Twelve

The End

'Battle is an orgy of disorder.'
General George S. Patton

During December 1944, Adolf Scheckenbach had been granted two weeks' leave, the last he was to have during the war. Shortly thereafter, 2nd Battalion, Fallschirm-Panzer-Regiment 'Hermann Göring' began upgrading from Panzer IVs to the newer Panthers.

> After Christmas 1944, my 7th Company was sent back to Putlos, to the east of Kiel, for re-equipping and training with new Panzer Vs, the Panther, and to my great joy I finally managed to get posted back to them. My reunion with them was short-lived because, at the time, they had no use for us there so the whole company was sent home on leave. For me it was the last leave of the war. The two weeks' leave and the following training were over very quickly. Some of us were specialised as drivers and radio men while the rest of us were trained as tank commanders, loaders and gunners, but they didn't give us any new Panthers.
>
> By now it was the end of February 1945 and we went back to the barracks at Berlin-Reinickendorf. We weren't happy about this as we knew that if we stayed there, we would only be cannon fodder for Berlin as it had already been declared a fortress. An *Oberfähnrich* brought orders that we were to move to a division assembly point at Königsbruck in Saxony, which is a little to the northeast of Dresden. There, on the night of 13 February, we saw and experienced the fire-bombing of Dresden. It was at that point that I knew that the war was lost but I was with my comrades and that was what counted – and in those times it was better to be in company as being alone or isolated made you a target of the Chained Dogs, the Military Police. A 'War Tribunal' was done quickly and also quickly done . . . Back

> with my company and the division, they remembered that I was an electrician and I went straight to work in the mobile workshops, repairing electrical problems on our vehicles.
>
> By the 20th we had moved up to the front and rejoined the division at the River Neisse, in the Muskau Bridgehead where the situation in Upper Silesia had become critical. We fought defensive battles against the Russians and all the while we were receiving new trucks, artillery, armoured cars and supplies but we never had enough fuel.[1]

Following the retreat to the Oder in late January, Necker relinquished command of the division to return to the Führer Reserve, replaced in early February by the experienced Heer Knight's Cross holder Oberst Max Lemke who had begun his military career with the Uhlan cavalry in 1914.[2]

By March Lemke's division had retreated through Sprottau and Sagan to avoid encirclement, still part of Panzerkorps 'Großdeutschland'. At Sagan on the Bober River, as the 'Hermann Göring' rearguard came under strong Soviet pressure, the Kaiser Wilhelm bridge was primed for demolition as the last troops withdrew to the western bank. With Russian soldiers only twenty metres from the bridge, the engineers of the demolition team were hit by small arms fire and incapacitated. Squad leader Gefreiter Emil Rademann immediately raced from cover and, despite intense enemy fire, reached the badly wounded men and ignited the prepared charges, blowing the bridge and providing valuable breathing space for the disordered division as it hastily prepared a new temporary defensive line. Rademann was awarded the Knight's Cross for his bravery on 23 February 1945.

At Sorau, during the steady retreat, the battered division was briefly restructured as a functional *Kampfgruppe* before being withdrawn from the front line to Weisswasser and reorganised once more as a division. The German retreat had not ended with the entrenched fighting at the Oder and Neisse Rivers, OKW attempting to fortify the western banks while maintaining four small bridgeheads on the eastern banks. Each of these bridgeheads comprised heavily manned trench networks, interwoven among fortified strongholds created within any buildings still standing, all approach roads being mined and strewn with obstacles as far as possible. At the eastern bridgehead near Bad Muskau, on the Neisse River north of Görlitz, the Fallschirm-Panzer-Division 'Hermann Göring' fought strong Soviet spearheads from the end of February to the middle of March.

On 13 March, the commander of Panzerkorps 'Großdeutschland', General der Panzertruppe Georg Jauer, issued the following message to Lemke's men:

> On 10 and 11 March 1945 you conducted a great defence of the Muskau bridgehead. The strength of a Bolshevik rifle division, reinforced by tanks, was shattered by your strong-willed defence, steadfastness and bravery. If Obgfr. Willi Ritsege and Gfr. Fritz Blien of 5th Company, Fallschirm-Panzergrenadier Regt. 1 'HG' achieved twenty-nine sniper kills in those days alone, and when seven tanks, including two Josef Stalins, were destroyed, then this is the best proof for me of your willingness to fight. I want to express the highest appreciation to your commander, Oberst Lemke, for his overall leadership, and to all of you for your exemplary commitment.

Following the division's withdrawal to Weisswasser, an armoured strength return of Rossmann's Panzer Regiment from the middle of the month listed twenty Panzer IVGs (all bar one fully operational), twenty Panthers (twelve operational) and a single Tiger I, although this was non-operational. From there Fallschirm-Panzer-Division 1 'HG' entrained to Görlitz and moved towards Neisse in Upper Silesia. There they passed from Jauer's command and into General der Panzertruppe Sigfrid Henrici's XL Panzer Corps

On 17 March the first rail transports carrying the advance elements of the division arrived in Ottmachau, west of Neisse, where they were to undertake a surprise offensive against the western flank of the armoured Soviet wedge advancing in the direction of Dresden. However, by the time the necessary trains had shipped the division to its destination and combat units had assembled, the opportunity for success had passed. With 20th Panzer Division on their left flank, the 'Hermann Göring' troops instead advanced to Rotthaus and Mansdorf, Lemke establishing his headquarters in the town of Konradsdorf on 18 March.

However, despite Jauer's previous praise for the division, a visit by the commander of Luftflotte 6, Generaloberst Ritter von Greim, under whose logistical jurisdiction the division fell, revealed that Generaloberst Ferdinand Schörner (commander of Army Group Centre) had criticised the 'mediocre leadership' of the division during an internal staff meeting on 19 March in Jermer-Josefstadt. Greim spent time with Lemke before travelling to visit the newly promoted Oberstleutnant Rossmann at his forward command post. A regimental report of 21 March recorded:

> Fallschirm-Panzer-Regiment 'HG' was just attacking Schnellwalde when Commandant Luftlotte 6 arrived at advanced regimental command post.
>
> During the course of the day, nine of the regiment's tanks were lost. A police battalion in the area was assaulted by a Russian squad of twenty-five men.
>
> Regiment has destroyed twenty-three anti-tank artillery pieces and seventeen tanks since 17 March. Regiment is bitter about treatment by the army. They want to take our cuff titles away from us.

The inter-service rivalry for logistics that had long bedevilled every branch of the Wehrmacht and Waffen-SS also extended to each arm of service's reputation, and the 'Hermann Göring' troops would seem to have been intrinsically tied to their namesake's own fortunes. This can be further evidenced by a diary entry made by General der Flieger Karl Koller, Luftwaffe Chief of Staff, in the Führer Headquarters in the bunker beneath the Reichs Chancellery.

> 21 April: In the evening between 8:30 p.m. and 2:00 a.m. [Hitler] is on the phone again: 'The Reichsmarschall maintains a private army in Carinhall. Dissolve it and use them immediately. He doesn't need a private army.'
>
> I reply that there was no private army in Carinhall, but only the 'Hermann Göring' division, which was available to the local front command of the army, and that most of the division's forces were already deployed. Hitler denies this, claiming to be well informed about the presence of strong forces in Carinhall.
>
> My research shows that apart from a single battalion, all parts of the division are already in combat. I report this to Hitler, he orders: 'Immediately place SS Obergruppenführer Steiner in command of the battalion' and ends the conversation.
>
> As I am still wondering what exactly this means, Hitler calls again. 'Every available Luftwaffe man in the area between Berlin and the coast to Stettin and Hamburg should be included in the attack I ordered in the northeast of Berlin.' On my objection that we

> could not deploy troops unused to fighting, and when I asked where the attack is supposed to be, there is no answer; he has already hung up.
>
> I have no idea of such a planned attack, and I also believe that our strength is too low for success to be achieved. In a series of phone calls, I try to clarify things. I learn from Generalmajor Freigang from General Conrath's Staff ('Hermann Göring' Division), Carinhall, that he has heard that Obergruppenführer Steiner will lead an attack from the Eberswalde area to the south.
>
> 22 April. Another call from the Führer's bunker. Holy smokes! I can't help people! Instead of Steiner, Conrath and Freigang, who I am looking for, I catch a *Hauptmann* of the 'Hermann Göring' division on the phone, who has just been with a battalion that is to take part in the attack. He tells me that the attack has not yet started, when is it? He does not know when it should start . . .

On 20 April, Hermann Göring left his Carinhall sanctuary for the last time. After shaking hands with his former staff and exchanging salutes with officers of his guard, Göring climbed into his car and left the area while the few soldiers of the Begleitbataillon 'Reichsmarschall' who had remained to guard their commander-in-chief before his summons to Berlin, began mining the buildings. Until the explosives were detonated the following day they took the opportunity to wander the halls of the expansive estate, now emptied of its contents which had been trucked away with the Reichsmarschall. The demolition plans did not, however, include the sarcophagus of Göring's late wife Carin, which was subsequently broken open and looted by Red Army troops who arrived only hours after the last 'Hermann Göring' men had departed.

Before these events that marked the Reich's final days, Fallschirm-Panzer-Division 'HG' continued to mount a fierce fighting retreat after the failed offensive from Neisse. On 22 March, Soviet forces attacked from Oppersdorf and during the day twelve Panzer IVs of the Panzer Regiment were lost. Within two days Neisse was captured by the Red Army as XL. Panzerkorps gave up hard-fought-for ground towards the west. On 28 March the division announced the award of the fourth Knight's Cross that month, to the veteran commander of Fallschirm-Panzergrenadier Regt. 1 'HG' Oberst Erich Bertram who five days previously had been killed in action by shell splinters 10 km west of Neisse.

The shattered division was pulled back to the northwest near Schweidnitz to rest and regroup briefly at the beginning of April, Max Lamke being promoted to *Generalmajor* on the 20th of that month. Losses had been considerable and, with little by way of reinforcement, companies and battalions were dissolved and amalgamated to provide units of a size and composition capable of combat. On 11 April, Griem at Luftflotte 6 announced the re-formation of Fallschirm-Panzerkorps 'Hermann Göring' as Schmalz's headquarters staff and Walther's Panzergrenadier Division were entrained from Berlin for Görlitz.

In the interim, Lemke's Panzer division was thrown once more into action against the Red Army's advance over the Neisse River in pursuit of German forces retreating towards Dresden. Still under the command of Panzerkorps 'Großdeutschland' the division, flanked by 20th Panzer Division, crashed into the southern edge of the Soviet advance north of Görlitz, hurling itself against Soviet troops emerging from forests east of Kodersdorf. Rossmann led his seventeen operational Panthers into action against the 1st Polish Armoured Corps, opening fire at a range of only fifty metres. Within twenty minutes, forty-three Soviet tanks had been destroyed or disabled and the remainder forced to retreat temporarily. Twelve disabled tanks – including four heavy Josef Stalins – were hurriedly repaired in divisional workshops, repainted with the Balkenkreuz and pressed into action against their former owners.

On 18 April the advance elements of Fallschirm-Panzergrenadier Division 2 'HG' began arriving in the area of Senftenberg to reunite with Lemke's Panzer Division. The commander of Army Group Centre, Schörner, began concentrating his units in the Görlitz and Reichenbach area, planning to launch a major counter-offensive against the southern flank of the Polish Army, halt their advance and break through to Berlin to relieve the trapped Ninth Army. He possessed, in total, elements of the Fourth Panzer Army; Fallschirm-Panzerkorps 'HG', 20th Panzer Division, Panzergrenadier Division 'Brandenburg', 17th Infantry Division as well as a *Kampfgruppe* of the remains of the 545th Volksgrenadier Division and the supply train from the 10th SS Panzer Division 'Frundsberg'. In total, he mustered what was at that time a force of considerable power; approximately 50,000 soldiers, 300 tanks, and 600 guns.

In one of the final armoured success of the Wehrmacht, Schörner attacked with his 'Görlitz Group' into a gap that had developed between the leading elements of the Polish 2nd Army racing for Dresden and those still engaged in fighting near Neisse. He astutely identified the inter-army boundary between the overstretched Poles and the Soviet 52nd Army around Bautzen and concentrated his forces at this point of maximum vulnerability. With his corps headquarters at Auerhaus, Schmalz coordinated his part of the attack, which began on 23 April. Although the German offensive was halted within five days, and comprehensively failed to break through to its ultimate goal of Berlin, losses to the Poles were particularly severe. 'Hermann Göring' troops near Bautzen destroyed large portions of 2nd Polish Army's logistical and communications train and severely damaged both the Polish 5th Infantry Division and 16th Armoured Brigade, both of which were struck in the rear and practically annihilated. Adolf Scheckenbach was with Fallschirm-Panzer-Division 'HG' as the German assault unfolded.

> On the 23rd we began our assault on Bautzen. Not far from our start points to the south we had a sharp engagement with some T-34s at Hochkirch and they came off badly. In the afternoon we, along with 20th Panzer and StuG Brigades 300 and 311, carefully rolled into the outskirts of Bautzen where we engaged the Poles and Russians. Our 'HG 2' Panzergrenadiers retook the city from the Russians, at a heavy cost, and, in the morning of the 24th, we rescued the remaining garrison. There were only 400 men left in an area of 150 × 150 metres.
>
> That afternoon, the 2nd Polish Armoured Brigade launched a counter-attack in the western approaches but they were soon halted and the Russian 24th Guards Armoured Brigade also withdrew, leaving the city and its surrounds to us. On the 25th we attacked northwards again, taking with us Panzergrenadiers from 'HG 2' and Regiment 112 from 20th Panzer. At about 1500 hrs the Russians counter-attacked but with the help of StuG Battalion 300, we drove them off and they retreated further than we expected. We met them again the next day in the village of Kleinwelka where we fought. Again, they came off second best and we captured a number of tanks including several more IS-2 Josef Stalin heavy tanks. We painted Balkenkreuzes on them and put them to good use as we advanced further. The sheer number of tanks the Russians had, had a quality of its own but I feel that German Panzers were individually superior vehicles in both armament and workmanship. We saw that if you're going to stage a war, it is important to have weapons and

seeing as we couldn't get our own Panzers, we used the enemy's – which were good enough.

I was very busy during this period, repairing vehicles both out on the battlefield and at our mobile workshops. It was dangerous work as the Russians were doing their best to kill us but I was able to repair electrical faults and get Panzers and other vehicles operational again. Our men fought hard which allowed the workshop sections to do their work – without having to resort to close combat – so the men could get their vehicles back.

We moved up through the villages of Luga and Holschdubrau where we got bogged down in woods which had been festooned with Russian and Polish tanks and PAKs. The general attack spread to the left of us with the Brandenburg Panzergrenadiers and parts of 20th Panzer also rolling north. They managed to encircle and destroy the Polish 9th Infantry Division. On the 27th and 28th, as we were not powerful enough to punch through the anti-tank gun line, we went over to the defensive and repelled Polish and Russian counter-attacks.[3]

Losses for 2nd Polish Army around Bautzen are accepted to have been approximately 5,000 men killed, 2,800 missing or taken prisoner and 10,500 wounded. Furthermore, they lost 170 tanks, 56 self-propelled guns, 124 mortars, 232 guns of all calibres, 330 vehicles, and 1,373 horses. Bautzen remained in German hands for the remainder of the war. However, although the steadily advancing Red Army included thousands of inexperienced men, tired soldiers who had been in almost constant battle for months and frequently dangerously worn-out machinery and equipment, they remained numerically overpowering for the German defenders. Despite the victory at Bautzen, German casualties in men and material could not be replaced and the Fallschirm-Panzerkorps 'HG' was moved back towards Dresden.

On the 29th we were relieved and during the night, railed to near Meißen, to the northwest of Dresden, on the northern side of the River Elbe and we marched to Auerhaus in the Friedewald to assemble in the cover of the forest. It was here we were properly reunited with our 'HG 2' Division and our Korpsbefehlsstand [Corps Headquarters]. By 2 May we were all in position to attack the Russians in the direction of Berlin, with the long-range objective of relieving the city.

The order to march was given early on 3 May and our entire corps quickly reached the Königsbruck–Großenhain road south of Lampertswalde. There was very heavy fighting as we crashed into and destroyed a Russian armoured spearhead, which included the 1st Polish Armoured Division. Apparently during the fighting, our regimental commander, Oberstleutnant Rossmann, and several of his officers drove into enemy-occupied Großenhain on our western flank. Surprisingly they were unnoticed and returned to us none the worse for wear.

At about lunchtime on the 5th our attack was stopped in open farmland near Ölsnitz, a little short of the border between the states of Saxony and Brandenburg. We lacked the reserves to punch through the seemingly endless supply of tanks and anti-tank guns the Russians had. During the night, we had to retreat so we could reorganise our units and lick our wounds for the fighting had been costly – and that was the end of our attempt to reach Berlin. We took up positions on the north of the Dresdener Heide and fought off the several attacks made by the Russians the next day. It was then that our company commander, Leutnant Knapp, while searching for a new position, was surprised by a Russian patrol and was killed in the ensuing fire-fight. His adjutant, a *Feldwebel* and an *Unteroffizier* were unable to rescue his body and were forced to retire to the main body of the company.

On 7 May, the Russians broke into what remained of Dresden from the east. We had to pull back quickly so we would not be caught on the northern side of the river. Apparently, our engineers had to use threats of force to stop the local commander from blowing our crossing point, the Loshwitz bridge, before we could get across. A bridgehead was formed at Loshwitz by our faithful Panzergrenadiers with the enemy all around. We and other 'HG' units, as well as others not associated with us, fought our way to the bridgehead and reinforced it, fighting off Russian attacks.

Apparently at about 1600 hrs Russian tanks reached the centre of the city and all the other bridges were blown. Now that the Russians had won the main battle for the city, they pulled back and generally left us alone while they celebrated victory with plenty of vodka. We formed ourselves up into proper units again and at 1700 hrs began crossing the river into the area of the formerly exclusive suburb of

> Blasewitz, though the whole area was now in ruins. We and other units, along with thousands of refugees, marched southeast out of the city with the Russians mostly ignoring us.[4]

Far to the north, Franz Lürbke of Fallschirm-Panzer-Ersatz-und-Ausbildungs-Regiment 3 'Hermann Göring' had been spared the fighting in Saxony as his unit retreated before the Red Army:

> The night of 26 April was extremely quiet again and the morning brought no change. Everything that was not urgently needed was put on the march to Welsow. Even a team of oxen was used to help us move. What a mockery of world history: ox teams in action in the front line! Those days I realised that we had finally lost the war. You cannot tackle and overwhelm a high-tech power with inadequate means. Nor can one destroy them with lies and false statements, only at the most hold them back with extreme heroism for a certain period of time, and that happened in our area.
>
> I was spared these battles and disasters. Fortunately, with the company squad and the rest of the train led by an *Oberleutnant*, I lost contact with the company on the night of 28 April because of an interim order. We marched around in circles several times, waited until dawn at an agreed meeting point and then gave up the search. The *Oberleutnant* was undecided what to do at first, but then he did what countless other soldiers around us did, and he started marching west with us.
>
> We were maybe two or three hours on the road when suddenly a Kubelwagen came to meet us on the street in Gollin, an officer from our division with a Knight's Cross, Major Hahm, standing in the passenger seat . . . He angrily hissed at the *Oberleutnant* . . . and threatened court martial – the worst possible consequences – and gave the order to turn back to the front immediately. He then drove in that direction, probably in the hope of being able to save something, although then he only had to retreat. The next evening Konstantin Hahm, who had married in Joachimsthal in March, fell.
>
> In any case, the *Oberleutnant* reacted as instructed that morning. But behind his back, one after the other, the men – including me – disappeared from the group in the thick bush that lined the pavement along the entire length of the road. Then we carefully continued our retreat in small groups. Officially, the entire front in our section

behind the Havel–Voss Canal was withdrawn on 28 April. Again, combat units to our rear had to be avoided. Generaloberst Heinrici had initially requested permission from OKW for this withdrawal order . . . but had been brusquely refused.

28 April brought me an unexpected reunion. Shortly after 'separation' from our *Oberleutnant*, I accidentally discovered a Panzer crew behind an anti-tank barrier on the road from Gollin to Vietmannsdorf preparing a Panzer IV lying in the ditch with engine damage for demolition. To my delight, they were old friends Werner Eggers and Walter Michaelis, also Gerd Mayer, known to me from Erlangen, and the tank commander, NCO Rudolf Schmidt. Only the loader was missing; the day before, under unfortunate circumstances, he was run over by his own tank through no fault of the driver. Rudolf showed me the letter he wanted to send to the parents, but the 'heroic death' described in it had no resemblance to reality.

The demolition occurred just before the arrival of some Volkssturm men. A few officers of the Waffen-SS also arrived too late, who thought that the Panzer's intact gun could still have been used against the Russians. However, because the Russians already seemed near, the dispute came to a quick end as everyone just wanted to leave in a hurry. Except for the Volkssturm men, who stayed behind with a few rifles and looked pretty forlorn in their civilian coats with their 'Volkssturm' armbands. What did they think when they saw the fleeing soldiers? In any case, it was a macabre situation and I can only hope that they realised the actual position and left.

Almost at the same time, Hermann Göring's Carinhall hunting lodge was destroyed by soldiers of the guard company a few kilometres south. A member of the demolition squad set off for Gollin immediately after the detonation. During his service at Carinhall he had met a young woman in Gollin and got engaged to her. But the short journey towards his bride-to-be was his doom. A few metres from his goal, he was seen and shot by Russian soldiers.[5]

The war was lost for the armies of the Third Reich. On the last day of April Hitler committed suicide himself in the depths of his Berlin bunker, one of his final acts being to strip Hermann Göring of his titles and decorations and order his arrest. Desperate men of the Wehrmacht and

Waffen-SS frequently attempted to head west to escape inevitable capture by the Red Army and surrender instead to American or British forces.

> The 'HG' Korps was ordered to occupy the crest of the Erzgebirge [Ore Mountains] to act as the rearguard for Kampfgruppe 'Schörner' which was retreating from Czechoslovakia. My company was part of the force that was ordered to go around the mountains to the other side, probably to somewhere like Teplice-Shönau to act as the vanguard of the corps and allow Schörner's Kampfgruppe to break free of pursuing Russians.
>
> On 8 May someone had organised rail wagons for us and we loaded up around Heidenau for much of the day while the rest of the corps continued heading up into the mountains to Glashütte. We soon rolled past Pirna and just a couple of hours later, our troop train stood in the Tetschen-Bodenbach station just inside Czechoslovakia. It was now the early evening of 8 May 1945. At the company roll-call our officers informed us that a cease-fire was in effect and that the war had ended.
>
> At this, our officers could no longer control the men. Most of them immediately started for their homes in the gathering dusk using the trucks and other vehicles we had brought with us. We, a section of ten soldiers of my company, took a Panzer, I think it was an old Panzer IV, off a rail wagon. Our intention was to go south, straight across the Sudetenland, through Czechoslovakia, and into Austria to fight in the Last Redoubt. We were too stupid to realise that fighting in Austria wasn't going to happen and that upon the collapse of the Greater German Reich, these countries regained their sovereignty. Austria and Czechoslovakia were once again independent and during our occupation they had endured many hardships. We were not going to be looked upon favourably, let alone while rolling through in a Panzer.
>
> We set off down the road and got many kilometres towards Prague before our Panzer ran out of fuel or maybe broke down and we couldn't figure out how to repair it, I don't remember which. That brought to us the realisation of how silly we had been, wanting to continue the war, so we left it there and began walking home. Shortly after this a young Sudeten German boy warned us that the Czechs were posted on all the roads and tracks. I recommended to

> my fellow travellers that we throw away all our weapons – we were only carrying our .08 pistols. About an hour later – it had been dark for a while – we were surprised by a group of Czech soldiers and taken to their nearest position. At the time we were surprised a few had forgotten to throw away all their ammunition and these were yelled at, abused and beaten up. Then, all our insignia was torn from us. Most of my group got rid of most of their uniforms along the way by swapping them for other clothes in empty houses but I kept mine.
>
> We spent the rest of the night in Raudnitz, a Czech city on the River Elbe about halfway between Tetschen-Bodenbach and Prague. The next day, we were set free and told to go home. As we marched west over the Elbe, a Czech on a bicycle yelled derisively to us, 'Home to the Reich'. That was a slogan which had been used in previous years by the Nazi Party for the return of ethnic Germans to the fold of the Reich after the annexation and invasions of Austria, Czechoslovakia, Hungary, Romania and Russia.
>
> A little way along we came upon a young Russian soldier on a horse who obviously wondered why we weren't being guarded by the Czechs. We told him that we were on our way home since, 'Stalin had ordered that German soldiers were to go to their homes.' This may have been so, but according to him, we weren't supposed to go until later. After our halt with this young soldier, who was perhaps eighteen or nineteen years old, we caught up with the retreating Kampfgruppe 'Schörner'. My group was stopped by a civilian patrol. These fellows were very interested in my black Panzer uniform and were looking for the blood group tattoo that all SS soldiers had on their upper left arm. At a range of about ten to twelve metres, a man stood on guard with a rifle at the ready. They couldn't find a tattoo so they let me go. But during the examination I felt very vulnerable and isolated.[6]

Of the 'Hermann Göring' commanding officers, Paul Conrath got out of Berlin and surrendered to the Western Allies; Wilhelm Schmalz and his corps staff were able to reach American troops before surrendering as was Max Lemke at the head of a portion of his division. However, the bulk of the splintered units were not so fortunate and the majority of the 'Hermann Göring' Divisions were captured by the Red Army after retreating towards

Geising and the Czech border. Due to the nature of their formation and the name they carried on their cuff-titles, they were generally classed in the same bracket as the SS by their Soviet captors and frequently treated with extreme harshness. Among them was Generalmajor Erich Walther, taken prisoner of war by the Red Army on 8 May and dying on 26 December 1947 in 'NKVD Special Camp 2' created on the site of the former Buchenwald concentration camp. These 'Special Camps' were subordinated to the Soviet Gulag system and operated a policy of complete isolation from the outside world. Though the prisoners were not used as slave labour, inmate mortality was high due to malnourishment and disease.

> The NKVD was most feared among the POWs. The NKVD conducted all interrogations and inquiries in any case of violation of laws and regulations. They selected the people to be sent away to special camps. The Russians started this action in September 1948, when they sent away from our camp 150 men to an unknown camp (according to a rumour this camp was supposed to be near Tiflis). I met a former POW who had been in the camp just next to this special camp. These two camps were separated only by barbed-wire fences. The POWs in this special camp were watched much more closely and in the death zone around the camp there were dogs patrolling. During the march to work the POWs were guarded much more strictly. The Russian guards had dogs with them and fired without warning if somebody left the marching column. I do not have any idea whether POWs of that camp were eventually released too. They sent away all former SS men, policemen, members of special army units like Großdeutschland, 'Hermann Göring', Brandenburg, etc. and former officers of the General Staff. They continued this action until May–June 1949. They picked out all people who had been in NSDAP organisations like SS, SA, NSKK, NSFK or in the above-mentioned army units or in the police or in the secret field police.[7]

Many of the more unfortunate members of the 'Hermann Göring' Divisions were sentenced to hard labour in the Gulag system, and it was not until the successful negotiations in Moscow by West German Chancellor Konrad Adenauer that the last surviving prisoners of war held within the USSR were released by the end of 1955. The number who died in the work camps remains unknown.

The 'Hermann Göring' formation remains one of the most enigmatic of the Wehrmacht. Of a clearly political origin, through service as Göring's personal police force, to anti-aircraft and, subsequently, anti-tank specialists until transformed into a bona-fide armoured formation, the reputation of the unit often overshadowed its actual achievements. This is true in both good and bad senses; its military prowess was, though perhaps patchy, undoubtedly valued by corps and army commanders who had its units on strength. Their wanton disregard for civilian welfare was equally obvious, though such massacres and ill-treatment were not characteristic of all men who bore the 'Göring' cuff-titles. Participation in anti-partisan drives and resprisals in Italy, as well as suppression of the Warsaw Uprising, will always stain those elements involved. Perhaps that is why the histories of the 'Hermann Göring' units so closely resemble that of the premier units of the Waffen-SS. Certainly Conrath faced the same accusations from some Wermacht officers – of fighting aggressive 'butchers' warfare' with limited tactical consideration – as those levelled at 'Sepp' Dietrich of the 'Leibstandarte', and Theodor Eicke of the 'Totenkopf' Division. That Conrath was held in the same regard by his men as those two SS officers were by theirs, and that, at least sometimes, his call for fanatical commitment in action achieved the desired results, perhaps further solidifies the comparison.

The sum total of the war experience of the 'Hermann Göring' troops remains a legacy and reputation that has endured long after the end of the Second World War and yet most of which was gained in less than two years of combat in Italy and the inferno of the Eastern Front. For better or worse, they left an enduring impression on both friend and foe.

Appendix 1

Hermann Göring Cuff Titles

'Hermann Göring' troops are frequently easily identified by their distinctive cuff-titles, generally positioned 1 cm above the right cuff of a service tunic, or 16cm above the right sleeve end on all cuffless garments.

The first was presented to Landespolizeigruppe 'General Göring'. The newly titled formation was authorised to wear a new cuff-title on the lower left sleeve: a dark green band with the words 'L.P.G. General Göring' machine-embroidered in white Gothic script, edged with white borders top and bottom for NCOs, executed in hand-woven silver-grey wire for officers.

Upon redesignation to Regiment 'General Göring' and transfer to the Luftwaffe, the cuff title also changed, now dark blue with 'General Göring' embroidered in silver wire for officers, with a silver border above and below, embroidered in matt grey thread for NCOs and without the border for enlisted men.

As the regiment grew to a brigade and then division, an order dated 22 May 1942 instructed all ranks to replace the previous 'General Göring' cuff-titles with the newly created 'Hermann Göring' one, to be completed no later than August. Still on a dark blue background, initial versions were written in Gothic script but superseded by block capitals shortly thereafter.

Additional Cuff Titles

Flak troops assigned to defend Fuhrer headquarters were allowed to wear the 'Führerhauptquartier' cuff title, 15 cm from the bottom of the left sleeve. This title was in gold gothic lettering with gold edging (both silver from 15 January 1941) on a black background.

Some troops attached to the Führer Begleit Bataillon, were permitted to wear the 'Großdeutchland' black cuff title with white Sutterlin script, again on the left sleeve.

The 'Afrika' cuff-title was permitted for all Luftwaffe troops who were serving in North Africa: 3 cm wide, dark blue background with 'Afrika' in embroidered aluminium for officers, woven matt grey fabric for enlisted men, positioned 16 cm from the bottom of the right sleeve and to be removed when transferred from the African combat theatre.

This was replaced for those men who had either served for six months in theatre, been wounded or received an award of the Iron Cross or higher, by the official Führer-approved campaign cuff-title in February 1943: 3.3 cm wide on khaki brown background with silver edging, the word 'Afrika' flanked by two palm trees in silver cotton.

Members of the Feldgendarmerie were also required to wear their service arm cuff-title on their lower left sleeve; a medium brown artificial silk band with grey edges and lettering.

Appendix 2

Knight's Cross Recipients

For clarity, I have only included decorations awarded while in either RGG or HG unit service.

Oakleaves and Swords

1 Feb. 1945	Oberst Erich Walther	commander Fsch.Pz.Gren.Div. 2 'HG'

Oakleaves

21 Aug. 1943	Generalmajor Paul Conrath	commander Pz.Div. 'HG'
23 Dec. 1943	Oberst Wilhelm Schmalz	commander Brig.z.b.V. (Pz.Div.'HG')
24 June 1944	Major Josef Fitz	commander I./Fsch.Pz.Gren.Regt. 1 'HG'
1 Feb. 1945	Major Karl Rossmann	commander Fsch.Pz.Regt. 'HG'
28 Feb. 1945	Oberstleutnant Bern von Baer	chief of Staff (Ia) Fsch.Pz.Korps 'HG'
15 April 1945	Major Hans Ostermeier	commander Fsch.Pz.Grn.Regt. 3 'HG'

Knight's Cross

4 Sept. 1941	Oberst Paul Conrath	commander Flak Regt. (mot.) 'GG'
6 Oct. 1941	Oberleutnant Rudolf Graf	battery commander 1./Flak Regt. 'GG'
12 Nov. 1941	Oberleutnant Karl Rossmann	commander 16./Flak Regt 'GG'
23 Nov. 1941	Leutnant Dirk Itzen†	reconnaissance officer 3./Flak Regt. 'GG'
18 May 1943	Hauptmann Eduard Kiefer	commander 2./Pz.Aufkl.Abt. 'HG'
21 May 1943	Generalmajor Josef Schmid	commander Division 'HG', Tunisia
21 June 1943	Hauptmann Kurt Schreiber	commander II./Gre.Regt. (mot.) 'HG'
21 June 1943	Oberfeldwebel Johannes Scheid	squad leader 11./Pz.Gren.Regt. 'HG'
2 Aug. 1943	Major Waldemar Kluge	commander I./Pz.Gren.Regt. 2 'HG'
2 Aug. 1943	Major Robert Rebholz	commander Pz.Aufkl.Abt. 'HG'
5 April 1944	Hauptmann Fritz Quednow†	commander 9./Jäg.Regt. 'HG'
5 April 1944	Leutnant Walter Knaf†	platoon leader 8./Pz.Gren.Regt.2 'HG'
18 May 1944	Obergefreiter Heinrich Witte	gunner 7./Fsch.Flak.Regt. 'HG'
9 June 1944	Major Konstantin Hahm	commander II./Fsch.Pz.Regt. 'HG'
24 June 1944	Oberst Hans-Horst von Necker	commander Fsch.Pz.Gren.Regt. 2 'HG'
25 June 1944	Oberst Georg-Henning von Heydebreck	commander Fsch.Pz.Gren.Regt. 1 'HG'
8 Aug. 1944	Oberfeldwebel Heinrich Schäfer	squad leader 4./Jäg.Regt. 'HG'
5 Sept. 1944	Feldwebel Karl Kulp	platoon leader 13./Fsch.Pz.Gren.Regt. 1 'HG'
30 Sept. 1944	Hauptmann Hans-Joachim Bellinger	commander 9.(StuG)/Fsch.Pz.Regt. 'HG'
30 Sept. 1944	Hauptmann Hans Thor†	commander I./Fsch.Pz.Gren.Regt. 2 'HG')
6 Oct. 1944	Hauptmann Fritz-Wilhelm Schmidt	commander II./Fsch.Pz.Gren.Regt. 2 'HG'
10 Oct. 1944	Oberleutnant Hans-Georg Lehmann	commander Sturm Kompanie 'HG'
18 Oct. 1944	Major Hans Sandrock	commander II.(StuG)/Fsch.Pz.Regt. 'HG'

18 Oct. 1944	Hauptmann Wolfram Stronk	commander 6./Fsch.Pz.Regt. 'HG'
19 Oct. 1944	Oberfähnrich Fritz Birnbaum	platoon leader 8./Fsch.Pz.Regt. 'HG'
20 Oct. 1944	Hauptmann Josef Francois	flak battery commander (and part of Pz.Gren.Brig. 'von Werthern')
29 Oct. 1944	Unteroffizier Siegfried Kalow†	squad leader 10./Fsch.Pz.Gren.Regt. 2 'HG'
20 Nov. 1944	Hauptmann Werner Stuchlik	commander II./Fsch.Pz.Gren.Regt. 2 'HG'
30 Nov. 1944	Oberleutnant Wilhelm Kuhlwilm	company commander Fsch.Pz.Gren.Regt. 3 'HG'
30 Nov. 1944	Oberleutnant Rupert Kraus	commander 2./Fsch.Pz.Regt. 'HG'
30 Nov. 1944	Leutnant Karl-Heinz Wallhausser	commander 1./Fsch.StuG.Abt 'HG'
30 Nov. 1944	Unteroffizier Werner Grunhold	squad leader 3./Fsch.Pz.Gren.Regt. 2 'HG'
30 Nov. 1944	Gefreiter Albert Plapper	squad leader 4./Fsch.Pz.Gren.Regt. 2 'HG'
30 Nov. 1944	Gefreiter Konrad Steets	battalion messenger II./Fsch.Pz.Gren.Regt. 2 'HG'
6 Dec. 1944	Hauptmann Joachim Renz†	commander I./Fsch.Pz.Regt. 'HG'
6 Dec. 1944	Oberleutnant Gerhard Tschierschwitz	commander 2./Fsch.Pz.Regt. 'HG'
14 Jan. 1945	Major Hans Briegel	commander Fsch.Pz.Gren.Regt. 2 'HG'
15 Jan. 1945	Unteroffizier Eckhardt Köppen†	commander 1./Fsch.Pz.Pi.Btl. 2 'HG'
28 Jan. 1945	Hauptmann Johann Wimmer	commander I./Fsch.Pz.Ers.u.Ausb.Regt. 'HG'
7 Feb. 1945	Unteroffizier Herbert Koepsel	squad leader 1./Fsch.Pz.Pi.Btl. 2 'HG'
8 Feb. 1945	Leutnant Heinz Koenig	commander 3./Fsch. StuG.Abt. 'HG'
11 Feb. 1945	Hauptmann Hans-Christian Hansen	commander II./Fsch.Pz.Gren.Regt. 3 'HG'
19 Feb. 1945	Gefreiter Lothar Schirner	gunner 19./Fsch.Flak.Regt. 'HG'
23 Feb. 1945	Gefreiter Emil Rademann	squad leader Fsch.Pz.Pi.Btl. 1 'HG'
28 Feb. 1945	Obergefreiter Heinrich Krappmann	gunner 19./Fsch.Flak.Regt. 'HG'
28 Feb. 1945	Major Heinz-Herbert Schweim	Ia Fsch.Pz.Gren. Div. s. 'HG'
12 Mar. 1945,	Oberleutnant Armin Klein	commander 15./Fsch.Flak.Regt. 'HG'
26 Mar. 1945	Oberfeldwebel Erhard Herbst	platoon leader II./Fsch.Pz.Regt. 'HG'
26 Mar. 1945	Leutnant Hans Lippe	platoon leader Fsch.Pz.Gren.Regt. 1 'HG'
26 Mar. 1945	Unteroffizier Heinz Probst	squad leader 1./Fsch.Pz.Gren.Regt. 4. 'HG'
26 Mar. 1945	Hauptmann Hans-Heinrich Richter	commander Fsch.Aufkl.Abt. 2 'HG'
28 Mar. 1945	Oberst Eric Bertram†	commander Fsch.Pz.Gren.Regt. 1 'HG'
5 April 1945	Hauptmann Wilhelm Schulze-Ostwald	company commander Fsch.St.Gesch.Abt. 'HG' (later changed his name to Wilhelm Leitzmann)
17 April 1945	Leutnant Helmut Leitenberger	platoon leader 3./Fsch.Pz.Regt. 'HG'
28 April 1945	Feldwebel Wolfgang Zander	squad leader Marsch.Kp./Fsch.Pz.Gren.Regt. 4 'HG'

9 May 1945	Oberst Friedrich August Meyer	commander Fsch.Pz.Ers.u.Ausb.Brig. 'HG'
(Recommendation Nr. 1493 made on 3 March, unfinished at end of war)		
9 May 1945	Leutnant Friedrich Behre	company commander I./Fsch.Pz.Gren.Regt. 1 'HG'
(Recommendation Nr. 1573 made on 14 April 1945, unfinished at end of war)		

Notes

Chapter One: Police

1. Another important step in the modification of Prussia's police force was taken during April 1933 when Rudolf Diels, head of the Prussian Political Police on Hitler's assumption of power, was appointed by Göring as chief of the new Prussian State Police Department 1A. Concerned with political crimes, the department was soon renamed Geheime Staatspolizei (Secret State Police), or Gestapo, and later, on 20 April 1934, handed over to the control of Heinrich Himmler's SS.
2. NARA T-315 Roll 2296.
3. Hsi-huey Liang, *Die Berliner Polizei in der Weimarer Republik*, p. 193.
4. Jakoby served as a senior signals officer for the remainder of the war, though severely wounded in the head on 17 May 1943 and periodically hospitalised thereafter. He ended the war as a *Generalleutnant*, was in hospital at the time of the German surrender and immediately released from Allied captivity. He died in Düsseldorf on 19 January 1967.
5. Eventually, in April 1943, this premier German airborne unit was redesignated 1st Fallschirmjäger Division.
6. www.dhm.de/lemo/zeitzeugen/friedrich-gerlach-meine-militaerzeit-beim-reiterzug-carinhall.html.
7. Rolf Wallburg's diary (www.billcarol.com/440197322).

Chapter Two: Early Successes in War

1. The battalion incorporated the Führerbegleitkommando which had been created in June 1938 with infantry from the 'Großdeutschland' Regiment.
2. In July 1940 control reverted to Staff, Regiment General Göring.
3. The two *Flakkorps* assigned to Army Groups A and B were not attached to any divisional-level unit, but directly deployed in support of advancing troops where required by the army group staffs. Vehicles of 103rd Flak Regiment were adorned with the II. Flakkorps insignia on vehicle bumpers: a black rectangle with white border and a white oakleaf and two acorns. The 3rd Battalion, RGG of I. Flakkorps used the corps vehicle insignia: a red shield with white border and white oakleaf.

4. 6th Battery had been detached from the regiment before Fall Gelb to form a new 3./leichte Flak Abteilung 73 (mot.), part of Flak Regiment 201.
5. At the beginning of December 1940, the officers of 3rd Battalion directly under Lindenberg were: Adjutant, Leutnant Baumgart; OC 11th Battery, Oberleutnant Gerhard Nagorny; OC 12th Battery, Oberleutnant Martin Lübke; OC 13th Battery, Hauptmann Gerhard Schmudlach.
6. Rolf Wallburg's diary.
7. After a period in charge of the V-1 programme, Walther Axthelm ended the war as General der Flakausbildung, attached to the Air Ministry; he was captured by the Americans but released on 1 July 1947.
8. Among the new officers who had been transferred to 4th Flak Battalion in July 1940 was Lt. Heinz Göring, Hermann Göring's nephew (his father, Heinrich, was the Reichsmarschall's brother).
9. Several of the bunkers were bypassed and their defenders only beaten after three days of fighting. Sokal, a town that had witnessed anti-Jewish programs over the previous decades, got its first taste of what was to come on the day of its occupation by German troops when eleven random Jews were shot dead in front of the Polish cathedral. By the war's end, only fifteen of the original Jewish population of just under 6,000 – almost half of the town's population – were left alive.
10. Twenty-three-year-old Leutnant Friedrich Wilmskötter suffered severe concussion during the battle and was later hospitalised after suffering frequent debilitating headaches and vomiting. He was released from hospital on 11 November 1941 as fit for active service but given leave until 2 December 1942. Later promoted to *Oberleutnant*, he was killed in action on 16 July 1943 at Reitano, Sicily.
11. NARA, Roll 2296.
12. The dynamic Mikhail Kirponos was later killed in action during fighting at Kiev on 20 September 1941.
13. Rossmann had already received the Iron Cross Second and First Classes on 29 June and 17 July respectively.
14. '*Kurzberecht über Einsatz der Kampfgruppe Koch (I./Sturm-Regiment)*', 31 March 1942. NARA Roll T315, 2293, p. 156.

Chapter Three: Growing Pains

1. Rolf Wallburg diary.
2. Wilmskötter later transferred from the Schützen Regiment to 10th (Panzerjäger) Company as company commander during October 1942.
3. Though perhaps not officially or ceremonially recognised as a Brigade until that date, a *Führerbefehl* of 9 July 1942 refers to Brigade 'Hermann Göring', potentially placing it under Waffen-SS command as a contingency against what

Hitler believed would be possible landings by British troops on the Channel coast.

4. The dynamic Kiefer had replaced Leutnant Gerhard as leader of the Motorcycle Company. Knight's Cross-winner Kiefer was captured in North Africa in 1943 and made several escape attempts from an American POW camp in Colorado. Once, having dyed his uniform with brown vegetable juice, he made it as far as St Louis by train before being recaptured. After the war he changed his name to Tilman Kiwe and became a notable actor, including roles in *The Longest Day* and *The Great Escape*.
5. NARA Roll 2293, Frame 375.
6. NARA Roll 2293 Frame 162.
7. NARA Roll 2296, Frame 262.
8. Wilhelm Schmalz, *An Airborne Panzer Corps*, p. 2.
9. Hosted on the Luftwaffe artefact site: http://aufhimmelzuhause.com/id327.htm.
10. An OKW War Diary entry of 5 November records Rommel's request for both 5th Paratroop Regiment and 7th Flieger Division (later the 1st Fallschirmjäger Division) to be placed under his command to counter the overwhelming British superiority on the ground after Alamein.
11. Percy E. Schramm, *Kriegstagebuch des Oberkommandos der Wehrmacht, 1. Januar 1942–31. Dezember 1942*, II, 2, p. 956.
12. John Frost would later become best known for his and his men's gallant stand at Arnhem during Operation 'Market-Garden' in September 1944.
13. John Frost, *A Drop Too Many*, p. 125.
14. *Images of War*, Vol. 19, p. 523, recollections of Lieutenant Peter Stainforth.
15. Kempa, formerly OC of the Bicycle Platoon until it was absorbed into 10th Company as 2nd Platoon, was killed on 4 February 1943.

16 Nehring was surprised by Arnim's arrival as he had been unaware that he was being replaced. He had already made extensive battle plans for the expansion of the defensive perimeter around Tunis, plans with which Arnim agreed and implemented beginning on 9 December.

17. Christoph Werner, *The Battles of the 'Hermann Goering' Division in Tunisia (Jan–12 May 1943*, pp. 5–6.
18. Schmock later commanded Sturmgeschütz Brigade 394 and was awarded the German Cross in Gold on 28 April 1945.

Chapter Four: Tunisia

1. Werner, T*he Battles of the 'Hermann Goering' Division in Tunisia*, p. 9.
2. Mickley was a Knight's Cross holder, won while an Oberleutnant in command of 7th Company, 304th Rifle Regiment (2nd Panzer Division) on 13 June 1941. The 'T' designation was applied to the first five *Marsch* battalions deployed – A16, A18, A20, A21 and A23 – to denote their immediate employment as

static defence units around Tunis as distinct from the other *Marsch* battalions that would soon follow.

3. Gustav von Vaerst, *Operations of the Fifth Panzer Army in Tunisia (1943)*, p. 1.
4. *Images of War*, Vol. 19, p. 535.
5. The Bergen-Belsen concentration camp lay at the southeastern border of the training area.
6. NARA, 2296, frame 217.
7. The *Jäger* were gathered with elements of the 334th Infantry Division and 10th Panzer Division as part of Korpsgruppe 'Weber', under the command of General Friedrich Weber (334th Infantry Division).
8. Rolf Wallburg diary.
9. Rolf Wallburg diary.
10. NARA Roll 2296 Frame 904.
11. This was a light four-wheel drive vehicle, the PKW 2/40, designed for the maintenance squad with a foldable workbench in the rear equipment box. The spare wheel was placed below the workbench. A welding torch together with its hose was placed in the equipment box inside the vehicle.
12. The addition of nine Pzpflw II F is interesting. The original HG document (reproduced as Frame 743, NARA Roll 2296) clearly states 9 Pz II F as well as 9 75mm PaK 40 (on separate lines) which on the surface seems unusual. However, these were either official Marder II tank destroyers, as this was a Panzjäger Company, or an ad-hoc forerunner of the Marder II, the report appearing to predate Marders' deployment in action.
13. On 16 April Schmid recommended the promotion of Oblt. Fritz Quednow – former Adjutant to Knoche – commander of 5th Company, Jäger Regiment 'Hermann Göring' to *Hauptmann*. Quednow had commanded the company since 15 November 1942 and the creation of the ad hoc 2nd Battalion. Qudenow was killed in action at the rank of *Hauptmann* as commander of 9th Company, Jäger Regiment 'Hermann Göring' on 27 April 1943 and is buried in Bordj-Cedria military cemetery, Tunisia. He was subsequently awarded the German Cross in Gold on 22 May 1943 (his rank given as *Oberleutnant*) and, belatedly, the Knight's Cross on 5 April 1944.
14. NARA 2293.
15. Fortunately for Gerhart Schirmer, he was recalled to Halberstadt before the collapse in Tunisia to oversee the formation of a new 2nd Battalion for the Jäger Regiment, his place as regimental commander being taken by Hptm. Horst Zimmermann.
16. NARA 2293 Frame 471.
17. *Images of War*, Vol. 19, p. 524.

18. Schäfer returned to Germany after the war but died on 7 December 1963 from lingering effects of his military service and an infection he originally developed in Texas.
19. *Company Officer's Handbook of the German Army*, Military Intelligence Department, March 1944, pp. 11–12.
20. Münzner, an ex-Army Panzer trainee officer, was transferred to the 'Hermann Göring' Division's 1st Company, Panzer Regt. before its redesignation as 3rd Company, and promoted from 1st Platoon leader on 4 March, replacing Hptm. Martin Lübke as company commander. Lübke moved to command 2nd Battalion, Panzer Regt. 'HG'
21. Rolf Wallburg was later captured near Mateur and spent time in first a British and then an American prisoner of war camp, before being sent to a prison camp in Alabama. His diary – a red leather book wrapped in a plastic liner – was found in the saddlebag of an abandoned motorcycle that lay in a wadi by Master Sergeant Robert Schiers. Both Rolf and Robert died in 1980. Robert's son Bill eventually had the diary translated and returned to Rolf's widow Marie, who featured prominently within its pages.
22. Foreign Document Study C098, *Recollections of Tunisia*, Generaloberst Jürgen von Arnim, p. 113.
23. Frantz was decorated with the Knight's Cross on 18 May 1943, repatriated to Germany from prisoner of war camp in February 1945 and attached to Flak-Div. Leipzig for service matters. He died in Bad Homburg in January 1971. Schmid also received the Knight's Cross, on 21 May. Following his return, he was appointed provisional commander of XII. Fliegerkorps. He survived the war, dying in August 1956 at Augsburg.
24. Omar Bradley, *A Soldier's Story*, p. 108.
25. *Military Reports on the United Nations*, No. 10, 15 September 1943, Section II, Combat Intelligence in Tunisia, p. 53.
26. Neitzel, Sonke. *Soldaten*, Simon & Schuster UK. Kindle Edition. Location 5707, referencing TNA WO 208/4168, 'Interrogation reports on German prisoners of war'.

Chapter Five: Rebirth

1. Bogislaw von Bonin, *Critique of the Italian Campaign 1943–1944*, an attachment to Walter Fries, *The Battle for Sicily*, p. 3.
2. Hans von Greiffenberg and Paul Conrath, *Der Kampf um Sizilien*, 1951, p. 2.
3. Schmalz, p. 4.
4. Heinz Guderian, *Panzer Leader*, p. 300.
5. Adolf Scheckenbach letter to Alan Scheckenbach.
6. NARA 2296, Frame 673. Hahm was ordered to Berlin between 25 March and the beginning of April.
7. Bundesarchiv MA, RL 32, 30.

Chapter Six: Sicily

1. T-2, Kesselring's Comments on MS #T-2, Generalfeldmarschall Albert Kesselring, 1948.
2. T-2, Kesselring's Comments on MS #T-2, p. 11.
3. Fries, *The Battle for Sicily*, p. 10.
4. Thomas L. Jentz, *Panzertruppen*, p. 107.
5. Hellmut Bergengruen, *Division 'Hermann Goering' in Sicily (10–14 July 1943)*, p. 81.
6. Kesselring's Comments on MS #T-2, p. 11.
7. Jentz, *Panzertruppen*, p. 102.
8. Berengruen, *Division 'Hermann Göring' in Sicily*, pp. 8–9.
9. Wilhelm Schmalz, *The Battle of Sicily in the Sector of Brigade 'Schmalz'*, T-2, pp. 88–9.
10. Adolf Scheckenbach, unpublished memoir.
11. *Company Officer's Handbook of the German Army*, Military Intelligence Department, March 1944, pp. 72–5.
12. U.S. Army Intelligence Bulletin, Volume II, No. 3, November 1943, pp. 22–5.
13. *German Evacuation Order - Sicily*, Tactical and Technical Trends, No. 40, 16 December 1943; U.S. War Department, Roll 2296, Frame 0993.
14. 'Kesselring's Comments on MS #T-2', p. 18.
15. Conrath, *Battle of Sicily*, pp.5, 12.

Chapter Seven: Italy, 1943

1. Oberst Lothar von Corvin-Wiersbitzki now commanded Panzergrenadier Regiment 1 'Hermann Göring', appointed on 15 July. Fitz had previously received the Knight's Cross while commander of 1st Battalion, Panzer-grenadier-Regiment 74, 19th Panzer Division, for valour during a counter-attack against Soviet forces north of Vyazma along the Shisdra river in December 1941. He would receive the Oak Leaves to his Knight's Cross on 24 June 1944 for action near Anzio.
2. Among the successes at Salerno claimed by 3rd (Sturmgeschütz) Battalion, Panzer Regiment 'Hermann Göring' was a single hit on an enemy cruiser on 12 September by an assault gun from 9th Company. The battalion lost only four men killed in action during September, although one was Lt. Hans-Gottfried Rüdiger and another Hptm. Willi Schirmer (posthumously promoted to *Major*), killed on 25th of the month. Thirty-seven men were listed as wounded during the same period.
3. NARA Roll 2296, Frame 563.
4. Wilhelm Schmalz, *An Account of the 'Hermann Goering' Division at Salerno, 9–17 September 1943*, p. 65.

5. XIV Panzer Corps: 15th Panzergrenadier Division, 'Hermann Göring' Panzer Division, 16th Panzer Division. LXXVI Panzer Corps: 26th Panzer Division, 29th Panzergrenadier Division and 1st Fallschirmjäger Division.
6. Gerhard Schreiber, *Die italiensich Militarinternierten im deutschen Machtbereich*, p. 130.
7. XIV Pz.Korps Chef Ia Nr. 567/43 g.Kdos, 23 Sept. 1943
8. Panzer Division 'Hermann Göring' 1a, Div.Gef.Stand from 23 Sept. 1943, contained in daily report XIV Pz. Corps, 26 Sept. 1943.
9. NARA Roll 2296, Frame 517.
10. The primary Gustav Line ran across Italy from just north of where the Garigliano River flows into the Tyrrhenian Sea in the west, through the Apennine Mountains to the mouth of the Sangro River on the Adriatic coast in the east. The two subsidiary lines, the Bernhardt Line and the Hitler Line ran much shorter distances from the Tyrrhenian Sea to just northeast of Cassino where they would merge into the Gustav Line. Relative to the Gustav Line, the Hitler Line stood to the northwest and the Bernhardt Line to the southeast of the primary defences.
11. Appendix to G-2 Situation Summary, No. 45, 15 October 1943. Headquarters U.S. 82nd Airborne Division, Ike Skelton Combined Arms Research Library Digital Library, Ft. Leavenworth, Kansas, USA.
12. 'German Defense of the Volturno River Line', *Tactical and Technical Trends*, No. 45, 1 April 1944; U.S. War Department.
13. NARA 2293, Frame 627.
14. NARA, 2296.
15. Ibid.
16. Office of Strategic Services Art Looting Intelligence Unit (ALIU) Reports 1945–1946 and ALIU Red Flag Names List and Index.
17. 'Daily Reports of Argan, Romanelli De Thomasso', Michele De Tomasso, Capodivison per la protzone delle opera d'arte del Ministero, https://www.fold3.com/image/114/271454980.
18. Report on German Kunstschutz in Italy Between 1943 and 1945, Headquarters Allied Commission, 30 June 1945. https://www.fold3.com/image/270192848.
19. Schlegel subsequently lost a leg in a fighter-bomber attack north of Bologna in July 1944. After the war he was arrested for 'looting' the abbey and spent seven months in prison before British Field Marshal Alexander intervened on his behalf and demanded his immediate release for the safe rescue of Cassino's treasures.
20. Lebendiges Museum Online, Hermann Lohmann, 'Rekrutenzeit und Ausbildung in der "Panzer Division Hermann Göring"', www.dhm.de/lemo/zeitzeugen/hermann-lohmann-rekrutenzeit-und-ausbildung-in-der-Panzer Division-hermann-goering.html.

21. www.dhm.de/lemo/zeitzeugen/hermann-lohmann-einsaetze-bei-monte-cassino-und-anzionettuno-194344.html.

Chapter Eight: Anzio

1. Dreher was posthumously promoted to *Hauptmann*.
2. Adolf Scheckenbach letter to Alan Scheckenbach. The battalion commander, Major Konstantin Hahm, was awarded the Knight's Cross on 9 June for his command of 2nd Battalion during this counter-attack.
3. This corps had been created from II. Luftwaffen-Feldkorps, also commanded by Schlemm from October 1942, as a higher headquarters for various Luftwaffe field divisions.
4. Ralph S. Mavrogordato, *XIV Panzer Corps Defensive Operations Along the Garigliano, Gari and Rapido Rivers*, MS#R-78, Foreign Studies Branch, Office of Chief of Military History, Washington DC, November 1955. p. 69.
5. Anti-aircraft capability for Conrath's *Gruppe* was surprisingly light. Divided between the three *Gruppen*, to be employed in ground or air defence at the discretion of divisional commanders, were the following weapons: Pfeifer: 12 × 88-mm, 9 × 37-mm and 42 × 20-mm; Gräser: 43 × 88-mm, 18 × 37-mm and 108 × 20-mm; Conrath: 11 × 88-mm, 9 × 37-mm and 31 × 20-mm.
6. 3rd Infantry Division, 'Annex #2 to Field Order 3' (Combined Arms Research Library, Archives, Fort Leavenworth, KS, 29 January 1944), 1.
7. *German Operations at Anzio*, produced at GMDS by a combined British, Canadian, and U.S. Staff, 9 April 1946, p. 22.
8. Schmalz, *FallschirmPanzer Corps Hermann Goering*, p. 8, and Appendix with his parachute division timetable on p. 9 and onwards.
9. Frank van Lunteren, *Spearhead of the Fifth Army*, p. 220.
10. *German Operations at Anzio*, p. 54.
11. Loeben had transferred to the 'Hermann Göring' Division from the ranks of 17th Panzer Division with which he had served on the Russian Front.
12. *German Operations at Anzio*, p. 665 (original translation from Allied report).

Chapter Nine: Rebuilding and Counter-Insurgency, Italy 1944

1. Unpublished manuscript, pp. 21–2.
2. Christian Kurt von Loeben was considered by his superiors to be a fresh, lively and cultured officer, though unimaginative in command. He was later killed in action on 23 March 1945 on the Eastern Front. After the discovery in 1994 of hundreds of eye-witness statements to German atrocities locked away in the basement of the military general prosecutor in Rome, seven ex-'Hermann Göring' soldiers were brought to trial for these, and other documented massacres. The preliminary hearing was held in Verona on 5 October 2009, against defendants Gustav Brandt, Helmut Odenwald, Fritz Olgerg, Ferdinand Osterhaus, Hans Georg Winkler, Günther Heinroth and Wilhelm Stark. The

first sentences were issued, after 52 hearings, on 6 July 2011: life imprisonment for Leutnant Ferdinand Osterhaus (5./Panzer Aufklarüngs Abteilung 'HG'), Hptm. Helmut Odenwald (10. Flak Regt. 'HG') and Fw. Alfred Luhmann. Günther Heinroth and Horst Günther Gabriel had died during the trial. An appeal in 2013 initially acquitted Odenwald and Osterhaus, though the next year life imprisonment was re-confirmed for Helmut Odenwald. Ferdinand Osterhaus passed away in 2014.

3. Not until November 1944 did the Feldgendarmerie Trupp change its designation to Feldgendarmerie Trupp, Fallschirm-Panzer-Division 'Hermann Göring'. It had been established as Feldgendarmerie Trupp Panzer Division 'Hermann Göring' in March 1943, changing its title to Feldgendarmerie Trupp 1000 in line with all other Luftwaffe field division military police units, which were allocated four-digit numbers.
4. After the Second World War, nineteen former SS officers were again part of the Hamburg police force, among them Heinz Barz who became the Polizeirat, Kommando V, Schupo-Amt Hamburg 13, and later Leiter der Kriminalpolizei in Krefeld.
5. Kerstin von Lingen, *Allen Dulles, the OSS, and Nazi War Criminals*, p. 34. Quoting BA-MA, RH 19 X/35, H.Gr. C, Grundsätzliche Befehle Januar–Juli 1944.
6. Conrath, awarded the German Cross in Gold on 18 May 1944, served in these capacities until the war's end. Promoted to *General der Fallschirmtruppe* on 1 January 1945, he was briefly held in Allied captivity before being released in 1945. He died on 15 January 1979 in Hamburg.
7. Lebendiges Museum Online, *Hermann Lohmann: Als Soldat in der Toskana 1944*, www.dhm.de/lemo/zeitzeugen/hermann-lohmann-als-soldat-in-der-toskana-1944.html.
8. Wilhelm Schmalz, *Fallschirm-Panzer-Division 'Hermann Göring' in Italien*, p. 8.
9. Oberstleutnant Georg-Henning von Heydebreck was also awarded the Knight's Cross on 25 June.
10. Wilhelm Schmalz, *Fallschirm-Panzer-Division 'Hermann Göring' in Italien*, p. 16.

Chapter Ten: From South to East,and East to West

1. Hitler had gone so far as to order the name of the defensive line changed, reasoning that it offered too great a lure for German forces to retreat to and that if the Allies succeeded in breaking through, they would highlight the ostentatious 'Gothic' title to magnify their victory. Subsequently, Kesselring renamed it the Green Line.
2. David Irving, *Göring*, pp. 639–40.
3. https://www.dhm.de/lemo/zeitzeugen/hermann-lohmann-als-soldat-in-der-toskana-1944.html.

4. Stronk survived the war and would later become a respected local politician in Lohhof near Munich, passing away on 10 April 2003 in Unterschleißheim.
5. General der Infanterie Hans Reinhard's LXXXVIII Corps was responsible for this sector of the coast, the actual fortifications of which he considered in poor repair.
6. Memories of Franz Lürbke, *Weiße Spiegel,* www.franzluerbke.de/42182/42618.html.
7. Tettau attempted, and failed, to have Oelkers court-martialled for his actions. Oelkers who had begun the war with the Leibstandarte SS 'Adolf Hitler' Regiment, was in training at the SS-Unterführerschule Arnhem at the time of 'Market-Garden'. His *Kampfgruppe* for the Rhine crossing was designated 'SS-Battalion Oelkers' and on 12 October he received a certificate of recognition from the Commanding General of XII SS Army Corps, SS-Obergruppenführer Curt von Gottberg for his outstanding leadership in building the Rhine bridgehead. Oelkers ended the war with 17th SS Panzergrenadier Division 'Götz von Berlichingen'.
8. Quoted in M. R. D. Foot, *Holland at War Against Hitler*, p. 117. Banwell was a remarkable man of a varied military career – including acting as a double for General Montgomery in North Africa – before he joined the 10th Battalion, Parachute Regiment. Captured at Arnhem, he escaped with two officers and contacted the Dutch underground to act as weapons instructor on their mainly British armaments. Captured again, he was incarcerated in Neuengamme and then Auschwitz concentration camps before being moved to a Stalag at Fallingbostel where the Red Army liberated him at the war's end. He died on 25 July 1999 in London.
9. Franz Kurowski, *Fallschirm-Panzerkorps 'Hermann Göring'*, p. 263.
10. One of the perpetrators of the attack on Eggert and Sommer was among those rounded up in Putten. Willem van Heesen was arrested, though he did not identify himself to the Germans when the assembled villagers were asked if any culprits wanted to step forward and confess. He died in captivity.
11. www.oktober44.nl/foundation-oktober44-engels.
12. Memories of Franz Lürbke, *Weiße Spiegel,* www.franzluerbke.de/42182/42618.html.
13. Schmalz, pp. 9–11.

Chapter Eleven: Panzer Corps

1. A new Fallschirmjäger Regiment 16 was subsequently formed in the Netherlands during October 1944.
2. Karl Knoblauch, *Dem Ende entgegen*, pp. 21–2. Knoblauch had begun the war as a member of Radfahr Abteilung 195 of the 95th Infantry Division, transferring to the Luftwaffe as a navigator during 1941. By October 1943 he had received

the Iron Cross First and Second Classes, Front Flying Clasp in Gold for reconnaissance, silver wound badge and German Cross in Gold.

3. Wilhelm Schmalz, *Panzer Korps Hermann Göring; An Organisational Study*, p. 5.
4. The *Erhenschale* had been introduced by Göring on 25 June 1942 as the ground-unit version of the flying personnel's *Ehrenpokale*. Later wounded in action during April 1945, Sandrock was hospitalised and on his recovery joined his regiment's reserve detachment in Oranienburg. Although the bulk of the 'Hermann Göring' units were cut off and captured by Soviet forces, Sandrock made his way west, surrendering to United States forces. On 18 May 1945, he escaped from captivity and succeeded in reaching his family home near Bonn.
5. Gerhard Tschierschwitz survived the war to be captured by the Red Army on 3 June 1945. He was initially sentenced to death for his alleged participation in war crimes, this being commuted to 25 years' hard labour in April 1950. He was released as part of the diplomatic agreement with Germany on 8 October 1953 and died on 17 January 1997.
6. *Unterlagen der Ia-Abteilung des Generalkommandos des FallschirmPanzerkorps „Hermann Göring": Meldung zum Zustand des FallschirmPanzerkorps „Hermann Göring"*. Bestand 500 Findbuch 12475 Akte 7, stored at Central Archives of the Ministry of Defense of the Soviet Union (CAMO), now available through 'German-Russian Project for Digitalization of German Documents in Archives of the Russian Federation' https://wwii.germandocsinrussia.org.
7. www.klee-klaus.de/gumbinnen_bis_balga.htm#Politisierung.
8. Graf was posthumously promoted to *Oberstleutnant*.
9. General der Artillerie Maximilian Felzmann, *The Last Russian Offensive, 1945: XXVII Corps Sector*, Foreign Military Studies, 1947, p. 21.
10. Memories of Franz Lürbke, *Weiße Spiegel,* www.franzluerbke.de/42182/42618.html.
11. *Deutsche Nachrichtenbüro*, dated 3 April 1945.
12. Major Hans Ostermeier was moved to command Fallschirm-Panzergrenadier Regt. 3 'HG' and subsequently awarded the Oak Leaves to his Knight's Cross on 15 April 1945, one of only six 'Hermann Göring' men to be so decorated.
13. https://www.klee-klaus.de/gumbinnen_bis_balga.htm#Zinten%20am%2015.%20Februar%201945.

Chapter Twelve: The End

1. Adolf Scheckenbach, letter to Alan Scheckenbach.
2. In April 1945 Necker was transferred back to the Heer and placed in command of the troops at Swinemünde and on the island of Usedom. He surrendered to British forces at the war's end and was released from captivity in June 1947. He died on 27 February 1979 in Bad Münstereifel-Houverath.
3. Adolf Scheckenbach, unpublished memoir.

4. Adolf Scheckenbach, unpublished memoirs.
5. Following the cessation of hostilities Lürbke avoided capture by Soviet troops and walked home to Elberfeld, reaching his destination on 14 May after being periodically stopped and checked to see if he carried the SS blood group tattoo. Interrogated by American authorities regarding his service, he omitted the term 'Hermann Göring Division', stating instead that he had served in the 'Luftwaffe Field Division 'HG'. He received his official discharge from the Wehrmacht in October 1945 and is still alive at the time of writing.
6. Adolf Scheckenbach, unpublished memoir. Scheckenbach and his comrades obtained false papers stating that they were railway workers and managed to walk home without further interference from Russian soldiers. On 7 June Adolf reached his family home in Baldersheim. Reporting to American authorities, he was officially discharged from the Wehrmacht after completing the 131-point questionnaire designed to provide information about a person's activities under Nazism.
7. 'Prisoner of War Camps in Russia; The account of a German Prisoner of War in Russia', Russian Research Center, Harvard Unversity, 23 March 1951, p. 22.

Bibliography

Existing records of Fallschirm-Panzer-Division 'Hermann Göring' are reproduced on NARA microfilm rolls 2293–7 of National Archives and Records Service (NARS) Microfilm Publication T315.

Magazines and Periodicals

Company Officer's Handbook of the German Army. United States War Department, Military Intelligence Division, Washington DC, 1944.

Geissler, Erhard, and Jeanne Guillemin, 'German flooding of the Pontine Marshes in World War II: Biological warfare or total war tactic?', *Politics and the Life Sciences*, Vol. 29, Cambridge University Press, March 2010, pp. 2–23.

'Race For Tunis', *Images of War*, Vol. 19, Marshall Cavendish, 1989.

Intelligence Bulletin 1943, Volume II, United States War Department, Military Intelligence Division, Washington DC, 1943.

Military Reports on the United Nations, United States War Department, Mililtary Intelligence Division, Washington DC, 1943.

Nash, Douglas E., 'Rommel's Lost Battalions', U.S. Army Center of Military History, *Army History*, Vol. 84, 2012, pp. 6–24.

Sadkovich, James J., 'Understanding Defeat: Reappraising Italy's Role in World War II', *Journal of Contemporary History*, 1989, Vol. 24, No. 1, pp. 27–61.

Ziemke, Earl F., *The German Northern Theater of Operations, 1940–1945*, Department of the Army Pamphlet, No 20-271, 1960.

Books

Andrae, Friedrich, *Auch gegen Frauen und Kinder*, Piper, 1995.

Bach, Wolgang, *Die Geschichte der Fallschirm-Panzer-Ersatz- und Ausbildungs-Brigade 'Hermann Göring'*, Eigen Verlag, 1987.

Belco, Victoria C., *War, Massacre, and Recovery*, University of Toronto Press, 2010.

Bender, Roger James, and George A. Petersen, *'Hermann Goring' from Regiment to Fallschirmkorps*, R. James Bender Publishing, 1975.

Didden, Jack, *Fighting Spirit*, Radboud University, 2012.

Edsel, Robert M., *Saving Italy: The Race to Rescue a Nation's Treasures from the Nazis*, W. W. Norton, 2014.

Edwards, Robert J., *Scouts Out: A History of German Armored Reconnaissance Units in World War II*, Stackpole, 2014.

Foot, M. R. D., *Holland at War against Hitler: Anglo-Dutch Relations 1940–1945*, Routledge, 2012.

Frost, John, *A Drop Too Many*, Pen & Sword, 1994.

Ganz, A. Harding, *Ghost Division*, Stackpole Books, 2016.

Gillono, Claude, *German Armour in the Defence of Sicily*, ADH Publishing, 1988.

Gotzel, Hermann, *Generaloberst Kurt Student und seine Fallschirmjager*, Podzun Pallas Verlag, 1980.

Greene, Jack, and Alessandro Massignani, *Hitler Strikes North: The Nazi Invasion of Norway and Denmark, 9 April 1940*, Frontline Books, 2013.

Großmann, Horst, and K. Dieckert, *Der Kampf um Ostpreußen*, Gräfe und Unzer Verlag, 1960.

Guderian, Heinz, *Panzer Leader*, Penguin Books, 2000.

Historical Division, War Department, *From the Volturno to the Winter Line*, War Department, Washington DC, 1945.

Höhne, Heinz, *The Order of the Death's Head*, Martin Secker & Warburg, 1969.

Irving, David, *Göring*, Parforce UK, 2002.

Jentz, Thomas L., *Panzertruppen*, Schiffer Publishing, 1996.

Knoblauch, Karl, *Dem Ende entgegen*, Flechsig, 2007.

Knopf, Volker, and Stefan Martens, *Görings Reich: Selbstinszenierungen in Carinhall*, Links Christoph Verlag, 2015.

Knopf, Volker, and Uwe Neumärker, *Görings Revier*, Links Christoph Verlag, 2012.

Kurowski, Franz, *Fallschirmpanzerkorps 'Hermann Goring'*, Flechsig Verlag, 2007.

Lang, Hsi-huey, *Die Berliner Polizei in der Weimarer Republik*, De Gruyter, 2014.

Lingen, Kerstin von, *Allen Dulles, the OSS, and Nazi War Criminals*, Cambridge University Press, 2013.

Lucas, James, *Storming Eagles*, Arms and Armour Press, 1988.

Lunteren, Frank van, *Spearhead of the Fifth Army: The 504th Parachute Infantry Regiment in Italy*, Casemate Publishing, 2016.

Marti, Philipp, *Die zwei Karrieren des Heinz Reinfarth*, Historischen Instituts der Universität Bern, 2012.

Matronola, Martino, and Eusebio Grossetti, *Il Bombardamento Di Montecassino – Diario Di Guerra*, Pubblicazioni Cassinesi, 1997.

Otte, Alfred, *Die Weissen Spiegel*, Podzun Pallas Verlag, 1989.

Quarrie, Bruce, *Fallschirmpanzerdivision 'Hermann Goring'*, Osprey, 1978.

Rolf, David, *The Bloody Road to Tunis*, Pen & Sword.

Roth, Björn Gerhard, *Halt, Feldgendarmerie!: Die Ordnungstruppen der deutschen Wehrmacht 1939–1945*, Books on Demand, 2019.

Schlosser, Marwan, *Soldat bei den Luftwaffen-Divisionen Hermann Göring*, Weilburg Verlag, 1992.

Schramm, Percy E., *Kriegstagebuch des Oberkommandos der Wehrmacht*, Bemard & Graefe Verlag, 2002.

Schreiber, Gerhard, *Die italiensich Militarinternierten im deutschen Machtbereich*, Walter de Gruyter, 1990.

Unknown, *Prisoners of War Camps in Russia; The Account of a German Prisoner of War in Russia*, Russian Research Center, Harvard University, 1951.

Williamson, Gordon, *The Hermann Goering Division*, Osprey, 2003.

Yada-McNeal, Stephan D., *Places of Shame*, Books on Demand, 2018.

German Operations at Anzio, produced at GMDS by a combined British, Canadian, and U.S. Staff, 9 April 1946.

US Army Foreign Military Studies

Post-war personal accounts of German operations created from interviews with former German officers. Created prior to the establishment of the US Army Europe Historical Division they were obviously opinion-centric to each author, but nevertheless used as a basis for later studies and publications.

Arnim, Jürgen von, *Recollections of Tunisia*, 1951, C-Series manuscripts, C098,.

Bergengruen, Hellmut, and Hans von Greiffenberg, *Division 'Hermann Goering' in Sicily (10–14 July 1943)*, OCMH, 1951, MS C-087a.

Fries, Walter, Boguslaw von Bonin, and Wilhelm Schmalz, *The Battle for Sicily*, T-Series Manuscripts, European Theater Historical Interrogations, US Army Historical Division, 1947, T-2.

Greiffenberg, Hans von, and Paul Conrath, *Division 'Hermann Goring' in Sicily (10–14 July 1943)*, OCMH, 1951, MS C-087c.

Greiffenberg, Hans von, and Wilhelm Schmalz, *Division 'Hermann Goring' Questionnaire*, OCMH, 1951, MS C-087b.

Reinhardt, Hellmuth, and Hellmut Bergengruen, *Division 'Hermann Goring' Questionnaire*, OCMH, 1951, C-087d.

Schmalz, Wilhelm, *Fallschirmpanzer Corps Hermann Goering*, US Army Historical Division, 1948, B-628.

Werner, Christoph Walter, *The Battles of the 'Hermann Goering' Division in Tunisia (Jan–12 May 1943)*, US Army Foreign Military Studies, 1947, D-085.

Vaerst, Gustav von, *Operations of the Fifth Panzer Army in Tunisia (1943)*, 1947, D001.

Websites

Gerlach, Friedrich, 'Meine Militärzeit beim Reiterzug Carinhall', www.dhm.de/lemo/zeitzeugen/friedrich-gerlach-meine-militaerzeit-beim-reiterzug-carinhall.html
Klee, Klaus, 'Der Kampf Um Ostpreussen', www.klee-klaus.de/gumbinnen_bis_balga.htm.
Lürbke, Franz, *Weiße Spiegel*, www.franzluerbke.de/42182/42618.html
Schiers, Bill and Carol, 'The Diary. Bill & Carol', www.billcarol.com/440039322.

Glossary

Abteilung – Generally a unit up to battalion strength. Otherwise meaning 'detachment', e.g. *Korps Abteilung*, or, 'Corps Detachment'
AOK – *Armeeoberkommando*, 'Army High Command'
Arzt – medical doctor.
Aufklärungs – reconnaissance.
Ausbildung – training, or 'forming'.
Beamter – Army officials who were civilians in military uniform.
Begleit – escort.
Comando Supremo – common term for Italian military high command, though its correct designation was Stato Maggiore Generale (STAMAGE).
Ersatz und Ausbildung – training and replacement.
Fallschirm – parachute.
Fallschirmjäger – paratrooper.
Feldgendarmerie – military police, also known by the slang term '*Kettenhunde*' ('chained dogs') due to the gorget they wore as part of their uniform.
Freikorps – Independent paramilitary groups that existed during the eighteenth to twentieth centuries; in the context of this book they were right-wing militias formed after the First World War, predominantly from veterans, to fight communists.
Füsilier – heavily armed replacement/reserve unit capable of reconnaissance or assault.
GNR – Guardia Nazionale Repubblicana, fascist Italian gendarmerie.
Haubitze – howitzer; low-velocity high-angle artillery piece.
Heer – Germany Army
Ia – Operations officer
Ib – Quartermaster
Ic – Intelligence Officer
Kampfgruppe – combined arms battle group of indeterminate size and composition, frequently named after its commander.
Kettenhund – (slang) military policeman.
Kradschütze – motorcycle.
Kubelwagen – literally 'bucket wagon'; light four-wheel-drive utility vehicle, equivalent to the American jeep.

leicht – light; e.g. *leichte Feldhaubitze*, or 'light field howitzer'.
leFH – light field howitzer.
mot. – motorised.
Nachrichten – signals or communication.
NKVD – The People's Commissariat for Internal Affairs; Soviet secret police from 1934 to 1946 which also fielded armed units in combat.
NSDAP – National Socialist German Workers' Party (Nationalsozialistische Deutsche Arbeiterpartei), abbreviated to 'Nazi'.
OKL – Oberkommando der Luftwaffe; Air Force high command.
OKH – Oberkommando des Heeres; Army high command.
OKW – Oberkommando der Wehrmacht; Hitler's / Germany's supreme military command.
PaK – *Panzerabwehrkanone*; anti-tank gun.
Panzer – literally 'armour' or 'armoured'; frequent colloquialism for a German tank.
Panzergrenadier – infantryman of an armoured formation.
Panzerspäh – armoured reconnaissance carried out by *Panzerspähwagen* (armoured car).
Pionier – combat engineer.
Reiter Zug – cavalry platoon.
RGG – Regiment 'General Göring'
RSI – Repubblica Sociale Italiana, second and final permutation of Mussolini's fascist state, established in 1943 following the Italian armistice.
Sanitäts – Medical.
Schützen Kompanie – rifle company.
schwere – heavy; e.g. *schwere Artillerie Abteilung*, 'heavy artillery battalion'.
Schwimmwagen – amphibious Kubelwagen model.
sFH – heavy field howitzer.
Sonderführer – literally 'specialist leader'. Typically a specialist in a particular field given temporary command within the Wehrmacht, Waffen-SS or other bodies such as the Organisation Todt. Frequently given to men without military training, the rank of *Sonderführer* allowed the military to exploit the expertise of civilians who were paid at a military rank deemed equivalent to their role.
SPW – armoured personnel carrier, generally half-track.
Stab – headquarters, or staff.
Stabsarzt – military doctor of *Hauptmann* level.
Sturmgeschütz – (abbreviated as StuG), a self-propelled gun, typically a StuG III armed with 75-mm anti-tank gun; a turretless armoured vehicle cheaper than a conventional tank.
Sturmhaubitze – self propelled howitzer, typically a 105-mm howitzer mounted on a StuG hull in place of the 75-mm anti-tank gun.
Trupp – a section of ten or twelve men.

Versorgung – supply.
Verwaltung – administration.
Volkssturm – Germany's 'Home Guard'; a militia formed for home defence, typically from older men.
Wach – watch or guard.
Werkstatt – workshop.
Zug – platoon of 30–40 men.

Index of Personalities